D1090138

Guys Like Us

GUYS LIKE US

Citing Masculinity in Cold War Poetics

MICHAEL DAVIDSON

The University of Chicago Press • *Chicago & London*

MICHAEL DAVIDSON is professor of American literature at the University of California, San Diego. He is the author of two critical books, most recently *Ghostlier Demarcations: Modern Poetry and the Material Word*, the editor of *The New Collected Poems of George Oppen*, and the author of eight books of poems, including *The Arcades* and *Post Hoc*.

The University of Chicago Press, Chicago 60637
The University of Chicago Press, Ltd., London
© 2004 by The University of Chicago
All rights reserved. Published 2004
Printed in the United States of America

13 12 11 10 09 08 07 06 05 04   1 2 3 4 5

ISBN: 0-226-13739-2 (cloth)
ISBN: 0-226-13740-6 (paper)

Title page illustration: detail of photograph of Jack Kerouac (see page 15).

Library of Congress Cataloging-in-Publication Data

Davidson, Michael, 1944–
    Guys like us : citing masculinity in cold war poetics / Michael Davidson.
        p. cm.
    Includes bibliographical references and index.
    ISBN 0-226-13739-2 (cloth : alk. paper) — ISBN 0-226-13740-6 (pbk. : alk. paper)
        1. American poetry—20th century—History and criticism.   2. Cold War in literature.
    3. Politics and literature—United States—History—20th century.   4. American poetry—
    Male authors—History and criticism.   5. Political poetry, American—History and criticism.
    6. Homosexuality and literature—United States.   7. Homosexuality, Male, in literature.
    8. Masculinity in literature.   9. Gay men in literature.   10. Men in literature.   I. Title.
    PS310.C6 D387 2004
    811'.5409358—dc21

                                                            2003012948

⊗The paper used in this publication meets the minimum requirements of the American National Standard for Information Sciences—Permanence of Paper for Printed Library Materials, ANSI Z39.48-1992.

Contents

Acknowledgments

Guys Like Us studies the fortunes of masculinity in an age of consensus. As I indicate throughout this book, gender categories during the cold war were by no means unified, despite the prevalence of an enabling myth of domestic, heterosexual normalcy. In writing this book, I was often reminded of inaugural moments in my own experience of that era when fissures in the edifice of normalcy revealed themselves—when guys, to my straight, middle-class eyes, were not like "us." I am thinking in particular of certain teachers, Scout leaders, coaches, counselors, and adult friends—often ridiculed by friends and fellow students—who first introduced me to the poetry of Gertrude Stein and T. S. Eliot, cast me in my first play, gave me a book of modern poetry, taught me piano, and put my poems in the school literary magazine. To these nontraditional guys and gals, I owe the true origins of this project.

There have been many friends who read portions of this manuscript or who gave me advice along the way, but I want to give special thanks to Judith Halberstam, who has been a real stalwart at every stage of the process. Her own example in her writings on sexuality has been empowering, and her encouragement of the project has been invaluable. I would also like to thank Marjorie Perloff for encouraging many stages of this project and for giving me good advice on an early draft of the book. In addition, I want to acknowledge the help of Michael Rogin, Nancy Armstrong, Judith Stacey, King-Kok Cheung, Don Wayne, Peter Middleton, Lisa Lowe, Aldon Nielsen, Henry Abelove, Alan Golding, Curtis Márez, Ron Silliman, Susan Kirkpatrick, Ann duCille, Eileen Myles, Tim Gray, Kathryne Lindberg, and Michael Palmer, who read portions of the manuscript, offered bibliographical help, and gave generous advice.

Several of these chapters began as conference talks or papers, and I thank the organizers of those events for helping to frame early portions of this book. This includes Betsy Erkkila and Jay Grossman of the conference "Breaking Bounds: A Whitman Centennial Celebration" at the University of Pennsylvania; Philip Brett and Sue-Ellen Case of the conference "Cruising the Performative" at the University of California, Riverside; Tenny Natanson and Edgar Dryden at the *Arizona Review* conference in Tucson; Joan Retallack of the conference "Poetry and Pedagogy" at Bard College; and Al Gelpi and Marjorie Perloff, who invited me to present two of these chapters at Stanford University.

A version of chapter 1 appeared as "Compulsory Homosociality: Charles Olson, Jack Spicer, and the Gender of Poetics," in *Cruising the Performative: Interventions into the Representation of Ethnicity, Nationality, and Sexuality,* edited by Sue-Ellen Case, Philip Brett, and Susan Leigh Foster (Bloomington: Indiana University Press, 1995), 197–216. A version of chapter 2 appeared as "From Margin to Mainstream: Postwar Poetry and the Politics of Containment," *American Literary History* 10, no. 2 (summer 1998): 266–90; used by permission of Oxford University Press. A version of chapter 3 appeared as "The Lady from Shanghai: California Orientalism and 'guys like us,'" *Western American Literature* 35, no. 4 (winter 2001): 347–71. A version of chapter 4 appeared as "When the World Strips Down and Rouges Up," in *Breaking Bounds: Whitman and American Cultural Studies,* edited by Betsy Erkkila and Jay Grossman (New York: Oxford University Press, 1996), 220–37; copyright © 1996 by Betsy Erkkila and Jay Grossman, used by permission of Oxford University Press, Inc.

I benefited from two excellent readers' reports from the University of Chicago Press, one by Robert von Hallberg and another by Peter Quartermain. Both reviews challenged my more outrageous claims and provided detailed suggestions for revision. I thank my editor at the University of Chicago Press, Alan Thomas, and his assistant, Randy Petilos, who have been extraordinarily supportive of this project and who have monitored every step of its completion with great finesse. I also thank my copy editor, Jay Williams; in-house production editor Christine Schwab; designer Adrianna Sutton; production controller Joseph Claude; and promotions manager Mark Heineke for their help in putting *Guys Like Us* into the world.

This book is dedicated to Lori Chamberlain and our children, Sophie and Ryder.

Beginning to wonder
Whether it could be lake
Or fog
We saw, our heads
Ringing under the stars we walked
To where it would have wet our feet
Had it been water
     George Oppen

Ernie Kovacs as Percy Dovetonsils (Photograph courtesy of Edie Adams)

Introduction

THE FIGURE OF THE POET AS PANSY

One of my earliest images of "the Poet" was provided by Ernie Kovacs's television character, Percy Dovetonsils. Wearing a set of eyeglasses with bulging eyeballs, smoking a cigarette in a long black holder, and sipping a drink from which a daisy protruded, Percy would purse his lips, shake his head, and read lines like the following:

When I was a little child everyone said I was manly
I had a parakeet—a bicycle seat—
     and a dear little friend named Stanley.
His father's voice was somewhat high
     (something to do with a doctor)
His mother taught psychiatry, honest I could have
     socked her!
      (Walley 140)

Kovacs's portrayal of Percy as a pansy may have betrayed a pervasive 1950s homophobic stereotype, but it also conveyed something more subversive. At a moment when the Film Production Code forbade any televised images of gay men, Percy was a queer alternative to the masculine ideals of the day as embodied by John Wayne, James Dean, and Marlon Brando. Not only was he a feminized male in an era governed by strict sex and gender codes, he was extravagant, irreverent, and colorful. The badness of his poetry (most of which was composed in the "Roses are red, violets are blue" formula) was redeemed by the outrageousness of his self-presentation. That presentation offered a distinct contrast to the dour portraits of poets on the inside flaps of Oscar Williams's modern poetry anthologies of the 1950s or the macho photographs of Beat era figures like Jack Kerouac or Neal Cassady, shown lounging on the hoods of cars in the pages of *Life* and *Esquire*. And, as the above poem indicates, Percy's subject was gender, his "manly" character verified, not by acts or attributes, but by his "dear little friend named Stanley." The latter's dearness is marked by having been raised by an emasculated father and a working professional mother (the fact that the latter is a psychiatrist would have surely marked her son for gender troubles in the 1950s). As we shall see, Kovacs's rhyme, "manly"/"Stanley," joined more than similar syllables.

Ernie Kovacs's genius rested not only in creating memorable characters like Percy Dovetonsils but in using television as a relatively plastic vehicle for producing new realities. He exposed the medium's illusionism through a kind of televisual alienation effect, tilting the camera, or filling the lens with water, or filming through a kaleidoscope. With the camera on, he would walk into the control room and address the technical crew or cross in front of the stage, exposing the cameraman filming him. Props fell away, revealing equally unstable props; screens toppled, revealing more screens. Kovacs's signature sign-off, "it's been real," was the best joke of all because it directly contradicted what the viewer had just seen. At the same time, "it's been real" asserted that television could be made to create an alternative reality, a "real time" fiction that parodied the fictive representation of real time. Percy Dovetonsils was a reality effect of television that contested the more somber realities of the cold war era: nuclear paranoia, McCarthyism, communism, conformism, corporate anomie. But Percy was a reality effect of 1950s masculinity as well, a supplement to gender normalization that ensured the stability of traditional male roles.[1]

As this book will explore (and Percy Dovetonsils illustrates), poetry has often been the site of alternative—often perverse—gender positions, nowhere more so than during the repressive 1950s. But poetry is also the site where those gender positions are created, from Aristotle's validation of the epic as the poetry of heroic males to the medieval *sirventes*'s equation of his poem to the female body to Poe's belief that the ideal lyric subject is the death of a beautiful woman to Charles Olson's phallocentric projective verse.[2] Anne Bradstreet's Puritan anxiety that as a female poet she is "obnoxious to each carping tongue / Who says my hand a needle better fits" or Emily Dickinson's response to T. W. Higginson's corrections to her verse, "I am in danger sir," suggests the close relationship between the two areas of genre and gender that extends well beyond their shared linguistic root (Latin *genus*: race, kind) and exposes the importance of taxonomy in constructing both arenas. If a poet is a "man speaking to men," as Wordsworth said, then to whom does the woman poet speak? Even the terms for prosody—feminine or "weak" endings, heroic couplets, masculine rhymes—betray the degree to which gender delineates formal features—and reinforces unequal gendered structures beyond the poem.

If poetry has been a site of gender binarism, it also cites alternative gender positions by quoting or representing subjects that cannot be contained by conventional pronominal usage. In terms made familiar by Judith Butler, gender itself is citational, a performance that must be repeated over time in order to secure a material body within socially acceptable roles and norms. Gender performativity is not an isolated act but rather a "reiterative and citational practice by which discourse produces the effects that it names" (*Bodies* 2). The very fact of reiteration—the necessity that gender divisions be repeated and insisted upon—signals the instability of those divisions. Nor is gender something imposed upon a prior sex, a discourse on a prediscursive body. Rather, sex becomes one of the effects of this citational process, a fiction accessible only through the portals of gender. The discourse of gender binaries depends on cultural representations (in poetry, films, novels, theater) to perpetuate heterosexual normativity, and it is precisely in these venues that gender performance coincides with aesthetic performance. As I will show in my last chapter with reference to Theresa Hak Kyung Cha, this collision (or collusion) is often the overt subject of poetic works that also foreground their own linguistic operations. In *Dictee,* Cha cites the ways that certain forms of repetition—language instruction under colonial rule, Catholic catechism, immigration interviews—instantiate the subject as nonnative speaker, woman, colonized subject. The site of colonization—a space where geopolitical reality is maintained and perpetuated—is the (in this case, Korean) woman's voice who cites her own subject status by reiterating formulaic responses to imposed forms of linguistic, religious, and state power. Thus, the pun in my subtitle, "citing masculinity," collapses three dimensions of gender in poetry: masculinity as a site or spatiotemporal category marking gender divisions; masculinity as a visible representation of individuals who are seen or sighted as male; and masculinity as cited or quoted within processes of textual interpellation. And since poetry is a genre that foregrounds repetition through similar acoustic or thematic features, it is a particularly appropriate arena in which to observe linkages between social and aesthetic formations of gender.

The most thorough study of the gendering of poetry—and indeed of creative writing in general—is Sandra Gilbert and Susan Gubar's *The Madwoman in the Attic*. The authors ask the question, "Is the pen a metaphorical penis?" and answer it by exposing a number of ways in which authorship is gendered as male by demonizing (or domesticating) women as muses, monsters, or angels of the house (3). Authorship is founded upon ideas of paternity for which the biblical incarnation of God's spirit in his son's flesh is the primary model, a metaphor self-consciously deployed by poets from Dante to Robert Lowell. If women presume to write, according to Gilbert and Gubar, they must seize the phallus and revision it with new eyes. As Adrienne Rich formulates it in "The Burning of Paper Instead of Children," "this is the oppressor's language // yet I need it to talk to you" (41).

In the light of recent gender and queer theory, we might revise their question and ask, Is the penis a penis, and can it stand up, as it were, to the work of masculinity in its multiple forms? Is the possession of biological signs of masculinity the same as being masculine? At what point does the penis become the phallus, a free-floating signifier of authority capable of being possessed by both biological males and females? Gilbert and Gubar's reliance on a unitary women's literary tradition, resistant to oedipal anxiety and constructed around strong female predecessors, tends to dissolve the variety of female-identified persons into a single gynocentric category. Moreover, as Nancy Armstrong observes, they often separate the history in which women are oppressed from the history that women have made, thus treating gender as a relatively transhistorical term (8). In *The Madwoman in the Attic* the gendering of poetry is still configured under a binary model that leaves the hierarchy male/female relatively unchanged. While this division provides an important heuristic by which to measure the ways women's contributions to literature have been thwarted, it limits the historical specificity of gendered production during the period that this book studies.

That period is the American cold war era, from the Marshall Plan and the formation of the Truman Doctrine in the late 1940s to the beginnings of détente. I stress geopolitical boundaries of the period rather than literary historical ones (postmodern, contemporary) to stress the proximity of cold war ideology to a literary tradition usually defined by its disinterested relation to history. Nor was this proximity arbitrary. As recent studies by Frances Stonor Saunders, Robin W. Winks, Christopher Lasch, Noam Chomsky et al., R. C. Lewontin, Richard Ohmann, and others have shown, the cold war was fought out as much on the cultural as on the diplomatic front through collusions between federal agencies like the CIA and universities, literary magazines, arts organizations, public forums, and area studies programs. If there was a single ideology to the cold war cultural front it was the idea that, in Daniel Bell's famous phrase, we had come to the "end of ideology" and that the arts had to remain a bastion of aesthetic free enterprise against totalitarian censorship. The CIA's Congress for Cultural Freedom and allied organizations were created to reinforce this view, and the New Criticism provided much of its aesthetic rationale.

During the early stages of this period, from 1945 to the early 1960s, strictures about literary excess—the dangers of intention and affectivity, the threat of emotion and confession—were often linked to a national consensus about American political and cultural values. Poetic language, by its self-conscious emphasis on its contingent nature and by its formal manipulation, offered "asbestos gloves," as Adrienne Rich called them, to deal with materials too hot to handle (171). The New Critics' concern that poetry balance and contain rhetorical tensions could be read as rules for normative personal behavior; the question of excessive gestures or of confessionalism would be resolved by aesthetic fiat. In 1958, Delmore Schwartz excoriated the Beat poets for their unruly "howling" and their frontal criticism of American institutions, suggesting that such behavior would lead to a destruction of civilization as we know it: "Clearly when the future of civilization is no longer assured, a criticism of American life in terms of a contrast between avowed ideals and present actuality cannot be a primary preoccupation and source of inspiration. For America, not Europe, is now the sanctuary of culture; civilization's very existence depends upon America, upon the actuality of American life" (27). Poetry offered, as Richard Wilbur said, a "defensible retreat into indefensible positions," a linguistic suburb where tensions outside the poem were safely managed within a domesticated verbal realm (Breslin 23). The term *containment* may have derived from foreign policy concerns about the spread of communism, but it also described a more general attitude toward personal and domestic life threatened by forces unleashed at Los Alamos and Hiroshima.[3] Hence fears of personal or rhetorical display, of unmediated confession and testimony, may also be read as anxieties about the presence of such identities in one's actual world—the specter of Allen Ginsberg and Gregory Corso crashing your Upper West Side cocktail party.[4]

Although New Critics and New York intellectuals were often at odds politically, they agreed on the importance of maintaining what Arthur Schlesinger called a "vital center" of common values against the threat of bolshevism in its various modalities.[5] Forums in the *Partisan Review,* like the 1952 "Our Country and Our Culture," presented literary critics, historians, sociologists, and journalists banding together (with the significant exception of Norman Mailer) under the issue's editorial statement: "Politically, there is a recognition that the kind of democracy which exists in America has an intrinsic and positive value; it is not merely a capitalist myth but a reality which must be defended against Russian totalitarianism. . . . For better or worse, most writers no longer accept alienation as the writer's fate in America; on the contrary, they want very much to be a part of American life. . . . They now believe that their values, if they are to be realized at all, must be realized in America and in relation to the actuality of American life" ("Our Country" 284). Although this book questions the degree to which there was artistic consensus on consensus, most respondents to the *Partisan Review* forum agreed on a need to revise modernism for postwar America, trimming it of its more exotic plumage by invoking a mythic historical avant-garde against its debased variants in the Beats.[6] Alienation, that keyword of postwar philosophical discourse, had to be returned to its "authentic" forms in Kafka or Dostoyevsky so that it could not be applied to, say, contemporary popular films like *The Wild Ones* or *Rebel without a Cause.* Adolescent enthusiasm needed to be curbed in favor of grown-up (*mature* would have been the more common term) responsibility. Intellectuals and writers no longer saw themselves as *isolatos* or outsiders but aligned with American institutions against the twin dangers of mass culture and creeping socialism. And where an iconoclasm continued to express itself—as in the abstract painting of Jackson Pollock— it was quickly explained as the expression of American democratic individualism or, as in Clement Greenberg's criticism, as the latter-day manifestation of Kantian disinterestedness.

Histories of this era have tended to be written around anti-Stalinist intellectuals repudiating their communist or fellow-traveling pasts, reinforcing liberalism without losing sight of New Deal values. But those histories, as Robert Corber points out, seldom deal with issues of sexuality and gender that often underwrote narratives of national security. Corber's work studies film, fiction, and drama during the 1950s, but it is with poetry that the collusion between new critical aesthetics and liberal consensus can be most vividly measured. For it is over issues of what art must leave out that we may see the stakes in what it must contain.

THE GREAT WHATSIT: COLD WAR MASCULINITY

If Ernie Kovacs provides a contrast to the usual picture of 1950s masculinity, that picture has nevertheless endured as an enabling cultural myth through recent retro films like *Blast from the Past, Pleasantville, Far from Heaven,* and *The Truman Show.* That stereotype usually includes reference to the new "organization man" described by William H. Whyte Jr., or the alienated corporate drone represented in Sloan Wilson's 1955 novel *The Man in the Gray Flannel Suit* or by Willy Loman in Arthur Miller's *Death of a Salesman* (1949). His female counterpart is the patient, domestic helpmate, figured by June Cleaver or Harriet Nelson, self-sacrificing, supportive of her husband, mother of at least two boys. This couple is white, middle class, suburban, Protestant. The couple joins the PTA and Rotary Club, drives a late model American car, and owns a television set that occupies a central place in the living room. In his spare time, the man works in his shop, making hi-fi components that he buys from a catalogue. The mother participates in consumer surveys by testing various new products that she rates according to her family's response. She plans casseroles that feature sauces made of canned soups from recipes found in the *Betty Crocker Cookbook*. The man works in an office building downtown; the woman stays at home, surrounded by new, laborsaving appliances. Matters of sexuality and the body are controlled by the woman; matters of economy and production are controlled by the man. Occasionally sexuality threatens to move outside of the family or erupt in its teenage children, but fortunately there is a secondary story—made famous by Grace Metalious in *Peyton Place* (1956) or John O'Hara in *From the Terrace* (1958)—that locates the problem in bad parenting skills or the crossing of class or racial lines. Beatniks and motorcycle rebels provide a certain *frisson* of social disorder, but their threat is neutralized by their identification with (or dependence upon) a debased mass culture.

Historical scholarship by Joanne Meyerowitz, Stephanie Coontz, David Savran, Wini Breines, George Lipsitz, Donna Penn, and others has done a good deal to displace the consistency of this enabling myth by focusing on working-class, black, gay and lesbian, and immigrant men and women during this period or by exposing flaws in the nuclear family. The revisionist character of this scholarship can be seen in the titles to books such as *Not June Cleaver,* Joanne Meyerowitz's anthology of essays on postwar women and gender, or *The Way We Never Were,* Stephanie Coontz's book about postwar families. But if domestic normalcy has been somewhat of a myth, the stereotype is worth revisiting because it helped create a collective subject around which national agendas could be formed. What we find in this recent scholarship is that cold war gender roles were far from stable and that national security was often fraught with domestic insecurity.

That insecurity was felt at both the local and global levels as a loss of agency, a feeling that powerful, unseen forces were, as General Jack D. Ripper says in *Dr. Strangelove,* sapping our vital fluids. Timothy Melley calls this insecurity "agency panic" to describe the displacement of individualism onto anonymous social or corporate forces.[7] Characters in novels by William Burroughs or Don DeLillo feel that they are being controlled by addictions or engineered by bureaucratic systems that speak in the comforting bromides of middle-class upward mobility. Agency panic is brought about not by overt danger but by the absorption of threat into familiar landscapes. The Moloch that Allen Ginsberg denounces in *Howl* is monstrous not only because it consumes the best minds of his generation but because its visage is familiar, embossed on the "Robot apartments" and "thousand blind windows" of corporate America (131). Melley shows how agency panic is articulated by sociologists of consumerism like Vance Packard as well as by right-wing conspiracy theorists like J. Edgar Hoover. For the former, decision making in consumption has been displaced from the individual onto advertisers, marketers, and motivational research engineers, leaving the individual with a feeling of helplessness before products. John Kenneth Galbraith calls this the "revised sequence" in which the manufacturers and advertisers reverse the "accepted sequence" by which individuals are presumed to take the initiative in consuming. Now it is the manufacturer, rather than the consumer, who controls desires.[8] For J. Edgar Hoover in *Masters of Deceit,* individuals are constant prey to communists who control and train their victims through insidious educational campaigns, infiltration of bureaucracies, and forms of social engineering.

For both the consumer scientist and the FBI head, agency is presumed to be the domain of strong masculine figures; the transition of agency to society is viewed as a fatal feminization. Philip Wylie defined the ill effects of this transition as "momism" in *Generation of Vipers* (first published in 1942 but rereleased to a much larger readership in 1955). The book placed the loss of (male) authority on overly protective, domineering mothers, whose productive functions had been diminished by industrialization and whose primary activities now involved consumption and the repression of her family. As Michael Rogin points out, Wylie's momism was "the demonic version of domestic ideology" in which mother "dominated her husband and encouraged the dependence of her son" (*Ronald Reagan* 242). Most insidiously, her overly protective nature damaged national will, weakening the resolve of soldiers, making them vulnerable to brainwashing and causing the early termination of the Korean War, a scenario vividly rendered in John Frankenheimer's 1962 film, *The Manchurian Candidate*. Momism was, on the domestic front, what communism was on the political—a stifling ideology of control, masking as nurturance and guidance.

There were several significant attempts in the postwar era to diagnose the extent to which this crisis of agency—whether produced by Burroughsian mind control or castrating matriarchs—was related to flaws in gender normalcy. The first was provided by Alfred Kinsey, whose two reports on male and female sexuality of 1948 and 1953 brought sexual practices out of the closet and into the living room. Kinsey's research, based on extensive interviews, made the (by today's standards) uncontroversial claims that women experienced sexual pleasure, that people engaged in a good deal of extra- and premarital sex, and that homosexuality was more prevalent than previously thought. Kinsey's outing of sexuality received vitriolic criticism from both the Left and the Right, all of which predictably served to boost sales and encourage debate. What was perhaps Kinsey's most devastating revelation was that 40 percent of his male subjects reported that they had engaged in homosexual activities and that "persons with homosexual histories are to be found in every age group, in every social level, in every conceivable occupation in cities and on farms, and in the most remote areas of the country" (Corber 11). The implications of this fact for national security were not lost on heads of congressional investigating committees who felt that because gay men could not be distinguished from straight, they posed a security—if not sexual—risk for the country at large.

A second and more pertinent text for our concerns with masculinity in literary subcultures is provided by Norman Mailer's essay on the Beat hipster, "The White Negro." Published in 1957 in *Dissent*, the essay relates masculine alienation to the delayed effects of Auschwitz and Hiroshima. The American "existentialist," by his awareness of the psychic and human toll that the war had cost, becomes disaffiliated from society, a "rebel without a cause." Unmoored from middle-class domestic life and traditional political institutions, he "knows that if our collective condition is to live with instant death by atomic war, relatively quick death by the State . . . or with slow death by conformity with every creative and rebellious instinct stifled . . . why then the only life-giving answer is to accept the terms of death, to live with death as immediate danger, to divorce oneself from society, to exist without roots, to set out on that uncharted journey into the rebellious imperatives of the self" (584). This "divorce" from conformist America is reconciled for Mailer by a new marriage (the metaphor is significant) with black culture generally and black males specifically. Instead of the "slow death by conformity" the alienated white male may participate in cultural traditions more authentic because grounded in historic persecution and social violence. The Negro in this marriage brings a "cultural dowry" of jazz, primitive sexuality, and street-smart argot that gives "expression to abstract states of feeling which all could share, at least all who [are] Hip" (586). "Hipness" knits black and white males in homosocial bonds grounded in estrangement and primitive feeling. At the same time, by seeing the Negro as a fantasy of primitive sexuality with whom he can "mate," Mailer feminizes black males and inscribes this homosocial union within heterosexual terms. As I will point out in subsequent chapters, this heterosexualizing of male bonding becomes a compulsory feature of many cultural forms during this period.

Mailer's utopian merging may have been good for alienated white males (we will see it reemerge in writings by Kenneth Rexroth and Jack Kerouac), but it did little to ameliorate the condition of black males who, as I point out in chapter 5 with reference to Amiri Baraka, had to negotiate a more problematic relationship to hipsterdom. And what Mailer calls marriage could easily be called blackface. Eric Lott, in this regard, sees Mailer's cross-racial identification as continuing a tradition of working-class white appropriations of black culture (his example includes Elvis Presley and his imitators). Lott notes that although it has been acceptable for whites to put on blackface, it is scandalous for African Americans to perform in whiteface, suggesting that Mailer's appropriation of black culture is strictly a one-way affair (207). Intellectuals like James Baldwin have viewed Mailer's cross-racial desire as a kind of fetishization, an attempt to appropriate black sexuality to articulate white sexual insecurity: "Why malign the sorely menaced sexuality of Negroes in order to justify the white man's own sexual panic?" (297). Baldwin implies that it is all very well for Mailer to make himself over in the image of blackness, but in doing so he depends on an essential black innocence and inarticulateness that maintains, rather than controverts, racial divisions.[9]

What Kinsey's reports performed for sexuality and Mailer's "White Negro" for masculinity, Betty Friedan's *The Feminine Mystique* performed for women—at least for white women. Her 1963 book uncovered "the problem that has no name," a "yearning that women suffered in the middle of the twentieth century," unfulfilled by raising children, supporting a breadwinner husband, or owning a ranch-style home in the suburbs (15). By studying national women's magazines like *McCall's* or *Redbook,* Friedan showed how mass culture in the fifteen years following World War II reproduced a domestic ideal of true womanhood not unlike its mid-nineteenth-century counterpart. Women were taught that "truly feminine women do not want careers, higher education, political rights—the independence and the opportunities that the old-fashioned feminists fought for" (16). According to Friedan, women learned these things from mass cultural products—magazines, television, advertising—and especially from a new class of sociological experts and psychologists who told them how to raise children, decorate a home, and please their husbands. This education was all the more disturbing because it was promulgated in a politically vulnerable America "concerned over the Soviet Union's lead in the space race [where] scientists noted that America's greatest source of unused brainpower was women" (17).

Friedan's critique of what she called the "Happy Housewife Heroine" was instrumental in launching modern feminist thought, but it did so by reinforcing many of the stereotypes she set out to attack. As Joanne Meyerowitz says, Friedan "homogenized American women and simplified postwar ideology; she reinforced the stereotype that portrayed all postwar women as middle-class, domestic, and suburban, and she caricatured the popular ideology that she said had suppressed them" (3). Meyerowitz suggests that there was a great deal more diversity among women than Friedan allowed—that not all women were happy staying at home, relinquishing careers and education to raise children. Nor did Friedan's sample cover mass cultural publications that targeted working-class or minority women readers. Even within many of the same magazines that Friedan used, Meyerowitz shows that for every story about the "happy heroine" could be found an editorial or nonfictional article that expresses discontent and malaise. As my examples from early homophile magazines like *The Ladder*, movies (*Mildred Pierce, The Lady from Shanghai*), novels (*The Bell Jar*), and poetry (Gwendolyn Brooks, Sylvia Plath, Adrienne Rich, Elizabeth Bishop) point out, the "feminine mystique" may have itself mystified the full range of women's experience during the cold war.

However flawed, each of these documents contested views of gender normalcy at a moment when the idea of female orgasm or male-male genital contact or black/white sexual relations were undiscussable. They also served to shift agency panic from paranoia about nameless institutions and bureaucracies to fears of nontraditional gender roles or sexual behavior. The problem that faced Kinsey, Mailer, and Friedan involved getting beyond a paradigm of deviance by which subjects not containable by middle-class white ideals were considered abnormal, delinquent, or antisocial. Such abnormal behavior posed a threat not only to domestic normalcy but to national security. Beginning in 1950 and continuing throughout the next decade, congressional committees regularly pursued "sex perverts" in the government as posing security risks. Even one homosexual in a government agency "tends to have a corrosive influence upon his fellow employees," reads a Senate Investigating Committee report of 1950. These "perverts will frequently attempt to entice normal individuals to engage in perverted practices" (qtd. in D'Emilio, *Sexual Politics* 59). As John D'Emilio says, the "homosexual menace" was often linked to threats of communist infiltration that in turn led to dismissals from civilian and military posts, federal agencies, schools, and universities.

We can see some of the tensions between geopolitical and domestic cold war scenarios dramatically illustrated in Robert Aldrich's *Kiss Me Deadly* (1955), a film, fortuitously for my purposes, built around a poem. In the film's opening scene, Christina (Cloris Leachman) is fleeing from unknown pursuers who, as we learn later, want to extract certain "atomic secrets" from her. She is picked up on a lonely highway by the macho Mike Hammer (Ralph Meeker), driving a sleek sports car, who ignores her obvious distress. As they drive into Los Angeles Christina asks Hammer if he has ever read poetry. No comment. "You wouldn't," she continues; "you're one of those self-indulgent males who thinks about nothing but his clothes, his car, himself." It turns out that Mike *should* read poetry because the key to the atomic energy secrets— "the great whatsit" as it is called in the movie—that Christina hides is based on a line from a poem by Christina Rossetti. Christina repeats this line to Mike shortly before she is recaptured and subsequently tortured to death by mysterious agents. The obtuse Mike Hammer is too much of a guy to read poetry, yet in the end, while attempting to discover the cause of Christina's murder, he is forced to interpret the Rossetti line, "Remember Me," which leads him to a box of atomic materials hidden in a gym locker. The key to that locker had been swallowed by Christina after Hammer picked her up; Mike must retrieve it by literally "re-membering" her body at the morgue where it lies, a hermeneutic task that goes quite beyond the usual obligations bequeathed by the Muses of Memory.

Up until this point in the movie, poetry is a cryptic code, written and remembered by women, containing political meanings that man must decipher. In a rather elaborate inversion of the wasteland motif, Mike Hammer becomes a failed modernist quester, unable to answer important cultural questions that would lead to productive order. In attempting to solve the question of the "great whatsit" in the box, Mike relies on tough guy tactics of violence and intimidation rather than the subtleties of induction and intuition. He beats up potential informants and forces his secretary to use sex to obtain information. Hammer's failure to interpret clues is the result of his dependence on strict gender divisions that are reinforced by material objects by which his masculine power is objectified. Hammer's apartment is full of male toys—hi-fi components, golf clubs, modernist lamps, binoculars, abstract paintings—that insulate him from empathy or identification (an early tape answering machine screens his calls) and blinds him to the deeper identities of the various Cassandras who enter his life.

In the film's famous denouement, the box of atomic material is stolen from the gym locker and taken to a Malibu beach house owned by the mysterious Dr. Soberin (Albert Dekker). But his accomplice, Lily (Gaby Rogers), who has been posing as Christina's roommate in order to obtain the secrets, becomes curious about the box's contents. Soberin warns her about what happened to Lot's wife, Pandora, and other presumptuous women, but Lily is not about to be dissuaded and, after killing Soberin, opens the box and sets off an atomic explosion. Aldrich's famous conclusion offers a dystopic view of both what happens when women procure atomic secrets (he could rely, in this respect, on his viewers' memory of the 1953 trial and execution of Ethel Rosenberg) and, more important, what happens when men are so involved in their masculine pursuits that they fail to learn lessons from poetry.

Much debate about the film centers on Robert Aldrich's personal relationship to the McCarthyist climate of the age. As commentators have mentioned, the film's screenwriter, A. L. Bezzerides, was blacklisted by HUAC, and Aldrich himself was graylisted.[10] Mickey Spillane's original Mike Hammer had been a commie-hating antihero, but Aldrich turns him into a parody of McCarthyist ends-justifies-means interrogation. The extreme violence of the film, its expressionist cinematography, disjunction of sound and visual tracks, and bizarre acting styles all signify an excess of cinematic information that cannot be contained by its hero alone. Ultimately the film argues for a restoration of geopolitical order by proper bureaucratic authorities. This point of view is manifested by Pat Murphy (Wesley Addy), Mike's friend and an FBI inspector, who chastises Hammer for his self-centeredness and urges him to let the "big boys" solve the matters of atomic material: "Now listen, Mike. Listen carefully. I'm going to pronounce a few words. They're harmless words, just a bunch of letters scrambled together, but their meaning is very important. Try to understand what they mean: Manhattan Project, Los Alamos, Trinity."[11]

Pat's advice is that of a cold war Sibyl. The names of atomic energy sites are cryptic fragments that the poet-quester, Mike, must interpret if national security is to be maintained. Mike's interpretation is more than a literary search for clues; it is a ritualized reinforcement of social coherence, managed by a benign bureaucratic power. This return to normalcy is purchased by substituting a rational, bureaucratic masculinity for Hammer's more hedonistic, individualist version. And although feminized poetry provides a valuable cultural key, it is shown to be inadequate to official power in the form of federal agencies and surveillance culture. The film's misogyny, far from being a distraction from its cold war theme, is a constituent feature of it, a way of legitimating consensus by showing the dangers of a feminized body politic. The fact that Hammer secures the key to "the great whatsit" from the body of a woman via the body of a poem written *by* a woman reinforces the triangular relationship between matters of national security, gender, and aesthetics.

THE BOY GANG: COMPULSORY HOMOSOCIALITY AND POETIC COMMUNITY

What is a poet? He is a man speaking to men . . . a man pleased
with his own passions and volitions
    William Wordsworth, preface to *The Lyrical Ballads*

"the musical phrase," go by it, boys
    Charles Olson, "Projective Verse"

According to Joyce Johnson in her memoir of life with the Beats, John Clellon Holmes sent a "Dream Letter" to Allen Ginsberg in 1954 that included the phrase, "the social organization which is most true of itself to the artist is the boy gang." In Holmes's dream, Ginsberg awakes and adds in his journal, "Not society's perfum'd marriage." As Johnson summarizes it, the "messages of the real Holmes seem to have remained consistent with those of the dream one" (79). What is interesting about this anecdote is not Ginsberg's differentiation of the boy's gang from marriage but the close relation between the two, the way that the dream of homosocial community depends on its differentiation from (1) society, (2) marriage, and (3) ("perfum'd") women. Dream letter and journal entry are joined in what we might call a "homo-textual" discourse of male bonding. This multilayered document, part fantasy and part material text, part dream and part personal narrative, could describe the palimpsestic character of much contemporary poetic discourse—from Jack Spicer's theory of dictation to Charles Olson's "Projective Verse" to Black Arts' scream. Joyce Johnson's aptly titled memoir, *Minor Characters*, affectionately—but critically—studies the marginalization of women within this discourse and the ways that retrospective accounts of the Beats perpetuate this same narrative. At one point she describes seeing a 1993 Gap ad based on a photograph of Kerouac wearing a pair of khakis. She sees that her own presence in the photo has been air-brushed out: "In [the photograph] well out of the foreground, arms folded, dressed in black of course, with a look on her face that suggests waiting, you would have found an anonymous young woman. It was strange to know everything about that woman who wasn't there, strange to be alive and to be a legend's ghost" (xxxi). In terms developed by Avery Gordon, the air-brushed woman implies a kind of social uncanny, a "seething presence, acting on and often meddling with taken-for-granted realities" (8). The critical study of cultural phenomena needs to be attentive to such ghostly matters—the woman who is not there and the feminized presence who is.

One such taken-for-granted reality can be found in the simile in my book's title, "guys like us," which is taken from Jack Kerouac's *The Dharma Bums*. In this novel, the narrator, Ray Smith, celebrates the "rucksack revolution" that he identifies with the poet, Asianist, and mountain climber, Japhy Ryder (Gary Snyder): "Think what a great world revolution will take place when East meets West finally, and it'll be guys like us that can start the thing. Think of millions of guys all over the world with rucksacks on their backs tramping around the back country and hitch-hiking and bringing the word down to everybody" (160). Kerouac's faith in a social revolution formed by "guys like us" is predicated on the existence of homosocial bonds so pervasive that they may serve as an all-purpose antecedent for any simile. "We" occupies the social, and thereby rhetorical, position from which all comparisons ensue. The simile expresses a presumption that in a world of men, it will be "guys like us" (and not like "them") who will bring the "word down to everybody." This is a form of populist elitism, a revolution of the few so that the majority might levitate. It was precisely the oxymoronic character of this position that inspired journalists and liberal pundits into scornful laughter, yet it gave rise to the revolution with which Kerouac was identified.

This book explores that revolution within the vicissitudes of "compul-

Jack Kerouac and Joyce Johnson (Photograph copyright 2003 Jerry Yulsman/Globe Photos, Inc.)

sory homosociality" by which I refer to the ways same-sex relationships were mandated during the 1950s and in which misogyny was often a component. I expand Adrienne Rich's formulation of "compulsory heterosexuality" to encompass same-sex relationships that, whether genitalized or not, are nevertheless obligatory for social formation and power. Although Kerouac's milieu contained numerous homosexual males, its social semiotic was based on a heterosexual model of heavy drinking, hard living, fast cars, sports, and sexual excess. The "boy gang" of which Ginsberg dreamed (ironically by means of another male, John Clellon Holmes) was distinctly *not* "society's perfum'd marriage," yet it was by no means a post-Stonewall sexual revolution either.

So what was it? How did homosocial bonds among males sediment both social revolution and sexual repression at the same time? I will argue that fraternal bonds were necessary for the creation of new artistic modalities and social positions based on what Eve Sedgwick calls "male homosocial desire" (*Between Men* 5). Her emphasis on "desire" over "love" marks the erotic character of relationships between men in contradistinction to their emotional or affective form. As such, desire delimits "structural permutations of social impulses," regardless of whether they result in genitalized sexuality (2). Homosociality, in Sedgwick's usage, implies a triangulated erotics between two men in which a woman serves as a shared object, a fulcrum of heterosexual legitimacy to mask repressed homosexual desire. The classic instance within Beat hagiography would be the triadic relationship of Neal Cassady, Jack Kerouac, and Carolyn Cassady in which the love between two artistic males was mediated through the wife with whom each shared a sexual relationship. Although this triangular structure is not systematically traced in each chapter, the book details the importance of homosocial desire in creating alternative subjectivities to the dominant ideologies of gender in the 1950s. I will also argue that the ideal of marginality was itself underwritten by cold war political scenarios concerning the dangers of subversion and nonconformism. As I point out in chapter 2, the term *marginal* had specific geopolitical meanings within national security debates and must be measured in relation to an intellectual "mainstream" of academic clerics, anti-Stalinists, and middlebrow pundits. As Johnson's memoir indicates, however radical these new positions may have been for society in the 1950s, they tended to be exclusive and conservative where women were concerned. Charles Olson's insular Black Mountain school, Jack Spicer's exclusive bar circle in San Francisco, Black Arts' cultural nationalism, bohemian subcultures formed around orientalism, poets who embraced Walt Whitman, early homophile movements—these sites of artistic and political agency involved acts of social disidentification whose insularity often protected what they attempted to thwart.

Homosocial community was a liberating factor in producing new forms of masculinity, but there were plenty of precedents during the 1950s for men to get together and do business. The ideology of liberal consensus, it hardly needs saying, went hand in hand with a joiner mentality from which literary bohemia was not immune. While same-sex relationships had been reinforced during the war, when servicemen or factory workers returned to civilian life, those links survived.[12] Within traditional masculine culture, this joiner ethos was manifest in the growth of all male fraternal organizations like the Elks or Moose Clubs, the expansion of do-it-yourself and hobby movements, the increase in popularity of the Boy Scouts, Pop Warner Football, and Little League, and participation in the (largely) male Rotary, Kiwanis, Oddfellows, and Chamber of Commerce. It was, as David Riesman famously described it, an era of the "other-directed individual" whose allegiance was less to himself than to his peer group—his neighbor, business associates, social milieu. It has been less acknowledged that other-directedness was a way of cementing institutional and corporate power along same-sex lines.

Poets may have shunned more traditional homosocial groupings, but they often created their work within a company of peers whose fugitive status and self-conscious marginality were essential elements in community formation. Speaking of his relationship to Jack Spicer, Robert Duncan says that "We were—Robin Blaser and I—in 1946–1950, for him, members of his secret boys' club, hero-friends and team-mates in this new game of poetry" ("Underside" 3). For Spicer in particular, poetry was not created in heroic isolation or democratic participation but in small circles of adepts, membership limited to insiders who knew the passwords and secret lore. Coterie poetry was hardly fashionable within an era that valued consensus and institutional conformism, but its production within such self-limiting, exclusive groups may have provided a necessary sense of solidarity. Not all poetry communities of the cold war era were as sectarian as Spicer's—owing largely to its protective function within an homophobic society—but the "boys' club" served an important function when more institutional forms of community (university affiliations, class privilege, religious affiliation) could not be assumed.

What are the literary consequences of treating poetry as an instrument of community formation? Doesn't this kind of consideration vitiate questions of literary value and lead to a valorization of writing based solely on its claims to group solidarity? Can one really speak of a "good" cultural nationalist, feminist, language-centered (take your pick) poem if its value lies in its address to a hypothetical, collective plural? These are valuable questions to ask, but they tend to presume the integrity of the single poem as starting point rather than the discursive field engaged by the work at hand. As I point out with reference to Jack Spicer or Amiri Baraka, the function of poetry during this period was often to perform and engage social alliances, not repre-

sent them separate from the poem. This may have led to the production of poems that seem, from a later vantage, overly hectoring, insular, or rhetor-ical,
yet as documents in emerging queer or black power discourses, they addressed specific constituencies without consideration of a larger reading
public.

Questions of art's relation to community offer a variation on avant-
garde discourse that has been similarly challenged for its function as illustra-
tive practice. As Paul Mann points out, the avant-garde (cubism, dadaism,
futurism) lives most vividly in the moment of its death, when questions of its
historicity and institutional role are most challenged. According to Mann, the
point when the avant-garde's demise is being debated is the moment of its
greatest productivity. "Art is always already bound up in discursive contexts,"
Mann says, and those contexts precede the production of the actual object (5).
Seen in this light, Duchamp's urinal or futurist manifestos are the belated
representations of a more pervasive disaffection with affirmative culture. To
raise the question of art's place in society (or museum or book) *by means of art*
is to fulfill art's most fundamental function: the questioning of its right to exist as something distinct from other forms of materiality. And, in like manner, poetry as a function of community formation testifies to its dialectical
relationship to failed social forms, for which the school or cell or circle become contestatory alternatives.

Since my focus is on poetic communities organized around a masculine, heteronormative model, those alternatives hardly seem to challenge the
status quo. What could be more traditional than a group of men doing business, even if it is poetic business? As I will point out, there were many
fissures in the edifice of heterosexual identity during the cold war, and the
business conducted among poets was hardly as remunerative as that in the
board room. More important for the question of poetic value, however, is that
poetry's very difference from instrumental language marks the inadequacies
of communicational conduits within which business is conducted. By looking at the collective milieu in which poetry is produced, we might see poetic
composition as a collaborative rather than an individual function, a conversation among writers alienated from each other or from the dominant versions
of community in the United States. As a form of collaboration, poetry displays the porous borders between the work of art and the work that art performs in shoring up consensus.

I would differentiate a poetics based around community from a more
familiar school-based criticism whereby poetry is examined in terms of a
shared credo. This latter form of analysis presumes group agreement on certain aesthetic tenets and ignores the fruitful role of dissension, disagree-
ment, panic, and erotic play that underlie group formation. As Jack Spicer
says, "the city that we create in our bartalk or in our fuss and fury about each

other is in an utterly mixed and mirrored way an image of the city" (*Collected* 176). To see Charles Olson's bombastic, name-calling reading at the Berkeley Poetry Festival of 1965 as an assertion of Black Mountain aesthetics is only to treat one element of the event ("Reading at Berkeley"). To see it as a theatrical manifestation of masculine power negotiations among new American poets is, as Libby Rifkin has shown, to see it as constructing "a verbal net that could rein in the [poetry] community's dispersion" (20). Olson's challenge of various poets in the audience (Lew Welch, Allen Ginsberg, Robert Duncan) was a way of establishing kinship while posing as the "boss poet" and "daddy" of this particular gathering. Olson was acknowledging the sectarian character of the Bay Area poetry scene by demanding its acquiesence to his blustery performance. These performative features must be considered as important elements of an aesthetic and political event for which the terms *school* or *aesthetic* are inadequate.

While sectarianism may not have been the pattern for all poets during the postwar period, it describes a pervasive feature of nontraditional writing.[13] Poets created imagined communities in bars, art spaces, little magazines, radio shows, or through the mails. The expansion of college creative writing programs through the G.I. Bill brought poets together who went on to start reading series or little magazines. Much important innovation of this era—the first happenings, debates about Action Painting in 10th Street bars, early formulations of "field" or "open" verse, postwar surrealism in its Deep Image incarnation, magazine and anthology wars, bebop and free-form jazz—was conducted within heavily restricted, masculine environments. Women who presumed to enter such enclaves often wrote within terms dictated, as my epigraph for this section indicates, by a man speaking to men. Francine du Plessix Gray remembers coming to Black Mountain College to study with Charles Olson, armed with short stories in which her protagonist "was always an adult male facing situations I knew little about—my favorite persona as a middle-aged alcoholic actor seeking salvation in a Bowery church" (346). As my discussion of Sylvia Plath and Elizabeth Bishop indicates, the poetic voice of many women poets of this era was often forged within similar masculinist scenarios. The poet who exorcised "Daddy" is also one who thematized her agon as a struggle to speak his language: "Ich, ich, ich, ich, / I could hardly speak" (Plath, *Collected* 223).

A PENNY FOR SOME OLD GUYS:
GENDER AND POSTMODERN POETICS

The term *guy* refers to the effigies of Guy Fawkes, leader of the unsuccessful Gunpowder Plot against James I, whose death is remembered in Great Britain on 4 November. A guy is a scarecrow, a "headpiece filled with straw," as T. S. Eliot imagined the hollow men of his generation: "Paralysed force, gesture without motion" (56). Modernism is filled with such empty males, paralyzed by self-consciousness and wounded by social forces over which they have no control: from Henry James's egocentric John Marcher reserving himself for something "rare and strange," to Proust's neurasthenic Marcel, to James Joyce's rootless Stephen Daedalus, to Ezra Pound's brittle aesthete, Hugh Selwyn Mauberley, to Eliot's J. Alfred Prufrock, to Ernest Hemingway's wounded Jake Barnes, to Wallace Stevens's "watery realist," Crispin, to Ralph Ellison's invisible man—a litany of males who, in Pound's terms, "Drifted . . . drifted precipitate . . . " in a modern wasteland (*Personae* 199). What such characters lack in masculine prowess is compensated by their authors' ability to achieve an adequate distance from them. In fact, they may have been created precisely to measure the distance between aesthetic sterility and artistic authority. If these modernist characters, through some failure of nerve, lacked the ability to "forge achaia" (*Personae* 198) it was no less a response to women who were increasingly running presses, writing successful novels, holding influential salons, struggling for the vote, and leading campaigns for reform. The women *were* speaking of Michelangelo, as Prufrock ruefully observed, and as a consequence probably would not speak to him. This is, of course, a rather restricted view of modernist poetry (Hugh Selwyn Mauberley could easily be replaced as a modernist type by any number of Pound's heroic Renaissance *condottiere* or Confucian patriarchs), but it does describe a persona with whom postwar poets were anxious not to be confused.

Postwar male poets who gave a penny to the old guys of modernism did so by reinstating an ideal of heroic masculinity and by returning to romanticism's cult of energy, orality, primitivism, and expressivism. This involved substituting the "headpiece [and codpiece] filled with straw" with Lawrence's phallicism or García Lorca's "Duende," replacing "endistanced" personae with an ontologically (and culturally) grounded voice. Early critics of postwar poets tended to make this revision of modernism the basis upon which to define a new postmodern poetics—and to differentiate this neoromanticism from more conservative trends during the period. Synoptic studies of contemporary poetry like those by Charles Altieri, Paul Bové, James Breslin, J. Hillis Miller, and Charles Molesworth focused on postwar poetry's revival of what Altieri called romantic "immanence" based on Wordsworthian numinous presence. In these critical works, postmodern poetic openness and process become enactments of natural and supernatural powers, latent in the world and discoverable by distinctive acts of attention. The poem serves less as modernist Image or Symbol than as instantiation of presence.

As these critical accounts define it, postmodernism is embodied in a new, expressive "I" fully invested with powers to testify ("I saw the best minds of my generation . . . "), educate ("I Maximus of Gloucester . . . tell you / what is a lance"), and confess ("My mind's not right"). According to the dominant reading, this new romantic subject was forged in the creative smithy of Blake, Shelley, and Whitman; it was *not* articulated through the highly ironic personae of Eliot or Pound. Nor was it the more moderated voice of mid-century formalists like John Ciardi, John Crowe Ransom, Louise Bogan, John Berryman, or Richard Wilbur, who attempted to balance informal discursivity with complex formal structure.[14] This was an "I" whose testamentary power lay in its ability to run on its nerve, as Frank O'Hara said, without looking back.

More recent studies of contemporary poetry by Alan Golding, Christopher Beach, Walter Kalaidjian, Maria Damon, Robert von Hallberg, and Libbie Rifkin have been less invested in differentiating a postwar "style" in contrast to modernist predecessors than in locating poets within postwar history or in testing the breadth of poetic production against the forces of canonization and institutional legitimization.[15] I would like to extend the historicist work of these scholars by focusing on the intersection of cold war geopolitical issues with gender, while returning to the important aesthetic issues raised by theories of poetic immanence. I want to complicate an expressivist reading of contemporary poetry in which a more-or-less autonomous "I" is poised against a series of obstacles and to see in the first person pronoun a series of hidden or suppressed pronouns that cannot be recuperated within a unitary subject. Rather than regard the testamentary "I" as a source or ground I prefer, as my subtitle indicates, to see it as a site or matrix of competing tendencies—some progressive, some reactionary—within the period covered by the Truman and Eisenhower administrations. As chapters in this book attest, cold war masculinity produces its actors in numerous sites and within specific historical contexts. I focus for the most part on poets and literary communities, but in order to test my theses I need to look at other forms of cultural production—film noir, Sylvia Plath's *The Bell Jar,* a nineteenth-century story by Ambrose Bierce, Kenneth Rexroth's *Autobiographical Novel,* Wayne Wang's film, *Chan Is Missing,* Ernie Kovacs's show—in order to see masculinity being produced in a variety of venues.

Chapter 1 discusses the compulsory character of homosocial literary communities, both hetero- and homosexual, in generating innovative poetic practices. By looking at the largely masculine communities surrounding Charles Olson's Black Mountain and Jack Spicer's San Francisco milieus, I show how the emergence of postwar gay male community was based on certain macho postures that contested the cultural status quo but did so in compulsorily heterosexual terms. And because both of these homosocial communities saw themselves in direct contrast to more public agendas of consolidation and consensus, they provide a lens for viewing larger ideas of American community.

In chapter 2 I extend the rhetoric of marginality associated with literary bohemia to speak of the relationship between global conflicts associated with the expansion of communism and the poetics of personalism and expressivism. Here, the specific character of what might be called a cold war lyric is investigated not in terms of references to national security issues but by its avoidance of those terms. My objects of study are lyrics by John Wieners, Robert Creeley, Gwendolyn Brooks, Edward Field, and Frank O'Hara. As Theodor Adorno points out, the lyric, by its refusal of the social, may be the best place to investigate the inadequacy of modern social formations. At the same time, this lyric often contains the seeds of a more liberatory stance, not because it refuses the social altogether, but because the lyric "I" is unable to dissever its placement within other competing ideas of subjecthood.

Chapter 3 takes another look at the homosocial character of literary bohemia, this time from the standpoint of region and race. In this chapter, I explore the role of orientalism among western writers from the late nineteenth century to the Beat generation. Poems and stories by Bret Harte and Ambrose Bierce depicted the threat posed by Asian immigrants to white immigrant labor from the East Coast, a threat that was reinforced by stereotypes of a feminized Asian male. Their representations of the "Heathen Chinee" helped perpetuate Asian male stereotypes, but did so by depicting a Wild West of cross-racial affectionate—and erotic—relationships among men that contested popular stereotypes that perpetuated labor unrest and exclusion laws. In this discussion I am interested in the role that the Asian other has played in forging western culture against a perceived East Coast effeteness. That other, whom I call "the Lady from Shanghai," turns out to be a variable fiction who is neither Asian nor a lady but a feminized male. The erotic potential of this figure animates significant work by West Coast writers from Kenneth Rexroth to Jack Kerouac and has spawned resistance in Asian American writers like Maxine Hong Kingston or Faye Ng and filmmakers like Wayne Wang. In this chapter I am interested in complicating theories of orientalism as described by Edward Said to include specific sites and locations of perceived oriental exoticism and threat.

Chapter 4 investigates the various ways in which masculinity in poetry was formed around the figure of Walt Whitman, not so much as the "good gray poet" of democracy, but as the gender-bending shape-shifter of "The Sleepers" and section 11 of *Leaves of Grass*. I first investigate Whitman's metaphors of cross-dressing in early editions of *Leaves of Grass*. I then discuss the ways that modern poets redressed Whitman, drawing on his innovative meters but deploring his rhetorical and emotional excesses. I then look at postwar poets who redressed Whitman as "our contemporary," seeing him as a countercultural figure whose multiple identities could be enlisted for purposes of social and political change. I focus specifically on Frank O'Hara, who sees in Whitman a more complex figure for male desire whose poems on adhesiveness or the love of comrades permits a category crisis that implicates the solidities of nation and race as well as masculine identity.

In chapter 5 I explore the role of homosociality within the context of cultural nationalism, specifically through the Black Arts movement of the late 1960s and early 1970s. Through the work of Amiri Baraka, I study the creation of a powerful but rather limited subject-position around which a new black aesthetic was formed. Baraka's idea of a unified African American experience—"the changing same"—contrasts with his own mutable identity as Beat hipster, cultural nationalist, Maoist, Marxist-Leninist, all reflected through shifting relations to gender and sexuality. I then turn to significant critiques of black masculinity, through feminist work by Michele Wallace, Audre Lorde, and Ntozake Shange as well as through intellectual forums in journals and periodicals, to show how the projection of black macho resulted in a significant critique of cultural feminism.

Up to this point in the book, I have defined masculinity largely in terms of biological males, but in chapter 6 I look at masculinity as it is represented by and in women. Building on the work of Esther Newton, Joan Nestle, and Judith Halberstam, I look at poetry by Sylvia Plath and Elizabeth Bishop as masculine women who fit neither a butch/femme lesbian model nor a heteronormal model. Early critics of Plath and Bishop sought to understand their work either by pathologizing their language (Plath) or fetishizing their formal control (Bishop), but more recent critics have turned to issues of gender and sexuality to enlist them into a feminist script. But it is not enough to situate both poets as being critical of traditional femininity; they must also be read against the era's attitudes about masculine women. To this end, I situate Plath and Bishop against the background of the emerging homophile movement as well as 1950s film icons like Joan Crawford and Eve Arden to show how gender-ambiguous women were being framed in more popular venues.

My final chapter concerns the role of cold war pedagogy in poetry, first through Charles Olson's early work "The Kingfishers" and, later, through Theresa Hak Kyung Cha's *Dictee*. Both poems are self-consciously pedagogical in providing a curriculum for understanding a wide range of social and historical issues concerning the formation of modern Asia. But both poems are framed around two very different versions of that region: for Olson, Mao's cultural revolution provides an alternative to cold war binarisms of U.S. and Soviet power; for Cha, the Pacific Rim implies more than an entrepreneurial zone but defines layers of cultural displacement experienced by Koreans under Japanese colonization, partition, and nationalism. Education is one of the key ideological state apparatuses within which individuals are naturalized as citizens, while gender represents the modality by which this naturalization process is lived. By looking at these two poems on either end of the cold war, we may see how the Black Mountain and Korean diaspora poet represent gender as a component in global affairs. It also offers an opportunity to conclude this book where it begins: with Charles Olson's projection of Black Mountain College and aesthetics as a homosocial "city on a hill" for future generations to emulate.

Making cameo appearances in many of the chapters is the genial presence of Frank O'Hara, who serves as a kind of docent on 1950s culture, a poetic flaneur who observed the crowd yet who was often happy to be *in* it. And like Whitman, his great predecessor, O'Hara gathered together various energies of American life, latent and overt, merging sexuality with consumerism ("The Day Lady Died"), race with nationalism ("Ode: French Negro Poets"), modernist fragmentation with personalist confession ("Easter"). While O'Hara is not the subject of this book, he serves, like Baudelaire for Walter Benjamin, as an allegory of late-twentieth-century America. But whereas Baudelaire bemoaned the emergence of the modern city, its renovated spaces and mass cultural corruptions, O'Hara celebrated the city's glamour, movement, and energy, the opportunities it affords for exceptional, extravagant behavior: "To be idiomatic in a vacuum / it is a shining thing" (*Collected* 282).

O'Hara offers a useful site for considering the relationship between sexuality and politics, not necessarily because he was an activist for gay rights but because he so richly embroidered the sexual as social idiolect, as a way of making his private speech public. He accepted his gayness in a homophobic time, marking its risks as well as its sectarianism. O'Hara also raises the issue of mass culture, which became a major issue among intellectuals of the 1950s. His notorious fusing of mass culture phenomena like James Dean, Billie Holiday, Coca Cola, and Jujubes with high culture idols like Rachmaninoff, Picasso, and Balanchine testifies to a crossing of cultures that paralleled a crossing of genders. Although O'Hara may have felt more comfortable in midtown museums and theatres, his poetry admitted downtown interests as well—the signage of 42nd Street, jazz clubs, sexual cruising, and gay bars that anticipate more complex mergings of social idiolects in recent popular culture. The same could be said for many other poets of O'Hara's generation—Jack Spicer, Bob Kauffman, John Wieners, and Allen Ginsberg come to mind—for whom poetry was a distinctly public venue and address to an audience a concern made palpable by the increased emphasis on poetry as performance.

What's in the *Daily News*? I'll tell you what's in the *Daily News*,
story about a guy who bought his wife a small ruby
With what otherwise would have been his union dues.
That's what's in the *Daily News*.
What's happening all over?
I'll tell you what's happening all over.
Guy sitting home by a television set,
who once used to be something of a rover
That's what's happening all over.

       Nicely and Benny's duet from *Guys and Dolls*

This book is being written at a moment when claims are being made for a new crisis in masculinity. Various causes have been adduced, depending on the commentator: the rise of feminism; the entry of more women into the workplace; the downsizing of industry and the loss of traditional male jobs; the shift from industrial to service economies; affirmative action and diversity programs; increased commodification and advertising directed at the male consumer; a series of localized, highly technologized wars (Korea, Vietnam, Iraq) without popular support or opportunities for male heroics; the marketing of supermasculine feminine ideals through exercise, bodybuilding, and body modification; the Viagra craze.[16] The direct manifestations of this crisis can be seen in various forms: a male backlash against feminism, increased legal claims by males denied jobs in the wake of the Bakke decision, the rise of the men's movement, the formation of militias and white male supremacist movements, the Million Man March, the Anita Hill/Clarence Thomas hearings, the Promise Keepers, family-values thinking in politics, the production of guy movies like *Goodfellas, Boiler Room,* and *Fight Club* that restore values of male bonding and competitive acquisition. All of these phenomena are being adduced as evidence that the rise of women, in the wake of feminism, has been the decline of men, the evacuation of fatherhood, the feminization of masculinity.

As can be seen from my epigraph from *Guys and Dolls,* not much seems to have changed since 1953—at least on the surface. If a guy is "reaching for stars in the sky" or exhibiting some other aberrant behavior, you can bet "that he's doing it for some doll" or at least because dolls are determining the firmament. The most significant document in the recent debate on masculine crisis—Susan Faludi's *Stiffed*—studies the current version of these events in a direct relation to gender roles of the 1950s. Faludi understands male crisis as an inverted reflection of that delineated by Betty Friedan; where

1950s other-directed corporate male was, there 1990s woman will be: "Men of the late 20th century are falling into a status oddly similar to that of women at mid-century. The fifties housewife . . . could be said to have morphed into the '90s man, stripped of his connection to a wider world and invited to fill the void with consumption and a gym-bred display of his ultra-masculinity. The empty compensations of a 'feminine mystique' are transforming into the empty compensations of a masculine mystique" (40).

The assumption behind this example of crisis thinking is that whatever the source of tension, there is a stable masculinity that can or must be restored or rediscovered. Despite the lures of what Faludi calls "ornamental culture"—accessories, clothing, and gadgets that confirm gender roles—males may repossess themselves of their original nature. Whether that state can be rediscovered by men beating on drums in the woods or forming support groups and political coalitions or rebonding with their fathers, the idea that some kind of masculinity needs shoring up is a given. It is not that men do not respect their fathers (growing up in the Depression or fighting in the war) but that "the culture they live in has left men with little other territory on which to prove themselves besides vanity" (36). The cold war male had John Wayne and Audie Murphy; the post–cold war male has the gender indeterminate Michael Jackson and the crassly sexual Bill Clinton. That women may feel similarly disempowered, that the same conditions lead to decreased job opportunities or decreased sense of self-worth, are possibilities seldom acknowledged in Faludi's book.

An equally powerful reading of masculinity crisis sees it, not as a recent phenomenon, but as the continuation of gender troubles that have been in place ever since the late nineteenth century, when sexologists, eugenicists, and doctors attempted to stabilize sexuality within normative rules and roles. Recent writings by Eve Sedgwick, Judith Butler, Kaja Silverman, Diana Fuss, Judith Halberstam, and others would suggest that this crisis of gendered identity has repeated itself cyclically every decade since Freud, that the crisis involves an attempt to stabilize or normalize categories that are then used as the basis upon which to erect juridical, social, and economic systems. The current mass cultural popularity of gender bending artists like Prince, Madonna, Michael Jackson, RuPaul; the vogue of voguing, unisex fashion ads, drag queen (and king) performances, and so on are adduced as signs that gender roles are breaking down and that the heterosexual basis upon which those roles depend is undergoing change.

The most radical implication of such thinking—by cultural producers and theorists alike—is the idea that gender itself may not be linked to biological sex, that there is no stable masculinity that could be put into a condition of crisis. As Judith Butler says, when "the constructed status of gender is theorized as radically independent of sex, gender itself becomes a free-floating artifice, with the consequence that *man* and *masculine* might just as easily signify a female body as a male one, and *woman* and *feminine* a male body as easily as a female one" (*Bodies* 6). It is just such a "free-floating artifice" that I am calling masculinity in this book, although rather than locating it in drag-queen balls or contemporary films I want to look at the modern crisis of gender when a putative model of normalcy was very much in place. That place or site of cold war normalcy was by no means stable, as my example from Ernie Kovacs verifies, yet its reiteration was necessary for certain geopolitical reasons. Now that the map has been redrawn around new global agendas, a lot of guys are still like guys, but they may not all be like "us."

1

Compulsory Homosociality: Charles Olson, Jack Spicer, and the Gender of Poetics

to be tumescent I

The affairs of men remain a chief concern

    Charles Olson, "The K"

THE POETICS OF GENDER

My title for this chapter conflates two influential revisions of feminist theory. The first is Adrienne Rich's diagnosis of the compulsory character of heterosexuality in marking gender divisions; the second is Eve Sedgwick's use of the term *homosocial* to refer to forms of same-sex bonding in which male interests are reinforced.[1] Both works represent a second or third stage of feminist theory based on the recognition that patriarchy roots its authority not only by excluding women from its orders but by basing its exclusions upon a heterosexual norm. When heterosexuality is regarded as the (untheorized) standard for evaluating gender differences, then the possibility of describing all forms of gender relations becomes moot. Such structural marginalization of others has political implications for a society in which certain types of homosocial bonding (board room politics, corporate networking, locker room badinage) are essential to the perpetuation of capitalist hegemony.

I have linked Rich's and Sedgwick's terms in order to suggest that in certain communities—literary circles or artistic movements, for instance— obligatory heterosexuality is reinforced even when those communities contain a large number of homosexual males. It is often assumed that because underground literary movements are marginal to the dominant culture, they are therefore more tolerant and progressive. Such assumptions need to be historicized by asking for whom progress is being claimed and by what aesthetic and social standards. As I will argue throughout this book, there was a lively debate in 1950s intellectual culture over which avant-garde was authentically advanced—whether the high modern formalist or the media absorbing beatnik, whether the artist who makes culture by repudiating social forms or the artist who gains identity through group identification and absorption into the popular media. Being progressive in cold war culture often meant different things to different constituencies. What remains constant within the largely male forums within which the avant-garde was debated was that the structure of homosocial relations, genitalized or not, often undergirds the production of new art forms and practices, even though that structure is often at odds with the liberatory sexual ethos that articulates those practices. One might, therefore, reverse Nancy K. Miller's question, "does gender have a poetics?" (xi), and ask, Does poetics have gender, and, if so, how do homosocial relationships participate in constructing both terms?[2]

Such questions become extremely pertinent when studying the formations of literary postmodernism where the attempt to go beyond the artisanal poetics of high modernism often replicates phallic ideals of power, energy, and virtuosity that it would seem to contest. Most commentators regard the shift in literary periods as one in which a model of literary performance regarded as realized totality—what John Crowe Ransom called "miraculist fusion"—is displaced by speech act (880). Poets of the late 1950s thought of their work as capable of effecting change—of doing rather than representing—by the sheer authority vested in the speaker, anticipating by several years J. L. Austin's theory of performative speech acts.[3] This authority is purchased not by establishing ironic distance or by invoking institutional or cultural precedents. Rather, authority derives from an ability to instantiate physiological and psychological states through highly gestural lineation and by the treatment of the page as a field for action. In the rhetoric of Black Mountain poetics, the poet scores the voice—and by extension the body— through lines that monitor moment-to-moment attentions. The poem's authenticity resides not so much in what the poem says as paraphrasable content but in the ways the poem displays its own processes of discovery. Many of the terms for such performance (gesture, field, action) derive from abstract expressionist painting for which the heroic ideal of physicality serves as aesthetic as well as communal precedent.[4]

I would like to study two literary circles of the 1950s in which homosocial relations were compulsory, even though each group consisted of numerous homosexual males. The groups in question are the North Beach bar scene surrounding Jack Spicer, who was openly gay, and the Black Mountain milieu surrounding Charles Olson, who was not.[5] Both poets wrote foundational documents in poetics that have become the basis for much discussion of postwar, nontraditional verse. Both poets developed their poetics within a group ethos of male solidarity and sodality that often betrayed homophobic qualities. Although women were sometimes associated with each group (Helen Adam and Joanne Kyger with Spicer, Denise Levertov with Olson), they were seldom acknowledged as literary innovators. While women were often absent from the centers of artistic and intellectual life in general during the 1950s, their absence in these groups was a structural necessity for the liberation of a new, male subject.[6]

Before focusing on particular cases, it is necessary to emphasize that compulsory homosociality was hardly limited to the Black Mountain or Spicer circles. One could say the same for Beat writers like Jack Kerouac and Allen Ginsberg who developed their ethos of cultural disaffiliation by rejecting momism and other vestiges of female authority (marriage, commitment, sexual fidelity). In his novels Kerouac fetishized the (hetero) sexual prowess of Neal Cassady and celebrated the rough camaraderie of men on the road. Ginsberg, in his most famous poem, elegizes those "who let themselves be fucked in the ass by saintly motorcyclists" while, at the same time, despairing over those who "lost their loveboys to the three old shrews of fate the one eyed shrew of the heterosexual dollar the one eyed shrew that winks out of the womb and the one eyed shrew that does nothing but sit on her ass and snip the intellectual golden threads of the craftsman's loom" (128). And in his most infamous confession of misogyny, "This Form of Life Needs Sex" Ginsberg despairs of woman, the "living meat-phantom, / . . . scary as my fanged god" who stands between him and "Futurity" (284).

The same could be said for poets of the Deep Image movement like Robert Bly and James Wright who developed their theories of the ecstatic, "leaping" image out of Jungian archetypalism and Bultmanian theories of matriarchal cultures. For Bly, the presence of the Great Mother sensitizes the male poet to his natural or childlike potential, but when She appears in her more medusan form as the Teeth Mother, her icon is the vagina dentata and her function is to destroy the male's psychic life (41). In both Beat and Deep Image movements, greater sensitivity or vision is purchased at the expense of women, even when her gender (as in more recent men's movement rhetoric) is invoked as a positive value. And where homosexuality is openly celebrated, as it is in Ginsberg, it is often in opposition not only to heterosexuality but to women in general:

Woman
      herself, why have I feared
          to be joined true
   embraced beneath the Panties of Forever
in with the one hole that repelled me 1937 on?
    (284–85)

The date recorded in Ginsberg's last line is important here beyond what it means for Ginsberg's sexuality. It marks a specific moment in the development of homosociality that coincides with a shift into what we now recognize as postmodernism. If Ginsberg was "repelled" by female genitalia, he could say so within a range of same-sex associations brought about by World War II. As John D'Emilio has pointed out, the war expanded possibilities for homosocial—and specifically gay and lesbian—interaction. The sudden removal of men and women from small towns into "sex-segregated, nonfamilial environments" such as the armed services or defense industries provided new possibilities for same-sex contacts ("Gay Politics" 458). Networks of gays and lesbians continued after the war as service personnel were demobilized in San Francisco, Los Angeles, or New York where the presence of bars and social services provided a hospitable environment. The inquisitorial climate of the cold war—from the House Un-American Activities Committee hearings of the late 1940s through the McCarthy committee—often linked political and sexual deviance, thus creating a greater sense of alliance among various "subversive" cultures. Many federal and state employees were fired for sexual misconduct and many more were subjected to surveillance. Gay community was challenged by increased police crackdowns on gay bars that, far from diminishing homosexual or lesbian activity, heightened awareness. Literary communities in Greenwich Village and North Beach were particularly affected by these developments because many of them evolved in the same bars that were the targets of police raids. And while regulars of those bars may have made distinctions between homosexual and straight patrons, the outside world and the mass media tended to link literary bohemia with sexual deviancy and dismiss both accordingly.

The expansion of gay and lesbian community during the 1950s was accompanied by the evolution of new, nontraditional masculine identities within the popular imagination: the *Playboy* swinging bachelor, the motorcycle renegade, the Hollywood cowboy, the pelvis gyrating rock star, and, of course, the beatnik. Many of these roles were explicitly misogynist in nature, women treated as little more than sex toys or castrating viragos. At the same time, these new masculine roles offered alternatives to the usual domestic scenario with its breadwinning male and housekeeping wife. Advertising saw the possibilities of the new male consumer and adjusted its agenda to

accommodate the single, discerning—even bohemian—purchaser of Marl-
boros, Hathaway shirts, and hi-fi components. Within the triumphant middle
class lay pockets of male resistance, whether in the white collar executive
who becomes a connoisseur of jazz or the truck driver who dons a leather
jacket on weekends. These alternative masculinities were commodities to be
purchased, even by those cultural producers who excoriated Madison Avenue techniques. Jack Kerouac writing about Beat hipsters "taking drugs,
digging bop, having flashes of insight" in the glossy pages of *Esquire* or *Playboy* seemed somehow appropriate to the times. The change of Allen Ginsberg, market researcher, to Allen Ginsberg, poet, may not have been such a
transition after all.

I make this point about the 1950s because theories of homosocial literary culture have often focused on its development in earlier periods. The
most significant treatment of the phenomenon, Eve Sedgwick's *Between
Men*, is devoted to "a new range of male homosocial bonds . . . connected to
new configurations of male homosexuality" that emerged in the nineteenth
century and helped to articulate stratifications within the new middle class
(207). The amorphous character of new class relations during this period
necessitated the reassertion of gender roles to give "an apparent ideological
distinctness" to an unstable social and economic context (207). That distinctness was—and remains—reinforced by an asymmetry between same-sex
groupings among women and men. For the former, same-sex bonding carries little of the social opprobrium that it does for the latter. This asymmetry
not only differentiates two kinds of homosocial groupings but ensures male
domination of women; whereas male-bonding often leads to material enrich-
ment, the same experience among women has no such material base.

Obviously, by the mid-twentieth century the unstable class relations
Sedgwick describes had become stabilized, and the asymmetries of gender
relations cemented into institutional and bureaucratic structures of great
complexity. Furthermore, the British class relations Sedgwick studies are a
good deal more stratified than those in the United States (for example, there
is no American equivalent to the aristocratic Oxbridge homosexual culture of
the sort depicted in novels like *Brideshead Revisited*), and thus any use of homosociality as a general concept of same-sex bonding must be defined within
its specific cultural formations.[7] The question of what it meant to be masculine in the 1950s must be set against those very bureaucratic structures—
giant, anonymous corporations, a new class of technical and intellectual expertise, a consensus ideology in institutional life—by which midcentury
America is known. The development of aesthetic models based on the body
and gesture, on voice and orality, represent a response to the increasing alienation of individuals within these social forms. What inheres between mid-
nineteenth- and mid-twentieth-century same-sex relations is the asymmetry

between male and female homosocialities and between their access to the same material conditions. What is unique to the movements that I will study here is the degree to which literary communities reinforced this asymmetry through gender-marked models of performance and action.

A CITY ON A HILL

The best place to begin studying the formation of male community in alternative poetics is Charles Olson's "Projective Verse" (1950). This manifesto advocates a theory of "open field" composition where the poet composes by attending to the physiology, breath, and breathing "of the man who writes as well as of his listenings" (*Collected Prose* 239). Even allowing for the gender inflections of the day, Olson's use of the masculine pronoun throughout the essay seems extreme. Speaking of the advantages of Pound's musical phrase, Olson advises "go by it, boys, rather than by, the metronome" (240); of the unity of form and content, "there it is, brothers, sitting there for USE" (240); of the advantages of using the syllable, "if a man is in there, will be, spontaneously, the obedience of his ear to the syllables" (242). The syllable is "king," and, when used properly, it is close to the mind, "the brother to this sister [the ear]" (242). Finally, out of this "incest" of male mind and female ear comes the line "from the breath, from the breathing of the man who writes, at the moment that he writes, and thus is, it is here that, the daily work, the WORK, gets in, for only he, the man who writes, can declare at every moment, the line its metric and its ending—where its breathing shall come to, termination" (242).

The highly subordinated and punctuated syntax of Olson's prose is as much a demonstration of projectivist poetics as it is a description. The prose is literally breathless with intensity as Olson maps the "breathing of the man who writes."[8] The work ethic implied by this impatience is reinforced by a productionist vision of poetry's effect on the social world, its "stance toward reality outside a poem" (246). It is here, in Olson's more utopian claims for projective verse, that his genitalization of performance most limits its practitioners: "It comes to this: the use of a man, by himself and thus by others, lies in how he conceives his relation to nature, that force to which he owes his somewhat small existence. . . . For a man's problem, the moment he takes speech up in all its fullness, is to give his work his seriousness. . . . But breath is man's special qualification as animal. Sound is a dimension he has extended. Language is one of his proudest acts. And when a poet rests in these as they are in himself . . . then he, if he chooses to speak from these roots, works in that area where nature has given him size, projective size" (247–48). It is clear that the body from which poetry is projective belongs to a male heterosexual whose alternating pattern of tumescence and detumescence, penetration and projection, dissemination and impregnation structures more than the poem's lineation. Despite his repudiation elsewhere in the essay of traditional figuration (the "suck of symbol") Olson uses a familiar metaphor of the male as generative principle operating on a passive female nature, "that force to which he owes his somewhat small existence" (25). Such sustained masculinization of poetry gives the first syllable of "Manifesto" new meaning.

Were "Projective Verse" the work of a single individual it could be seen as the product of an isolated sensibility in revolt against the New Critical strictures of his day. But the essay is, in fact, a collaborative work, constructed out of letters between Olson and Robert Creeley in the late 1940s. Portions of Creeley's letters are embedded in Olson's prose as are quotations and paraphrases of other authors (Pound, Williams, Fenollosa) that, as Marjorie Perloff has pointed out, make this less an original work than a collage enterprise.[9] The document has become the centerpiece for Black Mountain poetics, a movement composed largely of men, and although it involves several bisexual or gay males (Robert Duncan, John Wieners, Michael Rumaker, Jonathan Williams, Fielding Dawson) its cultivation of heroic expressivism betrays a strongly heterosexual bias.[10] Finally, "Projective Verse" is a pedagogical instrument, written at the beginning of Olson's teaching career and designed to educate a certain kind of student. Since, as we shall see, that student is gendered male we may assume that this collaborative project is not extended to female readers.

The recently published letters between Olson and Frances Boldereff suggest that there was a third interlocutor in the production of "Projective Verse" who may have exerted as much influence on the manifesto as Creeley. Boldereff was an independent scholar (she wrote books on Joyce and Blake), librarian, and typographic designer with whom Olson shared a long and intimate relationship. The letters between the two figures, written from the late 1940s through the late 1960s, testify to an intense intellectual and sexual involvement, especially during the period of Olson's apprenticeship as a poet. Olson sent Boldereff copies of poems and essays, and she responded with enthusiasm, goading him on to new discoveries and levels of inquiry. She seems to have introduced him to many key literary, archaeological, and anthropological books that he subsequently used in the *Maximus* series, and she was an avid reader of his earlier work on Melville. "Projective Verse" appears in an early draft among the letters, and it seems clear that Boldereff contributed certain ideas about language as action to the essay. The absence of any reference to this powerful woman intellectual can, of course, be explained (as Sharon Thesen does in her editorial introduction to the letters) by Olson's common-law marriage to Constance Olson during the early 1950s (xiv). But this occlusion of Boldereff's influence is also informed by Olson's phallic theory of literary inheritance that can admit the authority of Williams, Pound, Creeley, Dahlberg, and others, but not of strong women. Compulsory homosociality does not concern the biographical life of the male artist so much as the textual life he produces through homosocial associations. That textual life—what we call poetics—may very well be composed by biological male or female others, but its function is to replicate a continuum of male associations, colleagues, and fellow travelers. The implications of this continuum for Olson's larger view of *polis* and community are far-reaching.

Olson's belief that projective verse extends the private into the social body is demonstrated in *The Maximus Poems,* which claims to restore "that which is familiar" to an estranged *polis.* In his epic design, Olson sustains homologies between individual and community whereby the recovery of physiology and orality in one translates into the recovery of place and geography in the other. The capitalist entrepreneurs who threaten to dissolve the local fishing economy of Gloucester, Massachusetts, can be counteracted by the citizen who takes "the way of / the lowest," and learns thereby that "there are no hierarchies, no infinite, no such many as mass, there are only / eyes in all heads / to be looked out of" (33). Olson chronicles the tough, if flawed, lives of Cape Ann fishermen who embody the shattered remains of an earlier vibrant self-reliance that has been lost to commercial canning and corporate fishing. In this respect, Olson provides a sequel to Melville's *Pequod* in modern-day New England. However egalitarian, such treatment of hardy masculine figures is contradicted by Olson's epic stance as an "Isolated person in Gloucester, Massachusetts" who addresses "you islands / of men and girls" (16). Where men are men and women are girls, the possibilities for equal access to *polis* are limited. In Olson's imagination of social change, man is active ("The waist of a lion / for a man to move properly") whereas a woman is passive ("And for a woman, / who should move lazily / the weight of breasts" [39]). Thus the dynamic possibilities of a historical poetics based on local action are sustained by a myth of gender inequality.

In the early *Maximus* series Gloucester serves as a microcosmic example of lost American plenitude. Sites of resistance can be found in small enclaves of male community, from the Dorchester Company who first settled Cape Ann in 1624 to contemporary sailors in whom Olson sees limited possibilities for heroic action. In later books, Olson expands his field of interest to include archaic history and myth as performing on a cosmological scale what Gloucester performs on the local level. A central figure of the late *Maximus* series is the Cretan war god Enyalion whom Olson venerates as an ideal of male virtue (*arete*). His heroism is embodied in the fact that he "goes to war with a picture," a phrase that appears several times in the series as a statement of male rectitude:

              The only interesting thing
is if one can be
an image
of man. "The nobleness, and the arete."
     (473)

Enyalion's ability to imagine himself as man, able to act "with a picture" rather than a weapon means that he becomes redeemed potentiality rather than limited nature. And it is precisely this opposition between the male, reflected in his self-image, and feminine nature, as ground or material, that structures Olson's vision. The picture that Enyalion carries with him is quite literally of himself, "the law of possibility," and as such controls what he sees. Woman is left out of the picture, serving as " 'Earth' mass mother milk cow body / demonstrably, suddenly, MORE / primitive and universal" (333). Woman cannot hold an image of herself because she is the primordial condition out of which images are made.

     Olson's Jungian perspective in the late *Maximus* series represents not so much a departure from his earlier historical concerns as a universalizing of qualities first discerned in America's colonial past. The self-reliant homosociality of New England fishermen continues in Enyalion, an archetypal hero out of whom a new city, a *civitas dei*, might be constructed. Olson had no less of an aspiration for Black Mountain College, "the largest city I'll ever know," which in its last days consisted of fourteen people, significantly the same number as made up the original Dorchester Company ("On Black Mountain" 68). Such parallels were not lost on Olson, who often regarded Black Mountain as a "City on a Hill" and who linked it with earlier American social experiments. And as I develop it in chapter 7, he also saw Black Mountain in relation to other global experiments such as Mao's cultural revolution and Third World struggles in Latin America that seemed to offer social alternatives to Western capitalist institutions.

     At each level of *polis,* from the small town to the redeemed Jerusalem, community exists to reflect the aspirations of man, not simply as a generic category for humanity but as a gendered principle of power. In a late *Maximus* poem, Olson admits that there is a price to pay for visionary struggle: "I've sacrificed every thing, including sex and woman / —or lost them—to this attempt to acquire complete / concentration" (473). If this is a confession of vulnerability and limit on Olson's part, it is no less a statement of personal resistance by which "sex and woman" are kept out of a city they had yet to occupy.

     Female students who attended Black Mountain were not exactly kept out of Olson's classes, but they had a difficult time learning under his autocratic pedagogy. Francine du Plessix Gray, who came to the college in 1951, acknowledges Olson's importance but describes the difficulties that she and other female students had in dealing with Olson's Ahab-like authority. "You're still writing conservative junk!" she reports Olson as saying to her in class; "AND ABOVE ALL DON'T TRY TO PUBLISH ANYTHING FOR TEN YEARS!" (348). Gray proved to be a "dutiful daughter" and waited a decade before publishing her first story—in the *New Yorker*, of all places. Another Black Mountain student, Mary Fiore, reported that "in both [Olson's] classes and his private circle of followers he tended to perpetuate the standard Black Mountain 'straight' male view of women as alluring but largely vacuous creatures—'Me Tarzan heap big intellect, you Jane full of mysteries'" (Clark 210). When feminist scholar Nancy Armstrong showed up for the first day of Olson's modern poetry seminar at the State University of New York, Buffalo, she was told that the course was going to be about "Men's Poetry" and any women who wanted to attend would have to watch from the hallway.[11] Such dismissive treatment imposes a phallic test on learning that must be seen as a dimension of projectivism—an attempt to literalize the power of male speech by refusing women any interlocutory relationship within it. By relegating women to literal and figurative hallways, Olson could perfect the *civitas dei* after his own fashion (and image) and reinforce his Socratic authority.

If female students were relegated to the hallways, the male students who remained became acolytes in complex rituals of filial obligation that were not without their erotic charge. Fielding Dawson's memoir of his student years at the college describes both Olson and the painter Franz Kline as surrogate fathers who offered a measure of manhood based less on affection than upon competition and daring. "Measuring up" as student and son also meant negotiating challenges to traditional sexual roles. Dawson's ambivalence about his own sexuality begins the first day he enters the college: "when I . . . walked up that gutted dirt road towards the Dininghall, a feminine building (it held a lot), I walked into a different world" (2). This feminized space of difference permits him homosexual as well as heterosexual relationships, although his anxiety about the former leads him to self-recriminatory reflections as he seeks to conform his relationships with men to heterosexual terms. "Hell no . . . I'm married," he says in response to the renewal of contact with a former male lover: "Very well, I say bitterly to hurt yourself and pretend that game, remember the night in the shadows under the tree by the place where you saw the bee? Kitty was furious at you: '*Cut this faggot game out, Fee Dawson, you're not queer.*' I was ashamed" (36). The complex pronominal interplay of this passage embodies Dawson's confusion as he seeks to differentiate himself from the lover while remembering that version of himself that *does* remember the erotic "night in the shadows" with Kitty. Is he ashamed at his previous actions, his continuing homosexual desires, or his (current) heterosexual ménage? Against the assertion of heteronormalcy ("Hell no . . . I'm married") the narrator projects a set of alternative selves, chiding and qualifying his assertions.

The way that Dawson challenges such fears is by adopting a competitive attitude toward his teachers, especially Olson. The crowning expression of this is his description of a baseball game when he strikes out the 6' 7" rector. Olson "threw his bat in the bushes, cursed me, and stormed off the field" (18). Physical competitiveness extends to intellectual aggressiveness as the student apes the teacher's confrontational mode. When a new faculty member comes to campus, he is subjected to a withering attack from the students:

> Every now and again a Liberal showed up to teach. That poor social anthropologist and his pretty wife left fast, went down the road in shock. They had sat before the student body, some of the faculty stood around, we were a savage bunch, and the social anthropologist tried to answer our questions; it was probably because the guy had never heard of Frobenius that we wiped him out. His weak theories, limited possession of source material, lack of fieldwork and almost total lack of feeling for literature and the plastic arts, was the end of him. We sat silently, coldly staring at him.
>
> (41–42)

This description is a summary of Olsonian values: hatred of liberal intellectuals, the necessity for arts education, unquestioning faith in Poundian sources like Frobenius, cynicism about the social sciences, fetishization of "source materials," fieldwork as basis for scholarship. Olson's stance, articulated through Dawson, reflects a particular anxiety during the 1950s about the status of intellectuals. For many artists and writers of Olson's generation, disenchanted with New Deal or Socialist politics, the professionalization of knowledge (and collusion with State Department initiatives) had resulted in a "new class" of academically trained specialists. Ex-New-Dealer Olson, while hardly a neoconservative, nevertheless embodied a kind of populist intellectualism that betrayed many of the same suspicions of cold war liberalism of his more right-wing colleagues.[12]

Such suspicions of official intellectual culture are not without their gendered component. In *The Black Mountain Book* one such "bad" liberal intellectual turns out to be Paul Goodman, who taught for brief periods at the college and who had been considered for a permanent teaching position. As Dawson sees him, Goodman came to the college armed "with psychotherapy (his own), literature, history, community planning and sex, as weapons" (133). For Dawson, the openly homosexual Goodman is a tempter with whom the students must do battle, using weapons of verbal clarity and concision:

> Most of the things Paul said were right but he often told them badly, deliberately; he, characteristic of Liberal Intellectuals, used his brilliance as a whip. . . .

> That guy was loaded with guns, and when he fired it didn't altogether work, because we knew the words he used better than he did—which surprised him, calling a snake "You're a SNAKE!"
> "Yeah, I'm a snake. Watch out."
> (133–34)

Dawson distinguishes between figures like Goodman, who continued to live within the orbit of the university, and artists like Franz Kline or Olson, whose intellectual accomplishments are embodied in physical acts of painting and writing. The latter are "real guys," in Dawson's hagiographic memory, and their art is a direct expression of that reality.[13]

Dawson was describing more than his own homosexual panic in discussing Goodman's effect on the college. Olson also experienced Goodman as a sexual threat and said so in a poem written after that visit. In "Black Mt. College Has a Few Words for a Visitor" Olson plays upon the allegorical character of Goodman's name, transposing *goodman* (Olson may have been thinking of Hawthorne's guilt-ridden Puritan in "Young Goodman Brown") into *everyman* in order to display how ultimately banal his influence at the college had been:

Names names, Paul Goodman
                     or else your own
will be the Everyman of sugar sweet, the ginger cookie
to scare the Witch with you, poor boy—if we must have such classes
as "equals," the young, your lads, the fearful lasses
    (*Collected Poems* 268)

What Dawson describes as Black Mountain's positive leveling of distinctions between pedagogue and ephebe here becomes a dangerous mixing of instructions. When classes transform lads into lasses, then Olson's more hierarchical, masculinist approach to learning is destroyed; pedagogy becomes pederasty. In Olson's mind it is a short distance between the Platonic grove to anonymous cruising in Central Park. In Goodman's "ginger cookie," Olson discerns "a rougher thought . . . he could corrupt an army" (269). At the same time, Olson recognizes his own complicity in Goodman's sexual and literary intentions:

Look: us equals, that is, also sons of witches, are covered now with cookies
dipped in same from your fell poem. It fell, all right, four footed
with one foot short where five were called for—five, sd the Sphinx,
confronted with senescence and with you, still running running running
from her hot breath who bore you, Hansel Paul, to bore us—all.

(269)

These cryptic lines say a great deal about how Olson configures homophobia through misogyny, identifying with Goodman as "sons of witches"
and subject to Circe-like powers of transformation. But Goodman's poem
(he had written verses critical of Black Mountain after his sojourn at the
college) falls short; his "four foot" line is inadequate to grapple with the
Sphinx's riddle.[14] Olson's considerably longer iambic lines are, presumably,
the proper (phallic) form for this kind of male challenge. In the allegory of
Hansel and Gretel that Olson employs here, sons are vulnerable to witches
who may transform them into ginger cookies and emasculate their poetry.
Goodman's solution is to become the "Everyman of sugar sweet" and thus
evade battle with the Sphinx. Olson, as author of "a Few Words for a Visitor"
adopts an oedipal stance, refusing to run "from her hot breath" and answer
her riddle.

Black Mountain, as this example indicates, was both a place and an ideology, a community and a set of legitimating practices and forms. As a poetics, it was never far from a vision of social totality, and while this vision was
often progressive in its resistance to commercialism and conformism, it was
often limited in its incorporation of others. Olson's belief that the projective
act in poetry will lead "to dimensions larger than the man" was not hyperbole;
it produced a generation of poets that shaped literary history in the 1960s and
1970s (*Collected Prose* 247). If projectivism enlarged "the man" it also reinforced his position as subject looking out on a feminized universe of passive
objects. This specular position was by no means stable in the 1950s, as Dawson's memoir makes clear, necessitating an almost parodic reassertion of
masculine self-sufficiency. This may have been a cold war ritual that many individuals had to undergo at this time, even when they declared themselves
"Isolatos" from outposts in North Carolina or Gloucester.

"THE CITY THAT WE CREATE IN OUR BARTALK"

Or San Francisco. Jack Spicer's poetics of dictation, like Olson's "Projective
Verse," was never formulated in any systematic way but developed through a
kind of occasional workshop conducted in various North Beach bars and
apartments. It receives its most famous articulation in the Vancouver lec-

tures of 1963 in which Spicer describes poetry as being received from the "outside" rather than generated from within.[15] The poet is a medium or channel into which the poem comes from an "endistanced" source. In formulating his poetics of dictation, Spicer often alludes to Cocteau's movie *Orphée* in which the poet receives his poetry via his car radio and to Yeats's later experiments with mediumistic writing. This theory of poetic dictation thwarts intentionality by demanding that the poet remain open to what Spicer called the "low ghosts" who are constantly blabbering at the margins of discourse.

Such spirited metaphors for poetic reception have obvious precedents in romantic poetics and surrealism, but they also have practical implications for the bohemian culture in which Spicer lived. At bars like Gino Carlos and The Place, the Spicer circle lived out certain rites of exclusion, acceptance, and initiation in relation to a potentially hostile outside world. In the homophobic 1950s the group had every reason to fear that world where beatings, arrests, and incarceration of homosexuals were regular features of North Beach life. If the poetry/bar world was insular, it was also necessary, in a pre-Stonewall era, for developing gay community. I have discussed the significance of this sense of community in *The San Francisco Renaissance* but would add that such insularity of the Spicer circle did not prevent the development of its own forms of exclusion and homophobia.

The origins of Spicer's group ethos can be traced back to his college years at the University of California at Berkeley during the late 1940s. As students of medieval literature and history he, Robert Duncan, and Robin Blaser were fascinated by the lore of Arthurian knights, crusades, and secret societies. Contributing significantly to the Berkeley poets' sense of insular community was the influence of the medieval historian Ernst Kantorowicz who was teaching at Berkeley during the late 1940s and with whom the three poets took classes. He had been a member of the circle of homosexual artists surrounding Stefan George in Germany that included Kantorowicz's own teacher, Friederich Gundolf. During the famous loyalty oath controversy at Berkeley, Kantorowicz courageously refused to sign, moving to Princeton's Institute for Advanced Study. In Kantorowicz, the young poets found a model for homosocial community upon which their own Pre-Raphaelite Berkeley Renaissance was based.[16]

This cultishness of the Berkeley period continued into the 1950s when Spicer developed another male fraternity in North Beach bars. The poets in Spicer's circle, like those at Black Mountain, preferred a kind of hard-drinking, macho ethos, supplemented by sports, pinball, and verbal fisticuffs. Younger poets had to prove themselves to the more senior poets, and competition between individuals was encouraged. Many younger writers have testified to the competitive atmosphere of the Spicer circle and honed their writing through informal workshops conducted at various venues. Group magazines like *Open Space, J,* and *Capitalist Bloodsucker,* which published poetry by members of the circle, also printed satires and imitations of other poets and movements. Retaining one's marginal status meant maintaining a vigilant stand against the forces of cooption or what Spicer called the "fix": "Tell everyone to have guts," Spicer urges; "Come through the margins / Clear and pure / Like love is" (*Collected Books* 63). And, in his later poems, Spicer extends his metaphor of poetic reception to include baseball and boxing:

The poet is a radio. The poet is a liar. The poet is a counterpunching radio.
And those messages (God would not damn them) do not
    even know they are champions.
  (218)

The inability to spar within this circle meant that one lacked will, that, to adapt one of Spicer's favorite metaphors, Orpheus had lost direction by turning back to find Eurydice.

The title for this section points to much of this agonistic spirit. It is drawn from Spicer's *The Heads of the Town up to the Aether:* "But the city that we create in our bartalk or in our fuss and fury about each other is in an utterly mixed and mirrored way an image of the city. A return from exile" (*Collected Books* 176). Spicer is posing a link between Dante's projection of Florence into the *civitas dei* of the *Divine Comedy* by imagining a redeemed San Francisco formed out of the poet's North Beach milieu. Against communitarian ideas like those of Paul Goodman, Spicer's imagined community exists through contention, "our fuss and fury about each other." For Spicer, argument and conflict signal the fact that ideas are real and earnest, embodied in persons who find them worth fighting for. Much of that contention is related to power dynamics based around gender and is therefore rather distinct from Plato's ideal Republic.

Spicer's tough-guy stance configured homosexuality within an almost Calvinist sense of moral imperatives. The battle for poetry had to be waged against the twin evils of femininity and assimilation. Effete or effeminate forms of gay behavior were not permitted. When asked about Spicer's relation to poets of the New York school, Landis Everson said that he (Spicer) didn't like them, especially John Ashbery. Spicer "called him 'a faggot poet.' John's first book was called *Some Trees* and Jack always made it a point of pronouncing it 'Thumb Twees' " (Ellingham and Killian 65). Nor was homosexuality to be contained within institutional structures. Its revolutionary potential was not in solidarity but in solitude: "Homosexuality is essentially being alone. Which is a fight against the capitalist bosses who do not want us to be alone" ("Homosexuality and Marxism" n.p.). Although Spicer participated in a limited way with older, more established homosexual institutions like the Log Cabin and the Mattachine Society, at least one poem in *Language* warns of the dangers of too much assimilation:

Which explains poetry. Distances
Impossible to be measured or walked over. A band of faggots
     (fasces) cannot be built into a log-cabin in which all Western
     Civilization can cower. And look at stars, and books, and
     other people's magic diligently.
    (*Collected Books* 227)

Spicer equates "faggots" with fascists ("fasces") when their outsider status is accommodated within the rest of Western civilization.[17] He also detects a certain fascistic element in organized homophile movements, despite the fact that Spicer was somewhat active in the Berkeley Mattachine Society during its early days.[18]

Against feminized or assimilated versions of gay identity, Spicer mounted a group offensive among faithful followers. The enemy was official verse culture with its publishing center in New York, its magazines and academic venues, but the enemy was no less the heterosexual outside world, especially that which nightly invaded "his" North Beach in tour busses searching for beatniks. Part of the group offensive involved creating a frontal, unadorned image of gay reality that excluded not only a heterosexual viewer but a certain kind of homosexual as well:

For Joe

People who don't like the smell of faggot vomit
Will never understand why men don't like women
Won't see why those never to be forgotten thighs
Of Helen (say) will move us into screams of laughter.
Parody (what we don't want) is the whole thing.
Don't deliver us any mail today, mailman.
Send us no letters. The female genital organ is hideous. We
Do not want to be moved.
Forgive us. Give us
A single example of the fact that nature is imperfect.
Men ought to love men
(And do)

As the man said
It's
Rosemary for remembrance.
    (62)

This poem is based on a vertiginous logic that mixes homosexual desire, homophobia, and misogyny. Spicer seems to be saying that in a society where one's homosexual nature is defined as "imperfect" he has no choice but to love "faggot vomit" and feel that "the female genital organ is hideous." Moreover the authority of this logic demands that he refuse any ameliorating position; he will not be "moved," ideologically or emotionally. Once he accepts this logic, misogyny becomes a structural prerequisite by which difference can be constructed. Whether or not the "female genital organ is hideous" is a moot point; it is a position required within the heterosexist continuum by which homosexuality is marked as other. The preposterous nature of claims in this poem is part of the requirement. The poem is unpleasant and awkward, mocking rational claims for beauty and normalcy by displaying their parodic versions. If there is an element of homosexual self-hatred here, it is acknowledged as such within the rhetoric that heterosexuality speaks. The proposition that "Men ought to love men" contains both the hope that there might be a world where men *can* love men but also the realization that in a world where men *do* love men, men ought *not* to love women.

As I have recounted elsewhere, "For Joe" was written on the occasion of Denise Levertov's visit to the San Francisco Bay area and was designed to provoke the visitor as much as test the loyalty of the audience.[19] The poem is also dedicated to another poet, Joe Dunn, and as such introduces a second level of address into the confrontation. Many of Spicer's poems speak directly to specific individuals, often in the form of letters, and thus demand a highly specific act of decoding. Each letter "is a mirror, dedicated to the person that I particularly want to look into it" (55), Spicer declares in *After Lorca*, thus removing the poem from its identity as discrete lyric and placing it in a dialogic relationship to the reader. Single poems are "one-night stands . . . as meaningless as sex in a Turkish bath" (*Collected Books* 61). Against the isolated lyric stands what Spicer called the "serial poem," a suite or book of single lyrics, often incomprehensible by themselves but linked when read as a group. The serial poem becomes the literary analogue of sexual community, each separate lyric given identity by its combative relationship to the whole: "Poems should echo and reecho against each other. They should create resonances. They cannot live alone any more than we can" (61).

Spicer thematized the communal implications of the serial poem by developing each of his books around one or more models of male fraternity: cowboy mythology in *Billy the Kid*, Gnostic theology and Orphic legend in

Heads of the Town up to the Aether, Arthurian knights in *The Holy Grail,* base-ball teams in *Language,* and frontier explorers in *Book of Magazine Verse.* Un-like modernist uses of myth, in which cultural decay is offset by the salvific presence of prior narratives, Spicer rewrites classical and popular stories to enforce solidarity among a small group of adepts. It is precisely because the larger culture has become fragmented that the marginal culture, with its rules and local deities, becomes necessary. The social role of poetry lies not in the author's political views but in the degree to which he can create a linguis-tic alternative to the instrumentalized language elsewhere in society.

In *After Lorca* (1957) we see the most obvious blend of poetics, corre-spondence, and homosociality. The book consists of a series of translations and mistranslations of García Lorca's poetry, interlaced with letters written to and from the Spanish poet. In these letters Spicer confronts two versions of correspondence: epistolarity and metaphor: "Things do not connect; they correspond. That is what makes it possible for a poet to translate real objects, to bring them across language as easily as he can bring them across time" (*Collected Books* 34). Metaphor is not the substitution of one sign by another but the bringing "across language" of two discontinuous realms. By address-ing García Lorca, Spicer attempts to bring the dead poet "across time" so that he may "correspond" with him. By writing his own poems and calling them translations, Spicer suggests that García Lorca's poetry lives on in the poetics he created for subsequent poets to appropriate. Unlike Harold Bloom's the-ory of influence, which privileges an oedipal struggle between fathers and sons, Spicer's theory of correspondence links male poets through shared sex-ual and textual affinities. The living poet does not castrate the father in order to write the new poem but translates the otherness of the dead poet into the otherness of the living.

Most commentary on *After Lorca* has noted the parallels between Spicer's theory of correspondence and symbolist or other modernist forms of literary non sequitur. What must be added is the level of homosocial male de-sire that animates every level of this work. The object of the series, García Lorca, was himself a gay male, whose ambivalence about his sexuality is a central theme in *Poeta en Nueva York.*[20] Two of the poems Spicer "adds" to that volume are based on the Narcissus legend as a central tale of homoeroti-cism. Since most of the translations are dedicated to other homosexual males, Spicer is also "corresponding" to and within a closed world of male friendship. Finally, the terms for Spicer's correspondence theory are written in the rhetoric of homosexual desire: "How easy it is in erotic musing or in the truer imagination of a dream to invent a beautiful boy. How difficult to take a boy in a blue bathing suit that I have watched as casually as a tree and to make him visible in a poem as a tree is visible, not as an image or a picture but as something alive—caught forever in the structure of words. Live moons, live lemons, live boys in bathing suits. The poem is a collage of the real" (*Collected Books* 34). This passage would seem to be a classic statement of modernist aesthetics—a merging of Thomas Mann's *Death in Venice* with Russian formalist *ostranenie*. Yet far from textualizing desire by creating an aesthetic monad as displacement for lost beauty, Spicer recreates desire again and again in the complex deixis of his poem. To make the beautiful boy visible means creating a network of references to dead poets (García Lorca, Whitman, Rimbaud) and living (dedicatees include many of Spicer's friends) that blurs the distinctions between original and belated texts. The boy Spicer desires is brought into the poem as something "caught forever in the structure of words," not in their power to fix him in an image.

Oddly enough Spicer signals his own homosexual anxiety most fervently in the poem that is closest to the original. In his version of García Lorca's "Oda a Walt Whitman," Spicer re-creates García Lorca's conflicted view of New York, a city that embodies both Whitman's healthy "adhesive" comrades as well as those *maricas* or "perverts" who "sprout out along the beach of your dreams" (29). Although most of the poem is faithful to the original, Spicer displays a degree of linguistic license in those passages involving forms of homosexuality that are uncontainable within Whitman's masculine comradeship. García Lorca's poem excoriates

> vosotros, maricas de la ciudades,
> de carne tumefacta y pensamiento immundo,
> madres delodo, arpías, enemigos sin sueño
> del Amor que reparte coronas de alegría.
>   (124)

which in Ben Belitt's translation reads as follows:

> But you! against all of you, perverts of the cities,
> immodest of thought and tumescent of flesh,
> mothers of filthiness, harpies, sleeplessly thwarting
> the Love that apportions us garlands of pleasure.
>   (125)

Spicer's version is a great deal more frontal in its attack:

> But against the rest of you, cocksuckers of cities.
> Hard-up and dirty-brained,
> Mothers of mud, harpies, dreamless enemies
> Of the Love that distributes crowns of gladness.
>   (31)

And where Belitt translates García Lorca's "Esclavos de la mujer, perras de sus tocadores, / abiertos en las plazas con fiebre de abanico" (124) as "toadies of women, dressing-room bitches, / brazen in squares in a fever of fans," Spicer is more direct: "Slaves of women, lapdogs of their dressing tables, / Opening their flys in parks with a fever of fans" (31). Clearly Spicer wants to force García Lorca's language into more extreme statement ("abiertos in las plazas" is demonstrably not the same as "opening their flys in parks") to display not only the Spanish poet's fears of homosexuality but his own.

Spicer's radical rewriting of García Lorca, like his attack on female genitalia in "For Joe," represents his view that poetry must be a forum where exclusions and seductions in the barworld of San Francisco can be played out in a textual form that retains qualities of a public affront. Poetry must not merely depict such conflict but must perform, through its language, the unbridgeable gaps between subject and object. Traditional poetics has no adequate terms to describe this merging of the aesthetic and quotidian, and thus Spicer resorted to baseball, comics, magic, and pinball as metaphors for poetry. Such ludic pleasures insist on their own entertainment value and imply a fruitful tension between skill and chance. But linguistic performativity is enabled through a more complex performance of masculinity within the Spicer circle that, in order to allow the outside into the poem, had to re-create the inside as a bunch of guys, "heads of the town [who aspire] . . . to the aether."

GENDER BORDER CONTROL

One of the key links between Olson's and Spicer's poetics is objectivism (or what Olson called "objectism"): the attempt to escape the "lyrical interference of the individual as ego" by regarding the poem as a form of materiality within the world. This attempt to separate inside from outside should be seen not only as a restatement of Keats's negative capability but as a form of what Judith Butler, in *Gender Trouble,* calls "gender border control" whereby the integrity of the subject is discursively maintained "for the purposes of the regulation of sexuality within the obligatory frame of reproductive heterosexuality" (136). The discursive means by which both poets sought to differentiate realms involves the development of a poetics of gesture within which the poet could escape reflection and act on the moment. But what was reflection for these poets if not a feminized space of interiority and psychic boundlessness? What was lyrical interference if not the intrusion of seductive reason and beautiful rhetoric? Language-as-gesture was a defense against such feminization. It could reinforce the integrity of the male body by regarding its nonreflective acts as significant, even heroic, at a moment when the possibilities for heroism were in short supply. But in projecting the poet as object and the poem as unmediated gesture, both heterosexual and homosexual poets feared a reciprocal objectification—and feminization—against which only male community could serve as protection.

By studying compulsory homosociality as a structure of subject production rather than a value system or form of sexual preference I am arguing that even within the most progressive communities—whether homosexual or heterosexual—forms of misogyny and homophobia are often necessary to their continuation. By applying this analysis to Black Mountain and San Francisco literary communities, I do not mean to diminish the subversive and oppositional possibilities that these groups represented. In fact it is because these movements mounted such a significant challenge to traditional models of American social identity during the 1950s that we need to understand what ideological closures continue to speak through a verse so often characterized as open.

Olson's poetics of the body and breath led to a participatory, historically critical poetry that has been influential for gay as well as straight poets. Likewise, Spicer's foregrounding of the linguistic basis of identity, his recognition that "where we are is in a sentence," anticipates many recent theories of discursive identity construction. By linking poetics to ideas of community and social resistance, Olson and Spicer provided an important corrective to modernist narratives of artisanal authority and objectivity. But in their postmodern attempts to turn logos into low-ghost, discourse into performance, these poets and their followers often spoke less as prophets than as ventriloquists. As belated readers of this highly mediated speech, we must be sensitive both to the possibilities of community it projected and those it could not yet pronounce.

2

From Margin to Mainstream: Postwar Poetry and the Politics of Containment

Yet I ride by the margin of that lake in
the wood, the castle,
and the excitement of strongholds,
and have a small boy's notion of doing good.
　　　Robert Creeley, "The Way"

MANAGING THE MARGINS

The division between margin and mainstream has often organized literary histories of the 1950s. The standard version of this story concerns a series of writers, from various bohemian enclaves, who emerged in the midst of conformist 1950s America to establish a beachhead against more conservative, academically trained writers represented by John Ciardi's *Mid-Century American Poets* (1950) or the Donald Hall, Robert Pack, and Louis Simpson anthology, *New Poets of England and America* (1957). The literary "cold war" between what Robert Lowell diagnosed as "raw" and "cooked" poetries is now the subject of several recent books, but what I want to investigate is the presumed gap between margin and mainstream as it pertains to American culture at midcentury.[1] Like the open margins of much postwar poetry, social margins shift position each generation, forcing us to investigate not only the center but the periphery. For poets of the 1950s the term *marginal* had definite international implications relating to America's geopolitical authority following the war. Nor was the term *mainstream* an uncontested territory for the new consumer society being produced through advertising, electronic media, and global capital.

It may seem that the debate over margin and mainstream is a variant of a larger avant-garde discourse concerning inside and outside, bourgeois affirmative culture and vanguard visionary. Paul Mann points out that the "language of inside and outside is endemic to any discussion of the avant-garde" but that deconstruction—in its reliance on avant-garde art as a model for critical discourse—has remapped the territory, incorporating the margin and exposing the delusional fact of the outside (13). This "involution of the margin has been one of the chief historical purposes of the avant-garde," creating a paradoxical situation in which the constituent "centering" feature of a movement is its outsider status (13). The avant-garde is thus doubly marginalized, calling into question an aesthetic topography based on interiors, margins, limits, and boundaries. By so problematizing this topography, the avant-garde comments suggestively on (or helps foster) a larger historical episteme that maintains the status quo. In his important diagnosis of this doubleness of the avant-garde, Mann misses an opportunity to historicize its formation in the 1950s where the "involution of the margin" was conducted in highly specific cultural terms concerning the status of mass culture in a postwar and cold war economy.

Using the Beat generation as an example, we could identify two scenarios by which margin and mainstream were opposed: either the Beats resisted hegemonic American values, remaining outside the mainstream by refusing its terms (conformism, consensus, contract) or else, given the totalizing nature of postwar capitalism, they were assimilated into it. The first narrative is written by the poets themselves, the second by cultural conservatives, both Left and Right, who saw the Beats not as a distinct culture but as a reflex of larger forces they could not control. In order to test these scenarios we need to historicize the rhetoric of opposition in relation to the cold war era in which such movements emerged.[2]

On the matter of *mainstream*, we must first ask which mainstream we mean. If we mean the literary-industrial complex, dominated by East Coast publishers, Ivy League colleges, and debates conducted in the *Kenyon Review* or by the corporate boosterism of the Eisenhower business cabinet, then the new counterpoetries of the 1950s were definitely marginal, not to say often hostile to it. "Go fuck yourself with your atom bomb" is Allen Ginsberg's summary response to the version of America being written in the pages of the *Wall Street Journal* or *Fortune* (146). But there was another mainstream being defined (and deplored) during this same period, variously defined as mass culture or mass society in the pages of the *Partisan Review* or by members of the Frankfurt school. For Dwight Macdonald, the mysteries of Earle Stanley Gardner, the paintings of Norman Rockwell, and the articles in *Life* magazine, however technically proficient, are directed solely at the market, not at the sensibilities of individual readers. Such cultural products reduce individuals to "mass man," a fictional index of cultural homogenization and are thus vulnerable to ideological infection. In the work of Macdonald, Clement Greenberg, Theodor Adorno, Lionel Trilling, and others, mass society is the product of advertising, movies, radio, television, and rock 'n' roll, a culture numbed to great art by the replicated, kitsch versions being produced by the culture industries. Against *this* mainstream stands what Trilling called an "adversary culture" of intellectual guardians and academic clerics defending authentic aesthetic values from their instrumentalized versions in popular media (n.p.).

Early critics of the Beats like Trilling, John Hollander, John Ciardi, Delmore Schwartz, and Irving Howe liked to point out the similarities between Kerouac and company and the middle class, suburban society they excoriated. Irving Howe, speaking of writers of the San Francisco Renaissance, notes that they "illustrate the painful, though not inevitable predicament of rebellion in a mass society. . . . In their contempt for mind, they are at one with the middle class suburbia they think they scorn. In their incoherence of feeling and statement they mirror the incoherent society that clings to them like a mocking shadow" (435). And, summarizing his selection of poets for his anthology *Mid-Century American Poets,* John Ciardi reinforced this division by deploring the "barbaric yawp" that animated much nineteenth-century poetry. Drawing on a series of oedipalized metaphors, Ciardi speaks approvingly of the contemporary generation's "maturity," its relinquishing of European parents along with its adolescent populism to produce an independent literary tradition: "For pre-eminently this is a generation not of Bohemian extravagance but of self-conscious sanity in an urbane and cultivated poetry that is the antithesis of the Bohemian spirit" (xxix). In their contempt for the new bohemians, critics like Howe and Ciardi demeaned popular sources in American writing in general. In doing so they revealed limits to the liberal consensus and tolerance they otherwise endorsed, turning Trilling's "adversary culture" into another version of Brahmin elitism. In this context, the cultural mainstream became identified negatively with bohemian excess, a connection which the Beats often exploited.

Far from rejecting the cultural mainstream, the Beats embraced many of its more oppositional features. Kerouac's affection for Krazy Kat and the Marx Brothers, his love of fast cars and speed, his enthusiasm for all night diners and automats, and his belief in the lumpen underclass certainly invoke one version of an American mainstream represented as well in the films of Marlon Brando and James Dean. His willingness to write for masscult periodicals like *Playboy, Esquire,* or *Fortune,* his appearances on the Steve Allen show, and his embrace of farmers, Chinatown cooks, and black jazz musicians place him far more in the center of American culture than genealogists of Beat culture might like. One could say the same for Michael McClure's representations of motorcycle culture and cartoons in his plays, Frank O'Hara's love of movies, Jack Spicer's affection for the Oz books and pinball, Bob Kaufman's surrealist merging of popular black culture and voodoo, LeRoi Jones's (Amiri Baraka's) nostalgia for popular radio shows like *The Shadow,* and Allen Ginsberg's belief that Walt Whitman occasionally appears in a neon supermarket—such use of popular sources testifies to the resilience of the cultural mainstream in their work. The most famous press and bookstore of the period was called, after all, City Lights, not Unreal Cities Books.

What makes 1950s counterpoetries like that of the Beats so significant as a cultural movement is that they complicated the division between mass culture and aesthetic culture as it was being discussed in 1950s intellectual forums—a division that had haunted American intellectuals since Hawthorne and Emerson. Nor did the Beats identify strictly as an avant-garde movement in the terms made famous by Clement Greenberg—a movement dedicated to the creation of "'abstract' or 'nonobjective' art . . . something valid solely on its own terms" (4). Rather, the Beats sustained the historical avant-garde's merging of art and mass-produced materials, practices associated with Marcel Duchamp and the dadaists and with the Beats' contemporaries Robert Rauschenberg, Jasper Johns, and Andy Warhol. The Beats, to continue my first example, neither sold out to the mainstream nor rejected it; rather, they worked strategically *within* it to develop an immanent critique. They sampled mass culture in ways that never privileged the artwork over its popular sources, as was often the case for their modernist forebears. If in the process they were "marginalized" within the establishment it was because they became necessary adjuncts to a larger politics of totalization being waged beyond the literary establishment. In this larger political arena, margins could be manipulated in order to maintain the illusion of a continuous American national fantasy. The management of these margins was the province of a cold war ideology that had as its central premise the end of all ideology. The liberal consensus seemed satisfied with this assessment, but a number of marginal writers remained skeptical.

Given this book's emphasis on the reproduction of masculinity, it is worth remembering that one of the primary threats of mass culture is its feminization of modernist autonomy. If Jackson Pollock's drip paintings were, for Greenberg, signs of heroic, masculine independence, their reproductions in Formica tabletops, hi-fi speaker covers, and window shades represented their kitsch vulgarization in the domestic sphere. Although Macdonald, Greenberg, Howe, and others do not mention women in their excoriations of mass culture, it is clear that their references to the ill effects of popular magazines, Hollywood melodramas, romance novels, advertising, and fashion are code words for female consumerism—or for feminized male consumers. As Andreas Huyssen has pointed out, the "great divide" between high art and mass culture coincides with the emergence of consumer society in the nineteenth century, a new public sphere dominated by women. A foundational modernist work like *Madame Bovary* depends for its formal perfection on containing—and criticizing—that gendered (bourgeois) sphere of women. Flaubert distinguishes himself as male writer from his main character, reader of popular romances, and thereby ensures the continuation of artisanal purity. What Huyssen calls "the hidden dialectic" of avant-garde and mass culture is the attempt on the part of certain artists following World War I to merge art and mass culture into a critical art and to overcome the art/life dichotomy.

Cold war debates over mass culture shifted the ground from a threat to "institution art" via feminized consumerism to one concerning national security. Dwight Macdonald's famous essay, "Masscult and Midcult," is cast specifically around the "larger question of the masses" and the danger that totalitarian regimes may use popular culture as an organ of indoctrination (8–9). And Daniel Bell, in *The End of Ideology,* after summarizing various forms that mass society has assumed, concludes that the threat in each of his categories is that "propaganda can manipulate the masses" (25). The threat of Soviet manipulation of popular opinion may differentiate postwar from earlier debates over art and culture, but what remains constant is a certain squeamishness among critics over the appearance of popular icons like Marilyn Monroe, beer cans, or newspaper photos in the work of gay artists like Andy Warhol, Jasper Johns, or Robert Rauschenberg.

A word about genre. It might seem that the place to investigate tensions between margins and mainstream in poetry would be in Beat generation jeremiads such as "Howl" or satires such as Gregory Corso's "Marriage" or in epic ventures like as Charles Olson's *Maximus Poems* or Melvin Tolson's *Libretto for the Republic of Liberia.* Instead, I would like to look at these issues in lyric modes, seemingly the epitomes of convention, in which marginal identities are mediated by formal and generic containment. The 1950s saw a renaissance of the lyric, influenced by several forces: Pound's translations of troubadour and Italian verse, Williams's interest in quantitative meters and the variable foot, the valorization of seventeenth-century metaphysical poets and Elizabethan lyricists, New Critical emphasis on the lyric's formal integrity and autonomy, the appearance of new translations of the French symbolist poets. As my epigraph from Robert Creeley indicates, there was in this revival a self-consciously romantic pose adopted by many poets of the period that served as a vehicle for testing new attitudes toward gender. While academic formalists were perfecting a tightly woven lyric vehicle out of the symbolist and metaphysical models, poets as different as Creeley, Gwendolyn Brooks, John Wieners, and Frank O'Hara were exploring looser lyric forms in order to test a variety of new social idiolects. One could see this same tendency in early work by W. S. Merwin, Paul Blackburn, LeRoi Jones, Denise Levertov, Robert Duncan, Joel Oppenheimer, Galway Kinnell, James Wright, Ron Loewinsohn, and John Ashbery, for whom the lyric self-consciously alludes to its own generic conventions in providing indices of interiority and self-reflection. Thus by looking at forms of poetry that would seem to eschew the social, we may see an internally distanced view of what the social cannot accommodate.

EXECUTING DIFFERENCES

The opening of Sylvia Plath's *The Bell Jar* presents a conundrum for cold war culture: "It was a queer, sultry summer, the summer they electrocuted the Rosenbergs, and I didn't know what I was doing in New York. I'm stupid about executions. The idea of being electrocuted makes me sick, and that's all there was to read about in the papers—goggle-eyed headlines staring up at me on every street corner and at the fusty, peanut-smelling mouth of every subway. It had nothing to do with me but I couldn't help wondering what it would be like, being burned alive all along your nerves" (1). Esther Greenwood's perverse refusal of history, her absorption of the Rosenberg's execution into a fit of personal pique, has seemed to many a supreme indulgence. Moreover her voyeuristic interest in the physical pain of execution personalizes an epochal moment in cold war history.[3] Yet by the end of the novel Esther does indeed feel "what it would be like, being burned alive all along your nerves" through shock therapy treatments administered after her suicide attempt. What begins as a petulant refusal to engage history returns more ominously as an administered attempt to remove memory. The two forms of refusal have a common source in a cold war imaginary in which the threat of invasion from without is experienced as psychological trauma within. The cure for both social and personal pathology is the application of electrodes, but as Lady Lazarus says, "there is a charge / For the eyeing of my scars" paid by poet and audience alike (*Collected* 246).

This replacement of public by private pains is a characteristic move among poets of Plath's milieu (Lowell and Berryman are the obvious examples) and could serve as a more general feature of 1950s personalism. Such gestures are usually seen as reactions to New Critical values of distanciation and impersonality, but they are no less related to a kind of domestic cultural containment in which crises of national security are acted out as dramas of private insecurity. The expression of such insecurity was itself contained by critics of Plath's generation, often armed with existentialism or psychoanalysis, who pathologized what they took to be obsessive emphasis on internal states. In a like manner the Beats were demonized as perpetual adolescents, unable to mature into responsible tax-paying Americans. Much has been said about the more public attacks on the National Security state during the fifties by Ginsberg, Ferlinghetti, and others, but less has been said about the constitutive relationship between containment as it was theorized on a geopolitical level and as it was enacted on the domestic front. If the cold war, as David Campbell says, was fought on a discursive plain related to the production and reproduction of identity, what sorts of identities were produced (vii)? To what extent was that production dependent on "the inscription of boundaries which serve to demarcate an 'inside' from an 'outside,' a 'self' from an 'other,' a 'domestic' from a 'foreign' " (8)? Moreover, how were those identities represented in cultural artifacts having no apparent relationship to national security? For if containment requires the creation of consensus, it manifests itself most powerfully where identities cannot be secured, where, to invoke lines by Robert Creeley, "the unsure / egoist is not / good for himself" (125).

The architecture of cold war containment was provided by a series of national security documents written by George Kennan, Paul Nitze, Dean Acheson, and other State Department officials during the late 1940s and that served as the basis for American foreign policy regarding the Soviet Union. As Kennan described it U.S. policy toward the Soviets "must be that of a long-term, patient but firm and vigilant containment of Russian expansive tendencies" ("Sources" 119). From his base as a Sovietologist and head of the Planning and Policy staff, stationed in Moscow, Kennan created a view of Russians as irrational, insecure, and paranoid, whose goals for world domination depended on disrupting the internal security of Western powers. Later national security documents like the one penned by Paul Nitze in 1950 (NSC 68) reinforced the Manichean division between capitalist and communist systems by vaunting the former's "self-discipline and self-restraint" against the latter's moral and philosophical decrepitude (387). What is most important about Kennan's policy in terms of cultural hegemony was his recognition that military containment abroad depended on the maintenance of domestic order at home. In his "long telegram" of 1946 he declares, "much depends on [the] health and vigor of our own society. World communism is like a malignant parasite which feeds only on diseased tissue. This is the point at which domestic and foreign policies meet. Every courageous and incisive measure to solve internal problems of our own society, to improve self-confidence, discipline, morale and community spirit of our own people, is a diplomatic victory over Moscow worth a thousand diplomatic notes & joint communiqués"

(63). Kennan's language of health and infection, as Andrew Ross points out, places the drama of containment in medical terms. Society is a body threatened by infection from without; it must be quarantined, but must be protected from within as well by appropriate ideological medicine (46).

In order to monitor the health of the vulnerable domestic body a vast federal bureaucracy was created. A short list of new agencies would include the NIA (National Intelligence Authority) in 1946; the CIA (1947); the IAC (Intelligence Advisory Committee) in 1950; the NSA (National Security Agency) in 1952; the Hoover Commission Task Force on Intelligence in 1955; and the DIA (Defense Intelligence Agency) in 1961, not to mention special congressional committees like the McCarthy committee or the House Committee on Un-American Activities. These agencies policed the threat of subversion through loyalty oaths, congressional hearings, blacklists, surveillance technology, executive orders, union-busting legislation, INS restrictions, and general harassment. While in no way as draconian in their methods as the Stalinist gulag and show trials of the same era, such institutions had the specific mandate of maintaining domestic normalcy.[4] The immediate threat posed by the Rosenbergs was not only the nature of the information they (purportedly) leaked to the Soviets but also that they lived among "us." Alger Hiss, according to one journalist, "wore no beard, spoke with no accent, moved casually in the best circles. . . . Hiss looked like the man down the block in Scarsdale. . . . If this man could be a spy, anybody could" (qtd. in Whitfield 28).

It is the nature of this "us" that was perhaps the most enduring legacy of the cold war, a collective subject forged by the politics of consensus and finished on Madison Avenue. Sociologists like David Riesman, William H. Whyte, Talcott Parsons, and Vance Packard studied this new other-directed individual, providing a skeptical yet legitimating rhetoric for the new group ethos. The ideal of homogeneity was not only something advocated by civic leaders and politicians; it could be purchased materially in the new Levittowns and postwar tract developments that sprang up to accommodate the baby boom. If, to adapt Robert Creeley, "the darkness sur / rounds us," why not "buy a goddamn big car" (132)? Creeley puts in brief what American consumers were being asked to believe—that the postwar economy was prosperous and that further consumption could ameliorate the forces of undifferentiated darkness.

Thanks to the work of Elaine Tyler May, Barbara Ehrenreich, Stephanie Koontz, Lynn Spigel, John D'Emilio, and others, we now know a good deal more about the effects of containment ideology on domestic life, sexuality, and mass culture. What is developed in their writings is that the threat of communism was translated into a renewed concern over the stability of the American family threatened by forces unleashed by the war. Just as the government had to monitor Soviet expansion abroad, so individuals had to police their sexual, social, moral, and domestic lives for signs of breakdown. But if Ozzie and Harriet were the template for middle-class normalcy, there was trouble brewing with Ricky's guitar—gender trouble.[5]

What should the young
man say, because he is buying
Modess? Should he

blush or not. Or
turn coyly, his head, to
one side, as if in

the exactitude of his emotion he
were not offended? Were
proud? Of what? To buy

a thing like that.
    (Creeley 135)

Barbara Ehrenreich has pointed out that the male shopper, fully able to discriminate among products, was a novel phenomenon of the 1950s (*Hearts* 51–59). But the products he was being asked to purchase included more than those being advertised in the pages of *Playboy* or *Esquire*. In "The Lover," by Robert Creeley, the young man's indecision at the checkout counter stems not only from embarrassment at buying a feminine hygiene product but from having to adopt an appropriate attitude toward it. The anxiety over naming Modess derives from the young man's dual role as shopper and lover, the "exactitude" of whose emotion is registered in Creeley's highly enjambed, halting lines. His various attempts to find an action suitable to the occasion only serves to heighten his squeamishness.

    "The Lover" obviously has little to do with fears of Soviet expansion, yet the poet's constant interrogation of roles, manners, and discretions marks a pervasive national concern with appropriate masculine behavior in the face of darker forces. The fact that the lover registers his insecurity through a gender-marked product reinforces the sense that "to buy / a thing like that" can be profoundly unsettling when it is a component of one's emotional duties. Creeley often registers his insecurity over roles by creating a double subject, invested with the ontological features of a first-person speaker but able to adopt a third-person perspective when the going gets tough: the "unsure / egoist is not / good for himself" (125). This lexical insecurity should be measured against mainstream notions of gendered responsibility, vested in the male breadwinner and homemaker wife, the maintenance of whose roles serves a larger national purpose. Such congruence between domestic and foreign policies can be seen in the remarks of a male respondent to a 1955 research study who described his family in cold war terms. Marriage provided him with "a sense of responsibility, a feeling of being a member of a group that in spite of many disagreements internally will face its external enemies together" (qtd. in May, *Recasting* 166).

The coy, evasive rhetoric of "The Lover" is a bit like the lover's quandary over response. Yet the posturing of indecision registers a more profound insecurity about what it means to be male, an uncertainty held in check by the regular tercets and quatrains that dominate Creeley's work. The enjambment undermines the formal syntax, assisting at the level of lineation the poem's interrogation of positions that are tested, rejected, and resubmitted for view. And it is characteristic of Creeley's verse of this period to try out various poses of masculinity, all of which seem to come in prepackaged forms of address: the abject lover, the self-righteous husband, the picaresque hero, the existential hipster.

One of Creeley's most characteristic poses is a courtly or mock-heroic persona, embodied in the poem from which my epigraph to this chapter is drawn:

My love's manners in bed
are not to be discussed by me,
as mine by her
I would not credit comment upon gracefully.

Yet I ride by the margin of that lake in
the wood, the castle,
and the excitement of strongholds,
and have a small boy's notion of doing good.
    (168)

The poet sees himself as a character in a picaresque romance, but he is hardly the quester of modernist epic, seeking to shore cultural ruins against chaos. Rather, he feels endlessly inadequate to sexual challenges—as marginal as the lake whose edge he traverses. He responds by posing a kind of courtly deference and discretion that are threatened by overly ornate diction: "I would not credit comment upon gracefully." He has a "small boy's notion of doing good" and in saying so strips the heroic scenario of all claims to authority. Courtly romance becomes Boy Scout oath. The poem's final quatrain attempts to counter the limits of the mock heroic by adopting a tone of resignation:

Oh well, I will say here,
knowing each man,

let you find a good wife too,
and love her as hard as you can.
> (168)

The three stanzas do rhetorical battle with each other: the first offering a posture of modesty and deference, the second a self-abnegating innocence, and
the last a tone of tough realism. Yet it becomes clear that in adopting poses
the speaker's claim that he knows "each man" is preposterous because he
clearly does not know himself. The throwaway phrase, "Oh well," signals the
inadequacy of the speaker's ability to move outside of the "small boy's notion
of doing good" and achieve some form of self-awareness. And because his
"lover" is merely an occasion for self-inquiry, a "good wife" as ephemeral as
the lady in a tower, she cannot help the speaker out of his dilemma. Nor does
irony provide a convenient perspective upon his confusion because there
is no position *outside* of these poses to which the reader can look for a sign
of authority. The poem mocks its own title, "The Way," in displaying the
multiple *ways* that masculinity lives itself out through self-protective speech
acts.

Creeley's poetry of the 1950s is intensely concerned with domestic re-
sponsibilities and heterosexual codes. Although these codes provide a highly
unstable armature upon which to secure identity, they are familiar enough to
be manipulated on a playing field called heteronormalcy. Individuals not
defined within such categories were forced to create countercommunities of
difference during an era in which difference carried little of the cultural ca-
chet that it has today. For homosexuals and lesbians, the formation of community was complicated by the era's pervasive homophobia, despite the fact
that the war had provided significant new zones of homosocial contact. Just
as they had been subjects of military witch hunts during the recent "hot" war,
homosexuals and lesbians were targeted as security risks in the cold war by
officials who deemed them likely targets for corruption. "[One] homosexual
can pollute a Government office," says the 1950 Senate report "Employment
of Homosexuals and Other Sex Perverts in Government" (qtd. in Campbell
176). Against such threats, the maintenance of heteromasculinity becomes a
national imperative, one satirized as such by Frank O'Hara: "[You] were
made in the image of god . . . I was not / I was made in the image of a sissy
truck-driver" (*Collected* 338).

O'Hara's New York vantage within a supportive gay art community
may have allowed him a certain ironic distance from normative masculine
roles of the sort Creeley interrogates, but for John Wieners, writing in San
Francisco at the same time, such community was a good deal more furtive.
In the *Hotel Wentley Poems* (1958) Wieners creates a community of difference by paying tribute to marginal types who inhabit alternative social

spaces (the gay bar, the mental ward, the hustler's street corner) vulnerable to official scrutiny. In "A Poem for Vipers" Wieners celebrates this subterranean world where private rituals of drugs and sex are endlessly threatened by invasion:

> The ritual.
> We make it. And have made it.
> For months now together after midnight.
> Soon I know the fuzz will
> interrupt, will arrest Jimmy and
> I shall be placed on probation. The poem
> does not lie to us. We lie under
> its law, alive in the glamour of this hour
> (n.p.)

Wieners transforms terms for deviance into terms of personal legitimation. Poetry as a form of making is also a generative form of lying; sexuality and drug use are rituals, ways of "making it" in a world threatened by arrest and incarceration. The alliterative sequence from "lie" to "law" to "alive" to "glamour" suggests the lyric possibilities of acts shared by those who, as he says later, "hide words / under the coats of their tongue." The poem literally covers these acts like a blanket, converting official sanctions against sodomy or drug use into a covert law unto itself.

In "A Poem for Cocksuckers" Wieners extends the pun on *lying* to include transvestism and racial masquerade:

> Well we can go
> in the queer bars w/
> our long hair reaching
> down to the ground and
> we can sing our songs
> of love like the black mama
> on the juke box, after all
> what have we got left.
>
> > On our right the fairies
> giggle in their lacquered
> voices & blow
> smoke in your eyes let them
> it's a nigger's world
> and we retain strength.
> > (n.p.)

Wieners's wordplay on left/right ("what have we got left," "On our right the fairies") suggests that hierarchical relations among binaries produces an inexorable logic: if gay, therefore queer, if queer, therefore black, if black, therefore nigger, and so on. Such a logic parodies the rhetorical slippery slope established by congressional investigating committees that insisted that each fissure in moral character betrays larger faults beneath. Pink leads to rose leads to red. While the poem affirms homosexuality, its use of stereotyped terms for gayness acknowledges the degree to which sexuality, like race, is maintained within compulsorily heteronormal terms. The speaker not only identifies with blacks in a racist society ("it's a nigger's world") he gains strength from their example. In this sense Wieners anticipates more recent theories of queer identity, first by acknowledging his interpellation in a homophobic society by transforming a term of social opprobrium ("queer") into an oppositional sign. He reinforces this act of inversion by rearticulating queerness as blackness, seeing one form of social marginalization by means of another. He sings the blues "like the black mama / on the juke box" and in the process participates in a version of nature otherwise denied him:

The gifts do not desert us,
fountains do not dry
up there are rivers running,
there are mountains
swelling for spring to cascade.

     It is all here between
the powdered legs &
painted eyes of the fairy
friends who do not fail us
     in our hour of
          despair.
   (n.p.)

Wieners, unlike his North Beach colleagues Jack Spicer and Jack Kerouac, chooses not to configure homosexuality in heterosexual terms but, rather, revises nature ("rivers" and "mountains") as a kind of theatrical performance—as "powdered" and "painted"—and therefore undecidable within gendered norms.

If Wieners articulates sexual otherness via black women and feminized men, Gwendolyn Brooks, writing during the same period, was able to articulate racial difference by reference to stereotypes of white masculinity. In early sequences like *A Street in Bronzeville* (1945) and *Annie Allen* (1949), Brooks depicts the complexities of figuring race around images of white normalcy, especially when those images are used to define national authority. The sonnets of "Gay Chaps at the Bar," written at the end of World War II, describe black soldiers walking a tightrope between the uniforms that identify them as equals to white soldiers and the uniform racism they experience in the barracks. Poems in *The Bean Eaters* (1960) address a postwar climate of open racial conflict during the early days of the civil rights movement. The killing of Emmett Till, integration of Little Rock's Central High, and KKK harassment provide the historical background, but what Brooks foregrounds are the specific modalities of representation in mass culture by which racial norms are cemented. "Strong Men, Riding Horses," for example, relates codes of white masculinity identified with the Hollywood western to the geopolitical "West" being defended in the name of national security. Brooks observes

Strong Men, riding horses. In the West
On a range five hundred miles. A Thousand. Reaching
From dawn to sunset. Rested blue to orange.
From hope to crying. Except that Strong Men are
Desert-eyed. Except that Strong Men are
Pasted to stars already. Have their cars
Beneath them. Rentless too. Too broad of chest
To shrink when the Rough Man hails.
    (329)

This poem was written during a period when the cowboy western served as a central vehicle for cold war ideology, first by thematizing the West as a source of heroic vitality against effete eastern forces and, second, through its validation of neo–Manifest Destiny in the form of the Truman Doctrine and the Marshall Plan.[6] Heroic masculinity as represented in classic westerns like *Rio Bravo* (1959) or 1950s television shows like *The Rifleman* or *Gunsmoke* or through the Marlboro Man ad campaign did not, needless to say, include African Americans. The historical frontier being defended against communism is replaced by the silver range of the movie screen where "Strong Men are / Pasted to stars already." The celluloid cowboy can afford to be "Rentless" and independent, but the speaker, a black woman, is saddled on a different horse:

I am not like that. I pay rent, am addled
By illegible landlords, run, if robbers call.

What mannerisms I present, employ,
Are camouflage, and what my mouths remark

To word-wall off that broadness of the dark
Is pitiful.
I am not brave at all.

    (329)

In this poem and others by Brooks the poet's voice is an index of social pressures, not a mask for escaping them. She registers this fact broadly by referring to her mouth in the plural: "what my mouths remark / to word-wall off that broadness of the dark," suggesting that her defensiveness is matched by an ability to ventriloquize. As Brooks indicates, the voice that says, "I am not brave at all" speaks a "camouflaged" rhetoric when measured against the wide screen heroics of John Wayne and Ronald Reagan. Brooks, Plath, Creeley, and Wieners measure the impact of social normalization in the 1950s through strategies that acknowledge the mediated nature of private speech. Congressional hearings, electronic surveillance, and loyalty oaths increasingly sought to link the spoken word to patriotic ideals. In a decade when the question, Are you or have you ever been? often elicited elaborate strategies of evasion or coerced confession, claims for a new orality in poetry seemed therapeutic indeed.[7]

Brooks's awareness of how gender is performed through forms of mediated speech is treated at length in her poem on the murder of Emmett Till, "A Bronzeville Mother Loiters in Mississippi. Meanwhile, a Mississippi Mother Burns Bacon." The poem concerns the vicious murder of the fifteen-year-old black boy, Emmett Till, in Money, Mississippi, in 1955 for purportedly whistling at a white woman. Two men, Roy Bryant and his half-brother, J. W. Milam, were charged with the murder but were acquitted in a widely televised trial. The two mothers in question in this poem are Carolyn Bryant, wife of Roy Bryant, and Mamie Till Bradley, Till's mother. The two represent two versions of beset motherhood: urban black working-class woman from Chicago and white working-class daughter of the South. In the first and longest part of poem, Brooks utilizes the persona of Carolyn Bryant to penetrate the mind (and voice) of a woman who casts herself as the heroine of a southern romance:

From the first it had been like a
Ballad. It had the beat inevitable. It had the blood.
A wildness cut up, and tied in little bunches,
Like the four-line stanzas of the ballads she had never quite
Understood—the ballads they had set her to, in school.

Herself: the milk-white maid, the "maid mild"
Of the ballad. Pursued

By the Dark Villain. Rescued by the Fine Prince.
The Happiness-Ever-After.
That was worth anything.
It was good to be a "maid mild."
That made the breath go fast.

    (333)

Like Emma Bovary reading her sentimental romances, Carolyn Bryant configures her life around southern ballads of white womanhood under siege. The idea of being a "maid mild" gives her an erotic charge that "made the breath go fast" and links her with earlier, aristocratic traditions. But in this case the dark villain turns out to be "a blackish child / Of fourteen," and the hero turns out to be her own abusive husband whose brutal treatment of his children at the domestic breakfast table offers a bleak contrast to her romantic fantasies of virginity protected. In the background of the southern mother's mediated reverie is the trial itself in which her husband has been accused. His racist contempt for the northern news media that is making his life a spectacle is matched by his erotic pleasure in showing "that snappy-eyed mother, / That sassy, Northern, brown-black— // Nothing could stop Mississippi" (336). Nor does the ballad in which the southern mother imagines herself include possible identifications with that "other" mother from the North. The husband's sexual advances to his wife contrast with the decidedly nonromantic banality of the courtroom:

Then a sickness heaved within her. The courtroom Coca-Cola,
The courtroom beer and hate and sweat and drone,
Pushed like a wall against her. She wanted to bear it.
But his mouth would not go away and neither would the
Decapitated exclamation points in that Other Woman's eyes.

    (339)

    This last line is more than hyperbole; it refers to Mamie Till's desire that her son's brutalized body be seen in an open coffin at his funeral. This theatrical presentation of racist violence was considered an outrageous affront to decency by the southern press, but within the black community it was necessary, in 1955, to illustrate the enduring legacy of lynchings in the year following the passage of *Brown v. Board of Education* and to help launch the civil rights movement.[8] Brooks understands the degree to which the myth of outraged southern womanhood demanded a counterdiscourse in which gothic trappings of violated innocence include crimes committed on innocent children. The graveyard verse of Emmaline Grangerford, which provides comic satire in *The Adventures of Huckleberry Finn*, is now given its more complex rendition in the voice of a southern mother. When such fictions break down, the ballad as a cultural repository can no longer provide a safe haven for protected womanhood. The wife's hatred for her husband bursts "into glorious flower, / And its perfume enclasped them—big, / Bigger than all magnolias" (339). It is clear that Brooks understands the painful mixture of race and gender to be one involving inversionary rhetoric: the ability of individuals to inhabit metaphors differently.

Just as Brooks takes on the persona of a white southern mother in mourning for failed expectations, so she respects the privacy of a black mother by *not* speaking for her. Rather, in the last segment of the poem, titled "The Last Quatrain of the Ballad of Emmett Till," she writes in the third person:

Emmett's mother is a pretty-faced thing;
the tint of pulled taffy.
She sits in a red room,
drinking black coffee.
She kisses her killed boy.
And she is sorry.
Chaos in windy grays
through a red prairie.
    (340)

This intimate portrait is painted as directly as possible, without the gothic trappings of racial violation and sexual revenge. Its third-person perspective on Mamie Till's life after her child's murder contrasts with the first person of Carolyn Bryant. Yet Brooks refers to this as the "last quatrain" of the ballad, suggesting that it is part of that southern story, even though it is now set against the backdrop of the Midwest prairie. Despite its title, this last section is not a quatrain, suggesting that for Brooks the ballad is more than a form; it is a vehicle for localized meanings. In the larger context of the poem, the final section is a snapshot (reinforced by color contrasts of "red room," "black coffee," "windy grays," and "red prairie"), the denouement of a story about race in America whose origins lie in the larger history of the nation. Brooks's awareness of the function of the ballad in chronicling southern history is matched by the stark visual presentation of Mamie Till's northern, urban vantage. If, as Paul Gilroy says, "gender is the modality through which race is lived," Brooks's poem could be seen as the formal vehicle in which that modality is represented (83).

"LIGHT SEEMS TO BE ETERNAL": FRANK O'HARA AND THE COLD WAR

What I have been describing as Brooks's management of voices and social idiolects would seem rather distant from the new orality and physicality of poetry embodied in Olson, Snyder, Ginsberg, Duncan, Levertov, and others, yet both tendencies could be seen as attempts to wrest authentic speech away from its more mediated versions within surveillance culture. In the work of Frank O'Hara, on the other hand, the voice becomes a plastic medium for representing a variety of public selves that, lacking a central core, provide highly theatricalized solutions to chaos, "a number of naked selves / so many pistols I have borrowed to protect myselves" (*Collected* 253). In these lines, the gun-fighter's weapon is not the phallic defender of the American national fantasy but a projection of that fantasy's will-to-dispersal, an acknowledgment that in a world where identities are purchased like suits of clothes, forms of resistance and defense must be similarly tailored.

O'Hara is the last poet one might associate with cold war subjects. His personalist, camp sensibility seems oblivious to politics and social issues, and yet his manipulation of voice often serves to carnivalize the more public rhetoric in the daily news. In "Poem (Khrushchev Is Coming on the Right Day!)," O'Hara invokes a major cold war figure whose arrival in New York on 18 September 1959 was eagerly anticipated. It was a visit inspired by a meeting earlier in the year between Vice President Nixon and the Soviet leader at an international exhibition in Moscow. In the "kitchen cabinet" the two cold warriors sparred over the superiority not of weaponry or ideology but of domestic conveniences like refrigerators and dishwashers. In the debate, Nixon equated the capitalist virtues of choice and competition with the female homemaker's right to choose brands of kitchen equipment; Khrushchev, on the other hand, argued that in a communist system, a woman's choice was not to be restricted to the domestic sphere but could be exercised throughout the workforce. The confrontation provided graphic evidence of the degree to which the war of containment was being waged over the hearts and minds of domestic workers. Eisenhower, anxious to display such domesticity on native soil, invited the Soviet leader to the United States, and it is this event that O'Hara memorializes in his poem.

Khrushchev's appearance in New York was a media event exploiting the considerable interest in the first-ever visit by a Soviet leader. The occasion was designed by Eisenhower and his aides to reinforce American ideals of hard work (he would visit free-market factories), family (he would visit Eisenhower's home in Abilene), and community (he would visit Levittown).[9] O'Hara's poem partakes little in the boosterist spirit of the visit, setting Khrushchev's arrival instead among more mundane occurrences of his own lunch hour reverie:

Khrushchev is coming on the right day!

                              the cool graced light
is pushed off the enormous glass piers by hard wind
and everything is tossing, hurrying on up

                         this country

has everything but *politesse,* a Puerto Rican cab driver says
and five different girls I see
                    look like Piedie Gimbel
with her blonde hair tossing too,
                            as she looked when I pushed
her little daughter on the swing on the lawn it was also windy
    (340)

These are hardly the same details about Khrushchev's visit that appeared in
the morning *New York Times.* Whatever anticipation the State Department or
the press might have had about the "rightness" of the visit's political timing,
O'Hara seems pleased that the day is windy, busy, and distracting. The political importance of the event is subsumed by the poet's desultory reflections
on cab drivers, friends, and past events. But unlike poems such as "A Step
away from Them" or "The Day Lady Died," where the quotidian frames a con-
cluding memento mori, such random details are constantly punctuated by
references to Khrushchev's presence as a news item:

last night we went to a movie and came out,
                            Ionesco is greater
than Beckett, Vincent said, that's what I think, blueberry blintzes
and Khrushchev was probably being carped at
                            in Washington, no *politesse*
Vincent tells me about his mother's trip to Sweden
    (340)

If Khrushchev is demystified by being sandwiched between blueberry blintzes
and vacations in Sweden, he is also constantly in view and is therefore part of
the overall landscape. O'Hara is right to assume Khrushchev's bumptious
behavior was being deplored in Washington (the *New York Times* for 17 September makes numerous references to his "two handed gestures" and quick
changes of mood), but this fact is countered by his cab driver's sense that
such *politesse* is equally lacking in America. So much for cultural stereotypes.
O'Hara's list of people, events, and conversations offers a verbal correlative to
the wind that, in September, distracts and diffuses.

    I would agree with Marjorie Perloff that this poem is "not about Khru-
shchev," but I would not assume from this that he is thereby rendered incon-
sequential (*Frank O'Hara* 147). Rather, I see O'Hara validating the Russian
leader's importance as a cultural sign, someone around whom the quotidian
is constructed. If it is necessary to hope that Khrushchev comes on the *right*
day, then his centrality organizes the terms around which rightness and

wrongness are established. It is this cultural meaning of the Soviet leader that mutes O'Hara's otherwise celebratory conclusion:

> where does the evil of the year go
> > when September takes New York
> and turns it into ozone stalagmites
> > deposits of light
> > so I get back up
> make coffee, and read François Villon, his life so dark
> > New York seems blinding and my tie is blowing up the street
> I wish it would blow off
> > though it is cold and somewhat warms my neck
> as the train bears Khrushchev on to Pennsylvania Station
> > and the light seems to be eternal
> > and joy seems to be inexorable
> > I am foolish enough always to find it in wind
> (340)

These lines contain faint echoes of Shelley's "Ode to the West Wind," which similarly contrasts the wildness of natural change to historical stasis. But O'Hara's reference carries with it hints of a more recent western wind produced by nuclear tests, a wind capable of "blowing up the street" or "blowing off" one's tie and "blinding" one as much to New York as to the life of Villon. And the train that "bears Khrushchev on to Pennsylvania Station" hints of Lenin's closed train to the Finland Station in preparation for the Bolshevik Revolution. Given these (admittedly oblique) references to East/West foreign tensions, O'Hara's final lines seem a good deal less celebratory than they first appear. The satisfactions of this windy day make the light "[seem] to be eternal" and joy "[seem] to be inexorable." Why this qualification? Is it because light, as a source of life and clarity, has been neutralized by the atomic age? Is a thing of beauty in an age of atomic testing no longer a joy forever? O'Hara's brilliant image of New York as "ozone stalagmites" is both a recognition of the city's potential as a natural landscape (skyscrapers as sedimented deposits) as well as a sign of its stasis. Against such intractability, the speaker's intercourse with cab drivers, Vincent, and Piedie Gimbel provides salutary movement and change.

My willingness to read a cold war scenario into such an occasional poem is motivated by other poems and essays written at the same time. Notwithstanding O'Hara's love of Pasternak, Mayakovsky, Stravinsky, and Balanchine, his references to Russian subjects in poems written during September 1959 suggest an ongoing concern with Soviet-American foreign relations. "September 14, 1959 (Moon)," for example, invokes a nocturnal, romantic landscape that has been redefined by Sputnik. In the late summer "the warm running trains / of the South escape to sweet brooks / and grassy roadbeds underneath the / thankful and enlightening Russian moon" (338). The idea that heavenly bodies are now the province of sublunary political agencies offers a new twist to a romantic topos. In "Variations on Pasternak's 'Mein Liebchen, Was Willst Du Noch Mehr?' " written the next day, O'Hara invokes "walls, except that they stretch through China / like a Way, are melancholy fingers in the snow / of years" (339). Although the Berlin Wall was not yet built, the presence of a Germany divided by ideological walls "that . . . stretch through China" is very much the subject here:

I had forgotten

that things could be beautiful in the 20th Century under the moon

the drabness of life peels away like an old recording by Lotte Lenya

it is not lucky to be German and you know it, though doom has held off.

    (339)[10]

And in "Getting up Ahead of Someone (Sun)," written two days after the Khrushchev poem, O'Hara offers a solar counterpart to his lunar "September 14, 1959." He describes himself waking at dawn, smoking, reading, waiting for the household to emerge:

and the house wakes up and goes
to get the dog in Sag Harbor I make
myself a bourbon and commence
to write one of my "I do this I do that"
poems in a sketch pad
               it is tomorrow
though only six hours have gone by
each day's light has more significance these days
    (341)

Without the context of other poems surrounding it, O'Hara's conclusion might seem a variation on romantic personalist lyric ("This Lime Tree Bower My Prison"). But given that both moon and sun, staples of romantic naturalism, now signify a horizon marked by what journalists called satellite diplomacy, the fact that "light has more significance these days" achieves an additional level of historical resonance. O'Hara's reference to his "I do this I do that" method of writing now frames a meditation on the passing of time made palpable by a light capable of dissolving light, a nuclear sunrise that renders "significance" mute.[11]

All of the poems I have discussed thus far share a common investment in the lyric's ability to register momentary states of attention against the gradual withering away of significant interiority. Whereas Pound could invoke visionary moments of light, buttressed by Neoplatonic philosophy, or Eliot the redemptive light of the incarnate word, O'Hara's light is, as Charles Altieri says, "stripped of . . . ontological vestments" (110). Which is not to say that he lacks any critical position *about* such a withering away. The sheer weight of his enumerations testifies to the importance he attaches to forces threatening the present. As I have indicated, the personalist lyric of the 1950s acknowledges the complicity between the poet's voice and a world of highly mediated ideological messages. O'Hara's ironizing of an important historical event does more than dismiss its authority in a cold war narrative; it provides an alternate register—insouciant, queer, celebratory—to contrast with the instrumentalized voices that monitor Khrushchev's visit.

O'Hara's use of voice must be measured against other, more traditional poets of his generation who also deal with cold war materials but whose use of irony is put to very different purposes.[12] In terms that I have already developed, such poets view the disparities between margins and mainstream as an oxymoron to be resolved by rhetorical fiat, a "sensible emptiness" in Richard Wilbur's phrase, within which the poem could constellate new plenitudes (117). In the work of Wilbur, Robert Lowell, Randall Jarrell, W. D. Snodgrass, John Berryman, the "Tranquilized Fifties" offer a backdrop for meditations on such contrasts. Popular culture, advertising, or fashion provide a discursive field not to entertain but to rise above:

Moving from Cheer to Joy, from Joy to All,
I take a box
And add it to my wild rice, my Cornish game hens,
The slacked or shorted, basketed, identical
Food-gathering flocks
Are selves I overlook. Wisdom, said William James

Is learning what to overlook. And I am wise
If that is wisdom.
  (Jarrell 90)

Randall Jarrell's opening lines to "Next Day" might resemble the discursive surface of O'Hara's *Lunch Poems* (1964), but his attempt to differentiate himself from shoppers and their laundry detergents, via William James, marks the distance between the two poets. Unlike O'Hara, the voice here is underwritten by those "ontological vestments" that provide a reflective position on events that threaten significant speech. Similarly, Lowell, pottering around his house on "hardly passionate Marlborough Street," nostalgically reconstructs his earlier "fire-breathing" political moment as a conscientious objector in "Memories of West Street and Lepke" (91). In "For the Union Dead," he contrasts the contemporary boarded-up South Boston Aquarium and urban renovation to the heroic black soldiers of Robert Gould Shaw's Civil War regiment. Richard Wilbur's "Advice to a Prophet" warns the atomic age Jeremiah to "spare us all word of the weapons, their force and range," feeling that "our slow, unreckoning hearts will be left behind, / Unable to fear what is too strange" (6). Wilbur's lines might be addressing Allen Ginsberg, "[mad]-eyed from stating the obvious," when he makes his humanist riposte: "Ask us, prophet, how we shall call / Our natures forth when that live tongue is all / Dispelled, that glass obscured or broken" (6). This reflective voice (and its iambic cadences) may be powerless against atomic annihilation, but its ability to invoke the "live tongue" of a common identity against the "dispelled" voice of the lonely prophet creates a moral universe of its own.

For it is the fear of dispersal that links Kennan's national security agenda and late modernist literary culture, whether it is the threat of proliferating nuclear arms or the dangers of an expanding mass culture. O'Hara counters these fears by not paying attention to them and celebrating the quotidian, but Wilbur must display the mind's synthetic powers at work as a palliative. Sometimes, the two impulses clash, as they do in the work of Edward Field, a poet who is included in Donald Allen's *New American Poetry* of 1960, but who nevertheless manifests some of Jarrell's or Wilbur's distancing rhetoric. Field's "Ode for Fidel Castro" also covers one of Khrushchev's visits to New York, focusing on the Soviet premier's 1960 meeting with the new Cuban leader at the Hotel Theresa in Harlem. Field's speaker is enthusiastic about the event, but unlike O'Hara he is acutely aware of the difficulty of finding a voice appropriate to the historical event. He commands his muse to "give me strength not to lay aside this poem / Like so many others in the pile by my typewriter / But to write the whole thing from beginning to end / O Perfection, the way it wants to go" (65). Unlike O'Hara who would simply "write the whole thing from beginning to end" without reflecting on the fact, Field makes his inadequacy to history the central feature of the poem. If the Cuban Revolution offers a momentary sign of hopeful change ("and good riddance Batista"), the poem's reliance on literary conventions of apostrophe ("O Boy God, Muse of Poets"), simile ("Where the words ring like gongs and meaning goes out the window"), and self-conscious musings ("So you're not perfect, poets don't look for perfect") makes it into a more recognizable meditation on art. While Field suggests a more processual style through his use of vernacular language, free lineation, and references to current events, he everywhere reminds us of his art: "For I am going to write on World Issues / Which demands laughter where we most believe" (65).

This self-reflexiveness is not merely aesthetic, as it often is in Wilbur. It involves, among other things, a recognition of his own otherness as a white male. The fact that Castro met Khrushchev in Harlem permits Field to link worldwide socialism with an emerging civil rights movement in America. He realizes, however, that when the two leaders leave New York, racism will still be alive and well—and this implicates him as well:

I used to have friends up there
When I went to visit them if I passed a mirror
My whiteness would surprise me
The mind takes on darkness of skin so easily
(Of course being a Jew I'm not exactly white)
It is that easy to turn black
And then have to be in that awful boat the Negroes are in
Although it's pretty lousy being white
And having that black hatred turned on you.
    (68)

Field's awareness of his own racial identity as a Jew in a racist society is marked by shock at seeing himself as a white other in a black mirror. Otherness, far from being a bond of solidarity in a hostile world as it is for Wieners, is a liminal state between self-hatred and race-hatred. He can neither identify with blacks nor differentiate himself from them.

Field concludes his poem by contrasting the Cuban coup d'état with Christmas in New York. The Christmas tree in Rockefeller Center stands as a sacrificial monument to lost natural plenitude. Like the Cuban Revolution, the tree stands for the "gods who love freedom":

The world's largest Christmas tree which will never be Christian
Even if you cut it down, make it stand on cement, decorate it with balls
It will still scream for the forest, like a wild animal
Like the gods who love freedom and topple to the saws of commerce
The gods who frighten us half to death in our dreams with their doings
And disappear when we need them most, awake.
    (69)

The Christmas tree, stripped of its ideological props, asserts its roots in atavistic ritual and natural process. And, like the tree, Castro is vulnerable to the "saws of commerce":

By the time you see this, Fidel, you might not even exist anymore
My government is merciless and even now
The machine to destroy you is moving into action
The chances are you won't last long
Well so long pal it was nice knowing you
I can't go around with a broken heart all my life
After I got over the fall of the Spanish Republic
I guess I can get over anything
My job is just to survive.
    (69)

Unlike many intellectuals of his generation, Field maintains a romantic faith in socialist movements. Yet those movements have been crushed by the "machine" of capitalism and the National Security State, against which the only virtue is to "survive." In his final image, he imagines himself meeting Castro and taking Khrushchev's place: "And then you'll get a kiss that will make Khrushchev's be forgotten / A kiss of the poet, that will make you truly good / the way you meant to be" (69). According to Field, the kiss of the poet is all that the revolution needs—the humanizing force of an articulate survivor to tell the tale that the newspaper won't.

Field's poem forges an uncertain truce between the poetics of process and the politics of consensus, between self-disclosure and self-effacement. It utilizes the idiolect of everyman ("Well so long pal, it was nice knowing you") leavened by humanist cliché ("the Gods who love freedom"). Such poems offer what Maria Damon, speaking of Lowell, calls a "pathos of failed liberalism" in which the impulse to personal confession is the result of public failures and collective anomie (123). Like the desiccated Boston Aquarium in Lowell's "For the Union Dead," possibilities for a public voice are limited, the opportunities for heroic action neutralized by memories of recent holocausts.

"THE END / WILL COME / IN ITS TIME"

Both O'Hara and Lowell had as one of their mentors a poet who late in his life provided a powerful image of what it means to live in the cold war. In "Asphodel, That Greeny Flower," William Carlos Williams recognizes that

                The mere picture
                        of the exploding bomb
        fascinates us
                so that we cannot wait
                        to prostrate ourselves
        before it. We do not believe
                that love
                        can so wreck our lives.
        The end
                will come
                        in its time

                (321–22)

It is both appropriate and ironic that Williams's meditation on the culture of
the bomb should occur in a lyric, the genre seemingly furthest from history.
But as Theodor Adorno says, the lyric demand for the untouched word is in
itself social: "It implies a protest against a social condition which every individual experiences as hostile, distant, cold and oppressive. And this social
condition impresses itself on the poetic form in a negative way" (58). This
may be an overly aestheticized view of lyric negativity, but it helps explain
how certain lyric poets during the 1950s fought the cold war on their own
terms. "The end / will come / in its time," Williams says, the possessive pronoun referring both to the bomb and to love. The end will take its own time,
in an economy of the body, but the discourse of ends, of Hegelian history, was
forever changed by forces unleashed in the Manhattan Project and Los
Alamos. What is so prescient about these lines is Williams's emphasis on the
picture of the bomb, for it was as a representation that the threat of nuclear annihilation came into American households. And in like manner the threat of
subversion, because it could never be verified by Senator McCarthy's infamous list, had to be represented as a picture, an imagined community, discursively produced in order to be contained.

      But if a picture held us captive, to adapt Wittgenstein, it did not lie
solely in "our" language, but in a language being enlisted in a process of cultural hegemony. The age of the bomb created what Alan Nadel has called a
"nuclear gaze" through which "actions with ambiguous motives" or indeterminate causes could be seen—and contained (24). The eruption of new literary bohemias during the mid-1950s, their various challenges to the authority
of the nuclear gaze, was a sign that something in the picture could not be contained. To conclude where I began: "Go fuck yourself with your atom bomb"
was Ginsberg's nose-thumbing response to the culture of consensus. Yet in
the same poem ("America") he acknowledges that the rhetoric of containment could not be transcended by jeremiad alone. His more threatening at-

tack on the status quo, one still visible in the politics of ACT Up and Queer Nation, was to ape the language by which containment did its work: "I'd better get right down to the job / America I'm putting my queer shoulder to the wheel" (148). If the sentiment was threatening to the mainstream, at least its idiom was familiar. And therein lay the poem's danger.

3

The Lady from Shanghai: California Orientalism and "Guys Like Us"

"Alvah says that while guys like us are all excited about being real Orientals and wearing robes, actual Orientals over there are reading surrealism and Charles Darwin and mad about Western business suits."

"East'll meet West anyway. Think what a great world revolution will take place when East meets West finally, and it'll be guys like us that can start the thing. Think of millions of guys all over the world with rucksacks on their backs tramping around the back country and hitch-hiking and bringing the word down to everybody."

Jack Kerouac, *The Dharma Bums*

GUYS LIKE US

With the passage of Proposition 187 in 1994 restricting health and educational benefits to undocumented workers, California has revived a long-standing pattern of animosity toward those upon whose labor the state has depended.[1] Whereas supporters of the bill spoke of the economic impact of "illegal aliens" upon the state's budget, California's historical record shows that this budget has been heavily subsidized by Chinese, Koreans, Japanese, Vietnamese, Mexicans, Eastern Europeans, Pacific Islanders, and other immigrants who have formed a substantial percentage of the work force. By focusing on economic impact rather than racial conflict, proponents of immigration reform have created a seemingly value-neutral forum in which to assess issues of immigration, affirmative action, welfare, and entitlements. But as Alexander Saxton, Michael Rogin, Tomás Almaguer, Ronald Takaki, David Roediger, and others have pointed out, anti-immigrant sentiment has not historically been fueled by economic interests alone, but has rested on racial distinctions by which white settlers could differentiate their own immigrant pasts from those of darker-skinned neighbors. This is especially the case with immigrants from China who formed the largest nonnative portion of the labor force at the moment of the state's emergence onto the national scene.

Although the popular imagination regards the first Chinese as indentured servants, many arrived on the western shore as entrepreneurs, working in placer mining camps of the 1850s and establishing their own claims on Gold Mountain. When the gold ran out (or when they were run out of the placer fields by white mining interests), they worked in large numbers for the first transcontinental railroad and later in frontier towns running restaurants, laundries, and dry goods businesses. Although many Chinese moved to overcrowded urban Chinatowns, a substantial number achieved greater economic success in agriculture and harvest labor. Fear of an "Asian invasion" began with the annexation of California in 1848 and manifested itself through anticoolie legislation and exclusionary mining taxes, culminating in the 1882 Chinese Exclusion Law and sealed with the Immigration Act of 1924. Much of this sentiment has persisted, particularly during World War II with the incarceration of Japanese in internment camps and today with localized attacks on Koreans, Vietnamese, and Japanese. A recent bumper sticker, "Buy American: Remember Pearl Harbor," exhibits more than Kiwanis boosterism; it revives a century-old racist fear of cheap Asian labor, even when that labor no longer works on domestic soil.

While Asians have been demonized as the "yellow peril," they also form a major part of a larger western cultural imaginary. From Grauman's Chinese theater and the Babylonian Samson Tyre and Rubber Company building in Los Angeles to the Japanese tea garden in San Francisco's Golden Gate Park and pagoda variations on craftsman houses in the Berkeley hills, from Korean or Vietnamese signage on urban boulevards to the retro-chinoiserie of postmodern restaurants—the western city is also a Chinatown. Orientalist fantasies of exoticism, sexual mystery, and adventure persist in the works of writers from Jack London, Robert Louis Stevenson, and Joaquin Miller through Dashiell Hammett, Nathaniel West, and Kenneth Rexroth. Chinatown is both a movie and a heterotopic space in the western metropole where the "alien" can be contained and where the "alien within" white culture can be liberated. The interplay between these two spaces—between cultural representation and heterotopia—will be the subject of this chapter.[2] As it will become clear, however, heterotopias are defined not only by demographic features but through orientalist narratives about a gendered "east" whose boundaries extend well past the city.

Orientalism has been defined largely in terms of a European fascination with the exotic East, regarded both as a cultural designation and as a component of material civilization. Edward Said notes that orientalism exists as an "ontological and epistemological distinction" between Orient and Occident, a cultural rift that has been relatively unchanged since the eighteenth century (2–3). But, as Lisa Lowe remarks, such oppositions tend to "uphold the logic of the dualism as the means of explaining how a discourse expresses domination and subordination [and thus fail] to account for the differences inherent in each term" (*Critical Terrains* 7). In the case of California, those differences must include the constitutive role of Asians in the state's cultural and political evolution. They must also include the complex racial politics of a region settled and occupied by other constituencies, most prominently Mexican Californios, who were themselves "orientalized" by white settlers. Whereas in Europe the Orient was a colonial outpost from which material resources, labor, and images were imported, in California Asians were independent skilled and unskilled workers from the time of the state's annexation. One must also account for the multiple migrations of Asians from various parts of the world, each with highly specific cultural and political identities, at different moments in the state's history. As I will point out, one of the most significant moments for the emergence of Asians as a political and economic force in California occurred in the period between the Chinese Cultural Revolution and the end of the Vietnam War, a cold war epoch that resulted in the formation of the Pacific Rim.

Asian immigration in California is well documented, but the cultural residues of that immigration in the modern period require further study. I would like to pursue the form that orientalism takes in California at two moments in its history. First, I look briefly at a formative moment during the 1870s when anticoolie sentiment expressed itself through anxieties over white masculinity. Second, I explore western orientalism in the period following World War II at a moment when immigration laws were relaxed and global restructurings brought about by the cold war redefined the nature of East and West along new geopolitical lines.[3] To some extent the orientalism within both moments is played out locally as a narrative of western exceptionalism by which Orient and Occident are mediated through a second "East," that of the eastern seaboard with all of the cultural and symbolic weight that this region implies for the West. Gilles Deleuze and Félix Guattari see this remapping of America as the creation of a "rhizomatic West, with its Indians without ancestry, its ever-receding limit, its shifting and displaced frontiers" (19). The rhizomatic evolution of the West grows, not from the usual East-West trajectory, but from tendrils sent out from multiple sites: "There is a whole American 'map' in the West, where even the trees form rhizomes. America reversed the directions: it put its Orient in the West, as if it were precisely in America that the earth came full circle; its West is the edge of the East" (19). For frontier regionalists like Bret Harte and Ambrose Bierce, the creation of an indigenous literary tradition depended on supplanting the pretensions and anomie of the Gilded Age. For postwar writers like Kenneth Rexroth and Jack Kerouac, the formation of western bohemia around Asian cultural models during the 1950s provides a second version of this narrative. If the Asian East offers an exotic alternative to the American East Coast, it does so through a complicated form of racial cross-dressing in which white males, by interacting with Asian culture, can reconfirm homosocial community and heterosexual authority. In order for this to happen, as my epigraph from Jack Kerouac indicates, "guys like us" must bring the message of the East "down to everybody."

THE LADY FROM SHANGHAI GOES WEST

We can see the complex nature of California orientalism in Orson Welles's 1947 movie, *The Lady from Shanghai*. The lady in question is not from Shanghai, nor is she Chinese. She is Elsa Bannister, played by a blond Rita Hayworth, whom we first meet in New York where she is married to a successful but crippled lawyer, Arthur Bannister (Everett Sloane). While riding in Central Park, she is accosted by thugs who attempt to drag her off into the bushes. She is saved by an angry young Irishman, Michael O'Hara, played by Welles, who quickly falls for her. Serving as a mate on Bannister's yacht, Michael pursues Elsa on a cruise through the Panama Canal, up the western coast of Mexico and ending up in San Francisco. O'Hara's obsession with Elsa causes him to become embroiled in a convoluted plot by which Bannister's partner, Grisby (Glenn Anders), is killed and O'Hara is set up as the killer. As he is about to be convicted, O'Hara escapes from the courtroom and finds himself in Chinatown, hiding in a theater where a Chinese opera is being performed. At this point the movie's title resonates for the first time.

It turns out that Elsa has in fact lived for a time in Shanghai, enough to have learned Chinese and to have developed contacts in San Francisco's Asian underworld.[4] She uses these contacts first to drug and then to sequester the fugitive O'Hara in a boarded-up amusement park, where he finds himself with both Elsa and her husband in a mirror maze. The famous shootout between Bannister and his wife is a justly celebrated denouement to the movie, but its play on mirrors and reality is assisted by the movie's exploitation of Elsa's role as an orientalized femme fatale. She is not the victim of her husband's possessiveness, as O'Hara has been given to believe, but a mantis who preys on other men, using her Chinatown access to urban spaces—fun houses, theaters and mirror rooms—to confuse fantasy and reality.

As Gina Marchetti observes, orientalized films often involve the threat of rape to a Caucasian woman by a "villainous Asian man" (10). *The Lady from*

Shanghai offers a variation on this theme by making the white male the victim of the orientalized female's sexuality. In fact it is one of several movies—*Shanghai Express* (1932) and *Chinatown* (1974) come to mind—where the hero is lured into danger by a white heroine metonymically identified as Asian and thereby synonymous with sexual intrigue and familial disruption. The use of Hayworth as a metonym for Asia is a way of accessing certain aspects of race (its otherness and exoticism) without exposing the viewer to a miscegenous relationship. As Michael Rogin points out with reference to the silent film *Old San Francisco,* the use of "racial masquerade" in films displaces the threat of miscegenation by whitening one racial type while "darkening" another (*Blackface* 131–33).

The fact that Welles plays a working-class Irishman against the upperclass, orientalized Elsa adds another layer of complexity. Their ill-fated romance repeats a much earlier (but no less violent) conflict between two immigrant populations in the West—Irish and Chinese—that spawned anticoolie agitation within the working classes of the late nineteenth century. The bridge between ethnicities and across class lines is formed by Elsa's construction of herself as Chinese. At one point she quotes a proverb: "The Chinese say it is difficult for love to last long; for one who loves passionately is cured of love." Such fortune cookie wisdom becomes Elsa's carpe diem proposal to O'Hara who, as a romantic Irishman, fails to understand what it means to cross ethnic and class lines in the pursuit of love. Elsa's whiteness—given vivid point by Hayworth's dyed blond hair—permits her to be the focus of desires that are never threatened by miscegenation.[5] All of these cross-racial dangers are solved at the movie's end when orientalized femme fatale and crippled (probably Jewish) lawyer destroy various mirrors that reflect them, finally killing each other, leaving the solitary Irish male to walk out into the dawn's early light.[6]

In Roman Polanski's *Chinatown* a similar confluence of racial and sexual forces is literalized through the incestuous relationship of Evelyn Mulwray (Faye Dunaway) with her father, Wilbur Cross (John Huston). As the head of the Los Angeles water district, Cross has been involved in a devious scheme to divert water in order to develop the San Fernando Valley—a fictional scenario with plenty of historical parallels. As in *The Lady from Shanghai,* class differences separate Evelyn from the slightly sleazy detective, Jake Gittes (Jack Nicholson), whom she hires to discover the killer of her husband, a former partner of Cross's who had become suspicious of the water diversion scheme. Warning Gittes against getting involved with his daughter, Cross says, "You may think you know what you're dealing with—but believe me, you don't." Gittes responds ruefully: "that's what the D.A. used to tell me about Chinatown" (Towne 80).

There are several important connections between Evelyn and Chinatown that link sexual and urban economies in California. Evelyn has been the victim of her father's incest and has borne his child, so that to *know* her is to know both her sexual past as well as the incest between Los Angeles water interests and civic government of which Cross is the embodiment. Evelyn, like Elsa Bannister, also has Chinatown connections, which she uses to hide her daughter from her father. Gittes's attempt to save Evelyn, like O'Hara's attempt to free Elsa, leads him to Chinatown where he witnesses—and to some extent enables—her violent death.

The idea that in Chinatown "normal" logic and morality do not apply is part of the frontier hypothesis, an attempt to contain irrational elements within manifest destiny that are not so manifest. If we apply my regionalist thesis, we might say that Chinatown becomes the West's political unconscious, the place where the violence of exploration, development, and growth continues to be played out within a closed demographic area.[7] And since this violence was often perpetrated against racial others—in this case, Chinese—it becomes rearticulated through mass cultural representations of tong wars, opium dens, and Asiatic prostitution. White women who cross over into Chinatown like Elsa Bannister or Evelyn Mulwray become identified with that same violence and ultimately suffer its effects. Thus, through a rather circuitous series of substitutions, the Caucasian woman is ruined not *by* villainous Asians but by associating *with* them.

The Lady from Shanghai's trajectory from New York to San Francisco traces a national journey from the decadent East (as embodied by the wealthy Bannister and his alcoholic, possibly homosexual partner, Grisby) through Central America, to a San Francisco of new fortunes and sexual intrigue. The voyage to an orientalized West structures much California literature, but if the "Heathen Chinee" built the literal railroad that made this passage possible, they no less provided necessary cultural signs out of which literary culture could be forged, a fact recognized by Jack Spicer, a poet of the San Francisco Renaissance:

"The dog wagged his tail and looked wonderfly sad" Poets in America with
       nothing to believe in except maybe the ships in Glouchester Harbor
       or the snow fall.
"Don't you remember Sweet Betsy from Pike,
She crossed the big mountains with her lover Ike."
No sense
In crossing a mountain with nobody living in it. No sense
In fighting their fires.
West coast is something nobody with sense would understand.
     We
Crossed them mountains, eating each other sometimes—or the

heathen Chinee
Building a railway. We are a coast people
There is nothing but ocean out beyond us. We grasp
The first thing coming.
>   (*Collected* 263)

In this poem Spicer counterposes the East Coast literary scene (Charles Olson's Gloucester or Frost's rural "snow fall") to the West Coast, a place "nobody with sense would understand." Spicer had attempted to live in New York and Boston unsuccessfully during the early 1950s but returned to San Francisco, disgusted by what he perceived as the exclusive, effete character of East Coast literary life. Against a poetics of sensibility and humanism that he identifies with New England culture (and despite Olson's similar antipathy), Spicer posits the dangerous, often catastrophic western migration and in the process links the cannibalism of the early Donner party with the Chinese role in building the railroad. Like many a western writer before him Spicer adopts the thesis that the West was forged out of extremity and violence. As a homosexual poet in a pre-Stonewall era, Spicer fantasizes that in the West one grasps "the first thing coming," a key ingredient in his own imagination of a hypermasculine queer frontier for the San Francisco Renaissance. Among his cohort in North Beach bars, geographic margins were directly tied to sexual and poetic practices. To inhabit the western edge of the continent enabled the writing of a marginal poetry.

Spicer's reference to the "heathen Chinee" invokes Bret Harte's 1870 poem, "Plain Language from Truthful James" in which the violent confrontation between immigrant Chinese and white labor is set in the Gold Rush mining country. In the poem Harte's narrator describes a card game in which his partner, William Nye, attempts to cheat the "peculiar" Chinaman, Ah Sin. The joke is on the two white men, however, when it turns out that Ah Sin has a few cards up his sleeve as well. Dealt a hand by the unscrupulous Nye, Ah Sin's cards turn out to be identical to the narrator's:

Then I looked up at Nye,
>   And he gazed upon me;
And he rose with a sigh,
>   And said, "Can this be?
We are ruined by Chinese cheap labour,"
>   And he went for that heathen Chinee.
>   (127)

The nineteenth-century literary controversy surrounding this poem centered on whether or not Harte, by depicting Ah Sin as a clever card shark, makes him the equal of the white gambler or whether the poet simply trades in a more pervasive racial stereotype of the conniving Asian in pigtail. Harte was sympathetic to the Chinese during the period of anticoolie agitation, but he created a poem that participated actively in further demonization of Asian immigrants.[8] However we resolve the conflict over his actual intentions toward Chinese, Harte's poem provides a problem for much subsequent regional literature where "local color" is achieved at the expense of racial color, where the solidification of homosocial community is defined by isolating ethnic others. His success in depicting the wild life of "Roaring Camp" depends on creating a vivid image of oriental guile and trickery, even when that deceitfulness foregrounds the same behavior among white miners, a duplicity brought out in the poem's final lines:

Which is why I remark,
  And my language is plain,
That for ways that are dark
  And for tricks that are vain,
The heathen Chinee is peculiar—
  Which the same I am free to maintain.
  (131)

For a poem intended as a burlesque of frontier violence, these lines seem oddly self-reflexive in their blurring of boundaries between Ah Sin and speaker. The narrator's insistence on his own "plain talk" against the "dark ways" of the "heathen Chinee" seem forced—as if the narrator's assertions of reportorial authority are undermined by the resemblance of the Chinese to himself. "Ways that are dark" and "plain" language coincide in a ballad where vernacular humor attempts, but fails, to finesse racism.

  The solidification of male community—in this case between the narrator and Nye—that we see validated in "Plain Talk from Truthful James" is threatened when the "heathen Chinee" is treated as the object of sexual desire. In the masculinist culture of mining camps, the Chinese male, denied domestic cohabitation by federal legislation against immigration of Chinese women, becomes specifically marked as a focus for white sexual anxiety. As Tomás Almaguer points out, in this overwhelmingly male immigrant population "Chinese men were initially seen as menacing sexual 'perverts' that preyed upon innocent white women," a fact that led to the creation of antimiscegenation statutes in California during the 1880s (160). But those same anxieties about Asian males could apply to homosexual desire as well. In Ambrose Bierce's first published short story, "The Haunted Valley" (1871), this desire is witnessed through the eyes of a first-person narrator whose identity as "Easterner" is self-consciously set against the rough logic of frontier settlements.[9] He is traversing a barren stretch of road on the way to Mexican Hill where he encounters Whisky Jo Dunfer in his "hermaphrodite habitation, half residence and half groggery." As it turns out, the hermaphroditic quality of Dunfer's domicile refers to more than its structural function.

Dunfer is described as betraying "a deep-seated antipathy to the Chinese," an expression of racism that becomes so vehement that the narrator attempts to ameliorate it, whereupon Dunfer delivers an attack on eastern liberalism that, to contemporary ears, seems hauntingly familiar: " 'You young Easterners,' " he said, " 'are a mile-and-a-half too good for this country, and you don't catch on to our play. People who don't know a Chileno from a Kanaka can afford to hang out liberal ideas about Chinese immigration, but a fellow that has to fight for his bone with a lot of mongrel coolies hasn't any time for foolishness' " (118). On the surface this is the voice of historical anti-Asian sentiment directed against an eastern political establishment that expanded Chinese immigration in order to enlarge the railroad labor force. But Dunfer's racist diatribes are also a foil for moral panics that have driven him to drink. Some years earlier he had accidentally killed a Chinese worker named Ah Wee whom he employed on his property. Although Dunfer introduces his former employee as a "miserable pig-tail Mongolian," the narrator soon discovers the true nature of Dunfer's sentiments after coming accidentally upon Ah Wee's grave:

AH WEE——CHINAMAN
Age unknown. Worked for Jo. Dunfer.
This monument is erected by him to keep the Chink's
memory green. Likewise as a warning to Celestials
not to take on airs. Devil take 'em!
She Was a Good Egg.
(121)

The inscription, with its substitution of female for male pronoun, is a curious mixture of what the narrator calls "hardihood and tenderness," expressing in stone what Dunfer cannot in person. This monument stares out as a warning to the narrator who, as a potential Celestial himself, should beware of "tak[ing] on airs."

The case of Ah Wee, like that of Ah Sin, is more complicated than one of mediated desire. When the narrator returns to the same spot four years later, accompanied by a "queer little man" named Gopher who had also worked for Dunfer, a new level of complexity is added to this allegory of racialized desire. The narrator discovers not only that Dunfer had killed Ah Wee but that the deed was due to jealousy. Gopher explains that " 'W'isky thought a lot o' that Chink; nobody but me knew how 'e doted on 'im. Couldn't bear 'im out of 'is sight, the derned protoplasm! And w'en 'e came down to this clearin' one day an' found him an' me neglectin' our work—him asleep an' me grapplin' a tarantula out of 'is sleeve—W'isky laid hold of my axe and let us have it, good an' hard!'" (125). Although Gopher survives the attack by the jealous Dunfer, Ah Wee is killed, and out of his despair Dunfer turns to drink and ultimately to rabid anticoolie sentiments. The denouement comes when it is revealed that there was every reason for Dunfer to be jealous, for Gopher had *also* loved Ah Wee and had followed his beloved from San Francisco to this "haunted valley." In Gopher's last declamation, the substitution of pronouns on the tomb now achieves full operatic form: "'Nine years ago!' he shrieked, throwing out his clenched hands—'nine years ago, w'en that big brute killed the woman who loves him better than she did me!—me who had followed 'er from San Francisco, where 'e won 'er at draw poker!—me who had watched over 'er for years w'en the scoundrel she belonged to was ashamed to acknowledge 'er and treat 'er white—me, who for her sake kept 'is cussed secret till it ate 'im up!'" (127). The "woman" in question—the movable fiction I am calling the Lady from Shanghai—is in fact Ah Wee, rendered female and killed out of sexual jealousy. Ramón Garcia notes that the gothic qualities of popular narratives like "The Haunted Valley" contain a larger historical horror in postbellum America, one of violence against "racialized and gendered populations in the U.S." (2). In the above passage we see vivid confirmation of this fact in its depiction of triangulated desire of two men for an Asian male who is both a woman and a piece of property, won in a game of chance and memorialized in sentimental rhetoric. The chivalric desire to "treat 'er white" is applied to someone who is neither "her" nor "white" but who must be reconfigured as such in order to live on in the narrator's memory.

The process by which the Asian male is reconfigured as a heterosexual, white partner is performed by the narrator who, as an easterner, must adapt himself to new and threatening logics of the West. As in numerous stories by Poe, if the valley is haunted, its demonic proportions are in the mind of a visitor who must constantly rationalize events according to recognizable categories. As Cathy Davidson points out, in Bierce's stories the "certainties of class, trade, gender, or education fall away to reveal the natural man beneath who, bereft of rhetoric, impotently succumbs to inarticulate panic" (14). What distinguishes the regional character of Bierce's stories is less their use of local color and idiolect than their study of the psychological effects of shock upon a mind that must organize chaotic impressions into a coherent narrative in which race, sex, and gender retain their normative and normalizing functions.

These two examples of racialized frontier narratives are introduced by Jack Spicer's observation that as a "coast people" "We grasp / the first thing coming" (*Collected* 263). The extremity that Spicer notices about the western imaginary has little to do with the frontier sublime as represented by painters from Albert Bierstadt and Frederic Remington to Mark Tobey. Rather the West is everywhere inflected with sexual and racial anxieties present in popular genres—from Deadwood Dick to Charlie Chan and the hardboiled detective novel (the noirish aspects of both *The Lady from Shanghai* and *Chinatown* pay homage to this same tradition). Spicer's reference to "Sweet Betsy from Pike" acknowledges the role that popular genres like the ballad, gothic story, and the satire had in creating and domesticating violence. The appeal of such genres is not only to provide escape but to transform historical tensions into fantasy or humor.

THE LADY FROM SHANGHAI IS NOT CHO-CHO-SAN

In speaking about *The Lady from Shanghai* I said that the journey from American East to West was often framed by an orientalist narrative of seduction and exoticism. Bret Harte's and Ambrose Bierce's nineteenth-century versions of this narrative explicitly link the formation of a western mythos to the demonization (and eroticization) of racial others. In postwar versions this transcontinental narrative often takes on the character of heroic legend, the most famous version being Jack Kerouac's *On the Road*. In the case of Kenneth Rexroth, Kerouac's predecessor and sometime nemesis, the exodus from the East to California provides the basis for hagiographic self-construction.[10] For both authors, crossings of the West with Asia reinforce heterosexual male community against the pressures of East Coast sophistication and privilege.

Edward Said observes that orientalism is based on a distinction between cultural topographies of East and West that serve as a starting point "for elaborate theories, epics, novels, social descriptions, and political accounts." These cultural products not only represent but ultimately "produce" the Orient as a political and sociological entity (3). While forms of countercultural community are a by-product of this discourse (fin-de-siècle aestheticism, arts and crafts antimodernism, for example), distinctions need to be made between Kerouac's or Rexroth's masculinist bohemia and more tribalist versions propounded by Gary Snyder. All three of these authors are usually conflated under the general heading of the Beat movement, but there are important differences. Snyder is probably the figure most often identified with a fusion of Asian cultural values and the postwar counterculture. His work has been closely associated with orientalist features of western life, but Snyder is himself a product of orientalist discourse through Jack Kerouac's portrayal of him as Japhy Ryder in the novel *The Dharma Bums*. The poet's relationship to Asia is much more complex than Kerouac's romantic version, making it necessary to separate the historical Snyder from the fictive in order to find a more nuanced understanding of his contributions to the postwar counterculture.

Since I have discussed Snyder extensively elsewhere, I will focus briefly here on the differences between his relationship to Asia and that of his Beat generation colleagues.[11] Unlike Rexroth or Kerouac, Snyder did not make the westward migration I mentioned above, but was born and raised in the Pacific Northwest. His identification with the region of his birth has profoundly affected his work, from references to his rural, working-class family background, his close proximity to Native American cultures of the Northwest, his hiking and backpacking experiences in the western mountains, his various jobs as forest fire lookout, trail crew worker, and tanker sailor. As Snyder has stated in essays and interviews, his first imagination of the West was formed by looking at Chinese murals on display at the Seattle Art Museum when he was a boy.[12] The impact of these murals and their similarity to landscapes of the Pacific Northwest can be felt throughout his writing, culminating in his magnum opus, *Mountains and Rivers without End,* a work inspired by Lu Yuan's Ch'ing Dynasty scroll paintings. Unlike Rexroth, Kerouac, Ginsberg, and other figures who looked to the East for spiritual or social models, Snyder has lived closely within those models throughout his life. As a graduate student at the University of California, Berkeley, he studied in the Oriental Languages Program, becoming fluent in Japanese and Chinese and serving as a translator of Buddhist texts for the Zen Institute. He lived for significant periods of time in Japan, beginning in 1955, and has traveled extensively in China, India, and Southeast Asia. He has practiced Zen Buddhism all of his life (his first trip to Japan was sponsored by the First Zen Institute of America in Kyoto), studying with Roshi Oda Sesso and taking formal vows as a Zen monk. Much of his poetry is indebted to Japanese and Chinese poets, and he has made several translations from the Japanese (his Han Shan translations were read at the famous Six Gallery reading of 1956). He and his former wife, Masa Uehara, lived for a time on the Banyan Ashram commune in Japan, and since returning to the United States in 1968 he has lived in a communal compound in the Sierra foothills, modeled on the Banyan Ashram. He is a regular commentator on Buddhist religion and practice within religious studies venues and publications. In short, Snyder's involvement with Asia goes well beyond an antiquarian interest.

What sets Snyder apart more significantly from the more facile appropriations of Asian culture on the West Coast is his complex political and ecological involvement in the Pacific Rim as a bioregion. He has been a vocal critic of U.S. environmental policies, but he has been no less critical of China and Japan for their own contributions to pollution, deforestation, and faulty crop management.[13] He has been a tireless advocate for local control of geographical areas within the Pacific basin and has written extensively on the need for international cooperation in protecting natural habitats and wildlife. As Timothy Gray has pointed out, Snyder is a "poet-geographer" of the Pacific Rim who has mapped the biodiversity of the region through poetry and prose. He sees it not as an entrepreneurial zone for economic growth but as an "uneven playing field of human interchange" (29). Gray goes on to point out that the critical force of a book like *The Back Country* comes not merely from its exploration of East/West relations but from its study of "the poet's attitude toward women, work and leisure" that cannot be separated from the human geography of the region (29).

Although Snyder often frames his relationship to community and family in heterosexual—even paternalist—terms, he is a good deal more critical of the sexual politics by which Asia is framed by the West. Several sections of *The Back Country* cast a skeptical eye on Western interests in Asian culture ("To Hell with Your Fertility Cult") or sexual tourism in the East ("Six Years"), and in his various writings on Buddhism he has discussed the limits of patriarchal structures in India and Japan compared with the participation of women in Western Buddhism.[14] Snyder's poetic mythology includes references to female cults and myths but always in relationship to the cultures in which those figures are venerated. Ideas of tribe, regionalism, network, and other social models identified with Snyder may reinforce a more traditional heterosexual communitarian ideal, but he has been unusually attentive to the ways that biodiversity demands an equivalent social diversity. This is a far cry from Kenneth Rexroth's or Jack Kerouac's eroticized treatment of the figure I am calling the Lady from Shanghai and the community invoked in her name.

In his autobiographical writings Rexroth describes his fateful 1927 entry into San Francisco on the day that George Sterling, the city's leading poet, committed suicide. In Rexroth's account this event fortuitously leaves room for the younger poet to create a new bohemian enclave.[15] What he discovers in the West is another East, one more congenial because less contaminated by American provinciality. San Francisco, as he says, "was very much of a backwater town and there just wasn't anything happening," but the city's proximity to Asia makes it ripe for cultural change: "The West Coast is close to the Orient. It's the next thing out there. There are a large number of orientals living on the West Coast. San Francisco is an international city and it has living contact with the Orient. It also has an internal oriental life. Once a week you can go to see a Buddhist basketball game. . . . There are Buddhist temples all over the place. To a New Yorker this is all ridiculous, the Orient means dimestore incense burners. It is very unreal" (Meltzer 30).[16] Rexroth plays out multiple variations on this theme, excoriating the smugness of the New York literary establishment while making San Francisco cosmopolitan by moving it closer to the Orient.[17] Rexroth was unquestionably an inspiration for younger poets like Robert Duncan, Gary Snyder, Philip Whalen, and

Allen Ginsberg in their Asian interests, but his investment in the East is inflected by a gender narrative in which heterosexual male potency is purchased through a myth of oriental sensuality. As in the case of *The Lady from Shanghai,* racial otherness rearticulates heteronormativity.

In Rexroth's *Autobiographical Novel* (1966) discussions of Eastern literature and thought are invariably elaborated through scenes describing the author's sexual exploits. Speaking of an affair with the lover of one of his best friends, Rexroth merges middle European decadence and Asian sensuality; the event was "like a weekend along about 1912 in the most expensive Budapest whorehouse" (431). He describes the woman as being "what Dr. Freud would call polymorphous perverse, with great joy and zest. I had never met a white woman like her, nor have I since. Lying in bed and smoking kif, she explained why" (431). Although the woman described here is not Asian, this scene, redolent of Ingres and Matisse, is suffused with orientalist features. Rexroth first establishes his racial and sexual credentials ("I had never met a white woman like her") before explaining that the woman had been the favorite concubine of a Japanese prince "possibly because she was the blondest, and the only one who could talk to him about literature and art. . . . There was only one trouble. No American man could satisfy her—intellectually, socially, or sexually. After she broke with my friend, she became the lover of a very handsome lesbian doctor" (432–33). Rexroth's own sexual abilities notwithstanding, he trades in a familiar heterosexist view of lesbianism as the result of sexual frustration in "normal" (that is, heterosexual) relationships— here embellished with orientalist features. The woman's blond hair, intellectual accomplishments, and sexual athleticism qualify her for inclusion within Rexroth's harem. But her most compelling feature is her attractiveness to a Japanese nobleman whose criteria for "satisfaction" are equal to Rexroth's. Thus Rexroth can participate in an elaborate cultural daisy chain via a white woman, an Asian prince, and a lesbian doctor.

Rexroth's linkage of the Orient with sexual rapaciousness continues in a later scene that describes his "Japanophilia." Once again, he first establishes his racial tolerance: "In addition to being organizer of the Fillmore District Unemployed Council, and cosecretary of the small League for the Struggle of Negro Rights, I was the only Caucasian who had any contact with the Japanese community" (434–35). He then proceeds to chronicle his contributions to Japanese culture: his translations from the Japanese, his essays on Japanese literature, and his lectures in Japan, not to mention his own commitment to Shingon Buddhism. But this chronicle is only foreplay for describing his obsessions with a "girl, who was the finest koto player on the West Coast and . . . [who] still quickens my pulse whenever I see her" (435). "I have no desire to turn this autobiography into another Frank Harris's *My Life and Loves,* let alone the popular Victorian pornographic memoir *My Private*

Life. But I must say that with few exceptions Japanese women merit their reputation as lovers. . . . But at least in those days, undressed and in bed, they were dreams out of *The Tale of Genji*" (436). Although Rexroth wants to distance himself from pornography, he participates in it enough to submit female agency to boudoir sophistication. At the end of this section, Rexroth attempts to draw all of his themes together by connecting political radicalism with sexual prowess: "And today Japanese women are in evergrowing rebellion. As the great woman poet Yosano Akiko said, 'When women assert themselves, it will be Mountain Moving Day.' The mountains are beginning to move in Japan, and there are not many Cho-Cho-Sans running around" (436). Despite his demurral, it is clear from the importance Rexroth grants to the legend about Japanese women's sexual prowess that Japanese feminism is constructed as much around Frank Harris's memoir as around *Madame Butterfly*.

In dealing with Rexroth one must be careful in assuming a one-to-one correspondence between historical author and persona. As Linda Hamalian points out in her introduction to the *Autobiographical Novel*, most of the events of Rexroth's early life correspond in some loose way with those in the novel, but the speaker is, in large measure, a construct or extension of those events. By regarding Rexroth as a "construct," however, we risk obscuring the function of such performance in the validation of certain hierarchies of gender. Since Rexroth's self-constructions underwrite structures of value (Lawrentian heterosexuality versus effete homosexuality, decadent East Coast versus sensual Asia, "authentic" ethnics versus bourgeois white people) we need to see the assertion of fictionality as itself a fiction and thus subject to further invention. When, in his late poems on Chinese themes, Rexroth attempts to project himself into a Japanese woman, the problematics of such fictive self-construction come to the surface.

Most critics regard Rexroth's translations from the Chinese as among his greatest productions, works that advance Pound's theories of translation and provide a bridge for younger poets like Snyder and Whalen. Eliot Weinberger regards the Marichiko poems as well as the Li Ch'ing-chao translations as "master works of remembered passion" (51). William Lockwood regards Rexroth's late Chinese translations as being "graceful, astonishingly rich and clarifying poems" (130). Morgan Gibson feels that in his translations Rexroth, "like a Bodhisattva, . . . became oriental as well as European, and feminine in his versions of Yosano Akiko, Ono no Komachi, and Li Ch'ing Chao" (97). Rexroth is particularly revered for his translations of Asian women poets—*The Burning Heart: Women Poets of Japan* and then Chinese women in *The Orchid Boat: Women Poets of China* and *Li Ch'ing Chao Complete Poems*. Such assessments, however accurate to the poems in question, never attempt to relate Rexroth's translations to his autobiographical writings. This silence is understandable enough, given differences in genre, but it permits a division of his writings into two distinct modalities, the latter redeemed by the former. If Rexroth was a sexist who traded in racist stereotypes, so the logic goes, at least when he translated from the Chinese he transcended his more venal side. This is a little like excusing Pound's interest in fascism by pointing to his interest in Neoplatonism or Confucianism. I see the two impulses—autobiographical self-fabrication and lyric clarity—as variations on a common attempt to validate masculine authority through immersion in the East of the new West.

Although we could look at any number of Rexroth's translations to explore orientalist themes, it is in *The Love Poems of Marichiko* that the intersection of sexual fantasy and masculine performance merge most dramatically. Based on the writings of Yosano Akiko (1878–1942), the Marichiko poems embody states of sexual ecstasy and loss in a series of sixty short lyrics.[18] These poems tell of a love affair from the standpoint of a fictitious female poet whose ardors soon turn to resentment when her lover ceases to visit. In his notes to the sequence Rexroth asks his reader to notice "that the sex of the lover is ambiguous," but he misremembers at least one poem in which gender is specified:

Once I shone afar like a
Snow-covered mountain.
Now I am lost like
An arrow shot in the dark.
He is gone and I must learn
To live alone and
Sleep alone like a hermit
Buried deep in the jungle.
I shall learn to go
Alone, like the unicorn.
    (134)

The heterosexual character of Marichiko's desire is expressed not only by the masculine pronoun used to describe the absent lover but by various phallic metaphors ("An arrow shot in the dark"; "sleep alone like a hermit"; "alone, like the unicorn") that she uses to describe her position in the relationship. Marichiko's passion is defined in terms of incompletion, for which the (presumably male) lover will supply fulfillment—at times infusing her sexual experience with his own: "Spasms of longing suffocate me / And will not stop" (105); "before I met you / I didn't have anything to think about" (107); "making love with you / Is like drinking sea water / The more I drink / The thirstier I become" (108); "as I came from the / Hot bath, you took me before

/ The horizontal mirror / Beside the low bed, while my / Breasts quivered in your hands, my / Buttocks shivered against you" (121). Marichiko consistently takes the passive role in lovemaking; she waits "with the shoji open"; her lover "[parts] my thighs, and kiss[es] me" (110); "lying in the meadow, open to you / Under the noon sun, / Hazy smoke half hides / My rose petals" (112). Of course such passages could as easily describe lesbian sexuality— and Rexroth's note attempts to hint at that possibility—but the stress on passivity and openness, on vulnerability and incompleteness limit the scope and variety of sexual engagement.

Not all of the poems are about sexuality. Although he adopts the epistolary present, Rexroth is actually writing a kind of memento mori on lost sexuality from the standpoint of old age:

Now the fireflies of our youth
Are all gone
Thanks to the efficient insecticides
Of our middle age.
    (132)

The previous scenes of lovemaking that provide such sensual surfaces for the most vivid poems in the series here give way before an awkward metaphor that instantiates the older lover's feeling of emptiness. The clumsy rhetoric acknowledges the sense of detumescence it mourns. Marichiko's absent lover is, in fact, Rexroth's own lost potency, a fact registered by the shift in diction from scenes of heightened erotic passion to metaphors drawn from the marketplace. The male poet represents himself as viewed in Marichiko's mirror:

Without me you can only
Live at random like
A falling pachinko ball.
I am your wisdom.
    (135)

As accurate to the terms of Chinese diction and form as they may be, such poems participate in the orientalist fantasies that mark the *Autobiographical Novel*. Instead of showing a more "sensitive" Rexroth, one who identifies with the condition of women as social individuals, they present an idealized sexual partner, one whose subjectivity is framed by masculine desire. Utilizing the persona of an Asian woman enables him to participate in more recognizable forms of paternalistic sexuality while retaining his credentials as a western Asianist.

The fusion of modes in Rexroth's work—spare, Chinese lyrics and bar-room braggadocio—is central to his construction of an alternative western bohemian tradition, distinct from the "Ivy League fog" factories of the eastern seaboard ("San Francisco Letter" 8). Any assessment of his poetry must take into account his social project of naming an "alternative society" of Wobblies, longshoremen, and self-taught scholars, a society that is homosocial in its formation but that admits women in their orientalized form. As admirable as Rexroth's political vision of the West is, its sexual and racial formations are considerably less progressive. Asia is an ally in forging a new western bohemia, but it is an Asia modified by an eroticized gaze first seen in nineteenth-century fantasies about oriental women. If Marichiko is a Lady from Shanghai (or in this case, Kyoto) she is marked by her passage through Rexroth's Golden Gate.

According to Rexroth, when Jack Kerouac first visited the older poet in the early 1950s "he walked into my house, sat down in a kind of stiff-legged imitation of a lotus posture, and announced that he was a Zen Buddhist . . . and then discovered everyone in the room knew at least one Oriental language" (Meltzer 32). Although Rexroth enjoyed pulling intellectual rank where Kerouac was concerned, he recognized that the Beats had spawned a significant interest in things Asian to the point that, as he said, "there are so many Airedales running around claiming to be Buddhists nowadays" (*Autobiographical Novel* 435). Kerouac, like Rexroth, had also made his own heroic western journey to escape the stultifying domestic life at home in Lowell, Massachusetts. Both men were the products of second generation immigrant parents (German American and French Canadian), a factor that may have contributed to their romance of an orientalized West. But whereas Rexroth figured the Orient in terms of heterosexual union Kerouac linked it to the formation of male community.

Although his most famous transcontinental trips are memorialized in *On the Road,* it is in *The Dharma Bums* where the myth of orientalized California makes its most significant appearance. In this novel, the Lady from Shanghai is a white male in the form of Japhy Ryder (Gary Snyder), one of the "felaheen people"—hobos, Zen mystics, and wandering scholars—who express for Kerouac an independent, ascetic ideal. Japhy introduces the narrator, Ray Smith (Kerouac), not only to the new bohemia of San Francisco but to the "greatest dharma bums of them all, the Zen Lunatics of China and Japan" (10). For Ray, Japhy provides an alternative masculinity to the more chaotic, unstructured versions encountered in Alvah Goldbrook (Allen Ginsberg) or Cody (Neal Cassady). Japhy's monastic shack in Berkeley, with its straw mats, crates of scholarly books, and "peaceful cup of tea at his side as he bent his serious head to the Chinese signs of the poet Han Shan" present a domestic model of order and control that Ray desires but can never achieve (17). At the same time, Ryder synthesizes monastic introspection with what Ray takes to be "masculine" pursuits of mountain climbing, wilderness camping, and sexual experimentation.

Ray attempts to organize his life around this domestic ideal later in the novel when he serves, at Japhy's suggestion, as a forest fire lookout. But the enormity of the natural landscape and the solitude of the mountain lookout challenge Ray's abilities to replicate Japhy's monastic calm. Ray comforts himself not so much by communing with the mountains as by seeing himself reflected in Japhy's mirror: "'And this is Japhy's lake, and these are Japhy's mountains,' I thought, and wished Japhy were there to see me doing everything he wanted me to do." The construction of this sentence is typical of Kerouac's writing and serves as a warning to those who read his novels as Baedeckers for living the unreflective life. Ray wants to be seen as doing what others want him to do. He pursues monastic solitude based on the life of the poet, Han Shan, but it is clear that his reading of his mountain lookout has its origin in a China created in Marin County: "What a mountain! It had that same unmistakable witches' tower shape Japhy had given it in his brush drawing of it that used to hang on the burlap wall in the flower shack in Corte Madera" (183).

An important scene in *The Dharma Bums* involves Kerouac's rendering of the famous Six Gallery poetry reading where the major principals of the Beat movement first appeared publicly. This inaugural moment of the San Francisco Renaissance is followed by a "freeswinging" meal in Chinatown:

> This happened to be Japhy's favorite Chinese restaurant, Nam Yuen, and he showed me how to order and how to eat with chopsticks and told anecdotes about the Zen Lunatics of the Orient and had me going so glad . . . that finally I went over to an old cook in the doorway of the kitchen and asked him "Why did Bodhidharma come from the West?" . . .
>
> "I don't care," said the old cook, with lidded eyes, and I told Japhy and he said, "Perfect answer, absolutely perfect. Now you know what I mean by Zen."
>
> I had a lot more to learn, too. Especially about how to handle girls.
> (15)

Although Kerouac's friends and colleagues have made claims for the seriousness of his religious commitments, they seldom acknowledge his ability to situate and ironize his enthusiasms. Ray's attempt to solicit Zen koans from a Chinese cook has elements more appropriate to the Marx Brothers than to *Meetings with Famous Men*. The fact that Zen wisdom is confused with learning to eat with chopsticks or handle girls deflates the seriousness of Japhy Ryder's esoteric study and serves as an alternative to Rexroth's intellectual ranking. Where Rexroth posits himself as an authority on Asian matters, Kerouac frames himself as an outsider learning from the ground up.

Such passages suggest that the formation of a new literary community, of which Kerouac was the central figure, was inflected by orientalist themes having less to do with China and more to do with a cultural revolution on the West Coast. This revolution must be set within the context of several forces impinging on postwar life: American corporate expansion, prompted by postwar prosperity, neoconservative reaction in intellectual circles, and a growing cold war consensus over superpower dominance. Against the forces of conformism, consensus, and consumerism, the lure of Asia, whether the defeated empire (Japan) or the emerging revolution (China) offered an important alternative. But the cultural revolution of West Coast bohemia contains an important caveat, expressed as such in the passage above. If Ray appropriates Chinese identity for his own uses in bonding with Japhy, the cook's "I don't care" acknowledges a distance between the largely white literary community in North Beach and the workaday world of Chinese cooks, seamstresses, and small business owners on lower Grant Avenue.

THE LADY FROM SHANGHAI IS MISSING

If, as I have indicated, the Lady from Shanghai is neither Chinese, nor Cho-Cho-San, nor a lady, who is she? We glimpse her briefly at the end of Wayne Wang's *Chan Is Missing* (1981), standing on a porch in Chinatown, swaying back and forth in a gentle dance. Playing in the background is Rogers and Hammerstein's song, "Grant Avenue," sung by Pat Suzuki:

You can eat if you are in the mood
Sharkfin soup, beancake fish
The girl who serves you all your food
Is another, tasty dish.

The tension between the upbeat touristic (and sexist) tune and the stark, black-and-white presentation of a woman who very well may have come from Shanghai—or Taipei or Hong Kong or Beijing—offers an important corrective both to Rexroth's eroticized portrayal of the Asian West and to Kerouac's romance of white Asians. Wang's movie follows its two male protagonists, Jo and Steve, as they search for their partner, Chan Hung, who has absconded with $4,000 of their money. It becomes clear that not only is Chan missing from Chinatown but that what it means to be Chinese is missing in the

United States and has been displaced onto a series of postcolonial narratives—including songs like "Grant Avenue"—that make finding the "true" Chan impossible.

Chan's absence occurs within an Asian American bachelor society that poses a stark alternative to the more romantic homosocial community of Rexroth's or Kerouac's postwar bohemia. Whereas Kerouac's idealization of hearty masculine types like Neal Cassady and Japhy Ryder is often fueled by moral panic, the homosocial community depicted in *Chan Is Missing* is produced in part by immigration laws that, by excluding Asian women from immigrating with their spouses to the West, had historically produced a society of aging men. While this era, by the time of the film, is over, the residues of that bachelor society are still being visited on its sons. Kerouac's enthusiastic feeling that "guys like us" will bring the message of the Orient to "everybody" will come as a surprise to Chinese American "guys" who have already lived in the United States for a century and who populate the largely masculine mahjong parlors, social clubs, and family societies depicted in Wang's films.

This bachelor society is the explicit subject of Wang's *Eat a Bowl of Tea* (1989), based on Louis Chu's 1961 novel and set in 1940s New York at a moment when immigration restrictions on Chinese women had been loosened. At this time it was possible for younger males, many of whom served in the armed forces during World War II, to visit China and bring a bride to the West. The young protagonist of the film, Ben Loy (Russell Wong), is urged by his father, Wah Gay (Victor Wong), to return to his paternal village in China and marry the daughter of his father's best friend. The dutiful son follows his father's wishes and returns to New York with his Chinese bride, Mei Oi (Cora Miao), but intergenerational and cross-cultural problems soon beset the couple. Part of the problem lies with the complex structure of male society represented by the two fathers, a society constructed not out of compulsory heterosexuality, as it is for Rexroth and Kerouac, but out of laws and statutes that govern the traffic in women. The marriage is overdetermined by expectations among the aging bachelors who hang out at the social halls and mahjong parlors of Chinatown. They hope that the liaison of Ben Loy and Mei Oi will compensate for their own failed marriages and economic dreams.

One sequence of scenes depicts the tension between two economies of the postwar period—one sexual and one national—as Ben Loy attempts to fulfill his proper (Asian) masculine role within the context of what his father regards as being a big shot in America. The father's close monitoring of the young couple's progress toward parenthood has led to the son's sexual impotence, a crisis that threatens the marriage and ultimately leads to his wife's infidelity. In order to escape the father's voyeuristic gaze, the couple spends a weekend in Washington, D.C., where they visit national landmarks like the

Lincoln and Jefferson monuments. Flushed with patriotic zeal (and released from paternal prying), the couple retires to their hotel room where the son finally performs his filial and marital obligation. But the next scene shows them back in New York, lying in bed, their blank faces registering the continuation of domestic malaise. Wang cuts to the aquarium scene from *The Lady from Shanghai* where Elsa throws herself at O'Hara, shouting, "Take me quick, take me!" a gesture of erotic submission in dramatic contrast to the troubled sexual relationship between the young Asian couple. Watching this scene and aroused by Welles's display of sexual aggressiveness, the couple leaves the theater, but once home their lovemaking is interrupted by the unexpected arrival of the young man's former Caucasian girlfriend.

The subject of these scenes is the construction and deflation of sexuality based on competing cultural discourses—of sexual productivity constantly threatened by an Asian double consciousness. "Normal" heterosexual relations are fraught by familial expectations on the one hand—the production of male progeny for the perpetuation of a fictive family order—and an ideology of democratic institutions and unfettered libidinal expression on the other. Wang's use of Welles's aquarium scene draws together both of these narratives in its presentation of unmediated sexuality set against a fish tank in which rapacious sharks and eels provide silent commentary. The panoptical gaze of family and social morality in Wang's film is represented at the end of Welles's scene where the two lovers are interrupted in their embrace by a class of school children. Their embarrassed giggles interrupt Elsa's and Michael's intimate contact and darken the faces of Ben Loy and Mei Oi watching from the darkened theater. Film and filmic quotation overlap each other, indicating the ways that twin forces of Western cultural representations and Asian familial traditions intrude into the private sphere.

The historical background of both Welles's and Wang's movies is, as I have indicated, a racialized and sexualized cultural imaginary of (and in) the West set against repressive forces of the East Coast. Wang acknowledges the limitations of that imaginary within Asian American culture by quoting Welles's most ambivalent representation of an orientalized sexuality. But Wang provides his own version of the same Western fantasy in the final scene of *Eat a Bowl of Tea;* the young couple, now relocated in San Francisco, is shown having an all-American barbecue surrounded by both fathers and their new baby, with a second clearly on the way. This postcard representation of cultural resolution must be framed against the global restructuring occurring in the late 1940s as represented by the emerging cold war, which provides a subtext in both movies. In *The Lady from Shanghai* it is represented by the paranoid fantasies of Grisby whose desire to escape from cities like San Francisco is fueled by fears of bombs dropping in an imminent nuclear holocaust. In Wang's film, it is represented by the Chinese civil war and then by the Korean conflict; as the film makes clear, the latter event threatens once again to close the borders between East and West and perpetuate the bachelor society that immigration laws have helped to create. Thus at the moment when the West is represented as a haven from culturally narrow prescriptions associated with the East Coast, the Soviet Union and China are constructed as new "Easts," as demonic others to Western free trade and imperial expansion.

Wang's films represent one of numerous corrective gestures being provided by Asian American artists to the orientalism of Western literature, particularly in its postwar, romantic mode. One could, in this context, refer to the work of Genny Lim, Lois-Ann Yamanaka, Janice Mirikitani, Jessica Hagedorn, Shawn Wong, Frank Chin, and Fae Ng, all of whom revisit orientalist themes in the West within the critical frame of Asian immigrant history.[19] While the contributions of Western writers to an understanding of Asian culture must be acknowledged, so also must we recognize the ways that Asia functioned to construct a myth of Western exceptionalism—as pervasive, in its own way, as the Puritan salvational narrative that has dominated American literary history. It is against this latter "eastern" narrative that poets and novelists provided their own orientalist versions. Exceptionalist narratives are, by their nature, exclusionary, made the more so when other populations (Mexican Californios, Native Americans, Chinese and Japanese workers) have legitimate claims on the terrain. Whether demonized as the "heathen Chinee" or romanticized as the Lady from Shanghai, Western Asian history is, like the plate tectonics of the region itself, written on a shifting, unstable surface.

4

"When the world strips down and rouges up":
Redressing Whitman

Another self, a duplicate of every one . . .
Under the broadcloth and gloves, under the ribbons and artificial flowers,
Keeping fair with the customs, speaking not a syllable of itself.
　　Walt Whitman, "Song of the Open Road"

So we are taking off our masks, are we, and keeping
our mouths shut? as if we'd been pierced by a glance!
　　Frank O'Hara, "Homosexuality"

I always say you're born naked and the rest is drag.
　　RuPaul

"I TOO / THAT AM A NATION"

In his speech to the Republican convention in August 1992, Patrick
Buchanan described the previous month's Democratic convention as "that
giant masquerade ball up at Madison Square Garden where twenty thousand
liberals and radicals came dressed up as moderates and centrists—in the
greatest single exhibition of cross-dressing in American political history."[1]
On one level, Buchanan's invective is addressed to what he perceives as the
liberal platform of the Democrats—their inclusion of abortion rights, health
care reform, and environmental issues. On another level, it is addressed to
the increasing presence of gay and lesbian issues in American political life—
AIDS research, domestic partners legislation, job protection, artistic censorship—that challenge the family-values agenda of the religious Right. By regarding Democrats as political transvestites, Buchanan wanted to link sexual

and political identities so that (so-called) perversity in one sphere may be read as corruption in another.

It is worth keeping Buchanan's rhetoric in mind as we consider Walt Whitman's legacy to later poets if only to remind ourselves of the continuing and virulent strand of homophobia that permeates our current political debate.[2] When identity is regulated according to a heterosexual norm, when gender is policed by rigid binaries, then Whitman's radical view of the self as ensemble is jettisoned. It might also be worth keeping Buchanan's trope of cross-dressing in mind as we consider the ways that contemporary gay male poets have appropriated Whitman's sexual politics to speak for social identities that even the good gray poet could not have envisioned. Whitman's "glorious mistake," as Robert Duncan called it, is not that he believed in America but that he envisaged it as a nation of others—a queer nation—where private and social bodies could be linked under a common law.

Duncan, like many poets of his generation, understood that there was a price for linking the private and social:

> I too
> that am a nation sustain the damage
> where smokes of continual ravage
> obscure the flame.
> It is across great scars of wrong
> I reach toward the song of kindred men
> and strike again the naked string
> old Whitman sang from.
> ("Poem Beginning with a Line by Pindar" 64)

Duncan recognizes that in order to identify with Whitman, he must "sustain the damage" of a society in which he is not allowed to participate.[3] The price of nonparticipation, for both Duncan and Whitman, is painful vision, an ability to see "always the under side turning, / fumes that injure the tender landscape" (64). Whitman anticipated such mediated relations to the social body by describing himself perpetually "aft the blinds of the window" (38), gazing out at forms of nakedness and mutuality for which "democracy" was the most available term but for which "adhesiveness" proved the most potent. When he becomes the woman who "hides handsome and richly drest" (38) to watch the twenty-eight bathers or when he asserts that he is "the poet of the woman the same as the man" (21), readers have heard a sensible appeal to pluralism. The good gay poet, however, might hear in such lines not simply identity within difference but identity within identity, the adoption of one role to articulate another. Finding their literary and sexual identities in the years following World War II, gay writers *add*ressed Whitman by *red*ressing his problematic of identity in specifically gendered terms. Thus the perennial topic of Whitman's influence must take into consideration not only the "outsetting bards" he produced but the multiple identities from which he was productive.

Before considering Whitman's direct influence on subsequent writers we should consider the validity of using cross-dressing to describe his performance of gender. After all, there is no indication that Whitman crossed Brooklyn ferry in drag or even addressed the social practice of transvestism. I am using cross-dressing as a sign of what Marjorie Garber calls a "category crisis" in which the deliberate confusion of gender markers confuses definitional distinctions (male/female, subject/object, poet/reader, gay/straight) (16). According to Garber, cross-dressing is a pervasive phenomenon in social life, ranging in its forms from businessmen who wear women's underwear beneath their three-piece suits to gender-bending rock stars like Michael Jackson and Madonna to full scale drag balls. Its appearance threatens to disrupt narratives of gender and sexual differentiation not because it reverses roles but because it foregrounds gender and sex *as* roles. Far from representing the desire of one gender to reveal its "true" identity through the garb of the other, cross-dressing foregrounds the performative character of identity itself. The eternal debate over Whitman's "object-choice" has been framed narrowly within an identitarian (and heterosexist) logic—if interested in stevedores and boat captains, therefore not interested in women—thus limiting the poet's many claims to be "untranslatable" (89).

There are obvious risks to using cross-dressing as a term for textual practice, not the least is that it erases specific political and social meanings of transvestism within the gay and lesbian society. As social practice, transvestism functions as a critique of gender stereotypes or as a provocative attack on the sex/gender system. A great deal of queer theory (including Garber's book) and popular journalism has seized upon drag as a significant form of cultural production, but these venues often fail to acknowledge the milieu in which cross-dressing has the most dramatic social effects. The gay and lesbian community has long understood the subversive and oppositional possibilities of drag and has used them to confront homophobic society. It has debated the limitations of drag—its reinforcement of gender stereotypes and heterosexual roles—in forging a political movement. But cross-dressing involves the warping of codes that inhere on many levels, from the sartorial to the rhetorical. If a poet like Emily Dickinson adopts, as she often does, the role of a male when she wants to describe conditions of power unavailable to women in the 1860s, she is extending the possibilities of transvestism into a textual form that may or may not have implications for her own sexuality. Similarly, in 1855, Whitman's desire for other men literally had no name, in our contemporary psychological sense, and thus had to be represented through scenarios that did.

As Garber points out, the presence of transvestism in literature represents a "category crisis elsewhere" in society, a displacement of tensions in culture at large onto the normative logics of gender differentiation (17). As I will point out in the case of Frank O'Hara, images of cross-dressing in his poetry often articulate racial and national crises during the cold war period. In Whitman, the adoption of female personae signals the emergence of new emerging sexual categories in the postbellum period that were beginning to be defined in medical and psychological literature. These categories, especially those defined in phrenological and mesmerist tracts, challenged definitions of masculinity and homosociality that were part of America's expansionist development. But such displacements of crisis from one sphere of society onto the sex/gender system needn't result in a strict binarist conception. In Jennie Livingston's film about African American drag balls, *Paris Is Burning* (1991), what is revealing is not so much the presentation of males dressed up as women (in high style fashions or Las Vegas chorus line gear) but men dressed up as men in a variety of professional roles, from military cadet to professional executive in three-piece suit. The sheer range of cross-dressed styles, across genders, classes, professions, races, and attitudes in this film provides the best optic on how limited the term *cross-dressing* can be when confined to a simple replacement of one gender with its putative opposite. Although Livingston's film depicts a distinctly postmodern version of gender confusion (one dependent on the existence of large urban populations of African Americans and Latinos), it expands the possibilities of what transvestism *might include* as identity performance.

The most common gender-crossing scenario in Whitman is that in which, like the twenty-eight bathers section of "Song of Myself," the poet adopts a feminine position in order to participate erotically with other males. Sexual and textual acts interlink in ways that force the reader to become, as it were, a third participant in Whitman's mediated desire. Michael Moon describes such moments as those in which "woman and (male) speaker meet in the 'unseen hand' which is also a sign of the substitutive relationship in which the poem *makes* seen what is unseen (hidden or proscribed desire) through the substitution for it of language and writing" (47). This materialization of unspeakable identities in the text is often figured through a rhetoric of dressing and undressing in which the act of removing clothing reveals an identity hidden beneath. "Undrape! you are not guilty to me" is Whitman's most characteristic appeal to authenticity, yet such invocations of nakedness are framed by the clothing that must be removed (35). "Agonies are one of my changes of garments" (67) Whitman acknowledges in section 33 of "Song of Myself," and elsewhere he speaks of "thrusting [himself] beneath . . . clothing" (116) or of seeing "through the broadcloth and gingham" (35) in order to reveal the body underneath. He notes "the little plentiful manikins skipping around in collars and tail'd coats," but he acknowledges in them "the duplicates of myself" (77). For every claim that "what is commonest, cheapest, nearest, easiest, is Me," there is the countervailing awareness that the poet must "adorn himself to bestow [himself] on the first that will take [him]" (41).[4]

Whitman adorned himself in much more immediate ways than in poetic figures of speech. In hundreds of daguerreotypes and photographs taken throughout his life, Whitman constructed versions of himself to present to the public and to introduce each successive edition of his poem. As Alan Trachtenberg notes, his "pictures took on epithets of their own—'The Christ likeness,' the 'Quaker picture,' 'my sea-captain face,' the 'Lear photo,' the 'Laughing Philosopher,' and, inevitably, 'the mysterious photograph'" (67). It is hard to think of another writer of his era who so thoroughly exploited the possibility of the camera for staging versions of self, from Broadway dandy to rough-hewn outdoorsman, from kindly preceptor to visionary sage. In all of these representations, clothing, props, and body language are important adjuncts to the effect desired. And he compounded this visual self-presentation with a series of reviews and publicity blurbs of his own work, written by himself, in which the "myth" of Walt Whitman was created for the public. What is remarkable about all such performances is that Whitman saw them as serving an essential authenticity, analogous to the poetry that, as he wrote in one unsigned review, becomes "his own flesh and form, undraped, regardless of models" (777). If *Leaves of Grass* was to be an "indirect epic" of the American Adam, Whitman's self-conscious reinvention of himself may have been the poem's most indirect feature.

Perhaps the most famous moment of cross-dressing, aside from the twenty-eight bathers passage mentioned above, is that in "The Sleepers" where Whitman as dreamer becomes both female lover and male beloved, as well as the surrounding darkness:

I am she who adorn'd herself and folded her hair expectantly,
My truant lover has come, and it is dark.

Double yourself and receive me darkness,
Receive me and my lover too, he will not let me go without him.

I roll myself upon you as upon a bed, I resign myself to the dusk.

He whom I call answers me and takes the place of my lover,
He rises with me silently from the bed
    (426–27)

In the passage's opening lines, the speaker is female, but genders quickly change place as the darkness is invoked. By asking that the darkness "double" itself, the speaker demands both obscurity as well as duplicity in the erotic scene about to take place. By doubling the darkness, she/he may be released from all boundaries and "resign" her/himself to whatever happens. Robert K. Martin notes that the " 'I' of these lines is both active and passive" (10); the speaker desires both to "receive" as well as to "roll myself upon you as upon a bed." But Martin sees the female voice as a "pretense" that Whitman elimi-nates as the passage moves toward its sexual apotheosis, whereas I see the constant shifting of positional relations between woman, lover, and darkness as the displacement of a unitary voice released by sexual excitation and reen-acted in the dream.

This reading is supported by the subsequent section, omitted in the 1881 edition of *Leaves of Grass*, in which the complex deixis in the lines above is replaced by a series of metonymic substitutions for a sex act of an indeter-minate nature. The speaker finds him/herself naked and vulnerable: "no one must see me now! . . . my clothes were stolen while I was abed, / Now I am thrust forth, where shall I run?" (626). Revealed (and aroused) the speaker is now subject to (or subject of) a sexual act that, however explicit, is also wildly indeterminate with reference to the specific event taking place:

The cloth laps a first sweet eating and drinking,
Laps life-swelling yolks—laps ear of rose-corn, milky and just ripen'd;
The white teeth stay, and the boss-tooth advances in darkness,
And liquor is spill'd on lips and bosoms by touching
    glasses, and the best liquor afterward.
    (627)

Critics have regarded these lines as representing fellatio, based on phallic im-ages of corn and the ejaculatory "spill'd" liquor. But the very ambiguity of "laps" as noun and verb, as protective covering and oral stimulation, makes placing this act extremely difficult. What seems considerably more important than defining the ways Whitman's figuration "hides" a given sexual act is the way that it "reveals" the multiplicity of erotic possibilities made possible through the shifting of roles. These lines should be read in terms of the larger poem: a dream fantasy in which subject and object shift positions, leaving the speaker caught among multiple personae: "I am the actor, the actress, the voter, the politician" (426). When in the second section, Whitman, imagining himself dead, says, "It is dark here under ground, it is not evil or pain here, it is blank here, for reasons," he is speaking as much about the ambiguities of sexual identity as he is about mortality (427). It is precisely this "blank . . . for reasons," a sexual and textual surd, that subsequent writers have tried to fill in.

Most theories of influence explain Whitman's mediated relations to identity as an oedipal struggle with strong literary precursors. Harold Bloom's influential version of this model points to a tension between expansive acceptance and evasiveness, but he can only explain such vacillation as a sign of Whitman's filial anxiety over the dominating presence of Emerson. Hence the following passage exemplifies a rhetorical clinamen or "reaction formation against his precursor":

Apart from the pulling and hauling stands what I am,
Stands amused, complacent, compassionating, ideal, unitary,
Looks down, is erect, or bends an arm . . .
Looking with side-curved head curious what will come next,
Both in and out of the game. . . .
    (32)

By reading this passage as a conflicted response to Emerson's "Experience," Bloom avoids a more profound critical clinamen that would historicize this alienation (249). From another point of view, Whitman's "what I am" stands "apart from the pulling and hauling" not simply to defend himself from Emerson's authority but because he is institutionally prohibited from entering categories of self-presence that Emerson subsumed under the Transparent Eyeball. It was for Hart Crane to recognize the social stakes of Whitman's mediated gaze and begin a process of homosexual response that has continued into the recent period.[5]

I have characterized this response by the term *redress* to speak of at least two ways in which poets have "talked back" to Whitman, each of which is based on homosexual desire.[6] The first usage refers to the mode of redress as corrective or remedy by which modernist poets acknowledged Whitman's importance while attempting to neutralize his excesses. This is the mode of Ezra Pound, T. S. Eliot, and many New Critics who saw Whitman as an embarrassing American relative complicating their project of cultural *risorgimento*. "Mentally I am a Walt Whitman who has learned to wear a collar and a dress shirt," says Pound (*Selected Prose* 145), and in his "A Pact" we hear the young expatriate strike a grudging truce with his stubborn literary parent:

I make a pact with you, Walt Whitman
I have detested you long enough.
I come to you as a grown child
Who has had a pig-headed father;
    (*Personae* 89)

What remains unacknowledged in Pound's response may be his discomfort over Whitman's importance for those British poets of the 1890s—Robert ("foetid") Buchanan, John Addington Symonds, Algernon Swinburne, William Michael, and Dante Gabriel Rossetti—from whom he hoped to dissociate himself. Since several of these poets—Symonds, most famously—identified with Whitman's particular homosexual meanings, we may infer from Pound's swaggering posture a gendered male alternative to what he perceived as an effeminate British affectation.[7]

The question of Whitman's relationship to national identity is, of course, crucial for his reception among modernist writers. For poets of Pound's generation, forging a distinctive poetics out of native materials, Whitman posed a problem. On the one hand, his hearty masculine urbanism was an important alternative to nineteenth-century genteel verse of the Longfellow/Whittier variety. His faith in American institutions and characters, his break with the iambic pentameter and fixed stanzaic forms, his various writings on language, slang, and American vernacular would seem the epitome of what William Carlos Williams called writing "in the American Grain." Yet Williams concludes his historiographic book by that title not with Whitman but Poe, a poet whose formalism and stilted meters would seem to be the opposite of Williams's variable foot. In a letter to Kay Boyle, Williams calls Whitman a "magnificent failure" who "showed all the terrifying defects of his own method. Whitman to me is one broom stroke and that is all" (*Selected Letters* 135). Yet in Williams's letters, one detects a worry that the "broom stroke" by the largeness of its gesture reveals something else: "It is useless to speak of Whitman's psychologic physiognomy, his this his that. All of it is true and of no importance. As I say, he has (for me) only one meaning and that virtually a negative one. He cleaned decks, did very little else" (287). "His this his that." What does Williams mean by these excrescences if not that Whitman's "physiognomy" contained multitudes of sexual meanings he would rather not think about? George Oppen agreed, stating in a letter to Williams in 1960: "Tho Whitman has been no use to me. Perhaps arriving after you I didn't need him. I always feel that that deluge and soup of words is a screen for the uncertainty of his own identity" (*Selected Letters* 39). The bond that Oppen establishes with Williams across generations is one based on objectivist values of condensation and focus that Whitman's "deluge and soup of words" makes problematic. But instead of seeing this excess as a companion version of democratic individualism, Oppen sees it as the symptom of an unstable identity.[8]

Whitman's excesses, so embarrassing to an earlier generation, became his virtues for poets who came of literary age in the 1950s and 1960s. His direct address, sexual themes, and open forms offered a salutary alternative to literary and social formalisms. Oppen's concern that Whitman's identity was uncertain now becomes an affirmation of new social identities that had been forming since the 1960s. Taking Whitman's personal address to heart, young poets redressed him in contemporary garb, the term now used to mean "dress again." One can see the range of such appropriations in the anthology edited by Jim Perlman, Ed Folsom, and Dan Campion, *Walt Whitman: The Measure of His Song,* in which the poet is presented in a variety of contemporary settings: Whitman playing baseball (Jonathan Williams), selling hot dogs at a beach concession stand (Larry Levis), working as Native American ecologist (Joseph Bruchac), languishing in rush hour traffic (William Heyen), and arm wrestling with Louis Simpson (Dave Smith). And in perhaps the best known version of this redressed Whitman, Allen Ginsberg discovers him "poking among the meats in the refrigerator and eyeing the grocery boys." In Ginsberg's vision, Whitman is brought directly into consumer society, a ghostly shopper searching for images of American plenitude. The contemporary supermarket, with its "peaches" and "penumbras," becomes the reified version of that "lost America of love" (123–24) Whitman envisioned through comradeship, but which is tentatively available in Ginsberg's flaneurial gaze. In all of these refashionings, Whitman is a figure of loss whose historicity, ironically enough, lies in his ability to transcend his historical moment and reinvigorate the present. By redressing him as "our contemporary," poets have measured the failings of American political and social life and have created a space for themselves as, in Lawrence Ferlinghetti's phrase, "Whitman's wild children" (204). Whitman's legacy, in this reading, is based on a hearty spirit of masculine comradeship that both excludes women and reinforces homosocial community.

Whitman "our contemporary" was to some extent a project and product of an earlier cold war narrative engaged in shoring up American consensus during the 1940s and 1950s. Although Ginsberg and Duncan rightly saw in Whitman a populist homosexual voice in the mid-nineteenth century, the way for their readings had been paved through the resuscitation of Whitman in college curricula and academic discourse since the publication of F. O. Matthiessen's *The American Renaissance* (1941). In this pioneering work, Matthiessen establishes a canon of authors (Melville, Emerson, Thoreau, Hawthorne, and Whitman) who serve as "representative men" for American values at large. But in his preface he hints at his contemporary perspective when he sees these male authors as embodying the origins of American liberal tradition, the "possibilities of democracy," and a spirit of "reform" against capitalist exploitation (ix). Recent critics such as Donald Pease, Jane Tompkins, and Jonathan Arac, in arguing for an "other American Renaissance," have seized on Matthiessen's book as a key moment in canon formation that, while vaunting one form of democracy, excluded other forms of democratic and liberatory possibilities in slave narratives, abolitionist documents, and sentimental novels. But these critics have also shown how Matthiessen's use of a few good midcentury men to represent American literary mastery was a way of encrypting his own New Deal–Left credentials, raising Emersonian self-reliance against Ahabian totalitarianism. These readings have usefully pointed to the ways that liberal consensus rearticulated one midcentury literary tradition for a later one and in the process inaugurated American Studies as a discipline within the orbit of cold war intellectual history.

These readings have tended to focus on Matthiessen's use of Whitman as a foil for his own Left political views—his endorsement of the Popular Front of 1935, his support for the Henry Wallace presidency, his work as a Christian Socialist and union organizer. The fact that these political views are chastened—if not utterly closeted—in *The American Renaissance* could be a sign of Matthiessen's anxiety over constructing a canon out of overtly ideological materials in the wake of the Hitler-Stalin nonaggression pact. But as Michael Cadden has pointed out, the closet that hid his political views in the early 1940s might also be one that contained his homosexuality, the suppression of the former coinciding with the avoidance of the latter. In Cadden's reading, Matthiessen's reticence on the subject of Whitman's sexuality in *The American Renaissance* contrasts with letters written to his lover at that time, Richard Cheney. In these letters the author of *Calamus* is described in highly erotic terms. The tension between *The American Renaissance* and Matthiessen's letters to Cheney signals the division between the critic's public and private lives and defines the nature of the cold war closet in the early 1940s. This tension, as Cadden shows, also caused Matthiessen much pain, as he says in one letter to Cheney: "have I any right to live in a community that would so utterly disapprove of me if it knew the facts? . . . I hate to have to hide when what I thrive on is absolute directness" (32). And such remarks may reflect the successful efforts of his own colleagues at Harvard to ostracize and marginalize the closeted critic, merging the period's destalinization and antifascism with homophobia.[9]

Cadden's important discussions of Matthiessen's queer relation to Whitman may somewhat overstate the closed nature of the *American Renaissance* closet. While it is true that the critic does not "out" the poet, he nevertheless provides what Whitman might call "hints" of his own relationship to sexuality throughout his discussion. Seen in the light of my use of cross-dressing, we could read the essay—the longest in the book—as dealing extensively with homosexuality as something that must be rendered through indirection. In fact, Matthiessen devotes most of his essay not to Whitman's openness but to his elusiveness—his love of "musical effects" in opera, his "promulging," his "atmospheric" language, his "paradoxes," his circuitous routes of lively fancy. In the opening section, for example, Matthiessen focuses on Whitman's, at that time, relatively unknown writings on language and slang, such as "Slang in America." Matthiessen acknowledges Whitman's description of *Leaves of Grass* as an "indirect" epic but relates that indirection specifically to the ways that slang embodies "the power to embody in a vibrant word or phrase 'the deep silent mysterious never to be examined, never to be told quality of life itself'" (520). Whatever that "quality of life" might ultimately mean is hard to say, but it is clear that its power is verified through the force by which it is suppressed. Matthiessen goes on to note that Whitman, like Henry Adams, celebrated the "dynamic force of sex" against the backdrop of middle-class gentility where the "neuter gender" prevails. Yet if we were to see Matthiessen's own position within that form of gentility, then his own reticence is implicated in what Whitman otherwise avows: "Both [Adams and Whitman] were agreed, though the phrasing here is Whitman's, that particularly among the so-called cultivated class the neuter gender prevailed, and that 'if the dresses were changed, the men might easily pass for women and the women for men'" (524). Thus Matthiessen may celebrate Whitman's hearty comradeship, embodied through slang, as the "indirect" incarnation of democracy, yet he may also hint at his own role as Whitman's other. If Matthiessen maintains the position of neutrality and passes, then Whitman may avow a "male principle" that is by no means Emersonian. Some verification of this double articulation in Matthiessen can be seen when he addresses Whitman's ability to fuse "contrasting elements" in *Leaves of Grass* by conforming words to "concrete experience" while being "bathed in imagination, his statements become broadly representative of humanity" (526). Being "bathed in imagination" is an indirect reference to Emerson's "Nature," but the lines Matthiessen chooses to illustrate this tendency hardly seem neutral on the gender of "humanity":

I am she who adorn'd herself and folded her hair expectantly,
My truant lover has come, and it is dark.
    (526)

What we see in such examples is Matthiessen using Whitman to generate a consensus view of American exceptionalism while deploying a rhetoric of indirection, substitution, and transference. Other cold war critics have seen Whitman as a poet who celebrates the "commonness" of American life, but in Matthiessen's hands, such commonness means something exceptional. Poets who rediscovered Whitman in the years following Matthiessen's tragic suicide in 1951 may not have been conscious of his contributions to a Whitman revival, but they were certainly the beneficiaries of his willingness to raise Whitman to center stage.

Whether redressing Whitman, as many modernists did, by correcting his grammar and brooding over his bumptiousness or articulating Whitman through cold war political discourses, the poet's impact was experienced as a kind of sexual panic. There may be a third way in which Whitman is recovered, this time shorn of all ontological supports and invested with those gender-bending tendencies excoriated by Patrick Buchanan. It is this considerably transformed mode of redress that we find in the work of Frank O'Hara, who often invokes Whitman as a sign of American resilience and energy but whose chatty, cosmopolitan tone seems the very opposite of Whitman's bardic celebrations. O'Hara acknowledges Whitman in numerous poems and essays, but I am interested less in the earlier poet's direct appearance than in his absence—the ways Whitman's afflatus is ventriloquized through O'Hara's flexible, often theatrical voice. When O'Hara says that "only Whitman and Crane and Williams, of the American poets, are better than the movies," he is setting a standard for poetry based upon Hollywood, not tradition and the individual talent (498). It is by this (however parodic) standard that O'Hara's poetry achieves its particular relevance for homosexual identity insofar as it constructs its most profound moments of self-revelation through public figures like Lana Turner, Billie Holiday, and Norma Shearer or by means of the signage of modern urban life.

O'Hara's desultory, "I do this I do that" mode offers a plastic vehicle for addressing positional relations. Casual and insouciant, the poems often seem to be a kind of verbal cruising in which little is at stake and human contacts are ephemeral. But, as Bruce Boone points out, O'Hara's camp tone, far from trivializing homosexual identity, represents its presence as communal possibility, even its potentiality for opposition and transgression. Furthermore, the discursiveness of this style undercuts the bardic, testamentary features of the "new American poetry" with its faith in the redemptive powers of the (masculine) voice and body, and creates the possibility of a presence formed out of feminine as well as masculine identities.

If Whitman's "voice" does not seem immediately evident in O'Hara it may be because of the persistence of a certain identitarian logic that limits influence to thematic or tonal parallels. Robert K. Martin, for example, does not include O'Hara in his important book, *The Homosexual Tradition in American Poetry*, because the poet does not "use his homosexuality as an element of self-definition in the way that Whitman or Crane does" (xix). This seems an unnecessarily narrow definition of both sex and self, one that presupposes a unitary and recuperable identity not unlike the one upon which Harold Bloom bases his theory of influence. The self O'Hara sings is a good deal more fluid:

My quietness has a man in it, he is transparent
and he carries me quietly, like a gondola, through the streets.
He has several likenesses, like stars and years, like numerals.
My quietness has a number of naked selves,
so many pistols I have borrowed to protect myselves
from creatures who too readily recognize my weapons
and have murder in their heart!
            (252–53)

Any celebration of multiplicity here is less a sign of self-revelation than it is
an indicator of vulnerability.[10] When each proposition of self comes with its
own weapon, then the single voice—what O'Hara calls the "serpent" in his
midst—remains locked in infinite reflexivity. Once the self is recognized as a
"likeness," however, it can be manipulated to accommodate any occasion.
And, while this may offer a degree of control in a homophobic environment,
it may also lead to a sense of rootlessness and despair. O'Hara's only defense
is to regard dispersion and change as a kind of grace:

to be born and live as variously as possible. The conception
of the masque barely suggests the sordid identifications.
I am a Hittite in love with a horse. I don't know what blood's
in me I feel like an African prince I am a girl walking downstairs
in a red pleated dress with heels I am a champion taking a fall
I am a jockey with a sprained ass-hole I am the light mist
                    in which a face appears
and it is another face of blonde . . .

. . . .

and I've just caught sight of the *Nina*, the *Pinta* and the *Santa Maria*
                    What land is this, so free?
        (256)

These "identifications" may be sordid to the individual seeking a unitary center or ground, but for the gay poet in 1956 they may be necessary for
survival. O'Hara opposes the totalized frame of the masque to the allegorical
representations within it, the "cancerous statue" of the self to the multiple
"ruses" it adopts. In Whitmanian terms the opposition is that between the
"word en-masse," with its spatial image of linguistic colonization, and the
particularity of individuals listed in his catalogues. O'Hara inflects Whitman's national allegory and its manifest destiny overtones with a postcolonial narrative of domination, cultural fragmentation, and crisis. "What land
is this, so free?" O'Hara asks, speaking not from the explorer's ship but from
the about-to-be colonized shore. By staging an elegy for his feelings in terms

of colonization, O'Hara signals the limits to Whitman's expansive self and the barriers to truly democratic vistas. At the same time, he extends Whitman's logic of identification in which, by refusing to be contained by any single self-definition, he becomes a series of theatrical roles.

"In Memory of My Feelings" offers an interesting corrective to Buchanan's association of national and private identity. Whereas the spokesman for the Moral Majority thinks of America as having a continuous, national self whose autonomy is threatened by multiple others, O'Hara identifies the nation as a series of "ruses," the proliferation of which refuses a continuous narrative history. O'Hara suggests that, like sexuality itself, nationhood is an unstable category. It posits a uniformity of values that cannot be extended to the multiple others who live within the borders of Times Square, not to mention the United States. Eve Sedgwick makes this point by speaking of the variety of ways in which national identity is formed, based on the "others" who are excluded: "Far beyond the pressure of crisis or exception, it may be that there exists for nations, as for genders, simply no normal way to partake of the categorical definitiveness of the national, no single kind of 'other' of what a nation is to which all can by the same structuration be definitionally opposed" ("Nationalisms" 241). Because Whitman's poetry is part of a national cultural experience as well, invoking him often legitimates this "categorical definitiveness" by excluding his more subversive meanings. By acknowledging both national and personal self as "selves" or "transparencies," O'Hara redresses a certain valedictory treatment of Whitman's democratic ethos and refigures it as gender trouble.

This synthesis of nationalism and sexuality is the subject of O'Hara's most open invocation of Whitman, "Ode: Salute to the French Negro Poets," a poem that imitates the earlier poet's rhetoric and lineation, if not his expansiveness. Like the Whitman of "Out of the Cradle, Endlessly Rocking," O'Hara finds himself on the margins of the continent, reflecting on the origins of his poetic vocation:

From near the sea, like Whitman my great predecessor, I call
to the spirits of other lands to make fecund my existence
   (305)

This rhapsodic apostrophe and its celebration of democratic participation are swiftly undercut by a more jocular tone. O'Hara is "trying to live in the terrible western world":

here where to love at all's to be a politician, as to love a poem
is pretentious, this may sound tendentious but it's lyrical

which shows what lyricism has been brought to by our fabled times
(305)

When "love" is reduced to formulaic homilies in political speeches (sustained by rhymes like "pretentious"/"tendentious") then the force of Whitman's experimental epic is neutralized. For among other things, O'Hara's "Ode" is about genre: the ability to create identities through private forms like the lyric or more public forms like the ode. To some extent Whitman represents a heroic moment in American poetry when each genre (and its corresponding rhetoric) could accommodate both kinds of love: love of country and love of person. In order to heal the distance between these two forms of love O'Hara appeals to Afro-Caribbean poets like Aimé Césaire for their alternative visions of what it means to live "in the terrible western world." The legacy of Césaire and Whitman is not a vision of consensus and synthesis but of the "love we bear each other's differences / in race which is the poetic ground on which we rear our smiles" (305).

Written in 1958 at the height of the Algerian war (and during the U.S. civil rights movement), O'Hara's ode celebrates a "poetic ground" that refuses categories of nationhood or race:

the beauty of America, neither cool jazz nor devoured Egyptian heroes, lies in
lives in the darkness I inhabit in the midst of sterile millions

the only truth is face to face, the poem whose words become your mouth
and dying in black and white we fight for what we love, not are
(305)

In these last lines, "the beauty of America" (or for that matter France) cannot be defined in terms of cultural artifacts (cool jazz), sheer size (millions), or essentialized categories (what we are). Rather, beauty lives in a struggle for "what we love" among differences. O'Hara appropriates "darkness" as a space in which the racial and sexual other lives "in the midst of sterile millions." By linking Whitman and Césaire, O'Hara suggests a bond between American romanticism and Negritude surrealism that refigures the cultural character of the Americas. Both represent literary traditions that attempt to join words and physical acts. When O'Hara says that in such immediacy "words become your mouth," he implies that words are no longer empty signifiers, incapable of expression, but are one with the persons who speak them. At another level, he asserts that words are becoming to your mouth, in the way that lipstick enhances facial features.

Such sentiments are repeated in his mock manifesto, "Personism," where O'Hara advocates placing the poem "squarely between the poet and the person, Lucky Pierre style" (499). Poet and reader are thus "face to face" with the medium of poetry between them. Gregory W. Bredbeck reminds us that "Lucky Pierre" is gay slang for the person in the middle of a homosexual threesome and is like the text itself "both receptive and piercing" (272). In this context, the text is an active participant in the interchange between poet and reader, and because O'Hara often addresses his poems to specific lovers and friends, private address and public acknowledgement of affection create an odd pact with the general reader. It is much like Whitman's ability to address his reader through the mediating frame of his material book. Staring at his reflection from the deck of the Brooklyn Ferry, Whitman sees us as well, "face to face," between the pages of a book he has yet to write. As he looks into his reflection, so we see him in the "leaves" of his book.

O'Hara similarly suggests that future generations will read this "message / of our hearts," but must do so "in adolescent closets who once shot at us in doorways" (305). The furtiveness of such reading partly refers to the risks taken by youths who read the subtexts of marginalized literatures, whether sexually explicit (as Whitman's work was thought to be) or subversive of Western imperialism (as in Césaire's). Despite this Whitmanian faith in the reader, difference "in the terrible western world" continues to be treated as division and threat, enacted through violence. Brad Gooch points out that the reference to being shot at in doorways refers to an incident when O'Hara was mugged in the doorway of his apartment building. When the poet ignored the demand for money and continued to walk up the stairs, he was shot by his assailant (251). Although the race of the mugger is not stated in the poem (nor in Gooch's account) it is clear that for O'Hara the bridge across differences is still broken and the doors to sexual and racial closets remain closed.

O'Hara's deliberate appropriation of Whitman's idiom in "Ode" is part of a larger strategy of tonal variation in which the voice becomes not the medium for expression but the site of contestation.[11] "It is the law of my own voice that I shall investigate" (182), O'Hara says in "Homosexuality," a poem that directly confronts the performative character of idiolect in gay subculture. This is not the bardic afflatus many of his generation inherited from Whitman, but a voice conscious of its own contingent character, its own status as social discourse. Where others are, as he says in the same poem, "taking off [their] masks" in gestures of authentication and revelation (Ginsberg might be the model), O'Hara studies the social sites of speaking.

The critical possibilities of exploring the "law" of voice are much at issue in "For Bill Berkson (On Again Looking into *Saturday Night*)," where tone is used to deflect an overheard homophobic remark while representing one's powerlessness in the face of it:

"who did you have lunch with?" "you" "oops! how ARE you"

> then too, the other day I was walking through a train
> with my suitcase and I overheard someone say "speaking of faggots"
> now isn't life difficult enough without that
> and why am I always carrying something
> well it was a shitty looking person anyway
> better a faggot than a farthead
>
> (441)

Tone is everything in this passage. The affected speech with which it opens ("oops! how ARE you") is itself a defense against distraction, a way of countering the implicit accusation of having forgotten a recent luncheon. The voice continues in the incident that follows in which the same tone is parodied as specifically homosexual speech. O'Hara's comedic response to the overheard remark (" 'speaking of faggots' ") deflects its violence by reducing it to adolescent badinage. But the violence that undergirds such verbal fisticuffs is made explicit:

> or as fathers have often said to friends of mine
> "better dead than a dope" "if I thought you were queer I'd kill you"
> you'd be right to, DAD, daddio, addled annie pad-lark (Brit. 19th C.)
>
> > well everything can't be perfect
> > you said it
>
> (442)

The genealogical origins of social stereotypes and name-calling are exposed as O'Hara acknowledges their paternal source. He counters the authority of this imperative by turning "DAD" into the hipster's "daddio," thus deflating the threat involved. By participating in several rhetorical frames—camp banter, adolescent one-upmanship, paternal homilies—O'Hara may investigate gay identity both from the standpoint of the object of derision as well as the subject of new verbal and oppositional strategies.

This example suggests some of the costs of Whitman's participation ethos—costs that D. H. Lawrence could only interpret as Whitman's longing for death. But O'Hara sees Whitman's desire to merge with others as a way of confronting the static character of modern urban life, of making personal an otherwise threatening landscape. The phantasmagoria of New York becomes accessible as a heteroglossia of potential conversations. So it is for Whitman:

I too knitted the old knot of contrariety,

. . . .

Saw many I loved in the street or ferry-boat or public assembly, yet never
    told them a word,
Lived the same life with the rest, the same old laughing, gnawing, sleeping,
Play'd the part that still looks back on the actor or actress.
    (163)

This is Whitman the flaneur who sees every social type but cannot act on his own furtive looks and averted glances. O'Hara replaces those silences with signifying speech acts that testify not by any truth-value in the statements themselves but by their character as social discourse.

It is this Baudelairian Whitman that provides me with my title, taken from O'Hara's "Easter," a long quasi-surrealist poem that, although Whitman never appears, foregrounds a kind of urban incarnation similar to "Crossing Brooklyn Ferry" and portions of "Song of Myself." The poem plays variations on a motif of cross-dressing in which nakedness is replaced by cosmetic renewal: "When the world strips down and rouges up / like a mattress's teeth brushed by love's bristling sun" (97). Here the modernist imperative to make strange is countered by an aesthete's imperative to make cosmetic. O'Hara is not interested in paring away the familiar to reveal the primary ideograms of cultural order but in eroticizing the surfaces of an edifice that has become transparent—or invisible. The distinction may seem slight—that between stripping down and rouging up—but it marks a transition from a modernism of miraculist unities to one of constructed differences.

If the title of this poem is operative, it refers to an apotheosis from a transcendental to a secular plane. The word made flesh is literalized in a night of cruising, analogous to Whitman's rambles around New York but now invested with new dangers and excitements:

it's the night like I love it all cruisy and nelly
fingered fan of boskage fronds the white smile of sleeps.
    (97)[12]

The surreal catalogues that make up the bulk of the poem are like the ornate rhetoric of this couplet—attempts at creating a textual surface as sensual as the night itself. But there are risks to cruising in alternate identities, the possibility of encountering a "pubic foliage of precarious hazard / sailors / Silent ripples in a bayou of raffish bumpkin winks" or of meeting the "black pirate whose cheek / batters the heavenly heart" (97, 99). Erotic potentiality mixes with corruption and decay; boundaries between seductiveness and repulsion merge as the poem cruises among unmoored signifiers:

a marvellous heart tiresomely got up in brisk bold stares
when those trappings fart at the feet of the stars
a self-coral serpent wrapped round an arm with no jujubes
without swish
without camp

. . . . . .

I supplicate
dirty blonde mermaids leaning on their elbows
rigor mortis sculpting the figure of those iron tears
　　(97)

Marjorie Perloff has linked such lines to dada and surrealist poets like Tristan Tzara and Benjamin Péret for the way that they subvert causality and analogy through catalogues of dissimilar materials (*Frank O'Hara* 65–66). What links "Easter" to Whitman, however, is the way that this linguistic subversion derives from a social and sexual logic of "bold stares" and camp duplicity. O'Hara's juxtaposition of dissimilar (or exotic) images is a kind of verbal drag in which a world "drowned in flesh" is dressed up in "trappings" that deflate the presence of an informing Logos. Even the serpent in the garden is a kind of ornament, "wrapped round an arm with no jujubes." This secularized Eden offers no rewards in the afterlife; its trappings "fart at the feet of the stars," declaring a kind of independence through sumptuary display. The pun on "stars" as both heavens and Hollywood celebrities merges the two realms of this cosmopolitan incarnation and gives to O'Hara's surrealist surface a distinctly American character. O'Hara, like Whitman in "The Sleepers," casts himself as an expectant lover for whom wandering and waiting in Gotham City promise renewal through dispersion. O'Hara extends such merging, in a "sleep trooped about by paid assassins mad for kisses," bringing Whitman's homoerotic poetics of longing into a contemporary world of cross-dressed identities.

"CRUDE IMPERIAL PRIDE"

Thus far I have treated cross-dressing in somewhat celebratory terms, a reading informed by postmodern gender theories that privilege multiple identities as a salutary challenge to gendered hierarchies. I have also treated poets for whom Whitman's example expresses avant-garde positions, both culturally and poetically. There is, however, a more skeptical version of what I have been calling cross-dressing put forth by more formalist poets who utilize the thematics of ornament and dress to comment on the limits of deception. Where Whitman's use of open meters may coincide with more open attitudes toward gender, poets such as Richard Wilbur, John Hollander, Stanley Kunitz, Louise Bogan, Alfred Corn, Anthony Hecht, and James Merrill utilize regular meters and layered diction to parody social rituals. While one might not think of these poets as Whitmanian ephebes, they nevertheless deploy a cosmopolitan register and social idiolect similar to O'Hara's, albeit by more formal means. In each of these poets, formal language mocks its own superciliousness, flaunting a kind of social propriety while exposing its darker repercussions. We could see this formalism, as Robert von Hallberg has, as manifesting a kind of cosmopolitanism against the "raw" versions of expressivism in Ginsberg or Olson, but we could also see it as a fit of form against what form can't contain.[13] If, as I've argued, Whitman addressed a wide range of poetic voices, he has been redressed in forms that he might not recognize as his own.

Anthony Hecht's "The Deodand" (1979) is a case in point.[14] It imagines the mise-en-scène behind Renoir's 1872 painting, *Parisians Dressed in Algerian Costume*. The painting depicts a scene in which bourgeois Parisian women dress up as harem slaves. The poem as voyeur looks upon this tableau vivant, just as Renoir peeked into "the swank, high-toned sixteenth *arrondissement*" to view this "strange charade":

Swathed in exotic finery, in loose silks,
Gauzy organzas with metallic threads,
Intricate Arab vests, brass ornaments
At wrist and ankle, those small sexual fetters,
Tight little silver chains, and bangled gold
Suspended like a coarse barbarian treasure.
    (6)

The catalogue is fetishistic rather than inclusive. Articles of ornament and clothing are listed not out of a love of diversity but through an erotics of limit and repression. The constraints of Hecht's language—his balanced use of ten and eleven syllable lines, his alliterations and near-rhymes—reinforce the lush decor of this scene, creating a verbal texture for orientalist fantasy that both participates in as well as mocks those surfaces. Hecht's opulent language contributes to multiple levels of fiction, just as the cross-dressing women base their costumes on other paintings:

One girl, consulting the authority
Of a painting, perhaps by Ingres or Delacroix,
Is reporting over her shoulder on the use
Of kohl to lend its dark, savage allurements.
Another, playing the slave-artisan's role,
Almost completely naked, brush in hand,

Attends to these instructions as she prepares
To complete the seductive shadowing of the eyes
Of the blond girl who appears the harem favorite,
    (6)

Hecht repaints Renoir's canvas as a series of commentaries on orientalized Paris. The patterned iambs and graceful—but irregular—rhymes and near-rhymes combine to maintain the synthetic quality of the scene. As women paint their faces, so painters depict the exotic East, but much is lost in this process of dressing-up that returns to haunt the poem's second half.

Hecht suspends judgment on the painting throughout the first half of the poem, permitting his language to luxuriate in Renoir's lush setting, but his tone changes in the second half. The scene shifts from the drawing room to the stable, from the women's "fantasies of jasmine and brass lamps" to "a rude stable smell of animal strength, / Of leather thongs, hinting of viola-tions" (7). What had been a celebration of the commodity devolves into an economy of the libido. This shift in tone is accompanied by a reflection on the historical moment of this orientalist fantasy:

What is all this but crude imperial pride,
Feminized, scented and attenuated,
The exploitation of the primitive,
Homages of romantic self-deception,
Mimes of submission glamorized as lust?

Hecht wonders if these women remember another woman who liked to dress up, Marie Antoinette, "the once queen who liked to play at milkmaid" and who suffered for her "romantic self-deception" during the Reign of Ter-ror. This association allows Hecht to engage in a rather predictable associa-tion of bourgeois trappings with feminized culture, the spoils of empire appearing in apartments of the Right Bank. These idle women, like Marie Antoinette, become the epitome of aristocratic privilege, playing bucolic games while Paris burns.

Hecht's voyeurism on Renoir's voyeurism on Parisian women's voy-eurism on orientalist scenes exacts a price. A "Deodand," Hecht explains in a note, is "a personal chattel which, having been the immediate occasion of the death of a human being, was given to God as an expiatory offering" (89). To some extent Hecht's poem is itself a deodand, an offering of formal opulence for critical uses. This feature of the poem is evident at the end when Hecht leaves Renoir's painting to remember a moment during the Algerian War when a French Legionnaire was captured, dressed as a woman, and forced to recite a popular show tune:

They shaved his head, decked him in a blonde wig,
Carmined his lips grotesquely, fitted him out
With long, theatrical false eyelashes
And a bright, loose-fitting skirt of calico,
And cut off all the fingers of both hands,
He had to eat from a fork held by his captors.
Thus costumed, he was taken from town to town,
Encampment to encampment, on a leash,
And forced to beg for his food.
    (8)

This is the dystopic side of Renoir's painting and of nineteenth-century imperialist adventures; the return of repressed history in the brutality of postcolonial nationalisms. These lines rephrase Walter Benjamin's idea that nineteenth-century Paris was a phantasmagoria of gleaming surfaces whose utopian potential led not to an improved civilization but toward barbarism.[15] The bourgeois women who dress as Algerian slaves merge with a French soldier of ninety years later, now cross-dressed in feminine garb to mock *La Belle France* of Delacroix and David. Hecht's merging of two revolutionary moments, imperial and bourgeois, is reinforced by a rather ornate translation of Marx: "Those who will not be taught by history / Have as their curse the office to repeat it" (7).

My second example, James Merrill's "After the Fire" (1972), also involves certain limits to deception and ornament. It, too, is a poem about loss and repetition. The poem concerns Merrill's return to his home in Athens, following a fire that has caused some small damage. He has come to inspect the repairs that have been made to the house, but it becomes clear that he is still in distress over the termination of a recent love affair. He encounters the family of his housecleaner, Kleo, with whom he has been close but who is now having her own internal troubles with her ninety-year-old mother. The old woman rails at the world and her family, calling her daughter a prostitute and her grandson "a *Degenerate!* a *Thieving / Faggot!*" (296). The daughter has been wounded by the old woman's daily harangues, but it appears that the grandmother's "hindsight" about her daughter's sexual escapades is partially correct. Kleo's son, Noti, has become an aging queen who has been appropriating objects and clothing from Merrill's house during his absence. The fire, the poem reveals, was inadvertently set by the son while using the house for a sexual rendezvous. The tensions in Kleo's family, thus become the objective correlative for the poet's own sense of loss, his recognition that, as the opening lines declare, "Everything changes; nothing does" (296).

As with Hecht's poem, Merrill's depends on a good deal of irrelevant chatter, held in check by irregularly rhymed pentameters that manage to carry both conversational and more formal modes of discourse. Merrill's character-istic arch tone belies the sadness he feels over the loss of his earlier affair, an event that surfaces in brief asides ("my heart leaps out of habit, / But it is only Kleo" [296]) and sudden confessions ("[my] eyes brim with past evenings in this hall, / Gravy-spattered cloth, candles minutely / Guttering in the love-blinded gaze" [297]). When, at the end, he speaks of the recent fire, he ruefully observes, "[some] of those embers can't be handled yet" (298), a line that refers as much to his own life as to the lives of his Greek neighbors.

It is in the portrayal of Kleo's gay son that our metaphor of dressing and cross-dressing comes into focus. Noti (the diminutive of Panayioti), is a figure of declining sexual allure whose address to the returning poet is both generous and unsettling. Merrill remembers when Noti used to cruise "the Naval Hospital, / Slim then, with teased hair" Now he "must be forty, / Age at which degeneration takes / Too much of one's time and strength and money" (297). As Merrill reflects on this degeneration, he becomes aware that Noti is wearing some of his own clothes from the apartment:

Huge, powerful, bland, he rolls his eyes and r's.
Glints of copper wreathe his porcelain brow
Like the old-time fuses here, that blow so readily.
I seem to know that crimson robe,
And on his big fat feet—my slippers, ruined.
Still, not to complicate affairs,
Remembering also the gift of thumb-sized garnet
Bruises he clasped around Aleko's throat,
I beam with gratitude. Meanwhile
Other translated objects one by one
Peep from hiding: teapot, towel, transistor.
Upon the sideboard an old me
Scissored from its glossy tavern scene—
I know that bare arm too, flung round my shoulder—
Buckles against a ruby glass ashtray.
       (298)

The language here is like the Greek fuses, unstable and capable of failure at any instant. As Aleko apparently discovered, Noti is capable of violence, which may explain Merrill's unwillingness to "complicate affairs" by chal-lenging Noti's thefts. Merrill's discovery of a photo of "an old me / Scissored from its glossy tavern scene" becomes a reflection on Noti himself who has "translated" numerous objects from Merrill's home and whose physical changes may reflect on the author's own sense of loss. The embers of this re-cent fire are still hot:

(It strikes me now, as happily it did not
The insurance company, that P caused the fire,
Kleo's key borrowed for a rendezvous,
A cigarette left burning. Never mind).
Life like the bandit Somethingopoulos
Gives to others what it takes from us.

    (298)

What Hecht's and Merrill's poems contribute to our theme of cross-dressing and cosmetics is a concern with the management of tone in which verbal insouciance belies serious matters. Acts of dressing-up become synec-doches for the poet's verbal craft. The ability to contain the violence of colo-nialism or sexual loss in formal measures becomes, in itself, a sign of agency and order. Merrill's rhymed couplet, "Life like the bandit Somethingopoulos / Gives to others what it takes from us" poses in an offhand manner the trou-bling fact that others gain life by feeding on us. But Merrill is also saying that whereas life is purchased from loss, poetry often compensates by building claims of truth on "translated objects." Hecht's mannered portrait of six-teenth *arrondissement* women dressing as harem slaves or Merrill's desultory conversation with his neighbors come from poets who willingly inhabit an haut bourgeois world (its operas, summer homes, art collections) yet who recognize its veneer. Hecht's invocation of the horrors of the Algerian War can only appear after he has tantalized us with a portrait of bourgeois plea-sures; the imperialism upon which that portrait is based can be rendered only within the verbal terms of that embourgeoisement.

OUTING WHITMAN

My permission to use cross-dressing as a trope for the textual performance of identities is partially granted by Whitman who, in a letter to Emerson in 1856, used the term "dressed up" to describe (and dismiss) the dandified literature of his era: "There is no great author; everyone has demeaned himself to some etiquette or some impotence. There is no manhood or life-power in poems; there are shoats and geldings more like. Or literature will be dressed up, a fine gentleman, distasteful to our instincts, foreign to our soil. Its neck bends right and left wherever it goes. Its costumes and jewelry prove how little it knows Nature. Its flesh is soft; it shows less and less of the indefinable hard something that is Nature" (736).[16] The language of castration here notwith-standing, Whitman worries over a literature that is "dressed up" and there-fore "foreign to our soil" (in this sense, agreeing with Pound's anxiety over poetry of the 1890s). Sartorial and national metaphors link misogyny and xenophobia in a letter designed to extend fellowship among like-minded males. The presence of unlike-minded males helps Whitman mark his difference from those soft-fleshed types who have not been kissed by the rough beard of masculine friendship.

At the same time, Whitman recognizes the close relationship between men who feminize their identities and writing, which creates identities by dressing up. His feeling that such writing is "foreign" perhaps betrays its own form of homosexual panic, one that O'Hara dispels by indulging its theatrical possibilities. O'Hara acknowledges his "foreignness" to Whitman's discourse of nature ("I can't even enjoy a blade of grass unless I know that a there's a subway handy, or a record store or some other sign that people do not totally *regret* life" [197]), but he discovers another nature within the city, a nature fabricated out of the passing parade. Cross-dressing becomes a figure for the multifariousness of that parade, its existence as a series of costumes, attitudes, and positions. For every hearty assurance that "what is known I strip away," there is the countervailing knowledge that what is revealed is a blank, a conceptual chasm for which language is inadequate: "I do not know it—it is without name—it is a word unsaid" (89). It seems less important to "name" it as his homosexuality, as many critics have done, than to see it as an identity in formation, an identity in drag.

The family-values ideologues of the religious Right have, of course, named this identity and have sought thereby to restrict it to public view. Under their platform Whitman continues to stand indicted since although he celebrated, in "Song of the Exposition," "the same old human race, the same within, without," he also confessed a "queer, queer race, of novel fashion" in adjacent lines (199). No wonder he was offended at Symonds's attempt to bring him "out" in one form when, under his own terms, he was already out in a number of others. For poets like Frank O'Hara who took Whitman at his word—a word "unsaid"—stripping the world of its illusions also meant dressing it up as illusion.

5

The Changing Name: Writing Gender in the Black Arts Nation Script

THE NAME THAT DARES NOT SPEAK ITS SEX

I walk up the muggy street beginning to sun
and have a hamburger and a malted and buy
an ugly NEW WORLD WRITING to see what the poets
in Ghana are doing these days
      Frank O'Hara, "The Day Lady Died"

Among the numerous events chronicled in Frank O'Hara's most famous poem is the purchase of "an ugly NEW WORLD WRITING," one of a series of literary anthologies published by New American Library between 1951 and 1964. O'Hara's casual interest in the poets of Ghana is, like his fast-food lunch, consumed on the run. The book merges with other purchases (cigarettes, newspapers, a shoeshine) that punctuate a desultory Midtown lunch hour. It highlights the speaker's distraction by offering the abstract pleasures of distant African poets against his inability to remember "who will feed me" that evening. The multiplicity of choices and distractions cause him "practically [to go] to sleep with quandriness," a condition transcended by reading of Billie Holiday's death in a newspaper headline.

Although the poem is an elegy for Holiday, her name, like those of the Ghanaian poets, is never mentioned. Instead, her nickname is hidden in the poem's title, "Lady Day" inverted into "The Day Lady Died." She joins other unnamed black subjects in the poem—shoeshine boys, Ghanaian poets, *Les Nègres* of Genet—that frame O'Hara's lunch hour reverie. The use of absent black subjects to permit the private (white) individual a moment of clarity suggests the poem's continuities with modernism. Billie Holiday's singing invokes a prior moment or "still point" in which time is stopped: "she whispered a song along the keyboard / to Mal Waldron and everyone and I stopped breathing." The announcement of her death in the quotidian lunch hour organizes and focalizes the vitality of life for an otherwise alienated speaker.[1] As an elegy for a major gay cultural icon, "The Day Lady Died" celebrates a nascent, if closeted community, whose outsiderhood is articulated by black music. The same claims for community via similar cultural means would be made by the Black Arts movement within a decade, yet the meaning of those cultural forms for black poets could not be more dissimilar.

Written in 1959, "The Day Lady Died" could avoid naming black persons because to all intents and purposes they were invisible to white America, providing Ralph Ellison with a powerful metaphor for postwar African American alienation.[2] But to many of those invisible men and women, poets in Ghana could not be so easily be dismissed. Decolonization within Africa had yielded a number of new independent states—including Ghana—and a dialogue had begun between African American intellectuals and African leaders that was central to the civil rights and Black Power movements.[3] American black intellectuals and writers such as Richard Wright, Martin Luther King, Paul Robeson, Adam Clayton Powell, and W. E. B. Du Bois traveled to Africa, establishing political and cultural exchanges that were widely reported in the African American press. Ghana, which received its independence in 1957, was especially important in internationalizing the American black population. As a socialist state, organized around a People's Party with ties to Nasser's anticolonialism and with nonalignment movements elsewhere in Africa, Ghana was a focal point for black American interest. Ghana's leader, Kwame Nkrumah, sponsored the 1958 All-African Peoples Conference, with substantial participation from U.S. blacks as well as Franz Fanon and other radical intellectuals. Du Bois's settlement there in 1961 and Nkrumah's visit to Harlem in 1961 cemented the focus on Ghana as a major player.

O'Hara's use of unnamed Ghanaian poets to reinforce a moment of private reflection marks an important divergence between black and white poets in the late 1950s. Whereas white modernists had often used unnamed others to articulate cultural or psychological vitality (or ruin), new black poets saw this as a dimension of colonialism with which they could not participate. Many black poets turned to African culture, music, and religion to erect a countercultural edifice to contest modernist primitivism. Toni Morrison has defined modernist appropriations of "American Africanism" as a "way of talking about and . . . policing matters of class, sexual license, and repression, formations and exercises of power, and meditations on ethics and accountability" (7). To some extent O'Hara's personist aesthetics could be placed within this tradition, nowhere more obviously than in his invocation of the poet's friend, LeRoi Jones, in his "Personism" manifesto: "[Personism] was founded by me after lunch with LeRoi Jones on August 27, 1959, a day in which I was in love with someone (not Roi, by the way, a blond). I went back to work and wrote a poem for this person. While I was writing it I was realizing that if I wanted to I could use the telephone instead of writing the poem, and so Personism was born" (*Collected* 499). Here, the easy sliding between O'Hara's lunchtime companion, LeRoi Jones, and his blond lover offers insight into an eroticized public world that Jones was ultimately to find intolerable. Although O'Hara makes it clear that Jones was *not* his lover, the very distinction between intellectual and erotic inspirations becomes blurred in O'Hara's parenthesis. Jones's later hostility toward "faggots" and "queers" (as well as Jews and women) must be measured against a moment in which he was close both to gay and white writers.[4]

What I want to investigate here is what Kimberly Benston calls the "topos of (un)naming" within the Black Arts movement. Benston notes that what distinguishes much black nationalist rhetoric is "an act of radical unnaming that sees all labels formulated by the master society ('they') as enslaving fictions" ("I Yam What I Am" 151). In this sense, unnaming involves wresting from the master's slave name (for example, Malcolm Little, LeRoi Jones) a new afrocentric personhood (Malcolm X, Amiri Baraka). For Black Arts poets this unnaming could also mean recuperating a real historical Ghana from a white poet's "ugly NEW WORLD WRITING." For O'Hara, not naming Billie Holiday as black aligns her with his own minority position as a gay male; for Baraka, not naming himself LeRoi Jones saves him from being identified with white society, which he genders as feminine. But the act of renaming involves, as I shall point out, foregrounding sexual otherness, the establishment of gender hierarchies, that will trouble black nationalism in significant ways.[5]

The first stage in this topos of unnaming can be seen in two examples, the first by Ethridge Knight:

> The Convict strolled into the prison administration building to get assistance and counseling for his personal problems. Inside the main

door were several other doors proclaiming: Doctor, Lawyer, Teacher, Counselor, Therapist, etc. He chose the proper door, and was confronted with two more doors: Custody and Treatment. He chose Treatment, went in, and was confronted with two more doors: First Offender and Previous Offender. Again he chose the proper door and was confronted with two *more* doors: Adult and Juvenile. He was an adult, so he walked through that door and ran smack into two *more* doors: Democrat and Republican. He was democrat, so he rushed through that door and ran smack into two *more* doors: Black and White. He was Black, so he rushed—*ran*—through that door—and fell nine stories to the street.

(114)

Knight's kafkaesque tale of "Rehabilitation & Treatment in the Prisons of America" describes his own incarceration for six years during the 1960s. As a parable of penal authority, it defines what Foucault calls the "disciplinary regimes" by which the prisoner is classified, examined, and defined. Being forced to choose within a set of binaries provides the prisoner with an illusion of agency, while marking the panoptical control of an invisible authority. The parable also defines the experience of black Americans in the 1950s who had to negotiate competing claims for participation in white society by means of choices created in advance *by* that society. Although many actual doors were opened through civil rights legislation between the Brown decision in 1954 and the Civil Rights Act of 1964, the endurance of racism, unemployment, de facto segregation, restrictive covenants, and other forces limited the ability of these doors to open on real social liberation.

An earlier version of Knight's parable is provided by a young LeRoi Jones in his first published poem:

The train pulled into Hartsville, S.C., and an
        angel jumped out. . . .
It was dark and he was scared
And the only sound was the noise
The moonlight makes when it strikes the rails.

He picked himself up, brushed off his wings, and
        looked around for the 'John.' . . .
There were three of them, 'Johns'
That is, one marked MEN, one
Marked WOMEN, and the third marked OTHERS.

He hesitated momentarily, checked his credentials
        and murmured,

'I wonder, could they have known?'

("Slice" 16)

Written at a moment (1958) when southern restrooms were still differentiated as white or "colored," this poem marks the same concern with categorization as in Knight's parable. Only, here, the distinction is not between white and colored but between gender binaries and otherness. Although we know what otherness means for the person who would become Amiri Baraka, the fact that race is not specified in the same binarist way that gender is allows us to ponder what other forms of difference Jones was facing in the 1950s when he was closest to Frank O'Hara. In his subsequent career as Amiri Baraka, he specified exactly what that category might mean to a black American, but as LeRoi Jones he is like his angel, checking his credentials to see what those "OTHERS" could know.

One link between the two parables above is the emphasis on naming and definition. In numerous poems and manifestos of the Black Arts period, the question of what to call oneself (and how not to be interpellated by white society) was paramount. A new art would be responsible for renaming "Negro" as "black," "civil rights" as "Black Power," "community" as "Nation." Slavery had imposed the master's name on persons of African ancestry; now, as Don L. Lee (renamed Haki Madhubuti) says, "It all gets down to who has the power to define. We don't. So other people put on us their definitions. Nationalism means that people stick together and move together in the best interests of themselves" (*Directionscore* 21). And Malcolm X concurs: "As long as you allow them to call you what they wish you don't know who you really are. You can't lay claim to any name, any home, any destiny, that will identify you as something you should be, as someone you should become, a brother among brothers" (qtd. in Benston, "I Yam What I Am" 152). Black nationalism provided a common name under which to organize and struggle, but it often did so by collapsing differences, limiting "someone you should become" to a "brother among brothers."[6] For those who were decidedly not "brothers"— women, gays, and lesbians—this naming process was particularly problematic because it often reinforced patriarchal and homophobic attitudes already in place. The necessity for defining a black male subjectivity necessitated erasing those elements whose alternative claims to civil equality would dilute the afrocentric stream. In this sense, black nationalism shared common cause with many of the reactionary regimes it attacked.

Black Power rhetoric was famously homophobic and misogynist, and any account of its history must include the constitutive role that sex/gender played in the nationalist script. Eldridge Cleaver's idea that homosexuality is a sickness, akin to "baby-rape or wanting to become the head of General Motors" (*Soul on Ice* 280), or Stokely Carmichael's idea that "the only place for women in SNCC is prone," or Ron Karenga's belief that "what makes a woman appealing is femininity and she can't be feminine without being submissive" (qtd. in Scott 305) are only the most familiar expressions of a nationalism built upon patriarchal foundations.[7] Women were regarded less as producers than as reproducers of black culture, their place within the movement limited to nurturing, mothering, and domestic maintenance—duties that they had been performing within the white population for years. In more cultural nationalist versions such as Nation of Islam or Maulana Ron Karenga's Kwanzaa, women's roles were formally restricted to showing allegiance to their husbands, exhibiting deference and modesty toward other males.[8]

These attitudes were reinforced by white sociological descriptions of the black family as being dominated by an emasculating matriarchy. The Moynihan Report of 1965, to take the most famous example, located the crisis of black society not in racism but in the black family itself. The report cited statistics to show that almost a quarter of all black families were headed by women and that fatherless families were on the increase. Furthermore, this trend was seen as part of a longer historical pattern by which the Negro male had been the special object of scorn and humiliation, first through slavery, then through Jim Crow laws. Black women, on the other hand, were described as "deviant," retarding the progress of African Americans by establishing a stronger economic and social position than black men. This matriarchal authority, according to Moynihan, was "out of line with the rest of American society" (Rainwater and Yancey 29). The best solution for African American males was to join the armed forces, "a world away from women, a world run by strong men of unquestioned authority, where discipline, if harsh is nonetheless orderly and predictable, and where rewards, if limited, are granted on the basis of performance" (88). As others have observed, this advice was to have its grim repercussions in the number of soldiers of color conscripted into the armed forces—and killed—during the Vietnam War.[9] Moynihan's advice also helped displace the burden of blame away from the federal government or national racism and place it onto women, thus demonizing the constituency the report was meant to help.

Despite a strong negative reaction to the report among civil rights activists, its description of matriarchy and the emasculated male reinforced a certain gendered hierarchy within black nationalism and provided a set of allegorical types that Black Arts poetry would recycle over and over again.[10] Furthermore, Moynihan had drawn on black sociologists like E. Franklin Frazier for his matriarchal thesis, giving it a level of credibility within some circles it might not otherwise have had. As bell hooks observes, "militant black men were publicly attacking the white male patriarchs for their racism but they were also establishing a bond of solidarity with them based on their shared acceptance of and commitment to patriarchy" (99). By focusing on black women as emasculating matriarchs, this rhetoric diverted attention from the capitalist origins of racism and established rifts within the black community that would fester until the present day.[11]

If women were marginalized within the nation script, same sex relationships among men or women were beyond the pale. *Faggot* was a derogatory slur against any perceived male weakness or assimilation. Amiri Baraka's view of Roy Wilkins as "an eternal faggot" (*Selected* 115) or Reginald Lockett's call to "Die Black Pervert" (Baraka and Neal 354) offer the bluntest attack on any so-called "feminine" position.[12] Homosexuality was considered a violation of heroic black masculinity, as symbolized by the Black Panthers or Black Muslims, and same-sex relationships among women were seen as destructive to the black family. Ntozake Shange's *For Colored Girls Who Have Considered Suicide / When the Rainbow Is Enuf* (1975), with its appeal to black women to "love themselves," was attacked as a call to lesbianism, and a gay male author like James Baldwin was considered by Baraka as the "Joan of Arc of the cocktail party" (*Home* 117).[13] Homophobia and misogyny functioned as the means by which black males could efface a past aligned with white culture, whether that involved sex with white women, growing up in middle-class families, bohemianism, the cultivation of "sensitivity," or assimilationist political positions.

This masculinist, antigay imperative has been criticized by black feminists from Michele Wallace and Toni Cade (Bambara), to bell hooks, Angela Davis, and Audre Lorde and has inspired a powerful debate in numerous forums. This critique, while often acrimonious, changed both black liberation *and* feminism in ways that would alter the nature of 1970s social movements. Black males were forced to recognize gender as a key issue in the politics of nationalism while women of color were forced to define their differences from white middle-class feminism. Moreover, the limits to a top-down patriarchal nationalism have inspired a series of retrospective recantations and reconsiderations by Calvin Hernton, Manning Marable, Amiri Baraka, and other male activists that has broadened the base of black activism. Furthermore, it is all too easy to criticize the limits of sexual politics—white or black—during the 1960s from the vantage of the twenty-first century; it is harder to discriminate gender identities in a revolutionary period when the demand for solidarity outweighs the need for subtle distinctions. But if we want to look for reasons why black nationalism ultimately failed to unite the black community (if indeed such a concept exists at all), we need to understand the extent to which it was weakened by its own exclusionist rhetoric.

While for Amiri Baraka the "changing same" within black culture was an essential afrocentric nature, typified by its music, the changing *name* by which this essence was naturalized within black aesthetics was heterosexual male supremacy. Whether justified in terms of nationalism, family, or "the movement," male anxiety over feminization was the name that dare not speak its sex, the unspoken ground upon which all acts of renaming would be based. In terms developed in previous chapters, poetics is often founded on gender hierarchies that limit its political impact. Black women poets of the Black Arts movement were especially conscious of these limitations, and while celebrating the importance of solidarity, they began a revisionist critique of those hierarchies that would have a decisive impact on feminism itself. In the work of Audre Lorde, Sonia Sanchez, and Ntozake Shange, the realization that empowerment was often purchased at the expense of female agency becomes an important theme in their work. Poetics is not a neutral preserve in which matters of craft are defined and legitimated beyond the social. Social attitudes are naturalized within a poetics, and as the cultural arm of black power, Black Arts had a central role in articulating the multiple meanings of new nationhood.

ENGENDERING NATIONHOOD

Black Art is the aesthetic and spiritual sister of the Black Power concept. . . .
The Black Arts and the Black Power concept both relate broadly to the Afro-
American's desire for self-determination and nationhood. Both concepts are
nationalistic. One is concerned with the relationship between art and politics;
the other with the art of politics.

    Larry Neal, "The Black Arts Movement"

Larry Neal's understanding of the siblinglike relationship between Black Power and Black Arts underscores the importance of cultural production within a nationalist configuration of race. His gendering of the black aesthetic as the feminine counterpart to black power is significant in understanding the place of art in the movement. For many black activists, the role of art was questionable as social praxis and had to validate itself within the rhetorical field of social action. In this respect, black nationalism was similar to Chicano and Asian American nationalisms in relying first on unifying myths of cultural origin as well as cultural forms (theater, music, fashion) to provide a focus for what was, still, a mixed set of social goals. Earlier versions of cultural nationalism such as the Harlem Renaissance or Garveyite Pan-Africanism united less around economic and political empowerment than on projections of shared African heritage, lifestyle, art, and culture. But the Black Arts movement, for the most part, rejected the Harlem Renaissance for its presumed links to white patronage and support and for its intellectual elitism. And unlike Garveyism, with which it shares more similarities, 1960s nationalism did not forge its movement out of a specific place—Africa—so much as on a set of shared cultural attitudes.[14] The new renaissance would occur largely through the word, but the word not only as bearer of cultural heritage but as shout, as scream. The word would be performative, doing on the page and platform what urban riots, political organizing, and confrontational politics were doing on the street. This performative aspect of nationalist rhetoric was its greatest asset, but like any speech act based on extra-linguistic criteria, validity claims had to rely on the effectiveness of acts within a social matrix. And in the early 1960s this meant grounding acts within an identity politics those same linguistic acts had a crucial role in creating.

In a suggestive reading of Black Arts aesthetics, Phillip Bryan Harper sees this address to a collective subject as based on a rather unstable foundation. Referring to Baraka's inaugural poem in *Black Art*, "SOS," Harper feels that the poet's address to "all black people, man woman child [to] . . . come / on in" under the banner of Black Art interpellates "all members of the black diaspora" while restricting membership to specific constituencies (41). However generous the speaker's invitation, the addressee—"you"—is limited by being fixed to the "identity of the speaking 'I' " (48). Such subordination of collective others to the speaker precludes the constitution of an "effective black nationalist *collectivity*" because it is founded on an oppositional logic in which one term is unformed against an already established subject (48). This intraracial division within Black Arts poetry (he refers also to Nikki Giovanni, Sonia Sanchez, June Jordan, and Don L. Lee [Haki Madhubuti]) limits the inclusiveness claimed by the poetry.

This reading qualifies in important ways Black Arts rhetoric. First, it exposes the fact that much poetry of the period was not directed at a generalized *white* so much as a black audience in need of unity. Second, it shows how the address to a black "you," a shifter that changes in relation to the one addressing that pronoun, can only be as effective as the constitution of the "I." Given Baraka's notoriously changeable identity as Beat bohemian, black nationalist, cultural nationalist, and Marxist-Leninist, this constitution becomes difficult to sustain. I would add two qualifications of Harper's reading. The first would be the obvious point that Black Arts rhetoric was never designed to be read according to such subtle procedures of analysis. Its function was gestural, sustaining by the sheer force of address a large and diverse population. The second qualification would be to observe that the shifting pronominal usage Harper notices is made unstable by the fact that the "I" is constructed around hierarchically ordered gender divisions. It is not just that the unstable subject cannot "specify the referential field," as Harper claims, but that all constructions of nationhood within this referential field are already sexed and gendered. Thus the seemingly neutral address to a general-ized black audience is qualified by its position as a man speaking *only* to other men.

One can see a version of this address in one of Madhubuti's best known poem, "Don't Cry, Scream." Like many other poets of this period, Madhubuti uses John Coltrane to epitomize the nationalist ideals. Thus the call to national unity is made through a significant cultural producer, but as I will point out, not before fixing *him* in contradistinction to *her:*

into the sixties
a trane
came/out of the
fifties with a
golden boxcar
riding the rails
of novation.
      blowing
      a-melodics
      screeching,
      screaming,
      blasting—
           driving some away,
           (those paper readers who thought
           manhood was something innate)
    (*Directionscore* 94)

Coltrane's value, especially in mid-1960s albums like *Soultrane* and *Medita-tions,* lies in blasting through the more melodic contours and tight orchestra-tions of Ellington's "A Train." Madhubuti suggests that those who could not understand Coltrane's new sound were "paper readers who thought / man-hood was something innate."[15] Presumably manhood is something that "pa-per readers" (middle-class commuters, reading the *Times* on the A train to work) can take for granted, whereas the masculinity being forged by John Coltrane is being invented in the "WEEEEEEEEEEEEEEEE" of his tenor sax. Ma-dhubuti's attempt to imitate the scream of that horn in print links him to Coltrane as an artist, thereby distinguishing himself from a world based on "paper" rather than on the performative and oral tradition signified by Coltrane's music.

The bourgeois forms that Coltrane challenges release the speaker from the 1950s and its civil rights overtones and release him, as well, from the blues, here figured through Billie Holiday:

i cried for billy holiday,
the blues, we ain't blue
the blues exhibited illusions of manhood.
destroyed by you. Ascension into:

> scream-eeeeeeee-ing   sing
> SCREAM-EEEeeeeeee-ing   loud &
> SCREAM-EEEEEEEEEEEEEEEEE-ing long with
>   feeling

we ain't blue, we are black.
we ain't blue, we are black.
> (all the blues did was
> make me cry)
soultrane gone on a trip
he left man images
he was a life-style of
man-maker & annihilator
of attache case carriers.
> (95)

Here, the imperative of the title is made clear. Coltrane's avant-garde "scream" is contrasted to Billie Holiday's "cry," authentic, muscular manhood set against "illusions of manhood" produced through the blues.[16] Madhubuti's shifting lineation and indentations produce a kind of score (he calls his selected poems *Directionscore*) for performance, one that permits multiple voices to occur on the same page. Although Coltrane is presented in the third person in the opening of the poem, the effects of his music permit Madhubuti to shift to the second-person address ("illusions of manhood / destroyed by you") and at the end, to other black males, similarly transformed:

> can you scream—brother?   very
> can you scream—brother?   soft

i hear you.
i hear you.

and the Gods will too.
> (98)

Here, the second-person address unites both Coltrane and other "brothers," allowing for the possibility of apotheosis suggested by the final line. But the musical agent that makes this identification possible is not only John

Coltrane but the effacement of a female blues singer whose singing leaves no "man images" upon which to base identity. References elsewhere in the poem to "a faggot," "blonds," "snagga-tooth niggers," "negro cow-sissies / who did Tchaikovsky" and "ofays" constitute a chorus of negative, weak male images in contrast to the heroic version in Coltrane. The nose-thumbing gestures of the poem combined with quick changes of position, enjambment, collapsing of words, use of slashes, indentations, and parenthetical interjections reinforce on the page what Coltrane's music implies in acoustic space.

In his preface to "Don't Cry, Scream," Madhubuti makes it clear that he is writing for a specific audience: "Blackpoetry iswritten for/to/about & around the lives/spiritations/humanism & total existence of blackpeople. . . . Blackpoetry in its purest form is diametrically opposed to whi-te poetry. Whereas, blackpoets deal in the concrete rather than the abstract (concrete: art for people's sake; black language or Afro-american language in contrast to standard english, &c)" (*Directionscore* 85). And in her foreword to the volume, Gwendolyn Brooks—a longtime supporter of Madhubuti—reinforces the same impulse: Don Lee "knows that the black man today must ride full face into the whirlwind—with small regard for 'correctness,' with limited concern for the possibilities of 'error'" (79). However open his language, Madhubuti nevertheless relies on a rather schematic notion of black and white poetries. Concrete versus abstract, populism versus elitism—such categories contradict the radical implications that Madhubuti applies to Coltrane's music.

Although my reading relies on a rather subtle distinction about address, the poem's apotheosis through a diminished role for women can be seen in much of Madhubuti's writing. For him, woman "is an / in and out / rightsideup / action-image / of her man" (*Directionscore* 121). Speaking of the dangers of birth control, Madhubuti points out that this is one more white-authored attempt to undermine the black patriarchal family: "the entire white system is geared toward the total destruction of the Black man first—mentally, physically and spiritually. If the Black man is not allowed to take care of and build his family, where is the Black woman?" (qtd. in Marable 92). This same patriarchalism extends to Madhubuti's comments on women writers. Despite his support for Gwendolyn Brooks, his comments on Sonia Sanchez, Mari Evans, and Carolyn Rogers are condescending and patronizing. The writing of Sanchez is "good when she works for it, but she's better when she's personal" (*Dynamite Voices* 51). The need for women writers to remain personal and not engage in social poems is a constant theme. He is offended by Nikki Giovanni when she is "militant" (her poems "read like a first outline of a college freshman's essay" [73]), and Carolyn Rogers only succeeds when she celebrates manhood:

Check this! I quote the poem in its entirety. It is a hell of a tribute to a man:

a man, standing in the shadows of a
white marble building
chipping at the stones earnestly, tirelessly,
moving with the changes of the hours,
the days,
the seasons and years,
using the shadows to shield him
such a man,
can go un noticed . . .

. . . .

There is a commitment to craft and serious subject matter. This is one of the few poems in her new book that we take seriously.
(60)

Rogers's "commitment to craft" permits Madhubuti to take the poem seriously (signaled perhaps by his switch from first-person singular to plural pronoun) and offers him a formalist defense which diminishes the afrocentric and feminist implications of Rogers's poetry altogether. To be fair, Madhubuti is elsewhere critical of black macho in poems like "The Revolutionary Screw" and is capable of celebrating black womanhood in a poem like "Blackwoman." His support for women writers suggests his sympathy for women artists. But such sympathy does not accord women equal status with men in the nation-building enterprise that his poetry advocates.

"WHAT YOU FAGS THINK": AMIRI BARAKA

The gender politics of Amiri Baraka is a far more complex issue than that of Haki Madhubuti since the former has occupied multiple relationships both to white and black culture throughout his career. Baraka's famous move to Harlem in 1965 is regarded as the inaugural moment in the Black Arts movement, a journey of return and reconciliation that would motivate the rhetoric of many other writers. This exodus uptown entailed leaving his white wife and mixed-race children, his former Beat and Black Mountain colleagues, and his Lower East Side bohemian milieu. The journey is also marked as a class shift from middle- to working-class identifications. To some extent Baraka's various changes and moves have themselves served as a kind of bildungsroman of the black intellectual, his life serving, as Aldon Nielsen points out, as a "signifying event of equal importance with his verse" (220). In his autobiography, Baraka describes his arrival in Harlem as a kind of homecoming, akin to Aimé Césaire's *Return to My Native Land* or Franz Fanon's *The Wretched of the Earth:* "When we came up out of the subway, March 1965, cold and clear, Harlem all around us staring us down, we felt like pioneers of the new order. Back in the homeland to help raise the race" (*Autobiography* 295). Although he was to return "downtown" often in his subsequent years, he had moved culturally, first through his involvement in the Black Arts Repertory Theater and later through Newark's Spirit House.[17] Baraka's use of the term *homeland* to describe his cultural nationalism is interesting because it implies participating in a feminized domestic space that he excoriates in all of his writing. Like *nation, home* is an imagined space of safety whose associations with women or feminized men must be replaced and neutralized.

Baraka's transition to nationalism produced a series of important texts, marked most significantly by his trip to Cuba in 1960 ("Cuba Libre") and the publication of *Blues People* in 1963. The poetry and plays of this period are among his most significant and include his long poem for his sister, "Hymn for Lanie Poo," published in *Preface to a 20 Volume Suicide Note* and the "Crow Jane" poems of *The Dead Lecturer.* In both of these series poems, LeRoi Jones/Amiri Baraka looks back to his middle-class origins and his involvement in Anglo/European modernism, and in both a woman provides the metaphor for corruption. "Hymn for Lanie Poo" invokes, in a sardonic way, Eliot's neoprimitivism ("Throw on another goddamned Phoenecian"), and the Crow Jane series inverts Yeats's "Crazy Jane" to include castrating white womanhood. Baraka rejects what he takes to be modernist introspection and class *ressentiment* by focusing on the female agent that has provided the occasion for such alienation. He does this by inflecting modernist allusions with afrocentric meanings, rejecting his status as modernism's other (as primitive, as subaltern) and reinvigorating himself as a subject.

Both sequences build on the critique of the black bourgeoisie, offered by Baraka's former professor at Howard University, Franklin Frazier. For Frazier, the limits to black middle-class life are created by the feminization of the family. Males in black households are unable to play the "masculine role," hence they cultivate "personality" in order to win influence among whites. "In this respect they resemble women who use their 'personalities' to compensate for their inferior status in relation to men. This fact would seem to support the observation of an American sociologist that the Negro was 'the lady among the races'" (221). In Baraka's hands, this feminization of the middle-class black family is figured through his own sister, nicknamed "Lanie Poo" and memorialized in the last section:

my sister drives a green jaguar
my sister has her hair done twice a month

my sister is a school teacher
my sister took ballet lessons

.   .   .   .

my sister's boy friend is a faggot music teacher
    who digs Tschaikovsky
my sister digs Tschaikovsky also
it is because of this similarity of interests
that they will probably get married.

                              Smiling & glad/in
                              the huge & loveless
                              white-anglo sun/of
                              benevolent step
                              mother America.

(*Transbluesency* 14)

Lanie Poo's investment in "white-anglo" culture is a function of commodity society, fashion, and European culture. Baraka's satire identifies this black bourgeois position with a gendered but nonbiological mother America, "benevolent" but "loveless." Lanie Poo's boyfriend is, in Baraka's characteristic putdown, a "faggot music teacher." Marriage is construed not in terms of biological reproduction or affection but as a convenience, greased by aesthetics.

In this early stage of Baraka's career, positive images of blackness are lacking; they must be imagined out of negative, feminized images that are part of the class anxiety pervading all of his work of this period. Lacking a strong critique, based on affirmative models, Baraka falls back on modernist satire—the use of quotations in foreign languages (the poem's epigraph is from Rimbaud, "Vous êtes de faux Negres") and Eliotic interchange ("We spent the weekend at home. / I tried to get some sculpting done, / but nothing came of it. It's impos- / sible to be an artist and a bread / winner at the same time" [*Transbluesency* 9]). In short, Baraka accomplishes his critical retort to Eurocentric modernism utilizing the same means that this modernism bequeathed to him.[18] Not the least important aspect of this is modernism's use of the sterile, middle-class female and the emasculated, feminized male.

With the "Crow Jane" sequence in *The Dead Lecturer,* woman emerges in her new role as the castrating Devil Woman that will culminate in Lula in *The Dutchman* or the Devil Lady of *Madheart.* And like Lula, Crow Jane represents the fatal, sexualized allure of white culture. To this extent, as Baraka has said, Crow Jane is a Muse, but one whose inspiration leads not to Yeats's Byzantium but to the reified products of Western capitalism.[19] Building upon Yeats's own version of *la belle dame sans merci* Baraka weaves his version out of a blues lyric by Mississippi Joe Williams: "Crow Jane, Crow Jane, don't hold your head so high, / You realize, baby, you got to lay down and die" (*Transbluesency* 86). To some extent, Baraka's series is a ritual killing of Crow Jane in her role as white seductress of black men, but also in her role as the Muse of Western culture that seduced the young LeRoi Jones. She is, as Kimberly Benston observes, a "cleverly veiled personification of Southern racism's Jim Crow and as the typical faithless woman of the blues lament" (*Baraka* 116). As a variant on Yeats's Crazy Jane, she offers a sexuality that leads not to ecstasy or reproduction, but to death. The Irish poet's version merges the contradictory biological nature of sex and death into an ecstatic apotheosis ("For nothing can be sole or whole / That has not been rent" [260]). For Baraka, this fusion of sex and death has no ritual rending; Crow Jane is a "Dead lady / of thinking." She

> (Wipes
>
> her nose
> on the draperies. Spills drinks
> fondles another man's
> life. She is looking
> for alternatives. Me, once. Now
> I am her teller.
>
> (And I tell
> her symbols, as the grey movement
> of clouds.
>
> (*Transbluesency* 89)

Baraka recognizes that he was once one of her "alternatives," a victim of her search for novel sensations and experiences. But he has become now "her teller," and in this telling he diagnoses her movements as fickle as the shapes of clouds. Her "symbols," her sexual and cultural capital, vaporize for him as he contemplates a new Black Art identity, one forged not in the modernist image but in the oral tradition. To become a "teller," within the African American context, is to assume the position of speaker, signifying on "her symbols" rather than being signified *within* them.

In the final poem of the series, Baraka "canonizes" Crow Jane by consigning her body to the realm of objects. In this sense Baraka reverses the modernist trope of incarnation, removing any redemptive possibility of the flesh and turning it back into earth. Crow Jane becomes, a "trail / of objects. Dead nouns, rotted faces" (*Transbluesency* 91). These lines paraphrase Yeats in "Crazy Jane Talks with the Bishop": "'A woman can be proud and stiff / When on love intent; / But Love has pitched his mansion in / The place of excrement' " (259–60). Baraka extends this oxymoron of sexuality and excrementality to a kind of inverted benediction:

may the Gods,

      (those others
beg our forgiveness. And Damballah, kind father,
sew up
her bleeding hole.
    (91)

The gods Baraka addresses now are not the classical gods of Yeats or Pound, but the African god, Damballah, who expresses his "kindness" by sewing up "her bleeding hole." This violent image is not, of course, fantastic; it represents traditions of genital mutilation (infibulation) by which adolescent girls are prevented from sexual pleasure or premarital intercourse.[20] Baraka's prayer that a benevolent, patriarchal God will take sexual mastery over wayward sisters by limiting their bodily functions is performed by invoking African cultural traditions. By rewriting Yeats in afrocentric terms, Baraka revises modernism to suit new cultural materials. But in drawing on an earlier romantic topos of the femme fatale, Baraka reinforces racial difference by maintaining gender hierarchies. And by inverting Jim to Jane Crow, Baraka indicates the extent to which the separation of races is based on sexual fears held not only by white but by black males as well.

In this transitional period, Baraka is still building on modernist forms of objectification in which agonistic expiation could be carried by discrete images and metaphors. In his black nationalist phase, he rejects the "telling" of symbols for forms of performance that have no objective correlative. It is important to remember that the transition to nationalism was made largely through the theater in which Baraka received his first major recognition. His work with the Black Arts Repertory Theater School took writing off the page and placed it in a public forum. Language could be materialized as shout, scream, dialogue, and as such achieve a level of presence that the textual object could not. As Nathaniel Mackey observes, Baraka's rejection of Beat and Black Mountain writers was about their "failure . . . to live up to the extra-literary (especially political) implications of their poetics" (25). Charles Olson's feeling that projective verse offers a "stance toward reality beyond the poem" implies a subject-position that remains phenomenological but that, in Baraka's hands, is always political (*Collected Prose* 246).[21] Events such as the Harlem, Newark, and Watts riots provided a level of street theater that exerted their own impact on poetry as well. Whereas he figured his early poems as "indiscreet avowals," poems in *Black Magic* (1969) had to achieve the status of gesture:

Poems are bullshit unless they are
teeth or lemons piled
on a step . . .
.   .   .   .   .
                     We want live
words of the hip world live flesh &
coursing blood . . .
We want "poems that kill."
Assassin poems, Poems that shoot
guns.
     (*Transbluesency* 142)

As if to give body to this imperative, he begins to create a poetry that aspires to the condition of action. His rhetoric is not intended to refine or represent but to create experience, viscerally, on the page, a "black scream" often
framed around sexual violence.[22] In "Babylon Revisited," for example, this
gestural quality is used to attack white womanhood for her emasculation of
black males:

This bitch killed a friend of mine named Bob Thompson
a black painter, a giant, once, she reduced
to a pitiful imitation faggot
full of American holes and a monkey on his back
slapped airplanes
from the empire state building

May this bitch and her sisters, all of them,
receive my words
in all their orifices like lye mixed with
cocola and alaga syrup

feel this shit, bitches, feel it, now laugh your
hysterictic laughs
while your flesh burns
and your eyes peel to red mud
     (*Selected* 119)

This nightmare version of the "gaunt thing / with no organs" that "creeps
along the streets / of Europe" is the white Devil Woman that Baraka would
excoriate in numerous plays and poems of this period. To some extent, he is
exorcising his relationship with white women with whom he had formerly
been associated. But the level of rhetorical anger—not only toward women
but toward the effects of feminization on black males—cannot be located in

a single person. The fact that white womanhood lacks "organs" means that she is only a machine for desire, "nothing to make babies." It is not clear how this unnamed woman caused Thompson's drug addiction, but such considerations are mooted by a rhetoric designed to obliterate teleology, a "jihad against the devils," as Theodore Hudson calls it (136). Baraka implies that like King Kong, Thompson becomes a mindless product of American mass culture for whom desire is embodied in a white woman. Baraka's demand that "this bitch and all her sisters" receive his words as a form of torture is instantiated by the violence of his language.

Baraka's attack on white womanhood is also an attack on racist sexual ideology in which the white woman is the fetishized object of white sexual fears about black males. But Baraka's attitude toward the liberation of black women depends on her submission before male authority. In Baraka's revolutionary play *Madheart,* Black Woman is reborn from her dependence on white culture, represented by a white-inflected "Mother" and an equally bourgeois "Sister." Against these debased versions of African American womanhood, Black Man demands that Black Woman "Submit, for love":

I . . . I submit. (She goes down, weeping.) I submit . . . for love . . . please love. (The MAN sinks to his knees and embraces her, draws her with him up again. They both begin to cry and then laugh, laugh, wildly at everything and themselves.)

Black Man
You are my woman, now, forever, Black woman.

Black Woman
I am your woman, and you are the strongest of God. Fill me with your seed.
    (82)

Although Baraka is capable of providing successful comedy in his satire of the helpless Mother figure ("Tony Bennett, help us please. Beethoven, Peter Gunn . . . deliver us in our sterling silver headdress"), the real comedy, by current standards, consists in the image of Black Woman being reborn by submission to the male's inseminating design. The possessive pronoun instantiates through verbal contract what is implicit in the play as a whole: that the wresting of black male power from submission to white authority demands a reciprocal submission of black female power to patriarchy.[23]

The violence that underlies this scene is one in which physical abuse is normalized as a sign of affection and respect. *Madheart* may be, as Kimberly Benston characterizes it, a ritual allegory of male emancipation, but it depends on a legitimation of violence that has an all too real correlative in the social world (*Baraka* 221–22). In "20th Century Fox" the speaker remembers a "Dynamite black girl" enslaved to "shaky mansions of whiteladies," anonymous sex in hallways, "talked to by chalksissyghosts." But with the speaker, she

talks and talks
to me
kisses me
kisses me
makes love,

> we said awhile back
> Dynamite black girl
> swingin in the halls
> the world cant beat you
> and my slaps are love
> (*Selected* 87)

Baraka's invocation of black women imprisoned in white society is neutralized by his infantalizing rhetoric ("Dynamite black girl") and his attitude that *his* "slaps are love." To some extent this is a piece with other nationalist poems that celebrate "Beautiful Black Women," as he calls one poem, whose imperative is to ask for help from collective black womanhood from the standpoint of male guilt. "Help us get back what was always ours. Help us, women," he asks, but this return is less to positions of liberated womanhood than to a normative, heterosexual family (*Selected* 118).

What I have called the imagined home of Baraka's nationalism is predicated on patriarchy and is given its fullest expression in the essays published in *Home* of 1965. The book contains many of his most important essays, beginning with "Cuba Libre" and including "The Myth of a 'Negro Literature,' " and " 'Black' Is a Country." As I have said, his use of the domestic metaphor for this consciousness is significant since the book nowhere invokes an actual domestic space, preferring instead a cultural site that will replace the bourgeois household. This in itself could be a convincing argument for an alternative set of gender practices in which domesticity is not necessarily defined as feminine. But since there is no "place" for woman in any sphere outside of the domestic, Baraka fails to live up to his theories of "Revolutionary Love." In his preface to the volume Baraka sees himself as a "Prodigal Son," returning to blackness from exile in "whitie's books" and culture (10). In what becomes a leitmotif in all of his works, *home* also refers to an alternative cultural site to his own parents and sister, whose middle-classness stand as feminized weakness against his new afro-maleness.

In "American Sexual Reference: Black Male" Baraka combines themes of sexual emasculation with cold war themes of annihilation and homophobia: "Most American white men are trained to be fags. For this reason it is no wonder their faces are weak and blank, left without the hurt that reality makes—anytime. That red flush, those silk blue faggot eyes. So white women become men-things, a weird combination, sucking the male juices to build a navel orange, which is themselves" (*Home* 216). Using Marxian rhetoric of alienation and reification, Baraka sees white males as devoted to the "nonrealistic" and the "nonphysical," such that they can invent a form of warfare in which "whole populations can be destroyed by *pushing a button*" (217). White society can approach this level of abstraction because labor is performed by others, although some white ethnics (Irish, Jews, Italians) retain a level of "toughness" because they remain tied to labor. The intellectual fetish of existentialism, based as it is on alienation, becomes the white male's religion; thus white intellectuals can reject Euro-American culture by developing an antimaterialist stance while living comfortably within it, a reflection on Baraka's own bohemian past.

Baraka's analysis of bohemian or white intellectuals culminates in a homophobic image of the artist: "The artist is the concentrate, as I said, of the society's tendencies—the extremist. And the most extreme form of alienation acknowledged within white society is homosexuality. The long abiding characterization of the Western artist as usually 'queer' does not seem out of place" (*Home* 219). Here Baraka excoriates the artist's assimilation within the society he criticizes; to be an outsider is to become queer. While for John Wieners, as I said in chapter 2, black culture is allied with queer community in cementing alternative antihomophobic *and* antiracist formations, for Baraka, such correspondences are unthinkable. By a process of substitution the artist who removes himself from society benefits most from its disregard. The alienated (white) artist also benefits from social others (black) who do the world's work so that he may remain aloof. "But luxury reinforces weakness; a people who lose their self-sufficiency because they depend on their 'subjects' to do the world's work become effeminate and perverted" (*Home* 220).

The black intellectual or artist who retains an individualist rather than a collectivist focus is similarly marked as gay. In another essay from *Home* Baraka criticizes authors James Baldwin and South African writer Peter Abrahams for their individualism, but it is clear that his objection is as much to their homosexuality: "Again the *cry*, the spavined whine and plea of these Baldwins and Abrahams is sickening past belief. Why should anyone think of these men as individuals. Merely because they are able to shriek the shriek of a fashionable international body of white middle class society" (*Home* 117). And in an image drawn from Dante, Baraka claims that "we need not call to each other through the flames if we have nothing to say, or are merely diminishing the history of the world with descriptions that will show we are intelligent" (117). The author of *A System of Dante's Hell* utilizes *The Inferno*'s image of Guido de Montefeltro calling to Virgil through the flames of eternal perdition, an image Eliot used to inaugurate *The Waste Land*. Here, however, Hell is a closet, not a vessel of cultural malaise: "They [Baldwin and Abrahams] are too hip to be real black men, for instance this is only, let us say, a covering to register their feelings, a gay exotic plumage as they dissemble in the world of ideas, and always come home with the shaky ones" (118).

The sexual politics revealed in poems and essays from this period cannot be separated out from his nationalist politics. In recent essays and interviews he has been self-critical of these attitudes, but because self-criticism for him always implicates others, he is incapable of truly "coming around."[24] Rather, Baraka rearranges his various enemies in relationship to a "changing same" that is himself. The power of his poetry and plays lies in their uncompromising honesty that, if misplaced, is nevertheless necessary in an age of liberal tolerance. Yet the "black scream" of rage expresses anger not only at the condition of blacks in America but at social others who might be enlisted in that same anger.

"BEIN BETRAYED BY MEN WHO KNOW US"

Baraka's turn to black nationalism is figured as a return to a mythical homeland from which he has been dispossessed by white culture. His various transformations, political positions, and geographic movements cry out for an autobiography called "How I Became Amiri Baraka," except that his former wife has already appropriated that title for herself: *How I Became Hettie Jones*. Commenting on the latter in a new preface for his own autobiography (1997), Baraka describes the limits of his nationalist phase, citing its masculinism as a key defect. In order to establish solidarity with the women he disrespected over the years, he vaunts his new wife, Amina, against his previous (white) wife, Hettie, whose "strategy for harassment and undermining was that she would ingratiate herself with [his] parents . . . and thus create a hookup to undermine and disrupt [his] public life . . . " (xxi). Hettie Jones's memoir is hardly likely to "undermine" Baraka's public life, but it does present readers with a private identity for him that stands in stark contrast to the public one he has forged since the mid-1960s. Although the new preface is an important, if somewhat bizarre, self-critical statement on Baraka's part, its use of Hettie Jones to shore up a new socialist tolerance sustains trends I have already described.

When Audre Lorde writes *her* autobiography, it too concerns the act of unnaming, but unlike Baraka's it is formed around inclusions and multiplicities. She titles it *Zami: A New Spelling of My Name* and dedicates it to "the women who helped give me substance" and goes on to celebrate various real and mythological female figures (255). She defines herself as a "Sistah outsider" whose identity as a black lesbian places her not in a single cultural "home" but rather in "the . . . house of difference" (226). Addressing the 1976 MLA Convention Lorde declared she was "woman, poet, black, lesbian, mother, fat, sassy" (Hull 180). Such acknowledgment of plural positions suggests that renaming blackness need not be based on a single name, even when it is respelled as African. Lorde identifies not only as a black person but as a black lesbian mother and cancer survivor and thus makes the changing of her name an entry into several social spheres. Lorde's emphasis on the "spelling" of her name speaks of the need for black women to represent themselves, lest they be renamed by others.[25]

As I have indicated, much Black Arts poetry is underwritten by an atavistic view of women as fecund wombs in which the revolution will be born. Women must be protected while men must be reinstated in their roles as heroes, warriors, and leaders. Rolland Snellings (Askia Muhammad Touré), for example, asks

Where are the warriors, the young men?
Who guards the women's quarters—the burnt-haired women's quarters
And hears their broken sobbing in the night?
To endure, to remain—like the red earth—strong and fecund.
    (Baraka and Neal 327)

In this allegory, males have been "severed by the Nordic Meataxe" and forced into servitude, leaving women alone, and leaving the race vulnerable to miscegenation: "*only you remain!* / You whose Womb has warmed the European hills and made the Pale Snows tawny" (327). As if in answer to this allegory of black male emasculation, Audre Lorde, in "The Woman Thing," responds

The hunters are back
from beating the winter's face
in search of a challenge or task
in search of food
making fresh tracks
for their children's hunger
they do not watch the sun
they cannot wear its heat
for a sign of triumph
or freedom.

The hunters are treading heavily
homeward through snow.
marked by their own bloody footprints.

Emptyhanded the hunters return
snow-maddened
sustained by their rages

In the night after food they will seek
young girls for their amusement.
Now the hunters are coming
and the unbaked girls
flee from their angers.

    (*Undersong* 30)

Although Lorde's poem precedes Snelling's historically, it responds to numerous Black Arts poems that frame women's power in reproductive terms.
In Snelling's poem, the community is riven by slavery, the warriors emasculated by the "Nordic Meataxe." Lorde recognizes that males' inability to express masculinity outside of a heroic narrative can lead to violence against
the very women they celebrate. The poem's title, "The Woman Thing," represents the objectification of woman—whether as fecund womb or as sexual
surrogate—within a market economy. By not specifying race in her poem,
Lorde implies that violence against women is not limited to the black community. But the fact that her poem rearticulates a common trope within the
Black Arts movement suggests that she is, indeed, questioning the sexualiza-
tion of power at an early stage of black nationalism.

    In 1964 Lorde anticipates the limits to Black Power rhetoric:

Listen brother   love you
love you   love you   love you
dig me
a different colored grave
we are both lying
side by side   in the same place
where you put me   down
deeper still   we are
aloneness
unresolved by weeping
sacked cities   not rebuilt
by slogans   by rhetorical pricks
picking the lock
that has always been   open.

Black is
not beautiful   baby

beautiful baby   beautiful
let's do it again
    (*Undersong* 140)

Here, "Black is beautiful" is seen as a ruse for reinforcing subservience, a rhetorical trick to keep women in the same "colored grave." The repetition and alliteration of the phrase, "Black is beautiful" diminishes its power, turning it into a cliché for anonymous sex ("let's do it again"). Thus in Lorde's hands, the Black Power slogan simply means being "screwed twice / at the same time / from on top as well as / from my side," by white racism and black sexism. Lorde uses the rhetorical structure of her own poem to describe the ways that political action is often based on (and undermined by) "slogans" and "rhetorical pricks."

Lorde's emphasis on the limitations of black rhetoric is furthered by Sonia Sanchez who often draws upon vernacular speech to counter more official rhetorics. Many of Sanchez's poems build upon familiar discourse arenas in which talk challenges the imposition of formulaic speech—including the signage of black nationalism:

who's gonna make all
that beautiful blk / rhetoric
mean something.
             like
i mean
        who's gonna take
the words
        blk / is / beautiful
and make more of it
than blk / capitalism.
               u dig?
    (15)

Like Lorde, Sanchez uses the poem to satirize nationalist rhetoric, providing her own idiosyncratic lineation, spelling and indentation as a counter. Her own vivid performance style heightens the sense that talk necessitates an audience, one that is by no means passive in its response.

Joyce Ann Joyce calls Sanchez's inversionary use of public rhetoric "sounding," the "ability to pick up the insults and abuses of racism and turn them around in a creative and provocative way" (7). The poem above is not specifically about racism, but it does "sound" on one form of speech and transform it. Moreover this inversion exposes a relationship between two kinds of power—economic and sexual—that are keys to racial formation. The fact that one strand of black nationalism did regard Black Power as black capitalism reinforces her point. Sanchez says as much in "Indianapolis/Summer/1969/ Poem" which begins in the middle of a rap about prostitution:

like.
        i mean.
                don't it all come down
to e/co/no/mics.
                like. it is fo
money that those young brothas on
illinois &
        ohio sts
                allow they selves to
be picked up
        cruised around
                till they
asses open in tune
                to holy rec/tum/
                                dom.
        (21)

Sanchez goes on to describe the same economic imperative for female prostitutes in which black bodies are used to support a white racist economy. But she does not stop there. Rather, she directs her attack at the African American community, asking

        like if brothas
programmed sistuhs fo love
instead of
        fucken/hood
                and i mean
if mothas programmed
                sistuhs to
good feelings bout they blk/men
and i
        mean if blk/fathas proved
they man/hood by
                fighten the enemy
instead of fucken every available sustuh
        (22)

If these conditions could be met, Sanchez insists

then may
    be it wud al
come down to some
       thing else
like RE   VO   LU   TION.
      i mean if.
          like. yeh.
(22)

Sanchez transforms the adage about economics ("it all comes down to e/co/ no/mics") into an imperative about revolution, the two terms joined by breaking each four syllable word into its elements. But in order for the name to change, the black body has to be transformed from object into subject and the economic basis for human relationships transformed into respect. Like other Black Arts poems, Sanchez's excoriates white sexual usurpation of blacks ("those blond / wigged / tight / pants / wearen / sistuhs / open they legs / mouths / asses / for wite / dicks. . . ." [22]), but she also indicts black males for equating manhood with sexual supremacy.

The opening and closing lines of the poem above signal the discursive field in which sounding occurs. Revolution is her main theme, but it is meaningless unless it is experienced as a common struggle, available in daily discourse. Her use of vernacular speech ("i mean if. / like. yeh") and her emphasis on audience response offers an opportunity for assent and verification, a quality that one finds in the work of many Black Arts poets, male and female. This interest in speech genres for Sanchez is specifically related to previous women writers such as Zora Neale Hurston or Margaret Walker, but in an interview with Zala Chandler she acknowledges the powerful influence of women in her church and family. Whereas for Baraka, family represents a problematic site for black empowerment, for Sanchez it provides an inaugural experience of female agency and voice: "Of that period in my life, I also remember that Mama used to have the 'Sisters' (church women) over to her house each Saturday to talk, to cook for the Sunday dinners, to hear each other, etc. And these sessions were really important to me. I knew that those women were transmitting knowledge to me . . . wisdom to me that I could keep all my life. . . . I heard an awareness there. I heard a people very much assured" (354). This same assurance can be heard in Sanchez's numerous performances, recordings, and videos in which collaboration with other performers is central. Her spirited reading style, her use of the audience in call and response, suggests communal aspects of the poetry that the page can only partially represent.

A womanist background is the subject of Ntozake Shange's *For Colored Girls . . .* (1975), which provides a third index for seeing gender trouble along the color line. It also shows the degree to which poetry was at the center of this debate. Shange's "choreopoem" utilizes multiple voices of black women from various classes to describe their complex relationships to black men. But the poem is much more than a diatribe. It is also a plea for self-respect and toler-ance. As with Lorde's poetry, it explores the sources of self-representation within a gynocentric culture. Much of the poem is devoted to communal forms of female vocalizing, from skiprope rhymes ("little sally walker, sittin in a saucer") to Motown ("Dancing in the Streets" by Martha and the Vandellas). Such references provide a musical narrative of a young girl's development from childhood ("Mama's little baby loves shortnin' shortnin'") to adult sexuality ("we danced doin nasty ol tricks"). And, most prominently, the choreopoem dis-plays *different* female voices testifying to their own experiences. Each of the speakers is defined by a different color in the "rainbow" of the book's title, and their social interactions are not limited to the black community but extend into the Latino and Asian American communities as well. What began as separate poems in their initial cabaret recitation became, in the theatrical version staged by Oz Scott in 1976, dialogues, dozens, and dances among all seven female members of the cast. This theatrical polyvocality replicates the play's origins in women's bars, art spaces, and publishing venues of the early 1970s. At the same time, it offers a riposte to the masculinist male drama of Baraka or Ed Bullins.

The play's title utilizes the Jim Crow-era definition of African Ameri-cans as "colored," recycled by Shange as a form of endearment and common-ality among young women. Shange uses this term of condescension to mark a specific period of black history that would be easily identifiable to an earlier generation. She also revises the term to include other women of color who have experienced racism and abuse. And since the term is linked to the rain-bow, "colored" implies the multiple skin tones otherwise subsumed under the term *black*. At a moment when black was beautiful, Shange's celebration of a rainbow coalition of women was a distinct alternative and, for many, a threat.

The play's most controversial element is its frank discussion of rape. Shange is most critical of what would now, politely, be called date rape but which is given its larger cultural description by the "lady in red" who de-scribes males

who make elaborate mediterranean dinners
& let the art ensemble carry all ethical burdens
while they invite a coupla friends over to have you
are sufferin from latent rapist bravado
& we are left wit the scars
    (19)

What the "lady in blue" calls "bein betrayed by men who know us" is the greatest crime a culture seeking solidarity can perform. If Shange is somewhat obtuse about the historical nature of those times, she is caustic about male self-exculpatory rhetoric:

lady in blue
    that niggah will be back tomorrow, sayin 'i'm sorry'
lady in yellow
    get this, last week my ol man came in sayin, 'i don't know how she
    got yr number baby, i'm sorry'
lady in brown
    no this one is it, 'o baby, yaknow i waz high, i'm sorry'
lady in purple
    'i'm only human, and inadequacy is what makes us human, & if we
    was perfect we wdnt have nothin to strive for, so you might as well go
    on and forgive me pretty baby, cause i'm sorry'
lady in green
    'shut up bitch, i told you i waz sorry'
    (52)

Such irreverent humor is mixed with more tragic content as Shange uses her characters to tell stories about women who, as the title claims, "have considered suicide when the rainbow is enuf." LeRoi Jones's first book was *Preface to a 20 Volume Suicide Note,* but Shange's use of the word *suicide* rejects the self-mutilating stance of the alienated black bohemian in favor of sororal solidarity.[26]

These latter qualities inspired a vehement negative reaction among black men. In a 1979 forum "Black Male/Female Relationships" in *Black Scholar* many of the male respondents use Shange's choreopoem (and Michele Wallace's *Myth of Black Macho*) to decry what Robert Staples calls "the divisive effects of feminism in an oppressed community" (Staples 65). Terry Jones feels that Wallace's and Shange's works "offer one of the most serious threats to black people since the slave trade," a statement whose extreme hyperbole marks the seriousness with which gender divisions were being debated around these works (*Black Scholar* 48). Most troubling among the respondents is Shange's exhortation to black women at the play's end to "love themselves":

i found god in myself
& i loved her / i loved her fiercely
    (63)

Staples feels that this represents an appeal to "the culture of Narcissism" and the triumph of white existentialism over critical nationalism. He also feels that Shange is urging black women to "go it alone" in a separatist rejection of black men. What Staples, Harry Edwards, Ron Karenga, Alvin Poussant, and others see as Shange's "narcissistic" appeal to separatism is read differently by women responding in the same forum. Audre Lorde sees the conclusion of Shange's play as an "exhortation to black women . . . to extend that compassion and love at last to ourselves" (*Black Scholar* 18). And Juliane Malveau sees the poems as an attempt to throw off the characterizations of black women as "'bitch,' as 'matriarch,' as 'domineering/dominant,'" which come from "whites and black men as well" (*Black Scholar* 33).

This womanist stance, which male respondents see as separatism and women regard as feminism, is developed in Shange's preface to the play. She locates its inspiration not in Black Arts venues in Harlem or Watts but in women's coffee houses, publishing venues, and art spaces in which new, multiethnic constituencies were gathering in the late 1960s. The multiple voices that speak the lines of the choreopoem reflect the collaborative nature of that production. The play was first presented at the Bacchanal, near Berkeley, as a collaborative venture with Raymond Sawyer's Afro-American Dance Company and Halifu's The Spirit of Dance. Other poets were involved in the project as well, including Jessica Hagedorn and Joanna Griffin, the co-founder of the Bacchanal and the publisher of Effie's Press. Shange credits the "women poets, women's readings & a multilingual woman presence" in the poetry movement of the late 1960s as providing inspiration for *Colored Girls*' gestation. The influence of Women's Studies programs at Sonoma and San Francisco State Colleges, Halifu Osumare's The Spirit of Dance troupe, and the newly formed ethnic studies programs of Bay Area public schools also had their impact. Finally, the idea of constructing a poem around portraits of women was inspired by Judy Grahn's *The Common Woman* series in which "the realities of seven different kinds of women" was displayed.

I stress these geographic and historical contexts to counter what critics of the play felt were its monologic limits. Harry Edwards links the play to Michele Wallace's *Black Macho*, describing both works as "monologues, utterly one-sided in perspective, and devoid of creditable, systematically developed political and historical context" (*Black Scholar* 59). Robert Staples complains that the play lacks "a reasonable and articulate male point of view" (Staples 26). Yet the play is not a monologue; its most salient feature is its multivoiced quality. And if one were to add the various contexts described above—the nexus of multicultural women's arts and culture, lesbian identities, nontraditional art sources—many more voices are added. To be sure, the play represents Shange's "point of view," but rather than writing a monologic poem on the subject of women's oppression she writes a polyvocal play. And whereas Baraka's revolutionary plays allegorize black women into a set of stereotypes, Shange displays multiple class and ethnic subject-positions. Staples's argument that the play lacks a "reasonable and articulate male point of view" implies the very paternalism that the play decries. How, one wonders, would Staples have responded to the same plea from white readers of angry black nationalist literature for a reasonable and articulate *white* point of view?

The larger point to be made about these responses is that a poem by a woman provided a springboard for debates concerning the fate of the nationalist project. Furthermore, the diminishment of that poem/play uses the oldest of canards: that a poem is monologic and therefore cannot provide adequate ("reasonable and articulate") debate. To use the terms with which I began this chapter, the doors to black identity in the late 1960s had been binarized, leaving few choices for blacks who occupied several subject-positions. Shange's female speakers attempt to "name" themselves as plural, as others who are both black and female, lightskinned and darkskinned, straight and lesbian, mixed-race and black, mothers and daughters, working class and middle class, challenged the writing of the nation script and suggested that within it several languages were being spoken.

CONCLUSION: THE "BALANCE OF MISERY"

The copy of *New World Writing* that Frank O'Hara would have bought must have been number 15 (1959), which featured a special forum on Ghanaian poets. Among the poems featured is "African Heaven" by Francis Ernest Kobina Parkes, sounding a note that would not have seemed out of place within the Black Arts movement:

Give me black souls,
Let them be black
Or chocolate brown
Or make them the
Color of dust—
Dustlike,
Browner than sand.
But if you can
Please keep them black,
Black.

    (230)

The poem is an appeal to larger community, an invitation like Baraka's "SOS" to "come on in" and celebrate black solidarity. Although Ghana is never mentioned, the poem is clearly a celebration of the recently liberated nation, one which, as I have said, inspired a new Pan-Africanist spirit in both civil rights and black nationalist projects. What differentiates the Ghanaian poem from the Black Arts celebration of the same theme would be the poem's conclusion:

And dear Lord,
If the place be
Not too full,
Please Admit spectators.
They may be
White or
Black . . .

Twerampon, please, please
Admit
Spectators!
That they may
Bask
In the balmy rays
Of the
Evening Sun,
In our lovely
African heaven!
    (232)

Kwame Nkrumah, Ghana's leader, did precisely what Parkes demands, inviting "spectators" from throughout the African diaspora as well as Europe, Asia, and the United States to witness its independence. Poets in the United States, for reasons having to do with the country's own violent heritage of slavery, lynching, and enduring prejudice, could not tolerate the same form of spectatorship.

It is worth opening the *New American Writing* forum on Ghana if only to name one poet that Frank O'Hara did not. But it is also worth thinking of how another nationalist movement configured its public address around terms of inclusion and spectatorship. Although Parkes invokes blackness as core principle, he recognizes gradients and nuances among constituents. If his subject is nationalist, his tone has little of the black nationalist anger, resembling more the tone of Harlem Renaissance poems. The absence in Parkes of what I earlier described as performative rhetoric marks the poem's difference from African *American* poetry in the post–civil rights era. Its appeal to a bucolic, rural Africa of the past with its "native songs / The clang of woods on tin / The tune of beads / And the pealing drums" reminds one more of Langston Hughes or Countee Cullen than Haki Madhubuti or Amiri Baraka. Baraka's address is much louder and more hectoring, relying on sheer invective for its power. Because inclusiveness, for Baraka, implies backsliding, he must forge a poetics out of exclusions and excommunications. For women poets of the same era, nationalism posed a more troubling possibility that in naming blackness they would unname themselves as women. When their voices aspired to militant postures, they were urged, as Madhubuti demonstrates, to find more intimate and personal forms.

While I have been critical of the masculinist posture of the Black Arts movement, I recognize the significance of the movement as a whole in getting beyond a traumatic period in American history. Moreover, it spawned a renaissance of black art and social activism that continues to exert an influence. From the Watts Workshop in Los Angeles and the Black Arts Repertory Theater School in Harlem, to magazines, anthologies, reading series, art spaces, poetry-music collaboration, and Black Studies programs, the black aesthetic continues to influence the shape of African American culture. The best background for understanding the extreme rhetoric of Black Arts poetry is not only black literary history but the stark photographs of lynchings during the 1920s and 1930s, the defaced body of Emmett Till in his coffin, the headlines covering the murders of Medgar Evers, Malcolm X, and Martin Luther King. These are the embodied sources for a rhetoric about black masculinity that must be included in any literary history. The black scream begins here, and if it strives for a nonlinguistic state of presence it does so for political and not aesthetic reasons. Baraka noted that the "balance of misery" was his heritage, and like many black poets of his generation, he recognized that the time for reflection had not come. He would have to wait for a time

When flames and non-specific passion wear themselves
away. And my eyes and hands and mind can turn
and soften, and my songs will be softer
and lightly weight the air.
     (*Transbluesency* 54)

6

Definitive Haircuts: Female Masculinity in
Elizabeth Bishop and Sylvia Plath

GENDERED PEDAGOGIES

We are, I am, you are
by cowardice or courage
the one who find our way
back to this scene
carrying a knife, a camera
a book of myths
in which
our names do not appear.

> Adrienne Rich, "Diving into the Wreck"

Some years ago, while lecturing on Adrienne Rich to a high school honors class, I proposed what seemed at the time an unproblematic thesis about these lines from "Diving into the Wreck" (1972). I argued that Rich's use of pronouns grammatically complicates what had been a thematic ambivalence over gender roles throughout the poem. Rich rehearses the multiple positions from which she speaks as a woman (singular, collective, dialogic) yet refuses to ground her subjectivity in a unitary womanhood. As such, she must speak from a fractured grammatical space as "the one who find our way." I noted that this ungrammatical position, linking singular and plural identities, represents the crisis of women of Rich's generation who attempted to examine the "wreck" of identity when that submerged vessel is owned and operated by patriarchy. The "book of myths" may include women (Helen, Penelope, Eve), but their stories are not their own. Rather, they have served to reinforce and legitimate masculine power, an authority purchased by the ability to name and signify. The poem revises that book of myths in order to discover the "name" beneath the naming process.

In the discussion that followed my lecture, one student qualified my ornate reading, adducing as contrary evidence a footnote on the poem provided by the editor to her high school anthology. That editor, X. J. Kennedy, explained that the "wreck" of the poem's title referred to Rich's marriage, brought to its tragic end by the death of her husband, Alfred Conrad, in 1970. Therefore, the grammatical problems of the last stanza reflect the condition of a woman unmoored from her heterosexual union, forced to explore herself without the aid of her husband. The editor, ignoring (or suppressing) reference to Rich's feminism, her significant critique of "compulsory heterosexuality," and her subsequent formulation of "lesbian continuum," corrects the ungrammatical sentence, providing a common antecedent for all pronouns in a heterosexual family romance.[1]

This incident serves as a useful reminder of the ways that pedagogy reinforces heteronormativity in order to explain heterotextuality. But the incommensurable grammar of "Diving into the Wreck" is no more easily solved by replacing undecidable antecedents with terms like *androgyny* or *lesbian*. Critics, armed with Rich's essays, have attempted to do just this, and in the process have reinforced the very dichotomized gender model that "Diving into the Wreck" questions.[2] While it would be convenient to use Rich's formulation of a lesbian continuum to explain that the "wreck" of the poem's title is specifically female—a submerged women's community waiting to be discovered—this dissolves all confusions in the poem to a single, monolithic term.[3] Just as the term *feminism* does not describe all areas of women's self-awareness and struggle, so *lesbian* does not account for the multiple forms of homosocial community among women. This fact is especially true for the years during which Rich served her literary apprenticeship.

One form that lesbian identity took in the period between World War II and the writing of "Diving into the Wreck" is the butch-femme dyad, despised by 1950s homophile groups as a dangerous marker of antisocial behavior and rejected by later lesbian feminists as a replication of heterosexist roles. Yet butch-femme, as Sue-Ellen Case, Joan Nestle, Esther Newton, and others have pointed out, introduces a level of political theater and parody into relationships among women that unsettles heterosexual gender roles. This dyad also offers an alternate way of resolving Rich's deixis under the two versions—heterosexist or lesbian—that I have mentioned. Rather than allegorize her lines in terms of a unitary "woman's tradition," we might see the poem's underwater imagery ("And I am here, the mermaid whose dark hair / streams black, the merman in his armored body") in terms of an indeterminate gender position, somewhere between "heroic masculinity" and romanticized femininity. In short, we might read masculinity back into the poem as a structural principle governing the visibility of gender rather than a role that must be expunged from view.

In this book I have described masculinity largely in terms of biological males. The sexual panics that inform the work of Jack Spicer, Kenneth Rexroth, Amiri Baraka, Charles Olson, and Jack Kerouac, and the carnivalizations of masculine roles in Frank O'Hara, Robert Creeley, John Wieners, and Walt Whitman all presuppose a male body upon which gendered narratives are inscribed. During the 1950s, that body was draped in the highly coded national uniforms of global protectionism (John Wayne, Audie Murphy), youth rebellion (Elvis Presley, James Dean), corporate anomie (the man in the gray flannel suit), and suburban normalcy (Ozzie Nelson, Jim Anderson in *Father Knows Best*). White working-class male bodies like those of James Dean or Marlon Brando or black male bodies like those of Sonnie Ray Liston or Little Richard offered excessive, potentially threatening versions of masculinity that had to be monitored by parental vigilance and the Hays Office. In the pursuit of white masculine normalcy, it was essential that "guys like us" knew what guys were like. Even when men appeared as women, as in *Some Like It Hot*, their return to heterosexual manhood was an essential, if comic, denouement.

But what happens when masculinity is detached from a biological male and attached to a female body? What sites of masculinity do not depend on one's possession of a penis? What narratives of power and legitimacy are displaced when masculinity is represented by a woman? Is masculinity an identity, an image, a performance? Judith Halberstam responds to these questions by noting that "masculinity . . . becomes legible as masculinity where and when it leaves the white male middle-class body" (*Female* 2). In Halberstam's terms, masculinity is a series of "prosthetic" effects by which power is marked and privilege conferred. Like James Bond with his electronic accessories or Mike Hammer (in Robert Aldrich's 1956 film *Kiss Me Deadly*) with his sports cars, masculinity is produced through its excrescences.[4] Lacking these cultural markers, masculinity becomes a phantom, able to speak independently of the body it inhabits. For Halberstam, female impersonators (drag kings), passing women, stone butches, f2m (female-to-male) transsexuals, tomboys, and other masculine females point to the difficulty of locating masculinity strictly in males. Female masculinity is not a noun but a hermeneutic process that provides "a glimpse of how masculinity is constructed as masculinity" (1).[5]

Halberstam's work extends (and complicates) that of Esther Newton, Lillian Faderman, Joan Nestle, Elizabeth Lapovsky Kennedy, Madeleine D. Davis, and others who have examined butch styles within lesbian culture. What differentiates Halberstam's work from previous studies of lesbian history is its stress on mannish women, not as derivative of male roles and styles, but rather as a separate and distinct gender position. Neither a woman passing as a man nor a woman on her way to manhood, the masculine female is comfortable in her short-cropped hair, pants, and attitude and exploits its ambiguous gender positioning for purposes of critique, satire, or sexual pleasure.[6] Although female masculinity is obviously associated with lesbianism, it is not necessarily limited to women who desire women or who identify as lesbians.[7] As this chapter will argue, female masculinity occurs across a range of sexual identities and cultural forms, from a lesbian poet like Elizabeth Bishop who refused to identify as a woman (much less gay) poet to sexually ambiguous actresses like Joan Crawford, Greta Garbo, or Eve Arden to a (presumably) heterosexual poet like Sylvia Plath. Female masculinity may be read as a marginal position within assimilationist lesbianism or as a sign of butch power within working-class bar culture.

Halberstam's work on female masculinity deploys queer theory's emphasis on gender performance to study women who, through cross-dressing or theater, quite literally perform masculine roles. Drag kings like Murray Hill, Betsey Gallagher, or Elvis Herselvis use their bodies, costumes, and routines to parody various forms of masculinity. The poets I study in this chapter conduct their gender performance in considerably more restricted spaces and venues. Adrienne Rich's pronominal indeterminacy is, as I have indicated, a grammatical working-out of a more complex problem of gendered identity that one can see in many women poets of her generation. Neither Bishop nor Plath could be said to perform masculinity in the same way as the drag kings or transgender persons Halberstam or Esther Newton study, yet their poetry is marked by self-conscious assaults on gender binarism that, in the context of 1950s domestic ideology, were extreme. That this extremity was configured within aesthetic terms as Bishop's "reticence" or Plath's expressivism indicates precisely how successful that domestic ideology was in normalizing potential gender alternatives.

But what were those alternatives in the postwar period and to what extent was the masculine female readable as such? Before looking at the high(er) culture artifacts of poets it is necessary to look at the cultural milieu within which those artifacts were made. The period following the war was, as I have remarked in earlier chapters, a moment when gender norms were highly rigidified and juridical prohibitions against what was then regarded as sexual deviance reinforced. In the prewar period, women had lived in companionable relationships with other women without the same degree of scrutiny, but the various witch-hunts of the late 1940s and early 1950s made opportunities for gay interaction difficult, if not dangerous. Frequent raids on gay bars, fears over job security, the policing of entertainment and educational venues, and the incarceration of "deviants" created a mood of paranoia. As Audre Lorde remembers, "You could never tell who was who, and the protective paranoia of the McCarthy years was still everywhere outside of the mainstream of blissed-out suburban middle america. Besides there were always rumors of plainclothes women circulating among us, looking for gay-girls with fewer than three pieces of female attire. That was enough to get you arrested for transvestism, which was illegal" (*Zami* 187).

Several factors contributed to the scrutiny that Lorde describes. Within the national theater established by McCarthyism, homosexuality was directly linked to political subversion. I have already discussed the ways that national security interests linked homosexuality to political subversion. Gay men and women became targets of more-than-sexual interest by the FBI and congressional investigating committees, their presumed threat to national security based on their mental "instability," their vulnerability to blackmail by foreign agents. Federal agencies like the FBI attempted to purge gays from civil service and the military, but this task was made difficult by the fact that gays could pass and escape detection. The extent of such passing was verified by the Kinsey reports of 1948 and 1953, which exposed the range and variety of homosexual activity across a wide spectrum of class and racial backgrounds and among men and women. The report documented the fact that homosexuals lived in all areas of American life and, therefore, could not be regarded as "maladjusted" members of society. Kinsey showed that many—as much as one in two—heterosexuals had had same-sex contacts during their lives and continued to have them even while married. Furthermore, his research team discovered that sexual acts presumably limited to gays were also performed by heterosexuals, thereby calling into question forms of legislation based on sodomy. Thus the need to have a visible representation of the deviant was complicated by the fact that he or she lived among "us."

If male homosexuals were a threat to cold war heterosexuality because of their defiance of heroic masculinity, masculine women were doubly dangerous because, as Terry Castle argues, they challenged the "political, economic, and sexual authority of men over women" (62). As women who did not depend on men, lesbians and butch women in particular threatened the patriarchal economy, financial and sexual, of the family. When they were represented at all—as in pulp novels of the period or films like *Caged* (1950), *Walk on the Wild Side* (1962), or *The Killing of Sister George* (1968)—lesbians were demonized as sexual predators or prostitutes.[8] To some extent this demonization existed in inverse proportion to their social invisibility; because women had always lived and fraternized with each other in nonthreatening, socially acceptable ways, it was necessary for the media to create negative icons in order to make lesbians visible for purposes of control and surveillance. This attempt to identify lesbians strictly in terms of their "perverse" sexuality, the emphasis on psychoanalytic definitions of deviance and inversion, constructed the terms within which early homophile organizations inaugurated their project.

DEFINITIVE HAIRCUTS

The perils of adopting an openly lesbian stance have been well documented by historians of sexuality. Being butch in the 1950s was hardly unproblematic, however, even within the lesbian community. As Joan Nestle summarizes it, "Butch-femme was an erotic partnership serving both as a conspicuous flag of rebellion and as an intimate exploration of women's sexuality. It was not an accident that butch-femme couples suffered the most street abuse and provoked more assimilated or closeted Lesbians to plead with them not to be so obvious" (101).

One can see verification of this assimilationist ideal by reading early issues of *The Ladder,* the newsletter of the Daughters of Bilitis (DOB), one of the first openly lesbian publications and a centerpiece of early gay liberation. The journal began in October 1956 and, along with the *Mattachine Review* (representing male homosexuals), was an important contributor to the early homophile movement. Founded by eight women in San Francisco, *The Ladder* provided a much-needed forum for lesbian readers across the country. It featured a calendar of events, editorial column, book reviews, creative work, and, most important, a letters section that served as an informal billboard of events and opinion. The journal's letters also offered an outlet for women to critique and debate the various trajectories of an emergent lesbian lifestyle.

As a document of cold war (as well as lesbian) history, *The Ladder's* significance can best be seen in the level of secrecy that attended its publication and distribution. The editors regularly instructed potential subscribers that their names would be safe from federal subpoenas and that they would never pass subscribers' names to any other magazine. "Your Name is Safe," reads an article in the second issue, followed in the third issue by an editorial titled "Don't Plead Guilty," which advised homosexuals of their legal rights if arrested on vagrancy charges. News of police raids on local bars, summaries of hearings on California's vagrancy law, testimony from various court cases relating to lesbian and homosexual issues provided the bulk of the news items but also suggested the climate of fear and intimidation within which the journal was published. Perhaps the most vivid sense of the journal's relationship to the red-scare climate of the mid-1950s can be seen in the disclaimer printed in all early issues: "The Daughters of Bilitis is not now, and never has been, affiliated with any other organization, political, social or otherwise." This disclaimer was probably in response to the fact that the Mattachine Society, the gay male homophile group, had been formed by members and fellow travelers of the Communist Party of the United States.[9] No doubt, the DOB hoped to differentiate its own mainstream views from its brother organization. Although Henry Hay and other founders of the Mattachine Society were eventually purged from the organization, the taint of subversion remained.

The Ladder's response to the homophobic climate of the mid-1950s took several forms. First, the journal reinforced the medicalized versions of homosexuality being offered by psychologists, sociologists, and therapists. "Authorities" on lesbian and homosexual behavior from Bay Area hospitals and universities were regular contributors to the journal and were often the only commentators whose full names were used. The journal sponsored public debates on whether or not homosexuals are "normal" or "deviant" and even commissioned its own sociological survey of homosexual behavior and lifestyles. Reviews of literature on sexology, from Krafft-Ebbing to Kinsey, provided intellectual content for the journal, prompting spirited debates within the letters column. To post-Stonewall ears, the journal's use of terms like "invert" or "sex variant" to describe lesbians is alarming, yet it is a reminder of how much the naming of nontraditional sexualities was dependent on psycho-pathological science. No less disturbing was the editorial manifesto printed on the first page of each issue which stated that the primary goal of the DOB was the "education of the variant, with particular emphasis on the psychological, physiological and sociological aspects, to enable her to understand herself and make her adjustment to society in all its social, civic and economic implications."

This rhetoric of "adjustment" speaks to the second way that the journal addressed homophobia, namely, by adopting an assimilationist posture in which all forms of extreme or extravagant behavior were excoriated. Editorials and letters stressed the need for lesbians to strive for middle-class respectability, to be "thoughtful, public spirited, responsible types," whose purpose is "social, not anti-social ends" (4.2 [Nov. 1959] 15).[10] The "anti-social" is clearly meant to include butch styles and masculine attire. One letter warns that "the kids in fly-front pants and with the butch haircuts and mannish manner are the worse [sic] publicity that we can get" (1.2 [Nov. 1956] 3). To which the editors respond: "[Our] organization has already touched on that matter [butch styles] and has converted a few to remembering that they are women first and a butch or fem secondly, so their attire should be that which society will accept" (3). Another letter hopes that butch styles and "definitive haircuts" will eventually seem normal, but that at the present juncture, it is necessary not to alarm one's heterosexual friends: "Someday, I expect, the 'discreet' lesbian will not turn her head on the streets at the sight of the 'butch' strolling hand in hand with her friend in their trousers and definitive haircuts. But for the moment, it still disturbs. It creates an impossible area for discussion with one's most enlightened . . . heterosexual friends" (1.8 [May 1957] 27). This letter, signed L. H. N., was in fact sent by Lorraine Hansberry, the author of *A Raisin in the Sun* and a regular contributor to the journal. The same gradualist rhetoric was being used in the then-current civil rights movement. What these letters indicate is a complicated response to butch styles. On the one hand, Hansberry yearns for a moment in which "trousers and definitive haircuts" are visible; on the other, she worries over the ways that such visibility challenges potential allies within the heterosexual community.

As a movement without public spaces or a representative body, the DOB focused on bars, house parties, and educational forums where lesbians gathered. Although editorials expressed anger at random busts and bar closings, they also stressed the need for lesbians *not* to provide any "immoderate behavior" that might lead to greater visibility. After one series of bar closings, Del Martin summarized the position of the Daughters of Bilitis: "The DOB . . . is presently carrying on an educational program to discourage lesbians from dressing in male attire and to educate lesbians to the fact that it is not in their self interest to so attire themselves and that it simply encourages repressive action or conduct against them. One of the purposes of the organization is 'advocating a mode of behavior and dress acceptable to society' and emphasizing the importance of mode of behavior and acceptance of dress in establishing understanding with others" (4.3 [Dec. 1959] 24). Such conciliatory responses to a campaign of harassment and intimidation may seem, by current standards, woefully inadequate, but they point to the difficulty the homophile movement had in establishing a foothold. Such remarks also dramatize the climate of fear within which attempts to organize homosexuals were conducted. Much of this centrism depended on the enforcement of appearance of gender "normalcy" and indicates the threat that masculine modes of dress and activity posed.[11]

If butch-femme roles for women were marginalized within the institutional frame of the early homophile movement, they had, paradoxically enough, an important role to play within mass culture. Perhaps the most productive zone for investigating female masculinity in the 1940s and 1950s is where my ocularcentric metaphor (sighting/citing) is most constructive—in film. The Production Code of 1930 had made the depiction of homosexuality or cross-dressing illegal. Aided by the McCarthyite spirit of the early 1950s, scrutiny of filmic representations of same-sex behavior became an important subset of communist witch-hunting. Given these attempts to out gay men and lesbians as political and sexual deviants, it is little wonder that the lesbian was, as Castle indicates, sometimes "apparitional" during this period. Yet she was often right in front of us, "there, in plain view, mortal and magnificent, at the center of the screen" in the form of Greta Garbo as Queen Christina or Katharine Hepburn as Sylvia Scarlet (2). Her visibility however, was often assisted by means of supporting actresses whose gender indeterminacy provided a contrasting note to the otherwise heterosexual trajectory of the film. Patricia White notes that, in contrast to the leading lady, supporting actresses offered "a site for the encoding of the threat and the promise of homosexual deviance" (140). White locates this position in the "queer career" of Agnes Moorehead who starred in numerous supporting roles as nurse, sidekick, witch, and spinster aunt. We could adduce other actresses who fulfilled the same role—Mercedes McCambridge in *Johnny Guitar, Touch of Evil,* or *Giant,* Thelma Ritter as the no-nonsense stooge in *Pickup on South Street,* Gaby Rogers as a Pandora of atomic secrets in *Kiss Me Deadly,* Angela Lansbury as the bad communist mom in *The Manchurian Candidate,* and, most important here, Eve Arden as Joan Crawford's tough-talking partner in *Mildred Pierce.* As White notes, whether the actresses who played these roles were, in fact, lesbians is not the point; but "the characterization complements [the] persona" and that persona is marked as lesbian (140).

Mildred Pierce (1945), based on James M. Cain's novel, establishes a series of nontraditional female roles that point up the unstable gender status of the title character. Situated on the cusp of World War II when many women were returning from the wartime workforce to new and uncertain domestic roles, the film explores the fortunes of one woman who challenges the postwar domestic ideal by becoming a successful entrepreneur—and who suffers from that presumption. In the film's opening, Mildred (Joan Crawford) is shown being interrogated by police who suspect her of having killed her current husband in a beach house shoot-out. Her flashback narrative to the cops recounts the breakdown of her first marriage and her transformation from housewife to businesswoman. This is the noirish frame that surrounds what is, in fact, a melodrama of cold war womanhood. In the flashback that follows, we see Mildred in her apron, baking a cake, caring for her two daughters and husband. She is the embodiment of the postwar housewife, living in a new southern California housing tract, profiting from the wartime real estate boom. But that boom is going bust for her husband Bert (Bruce Bennett), a real estate salesman, who has just lost his job. His inability to find work, combined with Mildred's desire to provide material possessions for her demanding and spoiled older daughter, Veda (Ann Blyth), leads to a deterioration of the marriage. Once separated from Bert, Mildred uses her domestic cooking and baking skills to gain a job as a waitress and then to start her own restaurant. In order to launch this venture, she uses the financial expertise of her husband's former partner, Wally (Jack Carson), and the financial capital of a ne'er-do-well playboy, Monte Beragon (Zachary Scott).[12] The restaurant becomes a success, and Mildred is well on her way to becoming an independently wealthy woman, able to withstand the unwanted attentions of Wally and Monte and provide for Veda's increasing consumer desires.

This regendered version of the Horatio Alger success story unravels when daughter Veda's interest in material possessions becomes linked to her interest in Monte. She uses sexual blackmail to break her engagement to a wealthy boyfriend and becomes increasingly independent of her mother whom she likens to a domestic drudge. Mildred, desperate to keep her dysfunctional daughter in line and reestablish some fiction of domestic bliss, marries Monte who proceeds to bankrupt Mildred's restaurants. He goes further by making sexual advances to Veda, to which the daughter reciprocates. Mildred confronts Monte with this fact, and he calls Veda a tramp. Veda, who overhears these remarks, shoots Monte. Mildred tries to protect her daughter by claiming to the police that she—Mildred—is the killer, but they know different and arrest Veda. Long-suffering former husband Bert reappears at the end to offer his support, thus reestablishing the original domestic ménage.

Mildred, through her tailored suits, businesslike manner, and entrepreneurial skills, embodies one version of the masculinized female that has earned the film a privileged place in gay male camp. It is a version undermined by a series of alternative (and dysfunctional) female roles that enable Mildred's return to heteronormalcy. Her younger daughter, Kay, a tomboy who would rather play football than share in her older sister's interest in makeup and clothes, dies of pneumonia, presumably as punishment for Mildred's one night stand with Monte. Veda, her older daughter, is a spoiled, predatory creature, whose class resentment can be seen in the way that she links sexuality with the commercial world her mother pursues. Mildred's black maid, Lottie (Butterfly McQueen), is a parody of the domestic labor Mildred has left behind. Lottie's exaggerated deference and subservience racialize that domestic labor. The rich mother of Veda's fiancé is a parody of upper-class privilege, a woman whose domination over her weak son is an exaggerated inversion of Mildred's inability to control her daughter.

And then there's Ida (Eve Arden), a wisecracking career gal with no illusions about men, money, or family. In the novel version of *Mildred Pierce*, Ida is married, but in the movie her sexual status is ambiguous. Her queerness is given ample point by her sardonic asides and wisecracks to various men who pursue Mildred. At one point, Wally is leaving Mildred's office as Ida is walking in. Wally has been putting the move on Mildred (as he does throughout the movie) and, having just been rebuked, looks at Ida and says, "I hate women." "My my," Ida responds, archly, to which Wally adds, "Thank goodness you're not one." Ida is not a woman in Wally's sexualized sense, but, at a deeper level, she is also not a woman by pursuing the same entrepreneurial aspirations as Mildred. Neither woman shows any deference to Wally and therefore cannot be defined within the usual sexual orbit. In order for Mildred to return to the conventional heterosexual role with Bert, Ida must remain in the sympathetic but ultimately undefinable female role Mildred must leave behind.

Mildred Pierce subjects noir cinematic style—expressionist lighting, voiceover/flashback, a dangerous femme fatale—to a regendering process. The tough male hero is replaced by a tough guy woman and her masculinized sidekick. The detective to whom Mildred tells the story of Monte's murder deduces the truth of Veda's culpability, but we, as an audience, learn something different. We learn a second-order truth about the links between women and economics, the exchange of sexuality for property, for which the masculine woman is a danger. Mildred covers for her daughter's murder, but she also covers her own inadequacy as a woman and is thereby punished. In Pam Cook's terms, "Mildred Pierce is constituted as a sexually ambiguous film, an ambiguity founded on duplicity which is eventually resolved by the re-assertion of the patriarchal metadiscourse" (71).

Several subtexts to Mildred Pierce enhance its role as an important queer film, the most obvious of which is Joan Crawford's role as a gay male icon. One could also adduce her butch role as Vienna in Johnny Guitar and her friendship with lesbian director Dorothy Arzner. Another subtext more germane to our concern with female masculinity is provided by her role, during the war, in what might be called the domestication of the independent female, a campaign to depict actresses who played strong independent women (Joan Crawford, Ann Southern, Lana Turner, Claudette Colbert) in domestic scenarios, raising children, cooking, and cleaning house. "During the war," according to Elaine Tyler May, "[these actresses] were suddenly featured in popular magazines chiefly as wives and mothers" (63). Thus Mildred Pierce could be seen to be a postwar pendant to this campaign, permitting an image of woman in a man's role yet relinquishing that role by her association with other dysfunctional females. Whatever attempts may have been made to idealize the maternal in Joan Crawford were dashed by Mommie Dearest, Christina Crawford's memoir about her mother's abusive treatment of her during her childhood.

Although feminists have hailed Mildred Pierce for its depiction of a strong-minded, independent woman, it is also a cautionary tale about the limits to such independence. And although the positive same-sex relationship formed between Mildred and Ida has earned the film high marks from lesbians, its use of Ida's masculinity negatively to critique Mildred's sexual independence ultimately restores heteronormalcy. We could see *Mildred Pierce* as a sign of charged postwar domestic relations in which the presumption of masculinity in women is normalized through what Betty Friedan was later to call the feminine mystique. Challenges to that mystique within homophile organizations or within mass cultural productions like films were not easy to muster, any more than speaking self-confidently from a grounded subject-position in the work of poets like Adrienne Rich was easy.

"OMISSIONS ARE NOT ACCIDENTS"

If the masculine female was somewhat apparitional in public culture, she was all but invisible in high cultural productions like poems and novels. With the notable exceptions of the tomboy, Frankie, in Carson McCuller's *Member of the Wedding* or lesbian Vassar alumna, Lakey, in Mary McCarthy's *The Group,* there are few if any representations of lesbians, let alone butch women. In the world of poetry, these absences were assisted by the formalist credos of the then-reigning New Criticism, which insisted that representation of personal desires or passions needed to be remedied by the objective correlative. If the 1930s was an age of ideology, as Daniel Bell called it, the 1940s and 1950s was an age of criticism (as W. H. Auden called it), notable for its development of sophisticated techniques of analysis but short on personal revelations. Yet the formalism valued during this era provided what Adrienne Rich called "asbestos gloves" for materials too hot to handle (171). Nowhere were these gloves more in evidence than in the work of Marianne Moore and her protégé, Elizabeth Bishop.

Marianne Moore's epigraph to her *Complete Poems* (1967), "Omissions are not accidents," has been taken as an epitome of modernist economy and condensation.[13] It applies to more than Moore's vaunted formal control, testifying as well to her avoidance of the personal in her poems. Her life as a single woman, her seeming lack of romantic intrigue, her interest in the arcana of classical history, cartography, ornithology, travel narratives, and the Brooklyn Dodgers, her use of syllabics and verbal pastiche—all are taken as signs of a spinster aunt's eccentricities. Feminists like Adrienne Rich used such qualities to criticize Moore for offering few obstacles to male consumption.[14] According to Rich, Moore's fame was purchased by writing within modernist male values of artisanal control and impersonality. In a male poet, such values might seem signs of technical mastery, but in her they become charming pendants to a life whose contours are difficult to discover. She becomes the latter-day version of Emily Dickinson, safe in her alabaster chambers, gothic in her refusal of public life—a miraculist of the quotidian.

Moore is the classic instance of the woman poet whose sexuality cannot be named, whose "omissions" must be explained by formalist fiat. As Jeanne Heuvig says, Moore's "practice of reserve . . . is bound up both in what she *cannot* and what she *refuses* to say" (19). Such refusal joins her to numerous women poets at midcentury—Elizabeth Bishop, Sylvia Plath, Louise Bogan, Anne Sexton, May Swenson, Muriel Rukeyser, May Sarton, Angelina Grimké, Audre Lorde, Helen Adam, Adrienne Rich, the lines between whose homosexual and heterosexual lives are blurred and who, therefore, pose problems of classification. Although several of them—Lorde, Rich and Swenson most famously—have, in later life, acknowledged their lesbianism, others remain ambiguously situated. And whereas omissions and absences in the work of male writers like Henry James or Ernest Hemingway are read as indices of romantic loss or "injury," the not-said in women confirms a Freudian "lack" for which poetry serves as palliative—and symptom.

Attempts to unite these midcentury authors within a women's literary tradition often recuperate them within a rather narrow gynocentric model. Without denying the importance of cultural feminist readings of women authors, I would like to complicate the *cultural* part by looking at two poets, Elizabeth Bishop and Sylvia Plath, who do not easily fit into standard homosexual/heterosexual categories and who manifest elements of what I have been calling female masculinity. Bishop resisted all attempts to include her in women's anthologies and refused to identify with the feminist movement. Her letters selected in *One Art* contain no references to lesbianism, even though she spent most of her adult life in long-term relationships with women. Plath, although more directly critical of patriarchal authority, was nevertheless equally ambivalent about her gendered status. In her early journals she often portrays herself as an androgynous creature, capable of desiring other women with the "calculation of a man choosing a mistress" (qtd. in Rose 116). Plath identified with a masculine tradition in literature and figured artisanal power in a set of powerful male figures, both fictive and real. By reading Bishop and Plath under the sign of masculinity I do not mean to reconfigure them under masculine universalist criteria. Nor am I implying that either of them necessarily took on butch roles or passed as males. Rather, I am seeking to locate their ambiguous gender positions *between* rather than *at* one or another pole of a dyadic gender structure.

I have chosen to focus my discussion on Bishop and Plath because within more official poetry venues they are the most representative women poets of their generation and because both resisted the phrase "woman poet" almost successfully. Both achieved literary fame early in their careers, gaining the admiration of a male literary establishment, and both served as models for a new generation of women writers. Bishop received every prestigious award offered in the United States (the Pulitzer Prize, two Guggenheim Fellowships, and an Academy of American Poets Fellowship) and was published in all of the major journals and magazines. She served one year as the poetry consultant to the Library of Congress and ended her career by teaching at Harvard. Plath began publishing early and won numerous prizes while still in college, becoming a student editor at *Mademoiselle* in her senior year at Smith College and going on to attend Cambridge University on a Fulbright Fellowship. She later taught at Smith College, at which time she was married to the poet laureate of England, Ted Hughes. Although her published output was small, she appeared in both high art and masscult periodicals through-out her brief life. Both poets came from privileged educational backgrounds, each attending a prestigious woman's college and each moving easily in official verse culture.

It may seem odd to link two poets who, despite their common New En-gland origins and education, seem utter opposites. Bishop strove to efface her personality from her poems and lived for the better part of her literary life far from the centers of literary life. Queried about her relationship to the Confessional poets, Bishop responded, "[you] just wish they'd keep some of these things to themselves" (Schwartz and Estes 303). Plath on the other hand can hardly be spoken about *without* reference to her biography, a fact that has made the reception of her work almost as important as the poetry. Unlike Bishop who spent the bulk of her life at the peripheries of the Ameri-cas (Nova Scotia, Key West, Brazil), Plath sought the centers of literary pub-lishing in New York and London. Bishop's formalism seems to have protected her from the autobiographical elements by which Plath is known. Whereas Bishop's reticence about gender issues may have allowed critics to feel that she safely escaped ideology through the aesthetic, Plath's violent hy-perbole ("Every woman adores a Fascist") creates a semiotic excess for which appeals to *écriture féminine* seem inadequate (Plath, *Collected* 223). Finally, in terms of their family backgrounds, each poet seems the inverse mirror of the other. Although both women lost their fathers early in their lives (Bishop at one, Plath at eight), Bishop suffered the absence of maternal affection while Plath was overwhelmed by it, leading her to create two separate selves, one for her mother and a kind of antiself for her poetry.

What links both poets, despite these differences, is the degree to which they questioned the binary logic of gender, refusing to be placed in feminine or masculine categories. Their most famous poems—Bishop's "Man Moth" and Plath's "Daddy"—interrogate masculine aspirations from within a speaker who embodies many of those aspirations. Likewise, their poems about female self-identification—Bishop's "The Waiting Room" and Plath's "Lady Lazarus"—describe women shocked or charged by their identification with other women. These are hardly paeans to female solidarity, but their complex negotiations of gender relations suggest some of the limits to such solidarity. Rather than recuperate Elizabeth Bishop and Sylvia Plath within a "women's tradition," I would like to take their resistance to gendering labels as a decisive element in their poetics.

FINDING MISS BREEN: ELIZABETH BISHOP

In 1951 Elizabeth Bishop set sail for South America, a journey that would result in a fifteen-year period of expatriation and her most enduring relationship with a woman, Lota de Macedo Soares. The journey also represented a move away from McCarthyite America with its fierce scrutiny of what was then called the "sex offender" and "homosexual menace" in public life. Bishop had not undergone any such scrutiny herself, but she must have realized that the climate was hardly right for a woman in short hair and pants who had had several significant relationships with women.[15] Brazil was in the throes of its own revolutionary change, and Bishop would become embroiled in hemispheric politics, through Lota Soares's political work for Carlos Lacerda, the governor of the state of Guanabara and supporter of the military government of Castelo Branco.[16] Thus she experienced perhaps at close quarters the global anticommunist politics being exported from the United States throughout Latin and South America.

The first poem that she wrote about her inaugural view of Brazil, "Arrival at Santos," seems to be a straightforward touristic account:

Here is a coast; here is a harbor;
here, after a meager diet of horizon, is some scenery:
impractically shaped and—who knows?—self-pitying mountains,
sad and harsh beneath their frivolous greenery
    (89)

The poem continues in this desultory manner to describe details of debarkation, customs, foreign currency, and the quality of glue on postage stamps. Bishop's famous descriptive eye is active as she figures her transition from objective observer of the coast to explorer of the country's "interior." She recognizes that the change of scenery fulfills more than curiosity; it provides a response to her "immodest demands for a different world" (89). As in many of her poems, landscape is the backdrop for such demands. "Arrival at Santos" is less *about* the landscape of Brazil than about the defamiliarizing experience of novelty, the way that seeing something for the first time creates a phantasmic and surreal scene that uncovers subterrestrial veins of consciousness.

The center of the poem is occupied not by the port of Santos but a fellow passenger, Miss Breen,

about seventy,
a retired police lieutenant, six feet tall,
with beautiful bright blue eyes and a kind expression.
Her home, when she is at home, is in Glens Fall

s, New York.
    (90)

Miss Breen becomes a touristic sight herself, as exotic as the "green coffee beans" and "feeble pink" warehouses (89). She is the masculine woman, inveterate wanderer and expatriate who served as a prototype for Bishop herself. Miss Breen lives in Glens Falls *"when she is at home,"* suggesting that, like Bishop, she is displaced from conventional domestic spaces and roles. This slightly uncanny fellow passenger is physically imposing—over six feet tall—and has, as a "retired police lieutenant" worked in traditionally male roles. Brett Millier, drawing on letters sent by Bishop to friends in the United States, explains that "what Elizabeth got from this brief acquaintance was a vision of an accomplished and successful lesbian life, not at all secretive or ashamed" (239). The poem, of course, does not say this; rather, the thematics of arrival, novelty, and change are focused on a mannish woman whose "beautiful bright blue eyes" offer another kind of novelty and solace in a foreign port. What would ensue from this moment—an openly lesbian household with Lota Soares—would create a profound change in Bishop's life: "We leave Santos at once; / we are driving to the interior" (90). Written at the beginning of her fifteen years in Brazil and presented as the inaugural moment of her 1950s work, "Arrival at Santos" announces the links between exterior and interior, surface reticence and private sexuality, that would dominate her middle years. "Driving to the interior" defines a significant shift in geographic location, but because it extends from her meeting with Miss Breen it defines a psychic and sexual territory as well.

    The fault lines in what Lee Edelman calls "the geography of gender" were felt keenly by Bishop at this time. She had been regarded almost exclusively as a protégé of Marianne Moore whose reticence and modesty were certainly regarded as feminine traits. Moore herself reinforced those features in her mentoring of Bishop. In a review of Bishop's *North and South* (1946) entitled "The Modest Expert," Moore praises the younger poet's "tentativeness" and "religious faith," and in her private correspondence urges her to expunge the "unprudishness" of male poets like Thomas and Williams and other "vulgarities" in the poem "Roosters."[17] Robert Lowell, another close friend, had reinforced this reading of Bishop's essentially feminine poetics in a review of the same volume, saying that poems like "Roosters" and "The Fish" are "outside of Marianne Moore, the best poems that I know of written by a woman in this century" (qtd. in Schwartz and Estes 188). These famous remarks, although written by one of Bishop's closest friends, rankled for years, causing Bishop later in life to grumble in an interview, "at the very end they often say 'The best poetry by a woman in this decade, or year, or month.' Well what's that worth?" (qtd. in Schwartz and Estes 324).

The poems that inspired such conclusions by Moore, Lowell, and others do appear to be careful and reticent, yet even among her most descriptive early poems, gender tensions can be felt. Take, for example, "Cirque d'Hiver" from *North and South* (1946). The poem is based on the image of a comic toy that creates a bisexual figure, part male circus horse but bearing a "little [female] dancer on his back." A single "pole" pierces both dancer and horse, the object serving as an elaborate metaphor for the inseparability of male and female roles in a single figure. Most commentary on the poem sees the toy as a metaphor for the artist, the dancer representing the creative imagination, balanced precariously on the (masculine) horse's intellectual back. But when, at the end of the poem, the toy turns toward the speaker, the confusion of pronouns hints, as it does in the Rich poem quoted earlier, at a triangular relationship of "desperate" proportions:

The dancer, by this time, has turned her back.
He is the more intelligent by far.
Facing each other rather desperately—
his eye is like a star—
we stare and say, "Well, we have come this far."
    (31)

But how far have "we" come? The toy, after all, is artificial, a pure product of romantic fantasy. Male horse and female dancer, dancer and auditor, child and adult face each other in a series of positional frames, assisted by the rhyming play on "star," "stare," "say," "far." "He is the more intelligent by far" presumably refers to the horse, yet the position of this statement in the stanza could as easily refer to the dancer, which appears in the previous line. The tone of resignation that occurs in the poem's last line—"Well, we have come this far"—cannot be accepted on its own terms but as a statement of the complex facing and replacing that has gone on in the poem. What animates "Cirque d'Hiver," "The Gentleman of Shalott," "The Man Moth," and her other early poems is precisely this blurring of boundaries in poems whose object is the separation of genders.

In poems written during the 1950s and 1960s this division along gendered lines manifests itself through the image of a mirror. But instead of serving as the icon for poetic mimesis, the mirror in Bishop becomes a camera obscura, a vehicle by which conventional relations may be inverted and identities confused.[18] In "Insomnia" the poet invokes the moon admiring it-self in a "bureau mirror." Since the observer of this mirroring is an insom-niac, she inhabits the same nightly vision as the moon and is thus drawn into its orbit. Bishop utilizes the traditional feminine associations with moon and vanity, only to turn them on their head:

By the Universe deserted,
she'd tell it to go to hell,
and she'd find a body of water,
or a mirror, on which to dwell.
So wrap up care in a cobweb
and drop it down the well

into that world inverted
where left is always right,
where the shadows are really the body,
where we stay awake all night,
where the heavens are shallow as the sea
is now deep, and you love me.
          (70)

In this allegory of modulated resistances, the feminine moon, feeling "de-serted" by the universe (and perhaps by universal modalities of legitimation), enters that "inverted" world "where left is always right, / where the shadows are really the body." The early medical term for homosexuality, *inversion*, is briefly invoked, not to signify sexual roles but to identify increased vision. The reversal of roles, the dropping of cares "down the well," reveals a world in which love to another woman can be declared. Although the gender of the ad-dressee is never specified, we may discover it in the mirror where it is re-vealed to be a woman, a version of the speaker. On the one hand, the poem dismisses proprieties—tells the universe to go to hell and accepts life in a world of "inversion"; on the other hand, it recognizes that such a declaration of love, despite the support of the universe, is consigned to a mirroring in which universal definitions of left and right, male and female, are turned around.

Marianne Moore understood exactly the kind of confession that was being expressed here and found it distasteful, calling "Insomnia" "a cheap love poem" (Erkkila 138).[19] For Moore, such negative appraisal may have to do with the poem's expression of passion in the last line, but it may also have to do with the implications of an "inverted world." For Alan Williamson, these mirrorings are examples of a narcissism that is never framed by adequate form. His comments on the failure of "Insomnia" say a great deal about the ways Bishop unsettles certain readers—and about the terms by which she achieved her universal acclaim:

> The last line admits of two readings, neither very cheery: that you "now" love me (but how deep is the sea, when compared with the heavens?); or that the phrase "you love me" is one of a series of impossible propositions, conceivable only in the narcissist's mirror-world "where left is always right." But from the reader's point of view, what is most shocking about this grim assessment is the way he is led to it without the least hint that a "you" is at issue in the poem; and then— as if the subject were too painful to bear more than the briefest mention—suddenly dropped. The naked emotion of the ending is pointed up by the contrasting tone of jaunty insouciance, pretend-optimism, with which the sentence begins.
>
> (97)

By never acknowledging that this poem might address a female lover, Williamson cannot explain the tentativeness of address, the absence of a sufficient antecedent for "you." The impossibility of declaring love openly is, for him, a sign of solipsism—the very demon of so many modernists—not a recognition of the historical impossibility for a gay person to make such a declaration. He is "shocked" not that such declaration should be so difficult but that the poem has not adequately prepared him for the poem's address. Summarizing the failure of this and other poems from *A Cold Spring,* Williamson concludes that the poet "has been swept away by a monolithic, unarguable intuition of implacable fate" and is relieved that "Bishop was never guilty of such imbalances again" (8). Williamson's moralistic rhetoric (narcissism, imbalance, guilt, shock) betrays a more-than-formalist worry over poetic proprieties. Williamson suggests that not only has the poem failed to provide an adequate objective correlative for emotion but that the emotion itself is too vulgar for words.

What Williamson and others value in Bishop is not only discretion but some sign that such qualities are kept safely within a heterosexual frame. Yet many of her poems utilize the conventions of heterosexual romance in order to expose an incommensurable aspect of it. This is explicitly the role of allegory in "The Riverman," a narrative poem based on an Amazonian legend of a man who leaves his wife and descends into the river to encounter a serpentlike female figure called Luandinha. On the surface, the poem describes a witch doctor's rite of passage into visionary states (the poem's epigraph makes this point explicit). On another level, however, the poem permits Bishop to adopt a male role in order to encounter another woman.

In the story, the narrator describes being addressed by the river Dolphin, "a man like myself," who asks him to leave his wife and join him in the river: "I thought once of my wife / but I knew what I was doing." In a room beneath the river, the speaker is given cigars and something to drink. "Then a tall, beautiful serpent / in elegant white satin" (Luandinha) appears and speaks

in a language I didn't know;
when she blew cigar smoke
into my ears and nostrils
I understood, like a dog,
although I can't speak it yet.
    (106)

This watery experience with a serpent in white satin transforms him into a water spirit himself. Each night, he returns to the river, descending in order to enjoy the sensual pleasures of this subaqueous zone. His descent gives him a special insight into the serpent's world:

Her rooms shine like silver
with the light from overhead,
a steady stream of light
like at the cinema.
    (107)

In this primitive setting, the relationship between nature and cinema seems odd, yet this is a realm in which light produces fantasies and mirrors reflect unreality. As in Rich's "Diving into the Wreck," the mirror has been manipulated by others, forcing the speaker to seek

a virgin mirror
no one's ever looked at,
that's never looked back at anyone,
to flash up the spirits' eyes
and help me recognize them.
The storekeeper offered me
a box of little mirrors,
but each time I picked one up
a neighbor looked over my shoulder
and then that one was spoiled—
spoiled, that is, for anything
but the girls to look at their mouths in,
to examine their teeth and smiles.
    (107)

Oddly enough, the "virgin mirror" being sought is one into which gendered expectations have not written their script. The ethnographic tale is that of a male shaman enduring a dark night of the soul, but the female poet's variation is about a descent into masculine gender in order to address a femme in satin. She wants to heed the voice of a "man like myself" who asks him to descend into another relationship to the feminine. "Why shouldn't I be ambitious?" Bishop asks; "I sincerely desire to be / a serious *sacaca*" (107). But, as with Bishop's own life, to be serious is to live below surface appearances, manipulating them, via personae, in order to speak in a different voice.

The use of the masculine pronoun to look beyond gender receives its most thorough treatment in "Crusoe in England" (1964/1971), a poem that many commentators feel is Bishop's most autobiographical poem. Although published in 1971, it was begun in 1963, following Bishop's return from Brazil and the tragic suicide of her Brazilian companion, Lota Soares. Spoken by Crusoe in his old age, the poem rewrites Defoe's narrative in terms of Bishop's life in Brazil, incorporating, as Brett Millier says, many elements of her sojourn there.[20] But as Bishop, in the voice of Crusoe, attests, "None of the books has ever got it right" (162). Since *Robinson Crusoe* is one of those books, Bishop's version is an attempt to rediscover a familiar story, as it were, from the inside.

If Defoe's Crusoe was inspired by Protestant industry and frugality, Bishop's Crusoe is considerably more somber, brooding on solitude and insecurity. Natural beauty, so important elsewhere in Bishop, becomes a meager compensation for loneliness: "I watched / the water spiral up . . . like smoke. / Beautiful, yes, but not much company" (163). And if Defoe's Crusoe is supported by biblical injunction in his efforts at domestication Bishop's Crusoe makes his home out of introspection:

What's wrong about self-pity, anyway?
With my legs dangling down familiarly
over a crater's edge, I told myself
"Pity should begin at home." So the more
pity I felt, the more I felt at home.
    (163)

This solipsistic Eden produces a will to categorization that almost drives Crusoe mad. He dreams of "infinities / of islands, islands spawning islands" and knows that he has to live "on each and every one, eventually . . . registering their flora, / their fauna, their geography" (165). The nighttime version of this taxonomical imperative is a set of nightmarish confusions—the very dystopia of categorization: "like slitting a baby's throat, mistaking it / for a baby goat."

Then along comes Friday:
Just when I thought I couldn't stand it
another minute longer, Friday came.
(Accounts of that have everything all wrong.)
Friday was nice.
Friday was nice, and we were friends.
If only he had been a woman!
I wanted to propagate my kind,
and so did he, I think, poor boy.
He'd pet the baby goats sometimes,
and race with them, or carry one around.
—Pretty to watch; he had a pretty body.
　　(166)

This is remarkable not for what it includes but for its collapsing of Crusoe's life with Friday to a single stanza. The brief reference to him ("Friday was nice and we were friends") reduces this important relationship to utter banality. Since Bishop's Friday *was* a woman, Crusoe's desire for a heterosexual relationship "to propagate my kind" reverses itself. Now Crusoe, as woman posing as a man, desires Friday to be a woman so that under the guise of heterosexuality they may "legitimate" their same-sex relationship. But the reference to "baby goats" ("he'd pet the baby goats") reminds us of the previous stanza in which Crusoe's nightmare featured "slitting a baby's throat" instead of a baby goat. Phonetic similarities ("goat" and "throat") merge two kinds of death, refusing the possibility of any endistanced position. Now the act of procreation is confused with murder, desire for the feminized other transformed to the mother's gaze at the "pretty body" of a boy.

Joanne Feit Diehl notes that in this poem "the voice of the isolated man most clearly articulates Bishop's terrain of difference, for Crusoe's hardship is related as much to the claustrophobia of entrapment within an obsessive imagination as it is to the physical conditions of the island" (20). This seems the most pertinent way in which Bishop has updated Defoe's novel: by making the story of a man's life on an island a sign of distinctly modern solipsism ("I often gave way to self-pity"). Crusoe's obsession is to catalogue and order novelty by naming its components. The difference between the island and the consciousness of the island, between history and its record, can be glimpsed in the last stanza. Crusoe, now in England, says, "The local museum's asked me to / leave everything to them: the flute, the knife, the shriveled shoes, / my shedding goatskin trousers. . . . How can anyone want such things?" But it is the outside world, the ethnographic imagination, that wants "such things." The user of knife and shoes inhabits them differently, just as her life with Friday is not a subject for discussion or confession. "And Friday, my dear Friday, died of measles / seventeen years ago come March." By placing Friday among the objects destined for the local museum, the erotic experience between them is reduced to an anthropological curiosity. But it is also Bishop responding to those who may have been curious about her "exotic" life in Brazil—that it cannot be contained in words or that once home in England—another island—such experiences undergo sea change. Hence this poem that looks back to Brazil is also about what it leaves out—what it *means* to leave out.

I referred earlier to Marianne Moore's remark, "omissions are not accidents" to speak of the ways that absence of reference to sexuality may announce its refractive power. In Bishop, the presence of same-sex desire is often mediated through other forms—geography, animals, diction. Friday's importance for Crusoe as a same-sex companion is marked not by romantic apostrophe but by the brevity of his appearance and by the banality of Crusoe's phrasing. For once, the elaborate naming of natural flora and fauna by which Bishop is best known helps frame a passage in which what is *not* described stands curiously revealed.

The omission of poems on sexual themes is not always accidental. One example of this is "Exchanging Hats," a poem of 1956 that Bishop never reprinted after its appearance in *New American Writing* and which she omitted from her *Complete Poems*. It is her most overt reference to the mutability of gender roles:

Unfunny uncles who insist
in trying on a lady's hat,
—oh, even if the joke falls flat,
we share your slight transvestite twist

in spite of our embarrassment.
Costume and custom are complex.
The headgear of the other sex
inspires us to experiment.

Anandrous aunts, who, at the beach,
with paper plates upon your laps,
keep putting on the yachtsmen's caps
with exhibitionistic screech,

the visors hanging o'er the ear
so that the golden anchors drag,
—the tides of fashion never lag.
Such caps may not be worn next year.
    (200)

The poem's use of loaded terms like "transvestite twist," "anandrous aunts," and "anchors drag" caused Bishop some discomfort, although she was pleased when her friend May Swenson read it aloud in New York. The poem is a bit like the "unfunny uncles" themselves, disporting itself in jaunty rhymes and regular meters that belie the complex implications of their subject. The poem costumes as light verse the theme of transvestism among familiar relatives. As in Plath's "Daddy," the childlike rhymes and meters support the childhood perspective of the speaker, a niece addressing adults. Like Bishop herself who was raised by aunts and uncles, the speaker wonders what is implied when uncles become effeminate by putting on a woman's hat or when aunts become masculinized by wearing a captain's hat. Such relatives have now passed away, but the speaker wonders of her aunt, "with avernal eyes, we wonder / what slow changes they see under / their vast, shady, turned-down brim" (201).

The metaphor of hats is a nice example of how costume and custom construct gender. As Bonnie Costello notes, "Bishop speaks from inside a culture that cannot sustain the norms of gender identity but perceives their instability as 'abnormal' or perverse or experimental. In this sense the openly deviant poet who converts role-playing into troping becomes the only potentially joyous member of the family" (84). This is an important observation about the ways that Bishop reconstructs a family that, in her case, was always fractured and tenuous. Those "anandrous aunts" become models for the masculine woman not because, as the adjective implies, they lack men but because they are capable of carnivalizing gender roles, however fitfully. Hats (headdresses, miters, fedoras) are signs of masculine power that when wielded by the male signify authority but when "exchanged" by women signal their arbitrary character.

The footnote to Bishop's "The Man Moth" indicates that the title is a "newspaper misprint for 'mammoth'" (14). We could use this as a metaphor for the ways that Bishop deals with her lesbianism—not by "publishing" it in an autobiographical manner but by "misprinting" or refracting it to enact its playful script on her textual body. What had been "mammoth" (New York, its towers and activity posing forms of unattainable glamour) becomes "Man moth," a creature made out of two biological codes. The doubled or mirrored quality of her poems repeats this formula, and while commentators have admired her discretion as a way of transforming the power of the surreal urban experience, she alerts us that this reticence is a misprint, the use of one code to annex another, less speakable version. As we know, Bishop's man-moth returns to "the pale subways of cement he calls home," and if he is the prototype for the man in the gray flannel suit, he also offers a "tear" "from underground springs" that is an offering of his "only possession" (14).

My Life had stood—a Loaded Gun
>   Emily Dickinson, "Poem no. 745"

How would you like to be Mrs Buddy Willard?
>   Sylvia Plath, *The Bell Jar*

Elizabeth Bishop's lack of production became a measure of her success, a fact that she noted on numerous occasions. Writing to Robert Lowell, Bishop claimed, "I've always felt that I've written poetry more by *not* writing it than writing it" (Jarraway 244). And in an interview, she spoke of her relatively small output: "Sometimes I think that if I had been born a man I probably would have written more. Dared more, or been able to spend more time at it. I've wasted a great deal of time" (Schwartz and Estes 329). Omissions are not accidents of intention but products of gender as well. For Bishop, being "born a man" permits a certain latitude of production and innovation denied to women. Yet, despite her acceptance of gender limitations, Bishop refused to be labeled a woman poet, claiming, at one point, that her feminism consisted precisely in *not* appearing in women's anthologies.[21] Such refusal could be seen as a characteristic gesture among intellectuals of her generation to create an art beyond ideology, but it could also be seen as a frustration with the limiting character of gender choices for the mannish woman.

Sylvia Plath, while hardly mannish in outward appearance, also worried over the limits of categories. At age seventeen she writes: "I want, I think, to be omniscient. . . . I think I would like to call myself 'The girl who wanted to be God.' Yet if I were not in this body, where *would* I be—perhaps I am destined to be classified and qualified. But, oh, I cry out against it. I am I—I am powerful—but to what extent? I am I" (*Letters Home* 40). These lines from Plath's 1949 journals announce a desire for release from "this body" into a God-like omniscience. Early journal entries are filled with remarks of this sort, protesting the circumscriptions of female identity and questioning the social construction of gender: "I am part man, and I notice women's breasts and thighs with the calculation of a man choosing a mistress . . . but that is the artist and the analytical attitude toward the female body . . . for I am more a woman; even as I long for full breasts and a beautiful body, so do I abhor the sensuousness which they bring. . . . I desire the things which will destroy me in the end" (*Letters Home* 23). In the first entry Plath understands that she is "destined to be classified," and wishes to "cry out against it." Such phrases suggest a nascent feminism, but their protest, in the second entry, is mixed with desires that cannot be configured under a heterosexual "analytical attitude toward the female body." Her desire to become "more a woman" turns self-lacerating and violent—as though further investment in feminine beauty will produce the very forms of masculine desire she repudiates. Her conclusion is prophetic: "I desire the things which will destroy me in the end."

Early readers of Plath, including A. Alvarez and Ted Hughes, attempted to configure such desires in aesthetic terms. *Ariel,* Plath's late and most psychologically charged book, becomes an artisanal transcendence of her earlier gender troubles. According to this view, Plath's triumph as an artist lies in transforming such uncertainties into art. Appeals to transcendence may, as Joyce Carol Oates argues, reflect Plath's debt to romanticism, but they no less recognize that the "I" is a role or masquerade. She is a "girl who [wants] to be God," and because the place that God occupies is already inhabited by a man—Otto Plath, Ted Hughes—the woman serves, like the speaker in "The Colossus," as his amanuensis, dredging the "silt" from his throat so that he can speak.[22] In poem after poem, the presumption of speech produces a divided rhetoric whereby the male being addressed ("I shall never get you put together") becomes identified with the female subject speaking ("I shall never get myself put together" [129]). Poems that attack male power like "Daddy," "The Rabbit Catcher," "Amnesiac," or "The Surgeon at 2 a.m." often ventriloquize from within that power. If, like Emily Dickinson, Plath's life was experienced as a loaded gun, it was pointed as much at herself as at the male object of her derision.

The tensions produced by this identification with the male are literalized in Plath's editorial remarks published in *Mademoiselle* in the August 1953 issue. "We're stargazers this season, bewitched by an atmosphere of evening blue. Foremost in the fashion constellation we spot *Mlle's* own tartan, the astronomic versatility of sweaters, and men, men, men—we've even taken the shirts off their backs!" (Stevenson 43). Guest managing editor Sylvia Plath, Smith College '54, is speaking of the fashion phenomenon of that era in which women began wearing men's shirts. Although her tone reflects the buoyant style of popular women's magazines ("the astronomic versatility of sweaters"), Plath's particular phraseology will be easily recognizable to readers of "Daddy" or "Lady Lazarus." The eerie repetition of "men, men, men" becomes a hallmark of later poems in which the exorcism of male authority through repetition ("ich ich ich") is performed by the adoption of "his" pronoun. Just as the speaker of "Daddy" appropriates the German of the lost father, so the woman speaker puts on the clothing of patriarchy to test its cultural power.

My title for this section, "Wearing Gender," is a double-edged phrase; it refers to clothing and fashion but also to desiccation and decay. To take on the position of male power is wearing on the one who must see herself reflected continually in his gaze. "There is a charge," as Lady Lazarus says, "for the eying of my scars," but it is the erotic "charge" that the speaker receives from such a revelation that permits her to return for more. Nor is the wearing of gender a strictly rhetorical figure; it is a professional necessity, related to market considerations of Plath's literary milieu. For Plath, as for Bishop, literary fame is obtained by publishing in the right places and meeting the right people, wearing the right clothes for the occasion. But for Plath, unlike Bishop, the "right places" included masscult periodicals like *Seventeen* or *Lady's Home Journal* as much as the *New Yorker*. It is in such popular venues that young women's gender identity is formed and within which Plath's early style is honed. In letters and journal entries, she is critical of the "slicks," yet she wants to break into them as a sign of professionalism. Like an athlete preparing for competition, Plath studies magazine styles for characteristic features: "I admire the slick market in NYC and find the stories muscular, pragmatic, fine technically and with a good sense of humor," she says. Elsewhere, "I will slave and slave until I break into those slicks." And, again, "When I write my first *Ladies Home Journal* story I will have made a step forward. I don't have to be a bourgeois mother to do it either" (Rose 171). Because she *was* the product of a bourgeois mother, she had to differentiate herself as author from herself as daughter—a separation that, as a comparison between *Ariel*—the poems of a reprobate daughter—and *Letters Home*—letters of a dutiful daughter—indicate, was not easy.[23] The cultural life that Plath probes in such writings is 1950s domestic ideology. The failure of that ideology is the subject of *The Bell Jar.*

Most critics regard *The Bell Jar* as a roman à clef about Plath's own psychic deterioration following her guest editorship at *Mademoiselle,* but it is no less a novel about the limits of postwar feminine identity.[24] That identity, the feminine mystique in Betty Friedan's terms, is an idealized version of domestic, maternal bliss forged in women's magazines and reinforced by psychoanalysis, advertising, and self-help books. Failure to live up to this ideal, according to Friedan, creates a malaise, a "problem that has no name" so pervasive are its effects (19). The novel's heroine, Esther Greenwood, can name her many advantages—good grades, enrollment at an Ivy League school, boyfriends, a loving and protective mother—yet she repudiates them in acts of self-lacerating violence. Her suicide attempt, her contempt for her mother, and her cynicism about American success in general may seem unjustified, given these advantages, yet it is precisely the unnameability of options *beyond* such surface markers that creates Esther's crisis. Her unwillingness to accept either the career opened up through her tenure at *Ladies Day* nor her interest in marrying and becoming Mrs. Buddy Willard leave her in an uncertain psychic and social space. As Esther says, upon watching her friend, Doreen, being seduced by the radio DJ, Lenny, "I felt myself melting into the shadows like the negative of a person I'd never seen before" (8).

Esther consistently defines herself as a shadow or reflection of what she is not: she is "supposed to be having the time of [her] life" in New York, but the experience is a nightmare; unlike her roommate, the busty Doreen, she is "skinny as a boy and barely rippled" (6); she envies the female Russian interpreter in her double-breasted gray suit and wishes she could "crawl into her and spend the rest of my life barking out one idiom after another" (61); she wishes she had a mother like her literary editor, Jay Cee, who would tell her "what to do" (32); she despairs at becoming a famous writer because "I'd never had a love affair or a baby or even seen anybody die" (99). In a famous fantasy, Esther sees her life branching out before her with a series of untenable, unreachable goals: "From the tip of every branch, like a fat purple fig, a wonderful future beckoned and winked. One fig was a husband and a happy home and children, and another fig was a famous poet and another fig was a brilliant professor, and another fig was Ee Gee [Jay Cee, Esther's editorial mentor], the amazing editor and another fig was Europe and Africa and South America . . . and another fig was an Olympic lady crew champion, and beyond and above these were many more figs I couldn't quite make out" (62). This fantasy is the kind of floral display of female professions (complete with fashion accessories) offered in the pages of *Ladies Day*. What we might call Esther's negative identity politics comes from the failure of these female roles to coincide with her own desires. She views the domestic ideology of the 1950s through a bell jar, a distorting glass in which that ideology is defamiliarized.

Although *Ladies Day* magazine is designed to prepare young girls for heterosexual union and motherhood, these crowning moments are presented in the most glaringly negative lights. Womanhood is viewed by Esther as a series of trials (painful intercourse, painful birth, electroshock therapy, alienating suburbia) to be endured. At one point, Buddy Willard, a hospital intern, takes Esther to view a woman giving birth. She is unmoved by the delivery but profoundly disturbed by the drug administered by the obstetrician: "I thought it sounded just like the sort of drug a man would invent. Here was a woman in terrible pain, obviously feeling every bit of it or she wouldn't groan like that, and she would go straight home and start another baby, because the drug would make her forget how bad the pain had been, when all the time, in some secret part of her, that long, blind, doorless and windowless corridor of pain was waiting to open up and shut her in again" (53). Here Friedan's "problem that has no name" is literalized in a painkiller, developed by masculine science, that provides surface relief but stores subterranean pain. And while Esther is indifferent to the spectacle of childbirth, Buddy is sexually aroused by it. He takes Esther back to his room, gives her some wine, and exposes his genitalia to her. Esther's response, however, is as clinical as his display: "The only thing I could think of was turkey neck and turkey gizzards and I felt very depressed" (55). Her cynical views of motherhood and sexuality are not helped by Buddy's subsequent remark that "after I had children I would feel differently, I wouldn't want to write poems any more" (69). Buddy baldly states what Esther understands all too well—that childbearing is not only eased *by* a drug; it *is* a drug that numbs the creative abilities when it is a component of heterosexual marriage.

Esther's coldness to childbirth and sexuality must be set against the backdrop of the narrative itself, told as we learn in the opening pages by a "recovered" Esther who now has a child of her own. But her recovery is the result of an extensive series of purgations by which competing sexualities are excised and heterosexuality asserted. Furthermore, her remarks about her subsequent mental health show that Esther is capable of turning everything into a novel (as she had intended to do during her summer in the suburbs, prior to her attempted suicide). Like the drug that represses pain for a future agony, the present-tense narrator, however secure in her new domestic environment, is not out of the woods. "How did I know that someday—at college, in Europe, somewhere, anywhere—the bell jar, with its stifling distortions, wouldn't descend again" (197). *The Bell Jar* is as much about the narration of female identity as it is a diagnosis of femininity's failure to reproduce one woman in its image.

The production of heterosexuality, via magazines, mothers, and material culture, is countered by the masculine woman in the form of Joan Giddings, a former girlfriend of Buddy Willard's, who is a patient at Esther's sanitarium and who "makes a pass" at her.[25] According to Esther, Joan is her "double . . . specially designed to follow and torment me" (167). She is described as "horsey, with such big teeth and eyes like two gray, goggly pebbles" who hangs on Esther "like a large and breathless fruitfly" (177). Searching for some piano music, Esther comes upon Joan and another female inmate of the sanitarium in bed together. Joan's friendly greeting is met with Esther's disdainful reflection that "her cornhusk voice made me want to puke" (179). No doubt Esther's discomfort is reinforced by Joan's suggestion that after she and her friend are done with their sex play "I'll come play the bottom part with you." The reference is to music, but the sexual double entendre produces a "creepy feeling" that leads her to ask her female psychiatrist, Dr. Noland, "What does a woman see in a woman that she can't see in a man?" "Tenderness," the doctor responds, but Esther is not convinced. When Joan confesses that she "likes" Esther, the latter walks out of the room, saying, "You make me puke, if you want to know" (180). These grotesque versions of sexual panic say a good deal about Esther's attitude toward lesbianism, but they also indicate a trajectory that the novel must follow if it is to represent the successful purgation of same-sex desire from a heterosexist fantasy.

These uncomfortable encounters with Joan's lesbianism prompt Esther to lose her virginity and thus prove her "normalcy." She finds a male partner in Irwin, an assistant professor, whom she meets at Harvard's Widener Library. Their sexual encounter is loveless and painful, turning bloody when Esther begins to hemorrhage. Irwin, unable to deal with the consequences of his act, takes Esther to Joan for help who then takes her to the hospital. To this extent, Dr. Noland's diagnosis of the tenderness that women see in other women is fulfilled. While Esther is being treated, Joan leaves the hospital, and the doctor later reports that she has been found dead, having hanged herself. Joan thus successfully completes a suicide that Esther had unsuccessfully begun. In the larger sexual economy of the novel, heterosexuality must win out while lesbianism must be killed off, lest the bell jar—now fully revealed as the threat of same-sex desire—descend once again. Pat Macpherson summarizes this economy as follows: "If heterosexuality is the natural culmination of psychic development signaling adulthood and the end of adolescence, homosexuality is the corrupt and sickly wrong turn, a dead-end developmentally. . . . Lesbianism threatens the whole project of female adolescence: to secure gender identity irreversibly, by heterosexual initiation into womanhood" (81). If *The Bell Jar* describes a rite of passage from adolescence into womanhood, from psychic distress into mental stability, it is accomplished by relinquishing—literally killing off—the threat of alternative sexual roles.

Poems written contemporaneously with *The Bell Jar* also explore the productive apparatus for femininity:

First, are you our sort of a person?
Do you wear
A glass eye, false teeth or a crutch,
A brace or a hook,
Rubber breasts or a rubber crotch,

Stitches to show something's missing? No, no? Then
How can we give you a thing?

    (221)

In "The Applicant," Plath adopts the persona of an employer interviewing a female applicant for a job.[26] The position in question necessitates the adoption of limbs and appendages that will complete the unformed applicant. The interviewer wants to make sure that the applicant is "our sort of person," which means that she must conform to ideas of feminine "lack." Like a paper doll, she is offered various forms of clothing as prostheses to gender. Marriage is figured as a kind of ultimate domestic convenience:

Open your hand.
Empty? Empty. Here is a hand

To fill it and willing
To bring teacups and roll away headaches
And do whatever you tell it.
Will you marry it?
It is guaranteed

To thumb shut your eyes at the end
And dissolve of sorrow.
>   (221)

What had begun as an address to the applicant herself gradually evolves into an address to the prospective groom seeking a marriage partner. Now the employer turns from selling the applicant on the job to advertising the wonders of the bride to the husband:

It can sew, it can cook,
It can talk, talk, talk.

It works, there is nothing wrong with it
You have a hole, it's a poultice.
You have an eye, it's an image.
My boy, it's your last resort.
Will you marry it, marry it, marry it.
>   (222)

The final line is an imperative disguised as a question: "Will you marry it, marry it, marry it." Within the commercial idiom that the poem adopts, marriage and commodification are one in the same. What links the two is a set of identifiable gender characteristics that the poem, by its mixing of pronouns, deconstructs. Inevitably, this poem has been read as an allegory of Plath's marriage to Ted Hughes, a dystopic account of her "failure" as a proper wife. But it is no less an adoption of the masculine voice of the marketplace in which sexual roles are commodities that produce a whole person. Within the consumerist domestic ideology of the 1950s, identities are equated with kitchen gadgets.

"The Applicant" is one of numerous poems spoken by a male voice of authority whose creation is a cyborg female, part human and part science. One of Plath's favorite rhetorical ploys is to describe this creation in medical terms, the male doctor as an artist of flesh, the patient a helpless putty for the sculptor. In "The Surgeon at 2 a.m." (1961) the male voice of the surgeon occupies a godlike position of authority, not unlike Plath's Nazi doctors, men in black, and Frankensteins.[27] The opening stanza announces the synthetic quality of the hospital environment, one that she described in "clinical" detail:

The white light is artificial, and hygienic as heaven.
The microbes cannot survive it.
They are departing in their transparent garments, turned aside
From the scalpels and the rubber hands.
The scalded sheet is a snowfield, frozen and peaceful.
The body under it is in my hands.
As usual there is no face. A lump of Chinese white
With seven holes thumbed in. The soul is another light.
I have not seen it; it does not fly up.
Tonight it has receded like a ship's light.
　　　(171)

In these lines, the face has been reduced to a mask out of Chinese opera, with "seven holes thumbed in." It is lost in a sea of hygienic whiteness, virginal and cold yet as full of potential as the artist's blank canvas. The body is an Edenic landscape upon which the Adamic surgeon organizes a chaotic, feminized nature, "a garden . . . with—tubers and fruits / Oozing their jammy substances, / a mat of roots" (171). If the surgeon is godlike in his ability to remove himself from concerns of men he is also secular in his belief in the perfection of science, one for whom the soul must recede "like a ship's light" in order for him to operate.

The biblical references to creation and mastery are flanked by another set of images relating to secular history. The godlike surgeon respects classical civilization:

How I admire the Romans—
Aqueducts, the Baths of Carcalla, the eagle nose!
The body is a Roman thing.
It has shut its mouth on the stone pill of repose.

It is a statue the orderlies are wheeling off.
I have perfected it.
I am left with an arm or a leg,
A set of teeth, or stones
To rattle in a bottle and take home,
And tissue in slices—a pathological salami.
Tonight the parts are entombed in an icebox

Tomorrow they will swim
In vinegar like saints' relics.
Tomorrow the patient will have a clean, pink plastic limb.

(171)

Here Plath mocks the voice of scientific rationality that gains legitimacy for its work by quoting from the classics. The surgeon's admiration for Roman civilization signifies his enlightened sense of power, one that he exploits by treating the body as a "statue" or work of art. By reifying the body into an object, the surgeon perverts an enlightenment ideology of progress, based as it is on references to Greece and Rome. When the surgeon claims, the "blood is a sunset. I admire it / I am up to my elbows in it," he shows the extent to which he is implicated in world historical violence (I am up to my elbows in blood) while transforming the body into a garden of innocence. As with "The Applicant," Plath regards the outcome of commercial or medical art as the production of a "clean, pink plastic limb" that can be fetishized like a saint's bones—or worn like a prosthesis.

Of course, this is extreme hyperbole—a rhetoric of performance rather than description. Surgeons are hardly all Mengeles, but their intimate relationship to female biology provides Plath with a capacious rhetoric for the ways medical science is implicated in female biology. Although "The Surgeon at 2 a.m." does not name the gender of the patient, references to Edenic gardens and "mat of roots" suggests that the surgeon's material is not gender-neutral. This fact becomes explicit in another poem from the same year, "Face Lift," in which a female friend's cosmetic surgery permits Plath to reflect on the links between feminine vanity and masculine science. Although she herself never underwent cosmetic surgery, Plath's ability to identify with one who did permits her to interrogate the pursuit of feminine beauty from within. The speaker imagines herself "Nude as Cleopatra" in her hospital gown, being given anesthesia that erases her "like chalk on a blackboard." The woman with a face lift is reborn, her former face trapped "in some laboratory jar":

Now she's done for, the dewlapped lady
I watched settle, line by line, in my mirror—
Old sock-face, sagged on a darning egg.
They've trapped her in some laboratory jar.
Let her die there, or wither incessantly for the next fifty years,
Nodding and rocking and fingering her thin hair.
Mother to myself, I wake swaddled in gauze,
Pink and smooth as a baby.

(156)

Here the face lift has become an act of self-mutilation that is also self-generating. She wakes "swaddled in gauze, / Pink and smooth as a baby." Given Plath's tendency to demonize surgeons and doctors, "Face Lift" turns agency away from the doctor to the one seeking a new face. Self-creation—the making of art—is also self-mutilation, the killing off of "old sock-face" in order to rise from the ashes of a former self.

What these poems about the medicalized female body signify is a positioning in which Plath participates in the male gaze enough to objectify women. And because she is a woman herself, any pleasure derived from such objectification is experienced as a guilty pleasure. Woman as strip tease artist, whore, slut, bad girl, failed daughter are staples of Plath's iconography, not because she identifies with their victim status, but because to see them at all requires occupying the place of the male. As Jacqueline Rose summarizes this dynamic, "weighed down by [sexist platitudes] she moves into the protest of [proto feminist revolt], only to find herself circling back to, rejoining, the masculine sexual sub-text of the very ideology to which she objects" (117). This refracted vision, like Bishop's mirrors and Rich's pronominal play, means that even poems written from a female standpoint may be ventriloquized versions of a male voice.

An elaborate working-out of this problematic can be found in "The Fearful," a poem that deals with the breakdown of her marriage to Ted Hughes. Its focus is an infamous phone call that Hughes's lover, Assia Wevill, made to the household, prompting Sylvia in a fit of rage to tear the phone out of the wall. The event appears in a number of poems, including "Daddy" ("The telephone's off at its root"), "The Other," and "Words Heard, by Accident, over the Phone." According to Anne Stevenson, "Assia phoned Ted through a male colleague at her office," a ruse that brought Hughes to the phone, via Plath, but which also established the fishing metaphor that dominates the poem (251):

This man makes a pseudonym
And crawls behind it like a worm.

This woman on the telephone
Says she is a man, not a woman.

The mask increases, eats the worm,
Stripes for mouth and eyes and nose,

The voice of the woman hollows—
More and more like a dead one,

Worms in the glottal stops.
She hates

The thought of a baby—
Stealer of cells, stealer of beauty—

She would rather be dead than fat,
Dead and perfect, like Nefertiti,

Hearing the fierce mask magnify
The silver limbo of each eye

Where the child can never swim,
Where there is only him and him.
    (256)

The act of masking one's voice, of covering one's gender, provides an image of deceit that has mortal consequences. The woman who uses a man's voice for access to the other man is a woman who is complicit in a sexual vortex; she has taken the bait even as she attempts to "fish" herself. The worm she eats now begins to gnaw from within, a reverse image of fertility that dominates the rest of the poem.

In the second half, the identification between the "other woman" and the speaker begins to emerge. At exactly the midpoint of the poem, "she" takes over from her pseudonymous version. The "worms" that invaded the voice of the other woman are now replaced by babies and other signs of fertility. Unlike the speaker, the other woman "hates // The thought of a baby" and would "rather be dead than fat." Plath, mother of two children, casts herself in the role of the life-giving, protective mother against the "dead and perfect" Egyptian queen, Nefertiti. Plath never uses the first-person pronoun, however, permitting both women to revolve in the same orbit of masculine authority, one given explicit point in the last line: "Where there is only him and him."

In one of the poem's most difficult images, "hearing the fierce mask magnify / The silver limbo of each eye," Plath fuses sensory realms of sound and sight to imply that the voice of deception reinforces a synthetic world in which there is only "him and him." Read as an allegory of Hughes's adulterous relationship with Assia, this means that the other woman can only focus on the male object of desire, not on the procreative familial life he shares with Sylvia. Read as an allegory of Plath's own gender uncertainty, the lines suggest a more "fearful" train of thought—that in a world where there is only "him and him" all subject-positions are "pseudonyms," all claims for a more natural, nurturing position as woman are subsumed in the "fierce mask" of patriarchal authority. Sylvia Plath, who had adopted a pseudonym herself as Victoria Lukas (in *The Bell Jar*), knew what it meant to distance herself from own personal vindictiveness and could identify with acts of mediated speech.

Confronted with the excesses of such vindictiveness, critics have deployed various forms of myth criticism—some of them based on Plath's own interests in Jung, Freud, and Robert Graves. In these instances, Plath's rage and anger involve the woman as bitch goddess, Medusa, or destroying angel of the house who reclaims her rightful site of power and creativity. As a historical myth, it involves the notion that cults of nature and fecundity are overridden by Christian prudery and patriarchy. In order for female power to reassert itself, it must become phallic, take on the destructive—as well as creative powers—of man, producing terror and pity in its beholder. But this myth, Freudian to its core, is underwritten by the phallus itself, configured in terms of a dyadic structure of masculine and feminine in which indeterminate gender choices are left out. In "The Hanging Man," for instance, a figure from the tarot pack, used as well by Eliot in *The Waste Land*, is transformed from a myth of redemptive fertility (Christ as hanged man) to an allegory of female masculinity:

By the roots of my hair some god got hold of me.
I sizzled in his blue volts like a desert prophet.

The nights snapped out of sight like a lizard's eyelid:
A world of bald white days in a shadeless socket.

A vulturous boredom pinned me in this tree.
If he were I, he would do what I did.

     (142)

Plath is here remembering her sessions of electroshock therapy administered following her first suicide attempt. Unlike Eliot's fisher king, wasting by the side of the dull canal, this figure "sizzle[s] in his blue volts like a desert prophet." Plath's rewriting of modernist fertility myth fuses the suffering god on the tree and god of electroshock therapy. The price of prophecy is torture (just ask the Cumaean Sibyl). Yet, as Plath implies, if the tables were turned and god were in her shoes, "he would do what I did." Such acknowledgements of complicity in Plath are more than confessions of guilt; they are representations of pleasure. Faced with the "vulturous boredom" of female subservience, better to be a prophet and sizzle.

Writing about Sylvia Plath's poetry in terms of female masculinity runs certain risks, as Jacqueline Rose discovered upon the publication of her book, *The Haunting of Sylvia Plath,* in 1992. Arguing that a poem like "The Rabbit Catcher" displays the author's uncertainty about Plath's sexual object choice, Rose incurred the wrath of Olwyn and Ted Hughes. In her book, Rose suggested that the opening lines of the poem display Plath's characteristic view of powerful nature, ravishing the speaker. But the question of who is ravishing whom is not resolvable in heteronormative terms. The line "the wind gagging my mouth with my own blown hair" could render an act of oral sex experienced both by a male or female body. "Who—man or woman—is tasting whom? . . . For Freud, such fantasies, such points of uncertainty, are the regular unconscious subtexts—for all of us—of the more straightforward reading, the more obvious narratives of stable sexual identity which we write" (138).

Responding to Rose's reading, Ted Hughes wrote an angry letter to the *TLS*, arguing that "Professor Rose distorts, re-invents etc. Sylvia Plath's 'sexual identity' with an abandon I could hardly believe—presenting her in a role that I vividly felt to be humiliating to Sylvia Plath's children" (15). In an interview with Janet Malcolm, Rose makes it clear she does not equate the various personae of Plath's poetry with Plath herself: "I'm in no sense speaking of Plath's lived sexual identity in the world about which I know nothing. I'm only discussing fantasy" (149). But of course "only" fantasy hinges on social realities that produce it. Hughes must stick to the fantasy that his children could be harmed by Rose's reading, just as Rose herself must defend herself by separating "fantasy" from Plath's biography. The fear that Plath might have been representing a sexual act as anything other than heterosexual offends the father and former husband, but what Rose calls the "dangerous pleasures she has allowed herself to enjoy" cannot be erased by making them conform to a heterosexual allegory. Like the editor whom I invoked at the outset of this chapter, Hughes in his various responses to critics, biographers, and journalists, has protected the "literary" worth of Plath by denying the very personal ambiguities that make it literary.[28] The ghost in the closet is not Plath's animus toward men—this is an easy mythological trope—but that she could identify so richly with masculine subject-positions. This would take Hughes's own role as power source, father, and lover, away from him and remove it to Sylvia's side of the bed. Hughes may be trying to protect his children in an odd appropriation of maternity, but he is also trying to protect himself as the arbiter of the sexual politics of the Plath myth. Controlling *that* became a lifelong preoccupation.

READING PRACTICES

In fact, Ted Hughes's attempt to protect his ex-wife from mythologizing has affected the writing of this chapter. In his *TLS* article, Hughes imagines future scholars who, upon reading Rose's fantastic interpretation of "The Rabbit Catcher," would build upon its homoerotic thesis and broadcast it as truth. "For most unsophisticated readers, Professor Rose's 'fantasy' will be an attempted interpretation of the truth—therefore a 'fact.' As part of the teaching of Sylvia Plath's poetry world-wide, such a titillating 'revelation' will become, for almost everybody taught, a kind of 'fact' " (15). Rose's "titillating 'revelation' " that Plath may be imagining a sexual position other than missionary worries the father of two children (now in their thirties) who might be shocked by such facts. By furthering the erotic duplicity of Plath's language in "The Rabbit Catcher" (and other poems) I, as a reader of Rose's book, must be participating in her fantasy.

Hughes is correct to think that interpretation is at the center of the issue. Plath's biography *has* been the subject of her poetry since the beginning, and exegetes have created a mythic figure out of her words. That mythic figure could be called "Bad Heterosexuality," and it can be used to perpetuate a view of woman as avenging angel, Medusa, Lady Macbeth. Hughes prefers this version to the one that would introduce lesbianism into the picture. For Hughes, interpretation is an idle game practiced by heartless leeches on the body of a real woman. Yet Plath's poetry trades in precisely such (gothic) images to interpret male power as totalizing—so totalizing that she must use "his" voice to say so. Thus what Hughes attempts to censor is not Plath's same-sex desires for women but her role as a speaker and sexual subject outside of the oedipalized story he and other critics have prepared for her.

I began this section by speaking of Adrienne Rich's "Diving into the Wreck" and its dramatizing (and grammatizing) of gender ambiguities through the manipulation of pronouns. The incommensurability between one's sex and one's gender identifications creates an impossible sentence—one that poetry is uniquely qualified to speak. As I have indicated with reference to Plath, that incommensurability was channeled into a narrative of pathology and medical health whereby the aesthetic offers a compensatory response. In the case of Elizabeth Bishop, such incommensurability is finessed through her vaunted formal control and embodied in the fantastic armadillos, man-moths, rainbow fish, and roosters that populate her poetic menagerie. As a woman wanting not to be confused with "women" but wanting to express her desires for them, Bishop chose to create an aesthetic closet within which those desires could be mediated. Or perhaps it would be better to say that the aesthetic closet was already in place in the New Critical 1940s and 1950s to be the arena in which gender was negotiated.

An earlier generation of mannish women—modernists like Gertrude Stein, Djuna Barnes, Natalie Barney, Radclyffe Hall, Jane Heap, H.D.—seem not to have worried so much about their "definitive haircuts." To some extent modernist female masculinity was protected by class differences that permitted a certain latitude of acceptance around gender ambiguity, often covered by terms like "eccentricity" (in the case of Stein) or "androgyny" (in the case of H.D. or Barney). Nor did modernist women authors (of a certain class) worry so much about finding formal solutions—"asbestos gloves"—for handling dangerous materials. They were riding the fast moving train called modernism, throwing categories to the wind. Mina Loy, in her "Feminist Manifesto," argues that for "the man who lives a life in which his activities conform to a social code which is a protectorate of the feminine element is no longer masculine. The woman who adapts herself to a theoretical valuation of her sex as a *relative impersonality* is not yet feminine" (269). This is not to say that these women were not exposed to homophobia, but they did live in supportive social contexts (salons, companionate marriages, bisexual liaisons) where gender difference could be accommodated.

Citing masculinity, as I have said throughout this book, is to cite zones of power. A corollary proposition might be that citing female masculinity cites fissures in those zones of power. Hence, textuality makes legible what must be hidden from view, what constitutes visibility itself. When masculinity appears in women, power is challenged (or threatened, depending on your point of view) and orders of domestic normalcy undermined. If Mildred Pierce strikes off on her own, she must be brought back to heterosexual dependency by the end of the movie. The restoration of her middle-class status is a requirement of her legibility as a woman, and her brief foray into economic independence must be squelched. A more familiar version of this threat for intellectuals of the 1950s was Eleanor Roosevelt whose mannish dress and demeanor often reinforced attacks on her support of civil rights and other progressive causes. The fact that she was a mannish woman whose (crippled) husband's progressive social programs during the 1930s were being deplored in the 1950s was no small factor in the ways that female masculinity was kept in check. As Judith Halberstam notes, masculinity is often made "legible" when it leaves the male body and appears in women or when its inadequacy as a social sign is marked *by* women, as in the case of *Kiss Me Deadly*. It is this legibility of gender as a set of roles that is often marked in poetry by women for whom the assumption of power is explained as artisanal control or, in Plath's case, an aesthetics of rage.

Although I have deployed the rhetoric of critical gender studies to expose female masculinity in Bishop and Plath, I want to stress the role of hermeneutics in studying gender. One cannot speak of these two poets without referring to their importance within an academic, literary history whose reading practices were, to some extent, honed on their work. Their inevitable appearance in the high school anthology to which I referred in my introduction is an extension of new critical values, yet their connection to another woman poet in that same anthology—Adrienne Rich—must be read by a different optic: the feminism that dared not speak its name when Elizabeth Bishop was first corresponding with Marianne Moore. Developing interpretive methods for analyzing women poets must include the meanings that swarm around pronouns ("I am she: I am he") or the historical reasons for an ungrammatical sentence.

7

Hunting among Stones: Poetry, Pedagogy, and the Pacific Rim

To name it now so as not to repeat history in oblivion
> Theresa Hak Kyung Cha, *Dictee*

We are all members of the community of nations surrounding the Pacific.
The Pacific has become the 20th century's economic fountain of youth.
> George Schultz

FROM ORIENTALISM TO PACIFIC RIM

According to a well-known story, when J. Robert Oppenheimer witnessed the first atomic bomb blast in the Nevada desert, he quoted a passage from the *Bhagavad-Gita:* "If the radiance of a thousand suns were to burst into the sky, that would be like the splendor of the Mighty One . . . I am become Death, destroyer of worlds" (Canaday 183–84).[1] Like many intellectuals—and scientists—of his generation, Oppenheimer had been trained in the classics. He knew seven languages, including Sanskrit, and was fond of spending his leisure time while at Los Alamos hiking in the woods and writing poetry. His fusion of the apocalyptic and the oriental in marking the Trinity blast signals the end of modernity's claim to Enlightenment reason through the application of science to humanist ends. It also marks a shift in modernism's poetic project, for which quotations from the Upanishads, Confucius, or Japanese haiku were a constitutive feature. We do not tend to think of the two spheres—atomic fission and orientalism—as compatible, but in the years following the Trinity blast those two areas would become increasingly linked as the cold war divided East and West along geopolitical lines.

It is worth remembering the close relationship between the discourses of nuclear physics and oriental philology when considering the role of poetry within U.S. education as it was transformed by the bomb. In chapter 3 I discussed the links between orientalism and western literature, but I want here to show how two writers self-consciously contested orientalist cultural authority through a pedagogical poetics at odds with official literary study of the period. Within the cold war university the arts and humanities often served as bucolic outposts for disinterested study, contrasting with the applied sciences, physics, and math that dominated education of the 1940s through 1960s.[2] The New Criticism, with its emphasis on close reading of texts and its rejection of history and authorial biography, provided a practical pedagogy for the 2.25 million veterans who entered college on the G.I. Bill. Students who had recently "made" history in the Pacific and European theaters were now being asked to forget it in the theaters of Elizabethan and Jacobean drama. "A poem must not mean but be" or "poetry makes nothing happen" were the consoling bromides of a literary establishment with its head in the sand. New Critical theory, with poetry as its test case for literary indeterminacy, underwrote the disengagement of literature from history and provided what Andrew Ross has called a *cordon sanitaire* of "affirmative culture" in the midst of Eisenhower era consensus (43).

Poets who challenged this hermeneutic model, like Charles Olson, did so not by returning history to the poem (Eliot, after all, had advocated just such a practice) but by making historical speculation its subject. A poem like "The Kingfishers," written in 1949 at the dawn of the cold war, studies meso-American culture through accounts of indigenous peoples, trade, and archaeological remains. Olson's curiosity about early civilizations foregrounds his own acts of ruminating and reflecting as a counter to modernist attempts by Eliot and Pound to circumscribe repetition in history. His title inverts Eliot's "fisher king" as an ahistorical principle of Christian redemption, returning the kingfisher to its (no less redemptive) cultural role within Mayan civilization.[3] But Olson is betraying more than an anthropological interest in early peoples; he is using them to reflect on more recent global changes in Asia and the formation of spaces not yet determined by the West. Olson sees Mao's cultural revolution, recently triumphant over Chiang Kai-shek's nationalist forces, as offering hope for a social revolution with cultural matters first and foremost. But he also envisions East and West joined around principles of social change rather than separated by cold war superpower rhetoric.

Olson's "The Kingfishers" marks an early stage in what Christopher Connery, Arif Dirlik, Bruce Cumings, and others have called a Pacific Rim discourse, the second stage of which is provided by Theresa Hak Kyung Cha's *Dictee*, written shortly before her death in 1982. Both poems critique earlier orientalizing tendencies within modernism—Olson to Pound's use of Confucius and the Chinese character, Cha to the collusion of the United States with Japan in the colonization of Korea. Both poems quote extensively from historical sources, utilizing the materiality of documents, encyclopedia entries, photographs, and diaries to stress the inscripted form of historical representation. Most important for our concern with the cold war university is the fact that both are pedagogical poems that stress the role of education in producing citizen subjects. Finally, both focus on a key moment in cold war history—1949—when the cultural revolution in China and the Korean War brought a new focus to Asia, no longer as a site of exoticism and oriental desire but as an economic resource that needed to be contained—and exploited.

These two stages of cold war history—containment and Pacific Rim—offer a useful stratification of the postmodern as a cultural dominant under late capitalism. Olson's poem was written in the discursive arena of the emerging cold war when foreign policy was dictated by metaphors of disease (infection, containment) and contract (consensus). It is a binary system in which perceived threats to national security, like those in Cuba, Chile, North Korea, and other decolonized regions were regarded by the State Department as satellites on one side of a binary opposition. The development of East Asian area studies, heavily financed by the CIA, Ford, and Carnegie Foundations, played a crucial role in furthering national security interests within the university, treating geographical regions as potential markets or unstable political entities orbiting around one or the other superpower.

Cha's poem was written within a moment of heightened concern about the shift in global power and international relations in Asia. The Pacific Rim emerges in the mid-1970s as a new stage of cold war discourse that marks the Pacific as an entrepreneurial zone, what George Schultz called an "economic fountain of youth" for a global economy. As a metaphor derived from the geological and tectonic circle of volcanoes that ring the area, the phrase implies a kind of centerless network anchored by the U.S./Japanese entrepreneurial link and sustained by the Four Tigers (Taiwan, Hong Kong, South Korea, Singapore) and other newly industrialized countries (NICs). As Connery points out, Pacific Rim discourse does not depend on a cold war dyad, an othering process "grounded in specific histories of colonialism or imperialism" (32). Rather, it presumes a kind of "metonymic equivalence" in which each element is tied to every other in a mutually reinforcing support network, "neither the center of a hegemonic power nor the imagined fulcrum of a 'balance of power'" (32). It is within this metonymic network that *Dictee* is written, a text that exposes the history of colonial damage to a specific region—Korea—

and to its language, culture, and possibilities for empowerment. Although the Pacific Rim is usually synonymous with transnational corporations, *Dictee* poses an alternative form of "in-corporation" whose object is a physical body and a shared history of colonial rupture, migration, and dislocation. Cha is less interested in identifying sources of exploitation as in exposing the discursive means by which power inscribes itself on individual citizens. Olson writes from outside of the system he critiques, "offshore by islands in the blood," as he says at the opening to the *Maximus Poems*, better to see its effects and assess the damage. Cha writes from within the power matrix, utilizing a "broken tongue. / Pidgeon. Semblance of speech" to contest the instrumental language of colonial power (75).

Cha's ability to write from within matrices of power is gained not simply by her position as a displaced Korean citizen but as a woman whose voice has been culturally silenced and whose body has often been the site for the writing of national imperatives. To contest this subjugation, Cha creates an archive of resistant women, both Asian and occidental, who challenge patriarchal religious, political, and educational systems. Where the question of a woman's voice is a centerpiece of *Dictee*, Olson's poem remains silent on matters of gender. As I have stated throughout this book silence is never silent but often productive of homosocial alliances and genealogies. While Olson might not appear to be concerned with gendered features of conquest or revolution, his establishment of kin with various father figures—Pound, Eliot, Norbert Wiener, Rimbaud—suggests that the new intellectual formations he envisions are shaped around an oedipal model. Thus we could see the two long poems as providing cultural bookends to the cold war in which the shift from a Manichean superpower conflict to decentralized global reach occurs along gendered lines. And to continue the metaphor, the texts between these two bookends are narratives of an emerging Pacific entrepreneurial zone, distinct from what Ed Dorn calls "the North Atlantic Turbine" of late-nineteenth-century industrial capitalism. At the same time, the poems acknowledge that the Pacific region is a *product* of that turbine, indistinguishable from Euro-American interests, fantasies, and projects, a Pacific, as Arif Dirlik points out, "incorporated into the narrative of capitalism . . . rather than the other way around" ("Introduction" 5).

"I HUNT AMONG STONES": "THE KINGFISHERS"

I am interested in a Melville who was long-eyed enough to understand the Pacific as part of our geography, another West, prefigured in the plains, antithetical.

Charles Olson, *Call Me Ishmael*

"The Kingfishers" depicts the Pacific region through several overlapping pedagogical frames—textual, disciplinary, and pragmatic—that contribute to its composition and large-scale meaning. The textual frame includes the poem's publication in magazines, anthologies, and books and its circulation within a (counter) culture of readers; the disciplinary frame includes the poem's participation in institutional contexts of learning and knowledge production; the third, pragmatic frame involves the poem's function as a pedagogical instrument, its claims to instruct through a particular curriculum and rhetoric. This last frame would also include the poem's proximity to Olson's other writings of the late 1940s and early 1950s—*Call Me Ishmael*, "Projective Verse," and "Mayan Letters"—that also address the Pacific region and the pedagogical potential of verse. One might add a fourth frame as well—Olson's own history as a scholar and teacher who wrote his M.A. thesis on Herman Melville at Wesleyan and who studied in the American Civilization program at Harvard with F. O. Matthiessen, Perry Miller, J. Ellery Sedgewick, Frederick Merk, and others. And, in this context, we might remember that Olson was beginning the first of several visits to Black Mountain College where he would, in 1951, become its rector.[4]

The textual frame for the "Kingfishers" includes its first publication in the *Montevallo Review*, the editor of which, Robert Payne, was beginning his long career as an Asianist, author of numerous studies of China and someone who had interviewed Mao in the early 1940s. According to Robert von Hallberg, Olson owned a prepublication copy of Payne's biography of Mao, in which Olson underlined passages that showed the communist leader's interest in Western as well as Eastern thinkers and his support of a cultural, as well as political, revolution (21). Saying something positive about Mao was dangerous business in the early days of the anticommunist witch-hunts, but Payne's optimistic assessment of the Chinese communist leader reinforced Olson's interest and provided his poem with a sympathetic reader and first publisher.

"The Kingfishers" reached a far wider audience, however, as the inaugural poem in Donald Allen's *The New American Poetry* (NAP). In this 1960 volume, "The Kingfishers" established the literary heritage of Pound and Williams that dominated the anthology and that played a key role in launching a new poetics. The volume's cover, with its schematic rendering of the American flag, reminds us that the NAP was engaged in a project of national redefinition as much as a poetic one. It was, as Alan Golding has pointed out, "the single most influential poetry anthology of the post-World War II period," not because it was used in college classrooms, but because it collected the voices of several anti-academic schools and movements—Beat, Black Mountain, New York school, San Francisco Renaissance—that had been fueling a youth revolution in the late 1950s ("*NAP* Revisited" 180). The flag on the cover was partly patriotic but mostly satiric because it marked a set of alternative political and social positions to American consensus that would not be found in the reigning college anthology of the period, Brooks's and Warren's *Understanding Poetry*. As Golding and others have indicated, it was an era of "anthology wars" where poetic turf was being defended for the hearts and minds of English teachers in the expanded educational system of the 1960s.

The disciplinary frame for "The Kingfishers" is that of cold war area studies and the social sciences more generally. Originally developed during World War II as information gathering on specific geographical regions as well as language instruction for military advisers and diplomats, area studies emerged as the principle intellectual legacy of the Office of Strategic Services (OSS) and the Office of War Information (OWI), for which Olson worked during the war in its Foreign Language division. The need for more precise data on countries with which the United States anticipated having contact—and conflict—drove the government, with the help of various foundations (Ford, Rockefeller, and the Carnegie Corporation) to subsidize academic programs in specific regions but to do so without giving the appearance of sponsoring overt propaganda efforts. As we now know, through the work of Frances Stoner Saunders, Bruce Cumings, Sigmund Diamond, and Emmanuel Wallerstein, area studies were heavily subsidized by the federal government and were enlisted in containing—rather than studying—Soviet influence. Among the most important such institutes—Harvard's Russian Research Center, Columbia's Russian Research Center, or the Association for Asian Studies (the AAS was the first area organization in the United States)—contributed to the expansion of the social sciences and international relations in the three decades after the war and continue today in the post–cold war period in "development studies" or international relations. As Cumings points out, the idea of area studies, particularly in regards to Asia, "was to bring contemporary social science theory to bear on the non western world, rather than to pursue themes of oriental studies often through philology" (177). Far from providing disinterested scholarly research on lesser known regions, area studies programs collaborated with the federal government in gathering intelligence on communist influence and, secondarily, monitoring curricula and the ideological leanings of academics engaged in teaching courses in Russia, China, and the Third World.

Olson's formal academic training at Wesleyan and Harvard precedes the formal establishment of cold war area studies, but by the time he was working on "The Kingfishers" these programs were in place. Furthermore, Olson's graduate work on American literature and culture reflected the sorts of anthropological and historical work that characterized the emerging field of American studies. His M.A. thesis (1933) and later Ph.D. work (1936–39) on Melville's *Moby Dick* were radical in their challenge to disciplinary boundaries of literary studies, drawing upon histories of whaling, exploration, Native Americans, American history, economics, anthropology, and South Pacific voyages. American Studies, while technically not an "area study," such as Russian or East Asia studies, was nevertheless implicated in State Department initiatives and received corporate sponsorship and foundation monies. One of the founders of American studies, Norman Holmes Pearson at Yale University, was a friend of Bryher, H.D., William Carlos Williams, Ezra Pound, and other modernists and had been a member of the counterintelligence office of the OSS during the war. At Yale, and with the backing of the CIA, he helped found the first program in American studies and recruited a number of operatives for the CIA. His linkage of American studies with intelligence work was prompted by a feeling that it "allowed us to understand our unique fitness for our postwar role as the world's governor, and encouraged a finer appreciation of our cultural sophistication among the ruled" (Saunders 238). I am not suggesting that Olson's interdisciplinary interests in Latin America or China are tainted by such collusions of academia and intelligence, but I would say that this work must be set against the backdrop of increased support for history and the social sciences within the academy. Olson was the beneficiary of regional studies of non-Western, developing countries that formed a contrast to more ahistorical treatments of "the oriental mind" or the "theme of God in *Moby Dick*" that were common in literary study in U.S. universities.

If the research and institutional basis for "The Kingfishers" was implicated in issues of national security, the poem's pedagogical frame was rooted in the very opposite. This third frame—what I am calling the pragmatic— refers to the poem's address to a reader, its attempt to instruct by providing an alternative scholarly practice to that of the dominant literary culture. Olson saw "The Kingfishers" as an assault on Eliot's *The Waste Land* and, by extension, on the ahistorical poetics advocated in Eliot's essays. In this regard, Olson was following in the footsteps of William Carlos Williams, who had inveighed against Eliot in work from *Spring and All* through *Paterson*. A good deal of Olson's animus was directed against what he perceived as Eliot's evacuation of history from poetry by transforming the local into the symbolic. Olson's anti–*Waste Land* pedagogical imperative can be found in any number of his early works. *Call Me Ishmael,* his 1947 book on Melville, is an idiosyncratic mixture of sociological data (New England labor history, fishing demographics, political economy of whaling), theories of American history, and hunches presented in an elliptical, epigrammatic style. Its thesis, radical for its time, is that Ahab's megalomaniacal pursuit of the white whale is a symptom of the rapaciousness of nineteenth-century capitalism reinforced by America's territorial expanse. Melville, according to Olson, saw whaling as the first American industry, employing thousands of laborers at subpar wages in horrendous working conditions for a commodity—sperm oil—that fueled many corporations in the early republic. Furthermore, this industry existed far from the New England and mid-Atlantic business centers, becoming the nineteenth-century version of outsourced labor and deterritorialized capital that dominates more recent economics. "The Pacific as sweatshop" is Olson's collapsed formula for describing relations among the sailors of the *Pequod* (*Collected Prose* 26). As my epigraph for this section indicates, Melville's Pacific was also part of U.S. geography, "antithetical" to the western plains but no less implicated in the expansionist tendencies that mark American imperialism from the 1848 war with Mexico on.

If *Call Me Ishmael* was Olson's contribution to literary historicism, "Projective Verse" provided the means. As I have already pointed out, "Projective Verse" was less one person's document than a collaborative effort among several interlocutors (Robert Creeley, Kitsue Kitasono, Frances Boldereff) with whom Olson was corresponding during the late 1940s. One of its most important claims for pedagogy is that once the poet enters the field of the poem, he (and, for Olson, the poet was always masculine) "can go by no track other than the one the poem under hand declares" (*Collected Prose* 240). Most critics have related Olson's concept of field to Action Painting or field theory in mathematics, but given his interest in anthropology and archaeology during this period one would also add fieldwork as a model for poetic composition.[5] A related claim is that by constructing the poetic line around muscular and physiological ratios, the poet establishes a new stance toward reality in the world at large. Here, Olson is advancing a thesis, proposed by Edward Sapir and Benjamin Lee Whorf, that changes within language affect changes in consciousness. By conceiving the poetic line around speculative acts, by shaping its contours according to bodily movements (breathing, looking, walking), the poet seeks to bridge the gap between aesthetic and physical universes. His utopian hope is that once "the projective purpose of the act of verse is recognized, the content does—it will—change" (247). These various features of the essay (its collaborative composition, its model of fieldwork, its linguistic determinism) propose an ideal of the poem not as a cultural repository but as a mode of instruction and goad for further speculation.

These three frames—the textual, disciplinary, and pragmatic—allow us to see "The Kingfisher" as part of a multifaceted response to genteel literary culture whose separation of literature from social or biographical forces was the reigning orthodoxy in English departments. Against this static model, Olson proposes his primary ethos: what "does not change / is the will to change" (*Collected Poems* 86). Guy Davenport sees these lines as a rough translation of Heraclitus's Fragment 23, which he translates as "change alone is unchanging" (252). Ralph Maud feels that the lines are actually Olson's own words as derived from a longer prose fragment concerning the poet's withdrawal from a political career in Democratic party politics to one in poetry (36–37). Olson had worked in the Roosevelt administration throughout the 1940s and was active in the campaign to place Henry Wallace on the ballot as vice president for the president's fourth term. Portions of "The Kingfishers" were written after attending the 1948 Democratic convention, where he went to support the presidential campaign for Claude Pepper of Florida. With the failure of both the Wallace and the Pepper presidential bids of 1948 and with Olson's increasing cynicism about bureaucratic politics, the time was right for a change. Olson inverts Nietzsche's "will to power," which he had seen firsthand in Washington, to become a "will to change," a respect for process and organic growth based on quotidian moments.

One such quotidian moment, addressed in the poem's subsequent lines, is a remark heard at a Washington party spoken by a mysterious guest named Fernand: "who cares / for their feathers / now" (86). Fernand is talking about the kingfisher, a bird highly prized by the ancient Maya and a valuable means of exchange in meso-American culture. Fernand leaves the party with his question unanswered, but Olson uses the poem to provide his own extended response to the question, showing the extent of his care for the feathers and through such care his access to larger issues of cultural decay and rebirth.[6] This dialogic quality of the poem—the poet's response to a question—is an important element to the poem's pedagogical meaning because it shows the poet teaching through his own process of learning. In answering the question, the poem draws on encyclopedia entries on Mayan civilization, Plutarch's essay on the Delphic stone, an account of the nesting habits of birds, Mao's 1948 address to the Communist Party, Prescott's account of New World conquest, and early cybernetic theories of Norbert Wiener. As with his speculations on the meaning of the whale in *Moby Dick*, Olson's interrogation of the meaning of kingfisher feathers has much to do with political economy and the origins of trade among indigenous peoples.

We can see Olson weaving these materials in the opening to part two of the poem:

I thought of the E on the stone, and of what Mao said
la lumiere"
        but the kingfisher
de l'aurore"
        but the kingfisher flew west
est devant nous!
        he got the color of his breast
        from the heat of the setting sun!

    (87)

Olson creates an antiphonal interplay between a French translation of Mao's speech to the Communist Party in 1948 with quotations from the *Encyclopedia Britannica* concerning the kingfisher. Mao's utopian hopes for a new dawn and the encyclopedia's description of folkloric accounts of the origins of the kingfisher's breast combine to form an arc from East to West. The fugal interplay of passages in two languages spatially separates the two areas on the page while suggesting their intercourse as documents that define emerging and declining cultures. Olson's use of a French friend's translation of Mao's speech contributes to the mixture by stressing the Western reception of Mao's revolution in China and the mediated character of news about world-changing events. Figuratively, Olson's kingfisher flies between these various spatial and cultural areas, establishing one history in the moment of its erasure.[7]

Eliot in "The Four Quartets" treats the kingfisher as a metaphor for Christ and redemption, a principle of stillness against the dull round of "time present and time past":

> After the kingfisher's wing
> Has answered light to light, and is silent, the light is still
> At the still point of the turning world.
> (121)

Against Eliot's dehistoricized "still point" Olson proposes a materialist history in which birds are embedded in cultural change, the rise and fall of civilizations, the role of trade and exchange. Speaking through the persona of Yeats in "This Is Yeats Speaking," Olson had complained that Eliot's version of tradition is "too organized . . . his uncertainty before chaos leads him to confuse authority with orthodoxy," and therefore he is unable to manage uncertainties and doubts that are the stuff of historical knowledge (*Collected Prose* 141). And, in a letter to Robert Payne, Olson complained that Eliot in "The Four Quartets" had stolen the local history of Cape Ann where Olson lived: "the Lady of Good Voyage and of the longshore fisherman in TW [*Waste Land*] is a measure of his use of other experience, then he lacks economic root. And he will turn out to be romantic" (*Selected Letters* 94). According to Olson, Eliot had taken the local economy of New England and turned it into a metaphor, just as the kingfisher had been stolen from the culture in which it had meaning.

Olson's debate with Eliot has a good deal to do with their common origins in Cape Ann and their very different views of early American history. Olson's conflict with Pound is a good deal more oedipal. It is hard to imagine "The Kingfishers" without Pound's example, yet the poem signals a disaffection with the author of *The Cantos* that had been evolving since the end of

World War II. Olson visited Pound at St. Elizabeth's Hospital during the late 1940s but had become increasingly irritated by the older poet's continuing racist rant. "The Kingfishers" seems to address the poetic form that this rant was to take in the *Pisan Cantos*, published in 1948. Pound's hopes for a fascist millennium still lingered in the opening Pisan canto through his portrait of Mussolini hung "by the heels at Milano" in which the fascist leader is viewed as a kind of ritual sacrifice (*Cantos* 425). Against Pound's elegiac depiction of Mussolini as a "dead bullock," Olson asks "shall you uncover honey / where maggots are?"[8] It is not only Pound's continuing belief in Mussolini that sparks Olson's ire but his conflation of the fascist leader with unchanging principles of right order that he identifies with Confucius and the aesthetics of the Chinese written character. Olson counters Pound's oft-quoted example of the ideogram for Dawn, "The Sun Rises (in the) East" with his own version taken from Mao's address to the Communist Party in 1948: "the dawn light is before us; let us rise up and act." Olson's rendering becomes

The light is in the east. Yes. And we must rise, act. Yet
in the west, despite the apparent darkness (the whiteness
which covers all), if you look, if you can bear, if you can, long enough,

> as long as it was necessary for him, my guide
> to look into the yellow of that longest-lasting rose
(91)

Mao's revolution had been underway for some years at this point, and its potential against "dark" forces in the cold war West is great. Olson's reference to "whiteness" reprises his Melville thesis about the evils of entrepreneurial capitalism but now applies it to a specifically cold war rhetoric of East and West.[9] In the *Pisan Cantos* Pound had called Mao a "snotty barbarian ignorant of T'ang history," but Olson links him to possibilities of change and process, identifying him rather romantically with the recent science of cybernetics and the archaic mysteries of pre-Socratic thought. Writing from the Yucatan peninsula to Robert Creeley the next year, Olson returns to Mao, saying that "culture is confidence, & surely, Mao makes Mexico certain, ahead (Communism here, by the way is solid, but is, as not in the States, nor . . . in Russia or Europe either, is a culture Revolution, or a least the weapon of same" ("Mayan Letters" 79). This emphasis on Mao's *cultural* revolution against Pound's orientalism was very much on Olson's mind when he assumed the rectorship of Black Mountain College. In a BBC interview he speaks of the centrality of the arts in the Black Mountain curriculum and adduced Mao as a basis. Mao offers a "breakthrough in curriculum . . . the only communal invention that has substituted for the damn western conception of society" (qtd. in von Hallberg 17). As Robert von Hallberg says, "Black Mountain as Yenan: that equation might keep before Olson the hope if not always the faith that Black Mountain was 'the predecessor of the nation!'" (28).

As Olson indicates in his letter to Creeley, Mao "makes Mexico certain," by which he implies the potential importance of events at Yenan for Latin American social revolution. The poem measures Mao's success against the West's destruction of indigenous people in the New World. Olson draws on passages from William Prescott's *History of the Conquest of Mexico* that refer to Cortés's destruction of Tenochtitlan ("And all now is war / where so lately there was peace"), the use of bird feathers in Aztec artwork ("last, two birds, of thread and featherwork, the quills / gold, the feet / gold"), and human sacrifice ("the priests / (in dark cotton robes, and dirty, / their dishevelled hair matted with blood" [88–89]). These passages define a mosaic of forces at stake in the justification of New World conquest: a passive people, riches to be gained, primitive religions to suppress. But, according to Olson, there were other alternatives to Cortés:

(of the two who first came, each a conquistador, one healed, the other
tore the eastern idols down, toppled
the temple walls, which, says the excuser
were black from human gore)

hear
hear, where the dry blood talks
where the old appetite walks
    (91)

Olson's "healing" conquistador is Cabeza de Vaca, whose long march through the American Southwest and his involvement in native populations whom he encountered, stands as a distinct alternative to Cortés. The fact that the "idols" whom the early conquistadors toppled are described as "Eastern" permits Olson to link the destruction of Montezuma's armies with the larger early imperial goal of finding the Indies in the New World. What the early conquistadors conquered was not the West but the East.

Another linkage of East and West is provided by Olson's reference to Plutarch's second century A.D. essay on the E or epsilon carved on the navel stone at Delphi: "But the E / cut so rudely on that oldest stone / sounded otherwise, / was differently heard" (169). The E, according to Plutarch, is a rune containing Pythagorean mysteries, just as, for Olson, the kingfisher was used in rituals and ceremonies. The meanings of both runic inscription and ceremonial bird have been lost, although the poem, in Davenport's terms, offers a series of "scholia and conjectures" for understanding them. Olson cares less *what* the E means than that it can be made to sound "otherwise." In Olson's hands the E also means East, a reaffirmation of the principle of change established in the opening lines and asserted through pre-Socratic links between Asian mysteries and Greece. Given the fact that cold war architects like George Kennan and Dean Acheson were defining the Soviet threat as Asian closedness and secrecy against Western openness and free trade, Olson's attempt to raise a new East of potentiality becomes more than a speculation on an ancient rune.[10]

In the final section, Olson steps back from his scholarly conjectures about kingfishers' feathers and Mao to establish kin with other poets who, like him, "interest [themselves] / in what was slain in the sun" (93). Among the kin that Olson addresses is Arthur Rimbaud, who appears through a couplet from *Un Saison en enfer:* "si j'ai du goût, ce n'est guères / que pour la terre et les pierres" [if I have any taste, it is only for earth and stones] (92). Maud provides an excellent summary of Olson's interest in the French poet, showing that he represents a kind of heroic integrity and self-knowledge that would serve as a model for those who "hunt among stones" (95–97). It is worth adding that the kin that Olson establishes in these final lines is a male sodality of fellow ethnologists and poetic workers who, even when, like Pound, they take the wrong path, nevertheless offer an ethos of commitment and action. Although Olson maintained a steady correspondence with Frances Boldereff (who received almost daily references to the progress of "The Kingfishers"), she is never included as possible kin, nor is any woman adduced as participant in the world-changing developments from the sixteenth to the twentieth century that the poem discusses. Such developments, from early conquest to cultural revolution, are still, as he says in another early poem, "affairs of men" (*Collected Poems* 14). The absence of women—and the erasure of gender issues in conquest—is perhaps the true secret of the stones. In this context it is tempting to read Olson's disparaging remark about Fernand "lispingly" discussing "Albers and Ankor Vat" as a "weak" or effeminate response to the questions addressed by the poem. That Fernand is last seen "sliding along the wall of the night, losing himself / in some crack of the ruins" permits Olson to stay on and interrogate change rather than escape it. But Fernand is a cipher; like the runic E and the kingfisher feather, he remains to be incorporated into Olson's pedagogical project.

"SHE MIMICKS THE SPEAKING": DICTEE

As Guy Davenport observes, Olson's phrase the "light is in the east" announces a "dawn moment in history, the Cold War was beginning, a new age of technology (atomic power, polymers, jet flight, plastics) was beginning;

empires (British, Soviet, Chinese) were changing character and boundaries" (257). This "dawn moment" includes both changes in global power and shifts in technology that must be measured by some new historical optic, one not dependent on an Enlightenment myth of progress and development. Among the new technologies that interested Olson was the science of cybernetics as described by Norbert Wiener in his 1948 book, *Cybernetics: Or Control and Communication in the Animal and the Machine.* In that book, Olson discovered the term *feedback,* which describes how a system, mechanical or human, compensates for error and uses that compensation to refine its functioning. Radar, for Wiener, is the classic instance of feedback, a system whereby high frequency radio waves are transmitted into space, bounced off an object, returned to the transmitting source, and sent out again to map the trajectory of a moving object. By a series of incremental forays, the radio wave may measure the object's exact location and size based not upon its known features but by predicting its "performance characteristics" (6). In "The Kingfishers," feedback becomes a model for the kind of processual thinking that the poem endorses, a speculative interrogation of an unknown form (the inscrutable E on a stone, the feathers of a bird) not only to understand it but to understand forces that have participated in occluding its meaning. Furthermore, feedback implies using what one has learned to construct further knowledge:

Not one death but many,
not accumulation but change, the feed-back proves, the feed-back is
the law

        Into the same river no man steps twice
        When fire dies air dies
        No one remains, nor is, one

  (89)

Olson juxtaposes the principle of revolution, embodied in the new China, with Heraclitean notions of change, joining Eastern and Western thought at the antipodes of human history. The word *feedback* also relates to the kingfisher, which, as we learn in the poem, builds its nest out of "rejectamenta" and thereby constructs a home out of "excrement and decayed fish" (87). This law of change and recursive knowledge defines a new, posthuman epistemology, for which Olson used the term "post-modern."[11]

As I have pointed out, Olson's reading of global change in "The Kingfishers" can be seen through three frames that relate to the poem's pedagogical imperative. We might use the same pedagogical categories for Theresa Hak Kyung Cha's *Dictee,* but the trinity of textual, disciplinary, and pragmatic modes would have to be revised to accommodate a diasporic, gendered condition that changes what it means to be a student in a postcolonial context.[12] Cha's pedagogy treats errors or mistakes—what education seeks to eliminate—as signs of displacement and subjection. The title of the work itself, *Dictee,* is published without the necessary acute accent over the first *e,* one of many indications of the poet's "foreign" relation to languages. My title for this section, "she mimicks the speaking," used as a counter to Olson's more confident "I hunt among stones," contains a misspelling that embodies precisely the mediated condition of the displaced female subject. She must mimic official (Japanese, French, English) patriarchal speech rather than produce it in her own tongue; the spelling, "mimick," mimics proper spoken English while betraying its user's strangeness to it.

Cha's relationship to my trinity of pedagogical frames must be adapted to the late 1960s and early 1970s when her own educational and artistic formation begins. *Dictee*'s textuality needs to be read in light of the author's larger involvement in new forms of performance and conceptual art, for which the materiality of language as a sign system replaces its strictly expressive features. The book's material form—its use of photographs, documents, holograph pages, and letters—makes this a mixed-genre work, related as much to visual and performance art as to poetry. Furthermore the work's textuality is itself the subject of its critique of gender and ethnic categories, foregrounding the material features of language as it serves to compartmentalize and mark specific bodies. The disciplinary frame for Cha's work would have to include her own formative experiences as an immigrant Korean child, attending Catholic missionary schools and learning languages (French and English) as part of her movement to the West. One would also refer to her later undergraduate and graduate work at the University of California, Berkeley, in comparative literature at a moment when continental theory was announcing a linguistic turn in the humanities. All of which leads to the third frame, the pragmatic, which for Cha includes the poem's deformation and defacement of various language systems—from the dictation exercise that provides the work with its title to the Catholic catechism to the small spelling and translation errors that I have already mentioned. These errors and deformations testify to what Lisa Lowe has called an "aesthetic of infidelity" in which forms of repetition, improper grammatical usage, misspellings, and other verbal mistakes mark the colonial subject's incommensurability with educational, religious and linguistic expectations ("Unfaithful" 37). It would be tempting to read Cha's verbal experimentation as a sign of postmodern playfulness, a diffusion of the subject into linguistic indeterminacy. But, as Elaine Kim observes, this would erase the author's Korean heritage and critique of power relations, turning her use of multiple identities into a kind of "reverse Orientalism" (22).

If cybernetics is Olson's model for technological change, the equivalent field for Cha is occupied by film. And just as Olson's ideas of change tend to reinforce a masculine base of authority, so Cha's use of the filmic medium is informed by theoretical accounts of the male gaze and the female positioning within that gaze. As a student of film and comparative literature at Berkeley during the early 1970s Cha read French film semiotics and feminist theory, and the impact of these fields can be seen in her films, videos, and photographic installations.[13] Her years in Berkeley coincided with a period of student protests and activist politics, but they also occurred during the heyday of the university's Pacific Film Archive, where she worked for three years (1974–77) and where her acquaintance with film was formed. While at Berkeley she studied with a number of film theorists and literary scholars, and later, at the Centre d'Études Américain du Cinéma in Paris, her teachers included Jean-Louis Baudry, Raymond Bellour, Thierry Kuntzel, Monique Wittig, and Christian Metz. These filmic influences can be seen in the poem's use of photographs, documents, stills from Carl Dreyer's *Jeanne d'Arc*, anatomical diagrams, and references to theaters and movie houses. Although *Dictee* has been read, quite properly, as a postcolonial text, it is less often observed that it is structured like a film, using techniques of montage and cutting to embody the fragmented character of female gender within a diasporic context.[14]

The intellectual sources for Cha's films, performances, and textual work partly reflect the influence of French critical theory and feminist film semiotics and their critique of expressive theories of language. Wiener's model of communication, quoted by Olson in his poem, as a "discrete or continuous sequence of measurable events distributed in time," presumes an unmediated conduit between sender and receiver of messages (90). But Cha realizes that speech and signs are broken, their ability to signify mediated by various forms of power. And this has implications for the poem's exploration of shifting national identities. When she says at one point that "Japan has become the sign. The alphabet. The vocabulary. The meaning is the instrument," she suggests that for generations of Korean-born subjects under Japanese occupation, national and imperial authority have become language (32). To speak a language is to mimic its subjectification of the speaker. In order to contest this subjectification, Cha speaks from a number of different positions that she subsumes into the "*diseuse*," the French term for the female speaking subject—a "*she* without the separate act of uttering" (89).

If Olson thought of himself, as he titled his second book of *The Maximus Poems*, as an "archaeologist of morning," then Cha might well be the ventriloquist of the postcolonial. She too hunts among stones and glyphs for a lost past, but it is a past "fixed in perpetual exile" (81). The glyphs upon which she meditates in *Dictee* appear in the book's frontispiece in the form of a photograph of characters in Hangul script, etched by Korean workers on the walls of a Japanese coal mine. Existing significantly outside the body of the text, they are the only appearance of Korean language in a book filled with references to other languages (English, French, Chinese) and signal the erasure of Korean culture by multiple waves of colonial occupation and displacement. They spell out a narrative of desire: "Mother / I miss you / I am hungry / I want to go home" (Kim and Alarcon 107). This homelessness was experienced by Cha's own mother who was forced under the Japanese occupation to reject her native Korean language and speak Japanese, later leaving Korea to work as a teacher among other Japanese teachers in Manchuria. With the Allied victory over Japan in 1945, she returned to a country quickly partitioned along the 38th parallel and reconfigured by a cold war stalemate into a nationalist republic. The runes on a wall remain mute signs of a displaced mother tongue, the pronunciation of which, for Cha's mother's generation, was a crime.

Were *Dictee* simply an elegy for a lost homeland, it would join numerous poems written during the nationalist 1970s as acts of recuperating a precontact history in America, Atzlan, Africa. But Cha's text foregrounds the educational apparatus by which homelands are discursively erased. She illustrates this by devoting much of the opening section of the book to dictation exercises used in language learning. For Cha, whose early education occurred in French Catholic missionary schools, learning a new language is part of a national pedagogy by which the student is interpellated into colonial rule. Dictation, as a pedagogy of the oppressed, involves a strict application of the performative: "Écrivez en français" is a command whose fulfillment produces a submissive speaker. But as Lisa Lowe has pointed out, the translations that Cha provides from the French are full of errors and grammatical mistakes that mark the learner as foreign ("Unfaithful" 40). In one instance, the foreign student includes the teacher's punctuation commands as part of her translation from French into English: "Open paragraph It was the first day period She had come from a far period tonight at dinner comma the families would ask comma open quotation marks How was the first day interrogation mark close quotation marks" (1). Both the form (inclusion of the teacher's punctuation command) and content ("she had come from a far") instantiate the student's position as other, as recipient of authoritative commands. But, by including the marks, Cha hints at a counterdiscursive function of the poem: to expose a certain ideal of fidelity implied in translation. In Lowe's terms she is "unfaithful to the original," yet such infidelity exposes both the conventions of pedagogical orthodoxy as well as the epistemological inadequacy of originality as a guarantor of linguistic accuracy.

Cha intervenes in the dictation exercise, juxtaposing a passage in "proper English" concerning a day's journey from London to Paris to a passage of ungrammatical fragments:

5. She call she believe she calling to she has calling because there no response she believe she calling and the other end must hear. The other end must see the other end feel she accept pages sent care of never to be seen never to be read never to be known if name if name be known if name only seen heard spoken read cannot be never she hide all essential words words link subject verb she writes hidden the essential words must be pretended invented she try on different images essential invisible

6. We left London at half past seven and arrived at Dover after a journey of two hours. At ten o'clock the boat left the harbour. The trip across the channel took only an hour and a half. The sea was calm, we did not feel the slightest of motion. We made a stop of an hour at Calais, where we had luncheon. It was rather dear but well served. (15)

In example 6 the recounted journey from England to France is repeated in the dictation exercise's linguistic journey from French to English. The collective plural of example 6 instantiates the collective experience of native speakers who may presume a "common" language whereas the feminine third person of example 5 defines the isolated female, nonnative speaker, unable to organize all of the words into grammatical sentences. Here the performative circuit of teacher-to-student is broken, the pretense of fidelity revealed as deception. One hears a kind of desperation of a speaker unable to conjugate subject and verb, forced to "try on different image" of what it is to be a self-identical speaking subject. This speaker—the *diseuse* or female-speaking subject—mimics authoritative speech but cannot invoke a collective "we." Rather, she creates a metadiscourse out of communicational features—call and response, filmic montage, pages sent through the mails—that are traditionally left out of official histories. For Olson, in "The Kingfishers," feedback represents knowledge accumulated piecemeal out of novel experiences, but for Cha feedback is always mediated by the system that produces it. The absence of periods and other subordinating marks illustrates the free-floating, invisible nature of this grammatical subject. But at the same time that she is dispossessed of a social and grammatical body, the *diseuse* is freed as a writer to create new forms of address not bound by the dialectical pattern of the *dictée*.

Cha's use of the *diseuse* as speaker is linked to her larger attempt to create a genealogy of historical women whose speech has been similarly broken or disbelieved. This genealogy includes Cha's mother, Hyung Soon Hua, denied the ability to speak Korean under Japanese occupation, Yu Guan Soon, martyred in the March 1919 uprising, Joan of Arc, punished for listening to voices. All of these women become figures of resistance within patriarchal systems of politics and religion. But, as Juliana Spahr says, these antinomian figures are formed within texts and representations (148). The Joan of Arc that Cha depicts is taken from a still photograph of the actress Maria Falconetti in Carl Dryer's movie about Joan or from a photograph of St. Theresa of Lisieux playing Joan in a convent drama. Combined with other forms of textuality in the poem, these passages imply that the female subject speaks in the highly mediated voices of official speech genres. Gynocentric solidarity is obtained in the interstices of religious, political, and state discourses, not out of a cultural feminist project of recuperation.

Finding the multiple sources of the *diseuse* means rescuing the historical subject from various categorizations that contain her. It means finding a third way, a *tertium quid*, that resists the historical narratives of gender, nationality, ancestry:

From A Far
What nationality
or what kindred and relation
what blood relation
what blood ties of blood
what ancestry
what race generation
what house clan tribe stock strain
what lineage extraction
what breed sect gender denomination caste
what stray ejection misplaced
Tertium Quid neither one thing nor the other
Tombe des nues de naturalized
what transplant to dispel upon
     (20)

This catalogue of categories summarizes *Dictee*'s deployment of multiple identity-positions. What might seem to be natural categories of blood or ancestry are revealed as classifications that homogenize and neutralize differences while offering the outer trappings of differentiation. To be "naturalized," as Shelley Sunn Wong points out, "through the interpellative operations of colonial, religious or patriarchal discourses is to be decidedly unnatural" (124). And as if to demonstrate the workings of a *tertium quid* that violates the classificatory imperative, Cha provides her own fractured speech, "*tombe des nues* [thunderstruck] de naturalized / what transplant to dispel upon." I read this as challenging the immigration or visa form catalogue of identities by "transplanting" or "dispelling" identity onto language itself. Questions of national or familial origin come from "A Far," an estrangement reinforced by the division of *afar* into two words.

To some extent, the poem's sectional divisions based upon the nine Muses is an attempt to appropriate a certain taxonomic imperative in aesthetics, launched by Aristotle, in which various language uses can be fixed within formal and stylistic rules. Far from adopting Aristotelian categories, Cha questions the authority of generic groupings by placing them against the backdrop of history and memory. Under the heading "Clio/History" Cha provides a narrative of Japanese occupation in Korea and the 1919 uprising against that occupation. Under the heading "Calliope/Epic Poetry," Cha presents a narrative of her mother's exile in Manchuria. "Melpomene/Tragedy" deals with the partition of Korea into north and south and with Cha's own return to Korea after eighteen years. Each sectional division permits a new way of reading generic categories as they are inflected by gender. The Muses as feminine guardians of memory are rearticulated to speak for specific moments of cultural disruption. And even in her apostrophe to the muse at the work's beginning, Cha revises the usual invocation to memory; instead of invoking the Muse to tell of heroic deeds and bloody battle, Cha asks the Muse to "tell me the story / Of all these things, O Goddess, daughter of Zeus / Beginning wherever you wish, tell even us" (7). Clearly the stories that Cha tells will not be those of war and valor but of "these things" that pertain to her own history. Finally, the Muse will address herself to female listeners ("tell even us") who are seldom invoked as listeners to heroic stories.

Such blurring of traditional genres is accompanied by a blurring of the borders between private and political bodies. Cha uses the metaphors of blood and ink to describe fluids that both inscribe and sustain, mark and liberate, the national subject. The same ink that establishes citizenship on an immigration form also writes the work called *Dictee*. This blurring of boundaries can be seen throughout the work. Section "Urania/Astronomy," for example, is prefaced by an acupuncture chart of the body and concluded by a diagram of the vocal cords and breathing apparatus.[15] Here Eastern and Western medical sciences are contained within the genre dedicated to heavenly bodies. The body's surface is a text, just as astronomical bodies mark distances and spaces and internal organs form speech. As if to stress the connections between inner organs and outer inscriptions, the content of "Astronomy" includes a description of a blood test used for an immigration or visa application. The links between the blood that is withdrawn and the ink that establishes citizenship are combined in a common "stain":

Contents housed in membranes. Stain from within dispel in drops in spills. Contents of other recesses seep outward.
    Too long. Enough already. One empty body waiting to contain.
Conceived for a single purpose and for the purpose only. To contain.
Made filled. Be full. She pulls out the needle and the skin lifts.

*Should it happen that the near-black liquid ink draws the line from point
mark gravity follow (inevitably, suddenly) in one line down the arm on the
table in one long spill, exhale of a spill.*
(64)

Both biological and national bodies are porous; the passive national body receives a new identity through immigration and citizenship while the passive
physical body dispels its fluid identity into a stain. Cha's "fluid" writing, her
blurring of subjects and antecedents, tenses and modifiers, provides a verbal
instantiation of these interminglings and exchanges. Cha's reference to the
body's fluids and features to establish national identity hints at a darker history of taxonomization that has historically racialized individuals through the
pseudoscience of eugenics, the one-drop rule, or the final solution.

The opening page of the following section, devoted to "Tragedy," replaces the acupuncture chart with a map of Korea, divided along the 38th parallel in 1948, a substitution that may offer a visual rhyme between physical,
heavenly, and political bodies. This section also deals with the submission of
the body—the Korean body to Japanese occupation and then to cold war partition and then nationalist suppression of civil rights. It also describes submission to the aesthetic, a female viewer's anticipation of the beginning of a
film: "She could be seen sitting in the first few rows. She would be sitting in
the first few rows. Closer the better. The more. Better to eliminate presences
of others surrounding better view away from that which is left behind far
away back behind more for closer view more and more face to face until nothing else sees only this view singular. All dim, gently, slowly until in the dark,
the absolute darkness the shadows fade" (79). The juxtaposition of this passage of passive anticipation in a theater (the grammatical use of the condi-
tional form reinforces this aspect) with a map of Korea offers a problematic
reflection on aesthetic pleasure: is the viewer's passivity equated with the citizen's or is it an alternative immobility that permits greater vision, a critical
potential that Walter Benjamin felt photography offers the viewer? Cha does
not answer the question precisely, although she seems to feel that the film refuses totalizing forces outside of the theater: "The submission is complete.
Relinquishes even the vision to immobility. Abandons all protests to that
which will appear to the sight. About to appear. Forecast. Break. Break, by all
means. The illusion that the act of viewing is to make alteration of the visible.
The expulsion is immediate. Not one second is lost to the replication of the totality. Total severance of the seen. Incision" (79). In film theory, the notion of
suture is used to describe the ways that the film's cuts enlist the viewer in creating the illusionistic space of the film. Cha appears to be referring to the su-
turing of the viewer as an act of expulsion, the "total severance of the seen"
from the reality it reproduces. In relation to the map of Korea, this implies

making the division of north and south, so fundamental to geopolitics of the cold war, visible as an enforced cut or suture. At the same time, the film utilizes its montage not to suture a "natural" division in the national subject but to "make alteration of the visible." Laura Mulvey sees the viewer's passivity as being the condition of the female spectator in the face of an active male gaze, replicated in the main (male) character. But for Cha this immobility seems to be a sight for further vision and critique.

This possibility is reinforced in the next segment of "Tragedy" in which Cha reproduces a letter (or imitates a hypothetical letter) sent to her mother from Korea to which she has returned after eighteen years living abroad.[16] Her return journey has placed Cha in the midst of student protests that rocked South Korea and led to the Kwangju Uprising in 1980 against military rule. Her letter remembers similar events in 1960 before she left Korea: "Nothing has changed, we are at a standstill. I speak in another tongue now, a second tongue a foreign tongue. . . . But nothing has changed" (80). She is also remembering similar protests from her mother's time against Japanese occupation: "Our destination is fixed on the perpetual motion of search. Fixed in its perpetual exile. Here at my return in eighteen years, the war is not ended. We fight the same war. We are inside the same struggle seeking the same destination. We are severed in Two by an abstract enemy an invisible enemy under the title of liberators who have conveniently named the severance, Civil War. Cold War. Stalemate" (81). The diasporic subject, returned to a homeland that was never home, now sees her origins as constantly framed by "Civil War. Cold War. Stalemate." This passage illustrates a key difference between the passivity of sitting in a movie theater and the passivity of living under occupation. The first voids the silence so that one can hear, breaks the illusion of realism so that one can see; the second names the silence, divides it into two irreconcilable forms of power that lead to "Stalemate." The fact that she is writing to her mother bridges the generational and geopolitical gap, reestablishing a familial bond that exists despite the various partitions that the work describes. If she speaks a "foreign tongue," she is capable of remembering and writing that memory against forms of official memory.

"TO NAME IT NOW . . ."

I began this chapter by saying that the Pacific Rim is a discourse against which Olson's "The Kingfishers" and Cha's *Dictee* could profitably be read. This suggests a perhaps specious connection between global economics and aesthetics, but it is one that becomes necessary if we are to understand the material role of education in both works. At the very least, their poems, written at opposite ends of the cold war, take direct aim at a powerful orientalist project that dominates modernism. While neither poet uses the phrase

Pacific Rim, their interest in remapping the Pacific region is worth pondering for new cartographies of global space. The old axis of United States versus Soviet Union no longer applies (although its rhetoric has been retrofitted recently to deal with Islamic fundamentalism), but it was powerfully alive when Olson was writing "The Kingfishers." To some extent that poem registers the impact of this cold war binary at the same time as it tries to wrest the "East" away from the versions that were prevalent in the State Department. Olson's and Cha's poems both contest a core/periphery model of global geography by which powerful nations sediment their economic authority by relying on outlying provinces or production zones. Rather these writers map across historical periods and information systems to develop a new chronotope for which terms like *modern* and *postmodern* seem inadequate.

In thinking of the Pacific region as a discourse rather than a geographic area I am drawing on historians, sociologists, and cultural critics who have defined the Pacific as a dimension of late capitalism marked by decentered flows of exchange and technology. This change begins in the early 1970s with the end of the Vietnam War, the emergence of Asian countries as economic powers, the move to flexible production, and cross-national alliances such as NAFTA. Most descriptions of a Pacific Rim discourse describe it as an invention of Euro-American interests, what General Douglas MacArthur called "the Anglo Saxon Lake," both as a fantasy (tropical tourism) and an economic zone (cheap labor, unregulated production standards).[17] There are, to be sure, significant fissures in the Pacific Rim, brought to light recently in protests against the World Bank and the IMF meetings, diminished Japanese economic power, increased worries over Islamic fundamentalism in the Philippines and Indonesia, the revised trade status of China, and the gradual incorporation of Mexico and Latin America into the discourse as a "western" Pacific economic power. All of these changes may soon make the decentered "Pacific Rim" as outdated as the binary cold war. Yet the idea of the Pacific Rim still provides a way of historicizing cultural products such as "The Kingfishers" and "Dictee." Their "investment" in the Pacific region as a zone of new formations and epistemologies is obviously not based around First World capital development, and thus they may provide an internally distanced look at what the Pacific Rim cannot contain.

With the emergence of globalism as a grid of interlinking networks of exchange, information, and capital, the temporal, hermeneutic model, within which Olson's process-based poetry has often been treated by Heideggerian critics, begins to look more like its modernist predecessors.[18] Cha's crossgeneric work, its record of a diasporic trajectory across languages, borders, genres, national identities, and gendered identity, problematizes a temporal hermeneutics. For her, there is no Heideggerian "truth" (*aletheia*) to be uncovered through speculative acts and testimonials. Rather, there is a destination "fixed in perpetual motion of search." This oxymoronic position—fixed motion—has historical antecedents that she chronicles in the first part of *Dictee*. But the ability to speak of that history cannot be assumed as the act of an independent poet/pedagogue as in the case of Olson. For Cha, the phrase "I hunt among stones" is hard to pronounce; it is an assertion that needs to be subjected to the conditions of language acquisition and reproduction. In this, Cha's textuality differs most radically from Olson's orality. And although *Dictee* is profoundly concerned with memory—the need to recover a lost cultural heritage—it does so not by seeking a *better* past but by offering a frame for studying the mediated character of the present. I have described this frame as pedagogical in order to define how certain postmodern poems teach by example. In the case of *Dictee* that teaching includes the pedagogical structure itself—the various ways in which citizens are indoctrinated into languages, forms of behavior, and structures of assent. The map of a divided Korea or the Catholic catechism or immigration blood test become sites of identity formation, no one of which exists without the other. All are part of a disciplinary project through which the national and gendered subject is produced.

Charles Olson was one of the first writers to see the "new Pacific" as an industry, via Melville, but also as an alternative space for social formation, via Mao. Theresa Hak Kyung Cha takes on the multiply divided Korea as a metaphor for Asian women who speak in a "broken tongue." Although she does not invoke the sweatshops or sexual tourism that would locate women within capitalist Pacific "rimspeak," she does describe the condition of women in diaspora and poses a series of strong alternatives to the passive Asian woman stereotype. Her use of the *diseuse* as the female speaking subject represents the multiple spaces from which "woman" speaks—both as grammatical subject of sentences and as agent in history. Such treatment of the speaking subject as a grammatical form differs dramatically from Olson's self-assured "I" who can claim kin with Pound and Rimbaud. The *diseuse* exists outside of history, in the usual teleological sense, yet only by refusing to speak within the available forms of historical agency can Cha instruct her readers. As her many references to a "broken" or "divided" tongue attest, the process of speaking is painful—but necessary: "To name it now so as not to repeat history in oblivion. To extract each fragment by each fragment from the word from the image another word another image the reply that will not repeat history in oblivion" (33).

Afterword: Moving Borders

"To name it now so as not to repeat history in oblivion." For Theresa Hak Kyung Cha, naming her diasporic history saves it from repetition. As I have tried to show throughout this book, naming becomes increasingly important when pedagogical, juridical, and political systems have the power to redefine and disinform on a massive scale. The fact that Cha performs her acts of naming in a genre-bending work embodies her belief that previous histories—those that occupied and divided Korea for nearly a century—are inadequate. "Civil War. Cold War. Stalemate," she writes, but the history of Korean colonization is never simply a matter of shifts in political power; it is underwritten by narratives of submission and dominance, masculine militarization and passive domestic feminization that make borders necessary. Cha's linkage of poetics and categories of history serves as a template for contemplating post–cold war cultural scenarios.

In this regard, one wonders what Cha would have made of an image reproduced in the *New York Times* recently, depicting a ceremony in which a

South Korean boy wearing a black suit and bearing a single rose walks down a deserted railroad track toward a North Korean girl in a white dress who also holds a rose in front of her. According to the *Times* article, the two children exchange roses and hug, symbolizing the "thaw" in relations between South and North. The railroad track that ends at their feet represents the curtailed history of a unified Korea that presumably will change because of ceremonies like this. The idealized heterosexual union of two Korean children poses the hope for a marriage of states, railroad lines, and families across cold war borders. The larger context for this ceremony (conducted, it should be pointed out, on the southern side of the DMZ with South Korean children posing as symbolic unifiers) is the recent admission on the part of North Korea's leader, Kim Jong Il, that North Korean security agents had kidnapped eleven Japanese youths in the late 1970s and taken them across the border to work as language trainers or intelligence operatives. This admission of North Korean deception was followed by a reciprocal confession of remorse by Japanese leader Junichiro Koizumi for his country's thirty-five-year occupation of Korea. The two leaders were participating in a ritual of truth telling and apology at a summit conference blessed via satellite broadcast by Russian leader Vladimir Putin who, according to the *Times*, "urged Kim Jong Il to complete the North Korean side of the rail link as part of a vast network over which goods can move from South Korea through the North to Russia and on to markets in Europe" (Kirk). This bizarre reversal of roles—Koreans kidnapping Japanese, Russians blessing free market trade across borders—has become a hallmark of post–cold war theater, nowhere more oddly embodied than in the United States, which recently fought a war in Afghanistan that it vilified when conducted by its cold war enemy little more than a decade earlier.

When I began writing this book, the cold war was moving from the present to the past tense. "We" had won; "they" had lost. From the Balkans to Hong Kong to Jakarta, the toppling of the Berlin Wall began a festival of renamings and redefinitions, of which the Korean summit conference is only one example. The old East/West dyad no longer seems applicable when what David Harvey calls new "spaces of hope" have emerged to provide entrepreneurial access to global largesse. Exactly where that largesse is coming from and whom it will serve are difficult to find, but it is clear that a new free market is on the move, and its name is globalization.

In the days since September 11th, however, U.S. cold war rhetoric has been dusted off to do new work—this time not with a confederated superpower as enemy but with a decentered, diasporic entity. Unlike its Soviet predecessor, which was eager to purchase (or in a more familiar cold war narrative, steal) the technologies of modernism, "terrorism" attacks the signs of modernity itself—tall buildings, signs of corporate and military power, using the very means of modern progress (chemicals, cell phones, airplanes, email, trains) that it hopes to topple. Cynics who point out that Middle Eastern hatred of the West may be a response to Western support of dictatorships and oppressive rulers are shouted down as dupes or, worse, collaborators.

Not surprisingly, the rhetoric of the new cold war comes in gendered forms. Saber rattling State Department officials invoke the need for retaliation against Arab states in the name of suffering Muslim women, subject to primitive laws of Shariah and the dehumanizing burqa. Newspapers are filled with stories of women who have been stoned to death for committing adultery, raped by invading forces, burned by acid for disagreeing with their husbands. Against such primitive misogyny in the Arab world, retaliation seems only fair. On the home front, the war is being fought over new images of masculine heroism appropriate for the first ever major attack on U.S. soil. Firemen and policemen who gave their lives in the rescue attempt at the World Trade Center have been compared to the soldiers who raised the flag on Iwo Jima in World War II, and the acronym NYFD has become a ubiquitous logo on baseball hats and T-shirts across the nation. The first Broadway play on the subject of September 11th is titled, fortuitously for my purposes, *Guys* and deals with the difficulties of a female journalist (played by Sigourney Weaver) finding adequate words to describe the heroic actions of firefighters killed on September 11th. Tough guy rhetoric of J. Edgar Hoover or Richard Nixon over the threat of communist subversion comes out of the mouths of Donald Rumsfeld, John Ashcroft, and George W. Bush over the threat of Al Qaeda cells in U.S. neighborhoods. Weapons that the United States had used to subdue Japan into a peace agreement in 1945 or to maintain a nuclear stalemate against the Soviet Union are now being demonized as "weapons of mass destruction" when in the hands of Arab fundamentalists. And perhaps most familiar to ears trained on the years I have been discussing in this book is the idea that the enemy could be living "among us," hidden under protections guaranteed in the Bill of Rights, living in our neighborhoods and enjoying the religious tolerance that we take for granted.

The new global formations that are knitting old foes and dividing new allies have yet to find an appropriate narrative, although the gendered rhetoric that I have just mentioned is helping to write the script. As Cynthia Enloe points out, the end of superpower rivalry does not guarantee "an end to the militarization of masculinity on which it thrived. On the other hand, masculinity is not abstract, nor is it monolithic" (5). Enloe's qualifier suggests that what it means to be manly can no longer be taken for granted, especially in the new world protective order. She cites the example of UN peacekeepers who, in many cases, have replaced a national military presence in various parts of the world but who lack the authority, training, or firepower that marks a military male. And with increasing numbers of women in the military—as well as into various peacekeeping forces—the older model of masculine militarization must be reconsidered.

It is too early to tell what role literature will play in this shifting scenario, although cultural responses to the post–cold war period manifest something of the skepticism that I mentioned with regard to Theresa Hak Kyung Cha over the links between genre and gender. The idea that gender is a flexible category, socially constructed to map changing axes of power, has moved out of the academic journal and into popular culture, fashion advertising, and media. The seeds of social constructionism in gender studies can be found in the 1970s and 1980s, and thus the consolidation of literary movements around compulsory heterosexual masculinity no longer has credence within a wide area of cultural production. The study of masculinities has become a significant field of gender studies, as evidenced by books with titles such as *National Manhood, Manliness and Civilization, Engendering Men,* or *Constructing Masculinity.*[1] This important work has been aided not through a rediscovery of the men's movement's "inner male" but, as Cynthia Enloe observes, through the work of feminists who "start from the essential feminist discovery that we can make sense of men's gendered reactions only if we take women's experiences seriously" (20). Those experiences, as I have indicated in chapter 6, are by no means unitary but may very well involve the application of masculinities to women's experiences of power and sexuality.

A second issue raised by Cha's work concerns the nature of post–cold war national formations and the role of genre in framing them. A sense of how this issue of genre manifests itself can be gleaned by a personal example. In 1989, a group of American writers (Lyn Hejinian, Ron Silliman, Barrett Watten, and myself) were invited to what was then called Leningrad to meet with French, Russian, Georgian, Latvian, Armenian, and other writers in a conference entitled "Language—Consciousness—Society." It was a significant event for all of us, signaling changes that had begun during the Gorbachev era and that would result, at the end of the year, with the fall of the Berlin Wall. On our return, we decided to write a book about the experience, which we titled *Leningrad,* little realizing how quickly our title would become outdated. What was clear to the four of us is that the extraordinary changes in the Soviet Union of which we had seen a brief glimpse could not be told in a simple narrative history but had to be grounded, as our introduction states, "in a sense of community [connected] to progressive politics and new social theory" (Davidson et al. n.p.). We decided to write a collaborative work, based on shared observations, photos, documents, and anecdotes. The collaboration took the form of an elaborate exchange of texts, circulated according to a numerical formula based on repetitions of the number four. Each of us would write a section, pass it on to the next person who would then respond to it and pass it on again through four cycles. There were four possible routes of exchange, four circulations of four texts, leading to a total of sixty-four sections. The point was not a formal jeu d'ésprit but a recognition of the collaborative character of our poetics and our shared experience of the "new" Russia. Whatever our experiences of the Soviet Union, they had to take into account that larger (failed) collective experiment whose start was so auspicious in linking the arts to social emancipation. And since we relied heavily on remarks by our Russian friends, the collaboration incorporated their remarks to expand constituencies across borders.

I mention this example because post–cold war writing is, in various quarters, facing the futility of conceiving global narratives around national models, history-challenging events around bounded linear narratives, new social identities around gendered and sexualized categories. If one were to look for a shift in poetics since the period that this book describes it would have to be through the optic of, to adapt the title of a recent anthology of experimental women writers, "moving borders" (Sloan). Where cold war poetics was often dominated by polemics around public versus private (Allen Ginsberg's jeremiad versus W. S. Merwin's lyric), body versus mind (Charles Olson's projectivism versus Richard Wilbur's bounded tensions), confession versus containment (Sylvia Plath versus Elizabeth Bishop), individualism versus cultural nationalism (LeRoi Jones versus Amiri Baraka), borders seemed useful for differentiating guys like us from guys like them. With the fall of the Berlin Wall, the usefulness of walls to define structures of identity seems dubious.

The postmodern incredulity toward metanarratives of identity is equally a skepticism about the form that narratives have taken. Whether writing under the rubrics of *mestizaje,* hybridity, queer, or cyborg positionalities, poets of the last two decades have seen borders as movable fictions for which the formal collage one finds in *Dictee* is a harbinger. In anthologies of experimental writing such as the one I mentioned above, "moving borders" refers to cross-genre and collaborative writing among women who very well may be Asian American or African American lesbian or punk or "language-centered," but for whom such labels are not the defining point of any given writing. The works of Carla Harryman, Leslie Scalapino, Lisa Jarnot, Myung Mi Kim, Erica Hunt, Rachel Blau DuPlessis, Rae Armantrout, Laura Moriarty, Pamela Lu, Mei Mei Berssenbrugge, Eleni Sikelianos, Harryette Mullen, Lyn Hejinian, Renee Gladman, Dodie Bellamy, Eileen Myles, Diane Ward, Kathy Acker, and others pose a wide variety of shapes on the page, stage, website, CD-ROM, theater space, and radio wave.

Rather than take these developments as changes in formal methods or media, I would prefer to see them as changes in the ways that identities are cited within a larger public sphere, where the act of naming self-consciously describes the systems in which identities are reinforced. Describing her work, Leslie Scalapino speaks for many of the women named above: "The self is unraveled as an example in investigating particular historical events, which are potentially infinite" (Sloan 661). Writing is not a mimesis of self but a real-time enactment. As Scalapino continues, "I intended this work to be the repetition of historically real events the writing of which punches a hole in reality. (As if to void them, but actively)" (660). Nor is such repetition through a self-in-formation separate from political projects. Erica Hunt notes that "the consciousness of many oppositional writers of color, feminist writers, and speculative writers has been shaped in powerful ways by social movements" (Sloan 686). What has occurred among these writers is a considerably expanded palette of styles and discursive modes:

a woman began her poem with invitation (she said) we
had used our color to get inside but that was not the point
and I laughed. Or what is usually seen as laughter but
closer to measure. I felt uneasy and thought to empty
myself. She began her poem: we had used our color to get
inside though codes were undoing. And we crowded in.
Still talking about birds.
    (Gladman 68)

Renee Gladman's use of race ("our color") is "not the point" of the poem, as it had been during a period of black nationalism, yet institutional debates over race-based preferences are definitely a reference point for reading this poem. During an era when the dismantling of affirmative action programs raises issues of identity and merit, the question of who "we" are as persons of color is vexed. This becomes the focus of Gladman's pronominal confusion in speaking for a collective body and distinguishes her poem from Amiri Baraka's "SOS." She shifts from first to third to plural second person ("I felt uneasy and thought to empty / myself, She began her poem: we had used our color") and, in doing so, accomplishes across both race and gender lines what Adrienne Rich had attempted to accomplish around issues of gender in "Diving into the Wreck."

The challenges to identity politics, the opening of generic and gendered borders, the forging of new alliances among constituencies—these transformations have not happened without a certain loss of historical perspective about the various struggles of the past to claim identity, gender, and social cohesion. The recalibrations of gender and genre may mean that "poetry," as a model of literariness, no longer occupies the same buoyant role that it did in either New Critical curricula or antiwar activism. That centrality is held today by narrative, but the questioning of language's ability to name the unnamable will remain poetry's special realm, whether in the rap lyrics of

Le Tigre and Mos Def, the spoken word performances of Tracie Morris or Luis Alfaro, the signed poetry of the Flying Words Project, or the crossover work of Pattie Smith, Pamela Lu, and Heriberto Ypes.

Doubtless these poets are unknown to Dana Gioia who, in *Can Poetry Matter?* mourns the fact that "American poetry now belongs to a subculture" (1). He goes on to worry that "[no] longer part of the mainstream of artistic and intellectual life, [poetry] has become the specialized occupation of a relatively small and isolated group. Little of the frenetic activity it generates ever reaches outside that closed group" (1). Gioia's rueful observations remind me of similar remarks among New York intellectuals of the 1950s who imagined a halcyon time when poets were respected members of the establishment and when the avant-garde was synonymous with Thomas Mann and T. S. Eliot. But I take Gioia's disparaging remarks about subcultures as a positive recognition that poets of earlier times—especially the ones I discuss in this book—have taken their membership in a subculture as a badge of honor, a sign of disaffiliation. At a time when the official intellectual venues—presumably the ones that Gioia admires—were tainted by collusion with the national security state, subcultural identification may have been the only appropriate stance for poets to take. Gioia and other cultural conservatives who bemoan the loss of Kultur often use the professionalization of poetry through the growth of the creative writing program as a sign of poetry's decline, and as long as this is the only model by which poetry is measured he is probably right. But as this book has tried to demonstrate there are other, more public venues where poetry matters, not because it is part of intellectual life but because it refuses to feed the cultural machine that manufactures consensus.

In my introduction I invoked the face of Ernie Kovacs's Percy Dovetonsils—irreverent, bitchy, and fey—as my inaugural image of the poet. He was part of a collective cold war speech act in which "men like that" became "guys like us." Other faces have crowded in to complicate the picture: Beats pulling on cigarettes in T-shirts, New York dandies racing through cabs at rush hour, butch gals in short hair at the bar, black cultural nationalists pointing fingers at a crowd, Sylvia Plath wearing a man's oxford cloth shirt, Jack Spicer's pumpkin head cocked to one side and looking quizzically at his interlocutor. These images replace in my mind the portraits of John Frederick Nims, John Hall Wheelock, John Peele Bishop, and John Crowe Ransom on the covers of Oscar Williams's anthologies with which I grew up. But, having said this, I realize that the cold war generation of poets probably looks as tweedy and straight to the current generation as the original Oscar Williams's poets did to ours. Cary Nelson, speaking of the problem of cultural memory, notes that "we no longer know the history of the poetry of the first half of this century; most of us, moreover, do not know that the knowledge is gone" (4). One might say the same for the cold war era, but we might add that it was this era that perfected the art of forgetting, placing modernism safely beyond the veil of World War II where it would do no harm. It is in the interest of remembering the complexity of those cold war guys and their ways of creating community that that I have written this book.

Notes

1. Roland Barthes uses the term "reality effect" (*l'effet de réel*) to describe the realist novel's use of insignificant objects and details that contribute to the overall impression of verisimilitude. My use of the phrase to describe Ernie Kovacs's characters obviously skews Barthes's usage to suggest that television in its early stages created its own form of reality that normalized one form of masculinity by creating alternative, nontraditional characters—like Percy Dovetonsils. See Barthes, "The Reality Effect."

2. Giorgio Agamben points out that the medieval poet's equation of the body of the poem with the body of a woman extends to an analogy between metrical and anatomical perfection. Hence Dante "conceives of the structure of the *canzone* as founded on the relation between an essentially semantic, global unit and essentially metrical, partial units. [Dante] expresses this contrast through a bodily image: the feminine bosom, womb, or lap, with the implicit assimilation . . . of the *canzone* to a body constituted by metrical organs" (35–36).

3. On the origins of American containment ideology, see Campbell; Etzold and Gaddis; Gaddis; McCormick; and Nadel.

4. Although she does not describe a cocktail party, Diana Trilling describes a reading given by Allen Ginsberg and Gregory Corso at Columbia University that registers something of the anxiety produced by the Beat generation at more genteel gatherings. In her memoir, "The Other Night at Columbia: A Report from the Academy," Trilling expresses surprise at how well behaved and articulate Ginsberg was at the event, despite her fears that an appearance of the Beats at Columbia would provoke a riot.

5. Sidney Hook specifically links New Critical values of aesthetic detachment to fears of Soviet invasion: "If anything, one expects the intellectuals to see even more clearly that the relative autonomy of their craft is threatened by Soviet totalitarianism more completely than by any other social system in history" (570).

6. In this regard (and to contemporary ears) it is bizarre to hear Phillip Rahv speak in this forum of the avant-garde as being responsible for "most of the literary masterpieces of the past hundred years, from *Madame Bovary* to the *Four Quartets*" (310).

7. An earlier version of this phenomenon is described in Richard Hofstadter's "The Paranoid Style in American Politics," an essay written on the heels of the Kennedy assassination and one that looks retrospectively at earlier moments in U.S. history when panics over subversive activities dominated political life.

8. Jean Baudrillard discusses sociologists of consumerism such as Packard or Galbraith in his early essay, "Consumer Society." Describing Galbraith's use of the phrase "revised sequence," Baudrillard says that it has "the critical value of undermining the fundamental myth of the classical relation which assumes that it is the individual who exercises power in the economic system" (38). But Baudrillard goes on to point out that this reversal of producer and consumer presumes that consumers *could* exercise independent judgment were it not for the appearance of "artificial accelerators" from advertising and marketing that take over such judgment. Given Baudrillard's theory that a culture of simulation has replaced a prior "real" with fictions, such maintenance of the status quo as Galbraith proposes is itself a fiction.

9. The panic that Baldwin diagnoses may itself be a sign of distress out of which new versions of masculinity may emerge. As David Savran points out, Mailer's hipster is a prototype for a new type of postmodern subject, "a product of cultural miscegenation, a cross-dresser, neither completely white nor Black, masculine nor feminine, heterosexual nor homosexual, working-class nor bourgeois ... Embracing blackness, femininity, homosexuality, and poverty to declare himself white, masculine, heterosexual, and a man of independent means, he is unable, however, to stabilize any of these positions" (*Taking It* 52).

10. On background to *Kiss Me Deadly*, see Flinn, "Sound, Woman, and the Bomb."

11. Quoted in Telotte, "The Fantastic Realism of Film Noir" (13).

12. On homosexual and lesbian relationships during World War II, see Faderman (118–87) and D'Emilio and Freedman (239–74).

13. On the role of community formation in avant-garde poetry, see Beach; Silliman; and Rifkin.

14. For an excellent account of this formalist tradition, see Brunner.

15. The book closest to my own concerns is Edward Brunner's *Cold War Poetry*, which provides the most exhaustive survey of 1950s poetry to date. Unlike my book, which deals with "mavericks and renegades," Brunner's studies the "center" of American poetry during the 1950s (ix). Most significantly he provides a capacious survey of the "populist elitism" of much mainstream verse, which sought not modernist distanciation but, rather, accommodation to the mainstream reader. This is a significant transformation of the usual dichotomy between Beat bohemians and New Critical formalists because it opens up a third possibility for the poet, the professional academic writer, charged "with helping to quarantine a mass culture that other intellectuals viewed as out of control" (x). Although Brunner devotes a chapter to poems that thematize the atomic bomb, he does not spend a great deal of time on the causes or effects of the cold war itself nor to its impact on poetry, whether vanguard or mainstream.

16. The terrorist attacks of 11 September 2001 were initially followed by overwhelming U.S. support for retaliation against various Arab countries, but in the aftermath of this event support has wavered, especially in the light of the ongoing Palestinian-Israeli conflict. Hence the "crisis" over localized wars may not apply in the post–11 September climate, although the saber rattling that has continued by members of the Bush administration certainly looks like a restitution of an older model of masculine authority.

CHAPTER ONE

1. Rich discusses compulsory heterosexuality in "Compulsory Heterosexuality and Lesbian Existence" in Rich (203–24). Sedgwick's theory of homosocial desire is discussed in *Between Men* (1–20).

2. On the more general gendering of poetry, see Jed Rasula, "Gendering the Muse."

3. Austin's theory of the performative—a speech act characterized by "performing . . . an action" through contractual or declaratory means—is articulated in his 1955 William James Lectures at Harvard, collected as *How to Do Things with Words* (6).

4. For a thorough account of the vicissitudes of performance during the postwar era, see Daniel Belgrad, *The Culture of Spontaneity: Improvisation and the Arts in Postwar America*.

5. Although Olson led a heterosexual life, he often worried over the "troubles of Androgyne" in relation to his male students. Tom Clark reports that "he dreamed of ambiguous sexual encounters involving male students" (224), one dream of which may have been that described in "The Librarian" (1957). In this poem, the author of

Maximus discovers a "young musician" and librarian of Gloucester "in my parents' bedroom where I / found him intimate with my former wife" (*Collected Poems* 413). The replacement of young musician for husband, son for parents, librarian for poet, suggests a complex substitution of speaker and male other. Within this substitution set, every term of the poet's life—his patrimony, poetry, marriage—is met by a younger surrogate male. It would not be hard, then, to assume that the violation of the marriage bed is also a violation of the terms of heterosexual marriage as well, in which access to the female partner is blocked by the male.

6. I have discussed the relationship between literary communities and gender during the 1950s in *The San Francisco Renaissance*. Some of the discussion in this essay repeats that in my earlier book, but I now see some of the inadequacies of that earlier treatment and want to redress them here in the light of recent queer theory.

7. In *Epistemology of the Closet*, Sedgwick defines the darker effects of male bonding when structured within "a secularized and psychologized homophobia" (185). What Sedgwick calls the "paranoid Gothic" includes various forms of romanticism in which "a male hero is in a close, usually murderous relation to another male figure, in some respects his 'double,' to whom he seems to be mentally transparent" (186 n. 10). But it could also include early modernist "urban bachelor" novels of Henry James in which the central male character's inability to act is predicated not on indecision but on an overriding homosexual panic. Sedgwick's test case is James's "The Beast in the Jungle," but it would also include Freud's analysis of repression in the case of Dr. Schreber or modernist aesthetes like Pound's Mauberley or Eliot's Prufrock. Obviously homosexual panic means one thing for an era in which homosexuality is being invented and another for one in which it is being deployed as a threat to national security. Moreover Victorian novelists solved the problem of panic by creating a bachelor hero of indeterminate sexuality, whereas the homosexual anxiety that I describe in the cold war era is formed within communal networks, literary movements, and schools.

8. It is no little irony that the poet who staked so much on the unfettered breath was himself a chronic sufferer of emphysema, worsened by a lifetime of heavy smoking.

9. See Perloff's "Charles Olson and the 'Inferior Predecessors.'"

10. On homosexuality at Black Mountain, see Duberman (225–27, 330–33).

11. Interview with Nancy Armstrong, 27 Aug. 1993.

12. On intellectuals and the new class see Andrew Ross, *No Respect* (209–32) and Barbara Ehrenreich, *Fear of Falling* (144–95).

13. On Goodman at Black Mountain, see Duberman (329–33) and Horowitz.

14. On Goodman's poetry about Black Mountain, see Clark (224).

15. These lectures have been collected in Spicer, *The House That Jack Built*.

16. On Kantorowicz and the Berkeley Renaissance, see Ellingham and Killian (19–21, 32–33).

17. The reference to looking at "other people's magic" seems to refer to Robert

Duncan, who had been accused by Olson of dabbling in mysticism as a sectarian practice rather than as received truth. Olson's criticism appeared in an essay, "Against Wisdom as Such," which is mentioned in the previous poem of the series where Spicer aligns himself with Olson against Duncan's "gleeful, crass, and unworshipping / Wisdom" (226). Thus Spicer's attack on institutionalized homosexuality combines with his rejection of Duncan's "crass" wisdom in a complex form of male bonding with Olson.

18. On Spicer's relationship to early homophile organizations, see Ellingham and Killian (46–50).

19. This line inspired Denise Levertov to write her own critical response, "Hypocrite Women," which counters Spicer's rather outrageous claim as part of her own feminist response. I have discussed both poems in *The San Francisco Renaissance* (172–73).

20. García Lorca is a central figure in the poetics of the New American poetry. His "Theory and Function of the Duende" is often quoted in manifestos and essays of the 1950s and serves as a precursor to Spicer's theories of literary image. His poetry was translated extensively by poets, especially the Deep Image poets who searched for non-French versions of symbolism and surrealism.

CHAPTER TWO

1. The best discussion of the "poetry wars" between anthologies is Alan Golding's *From Outlaw to Classic,* which discusses Eric Torgerson's use of the phrase "cold war" to refer to literary debates (28).

2. By focusing on the Beats in these opening remarks I do not mean to exclude other important literary groups such as the New York school, Black Mountain, Deep Image, or Black Arts movements. But the Beats, more than these other groups, projected their marginality as a cultural sign that was incorporated and consumed by mainstream America.

3. In her journal entry of 19 June 1953, Plath echoes Esther's physical discomfort: "All right, so the headlines blare the two of them are going to be killed at eleven o'clock tonight. So I am sick at the stomach." Yet her response, unlike Esther's, concerns the larger national spectacle of electrocution: "There is no yelling, no horror, no great rebellion. That is the appalling thing." And her judgment of the Rosenberg's guilt is mediated by her awareness of the irony of electrocuting spies for passing along secrets whose content was mass destruction: "They were going to kill people with those atomic secrets. It is good for them to die. So that we can have the priority of killing people with those atomic secrets which are so very jealously and specially and inhumanly ours" (*Unabridged Journals* 541).

4. By comparing American McCarthyism to Stalinist purges I do not mean to blur important differences in actual effects. Obviously the Stalinist gulag caused far greater personal and social tragedy to the best minds of Mayakofsky's generation than

the red scare did to that of Ginsberg's. My point is to show that the politics of containment was not limited to foreign policy but affected the nature of private, domestic identities as well.

5. According to David Halberstam, Ricky's on-screen rebellion as a rock 'n' roll teen idol was orchestrated, to a large extent, by Ozzie Nelson, who saw the advantages of creating a sanitized version of Elvis for his younger television audience. But Ozzie's co-option of Ricky's rebellion caused rifts in the off-screen family (518–19).

6. On the relationship between westerns and anticommunism, see Savran, *Communists, Cowboys, and Queers* (1–19).

7. I have discussed the production of voice through electronic surveillance media in *Ghostlier Demarcations* (196–223).

8. On northern and southern press responses to the funeral for Emmett Till, see Ruth Feldstein (267–77). Feldstein notes that the various meanings of Till's death "pointed to the contested meanings of motherhood and respectability," and that what it meant to be a "good" mother was being managed differently by the black press in reporting on the trial and funeral. The fact that Mamie Till insisted on opening her son's coffin was an important intervention into domestic ideology: "in claiming her role as a grieving mother she helped inject motherhood more forcefully into the political landscape, but she could not control the terms of the debate or the ways in which she herself was a symbol" (266). This may be true as far as the historical Mamie Till is concerned, but Brooks does seem to understand this point by exposing the tensions between romantic conventions and racist realities.

9. The *New York Times* for 17 September 1959 is dominated by the Russian premier's visit—his trip to a model farm, his address to the National Press Club, Mrs. Khrushchev's opinions about Mrs. Eisenhower, what the Soviet leader would eat at State Department dinners. For our purposes, one of the most amusing news clips concerns a meeting between Khrushchev and Allen Dulles, the director of the Central Intelligence Agency. On being introduced to Dulles, Khrushchev said, "I know you. I read the same reports you do" (Mooney 20). To which Dulles replied, "I hope you get them legally." Given the fact that within a few weeks of this visit Gary Powers's U-2 surveillance plane would be shot down over Russia, causing a huge scandal in the intelligence community, Dulles's quip about legality has a certain hollow ring.

10. In an important essay on Pasternak, written around the same time as this poem, O'Hara speaks about Zhivago's refusal to "collaborate with society but with life. Soviet society is not alone in seducing the poet to deliver temporary half-truths which will shortly be cast aside for the excitement of a new celebration of nonlife" (*Standing Still* 103).

11. Although not written around the time of Khrushchev's visit, O'Hara's 1957 poem "Wind" also seems to address cold war containment:

Who'd have thought
             that snow falls

it always circled whirling
like a thought
                        in the glass ball
around me and my bear

Then it seemed beautiful
                        containment
snow whirled
                        nothing ever fell
nor my little bear
                        bad thoughts
imprisoned in crystal
    (269)

It is, of course, tempting to regard O'Hara's "containment" as similar to that used by
the State Department, especially when the scene depicted includes other signs of Russia: bears and snow. What seems more significant as a reference to the cold war is the
poem's sense that "beauty has replaced itself with evil / And the snow whirls only / in
fatal winds." Snow no longer falls within an innocent, contained world of a child's pa-
perweight but within a larger "cold" world of fate and evil, that winds from the east
blow west toward New York.

    12. For a more thorough overview of mainstream poets during this period, see
Brunner.

CHAPTER THREE

    1. California State Proposition 187 (1994) is one of several propositions passed
in the 1990s directed at ethnic minorities. Proposition 209 (1997) dismantled all
affirmative action programs, and Proposition 227 (1998) dismantled all bilingual education programs in public schools.

    2. The disparity between the historical presence of Asians in California and
their cultural representation can be illustrated by the fact that Kevin Starr, the state's
best known historian, devotes only four pages of his *Americans and the California
Dream: 1850–1915* (1973) to Chinese immigrants. At the same time he devotes an entire chapter to the Bohemian Club where members often satirized ethnic minorities in
their weekend retreats and high jinks.

    3. These restructurings were themselves enabled by orientalist discourse. As
Chris Connery points out, cold war rhetoric often figured the Soviet Union as an oriental despotism, its political and social goals shrouded in mystery, against the clear,
rational agendas of the West. The subsequent invention of the Pacific Rim as a "discursive and strategic Other" to the Soviet Union becomes a way of incorporating Asia
into the goals and aspirations of U.S. multinational capitalism (31–32).

4. There are good reasons why Shanghai is the city with which Elsa is associated. It was one of the first cities to be opened to the West and maintained a reputation as an international city. European-style café life flourished alongside massage parlors, opium dens, and houses of prostitution. Rey Chow notes that "Shanghai was distinguished not just as a modern city but also as a city of coexisting native and alien cultures. . . . Shanghai thus became in the eyes of many an alien China, ideologically and structurally in contradiction to the 'authentic' one" (37).

5. Another layer within the racial formation of *The Lady from Shanghai* is provided by the film's reference to Latin culture. Elsa's remark about short-lived love is made while on board Bannister's yacht as it travels up the Mexican coast, and it is in this portion of the film that Elsa's sexuality is dramatically exploited by Welles. Elsa is shown in a provocative swimsuit or walking the streets of Acapulco in a gauzy white gown. Mariachi music plays in the background, and peasants are shown in colorful native costumes. Coinciding with Elsa's sexual seduction of O'Hara, Acapulco provides the backdrop for Grisby's attempt to lure O'Hara into his own intrigue. The tropical heat of Mexico, exotic food, sensual music, and Welles's characteristically off-center camera angles create a mood of seductiveness that anticipates a similar cultural framing in San Francisco. Finally, the fact that Rita Hayworth is herself of Mexican origin, her hair died to remove all traces of Latin heritage, creates a tertiary layer of racial cross-dressing to this film.

6. Bannister's Jewishness is never spelled out, but it is clearly one of several cultural markers (disability due to polio, emasculated husband, devious lawyer) that Welles uses to emphasize his "weakness" vis-à-vis his wife. In *Citizen Kane* (1941), Everett Sloane plays the Jewish lawyer, Bernstein, who must manipulate Kane's shady business deals, adding credence to his Jewishness in *The Lady from Shanghai*.

7. This quality is vividly rendered in the silent film *Old San Francisco* (1927), in which Chinatown is depicted as a multilayered warren of narrow streets, opium dens, secret passageways, and dens of prostitution. At the film's climax the 1906 San Francisco earthquake levels the Chinese ghetto, destroying the film's cross-dressing Asian antagonist (Warner Ohland) and permitting urban redevelopment to rise from its ashes.

8. The definitive history of the poem and its reception can be found in Fenn, *Ah Sin and His Brethren in American Literature*. On the reception of this poem and Harte's response, see Takaki (105–6).

9. I am grateful to Ramón Garcia for introducing me to this story and for his own work on it.

10. Elizabeth Bishop gives a fair indication of Rexroth's relationship to easterners in a 1948 letter describing a writer's weekend at Bard College: "Those present were Richard Wilbur, [Richard] Eberhart, Cal [Robert Lowell], Lloyd [Frankenberg], Jean Garrigue, Dr. [William Carlos] Williams and Miss [Louise] Bogan and me, and a wild man from California in a bright red shirt and yellow braces named [Kenneth] Rexroth, who did his best to start a fight with everyone and considered us all effete and snobbish

Easterners. He never quite succeeded and finally had to prove his mettle or his reality or something by taking three of the prettiest undergraduates off for an evening in the cemetery" (174).

11. See *The San Francisco Renaissance* (95–112).

12. On Snyder's childhood relationship to Chinese landscape painting, see *The Real Work* (93–94). See also the introduction to *Mountains and Rivers without End.*

13. In section fourteen of "Logging" in *Myths and Texts* Snyder laments the clear cutting of timber in Asia and the West: "The groves are down / cut down / Groves of Ahab, of Cybele" (15).

14. See, for example, his interview with Peter Barry Chowka in *The Real Work,* especially 106–11.

15. See Rexroth's "Interview," in *The San Francisco Poets* (9).

16. I discuss Rexroth's role in the formation of a western bohemia in *The San Francisco Renaissance.*

17. In a 1957 article in *The Nation* Rexroth makes this connection between East Coast and Orient explicit: "The literary market place is far away in New York. Its cocktail parties and scalping expeditions and log rolling bees might as well be on the moon. . . . Its very remoteness helps make the city cosmopolitan. . . . Oriental interests come naturally, with none of the unwholesomeness of the occult. Several young SF writers read Chinese and Japanese, more are interested in Buddhism" ("San Francisco's Mature Bohemians" 160). I have discussed Rexroth's views of San Francisco's cosmopolitanism in *The San Francisco Renaissance* (11–12).

18. On the sources of Marichiko, see Gibson (83). In his note to the series Rexroth identifies Marichiko with Marishi-ben, an "Indian, pre-Aryan, goddess of the dawn who is a bodhisattva in Buddhism and patron of geisha, prostitutes, women in childbirth, and lovers, and in another aspect, once of samurai" (141).

19. It should be pointed out that the cultural efflorescence of Asian American literature since the publication of the 1974 landmark anthology *Aieeeee!* has not been achieved without its own gendered conflicts. The most famous instance involves the debate between Frank Chin and Maxine Hong Kingston over the latter's *The Woman Warrior.* Chin, along with his coeditors of *Aieeeee!* complained about the absence of heroic Asian American manhood and the proliferation of Asian stereotypes. Chin deplores Kingston's *The Woman Warrior* for its use of autobiography, a traditional "women's" genre, and for depicting Chinese American men as sexist. For further discussion of this debate, see King-Kok Cheung, "The Woman Warrior versus the Chinaman Pacific."

CHAPTER FOUR

1. *Los Angeles Times,* 18 Aug. 1992, A10. The radical Right has used the charge of transvestism to impugn liberals before. In the 1988 presidential elections, the Moral Majority's Jerry Falwell propagated a comic book, distributed by his son and

drawn by a "Christian cartoonist," depicting Democratic presidential candidate, Michael Dukakis, in a wig and dress. Responding to the potentially libelous nature of the representation, Falwell said that "it portrays the person in the context of what he is for or against" (Garber 54).

2. Nor is homophobia restricted to campaign rhetoric. Oregon's 1992 Initiative 9, the "Abnormal Behaviors Initiative," proposed to amend the state constitution to deny minority status to gays and lesbians and to restrict state funding or jobs to anyone who treats homosexuality as anything other than "abnormal, wrong, unnatural and perverse."

3. This damage, for Duncan, is not merely metaphorical but literal. In several of his poems, he refers to his youthful initiation into homosexual relations that resulted in a violent beating. I discuss this motif in *Ghostlier Demarcations* (187–90).

4. One could regard Whitman's catalogues as vast explorations of multiple identities in which the poet becomes so many things that the very unity to which his listings aspires is negated. Not only does Whitman identify with "the woman the same as the man" he also identifies with cities, mountains, animals, and gods (48). If a catalogue represents an attempt to enumerate for the purposes of cultural renewal, Whitman's catalogues, by their sheer diversity, call attention to the theatrical nature of identification. Although the poet may walk "with perfect ease in the capitol," he is not so much representative as a "representation":

Then the mechanics take him for a mechanic,
And the soldiers suppose him to be a soldier, and the
     sailors that he has follow'd the sea
And the authors take him for an author,
     and the artists for an artist,
And the laborers perceive he could labor with them
     and love them,
     ("Song of the Answerer" 168)

5. In this essay I am using the term *homosexual* to refer to same-sex relations among males. While not denying important influences by Whitman on both heterosexual women and lesbians, I want to limit my discussion to one specific form of identity construction involving masculine identity. In fact, it is because Whitman's ideal of same-sex relations is so specifically gendered as masculine that I want to study how later poets used him to confuse gender positions in their own work. On Crane's use of Whitman to develop his own homosexual text, see Yingling (4–7, 211–13).

6. I derive this phrase from Ed Folsom's excellent survey of literary tributes to Whitman, "Talking Back to Walt Whitman: An Introduction."

7. The mode of redress that I have identified with modernism does not end with Whitman's rediscovery in the late 1950s. Louis Simpson, in an essay setting out to "honor" Whitman, spends most of his time explaining how embarrassed he has

been as a poet by Whitman's "whooping it up," his "use of big-sounding words," his visionary tendencies and his desire that "young men . . . throw their arms about his neck" (Perlman, Folsom, and Campion 257–61). It is not that Simpson and his modernist forebears do not claim Whitman as a source for their poetry, only that in order to do so they must bring him down a peg, display their own good sense at Walt's expense.

8. Despite Oppen's dismissal of Whitman in his letter to Williams, he places the author of *Leaves of Grass* in a central location at the end of his long poem, "Of Being Numerous." In the last section of the poem—which chronicles Oppen's opposition to the Vietnam War—he quotes a letter by Whitman to his mother written during the Civil War which describes the Capitol Building by night, "a great bronze figure, the Genius of Liberty," which to Whitman looks "curious." Oppen ends his poem with this talismanic word to validate Whitman's speculative manner in his poetry but also his "curiosity" *about* everyday sights and scenes in the midst of war (*New Collected Poems* 188).

9. On the formation of American Studies and the anxious reception of *The American Renaissance* by Matthiessen's friends and colleagues, see Abelove, "American Studies, Queer Studies."

10. Whitman's variation on O'Hara's lines could be those in section 28 of "Song of Myself" in which the speaker's masturbatory fantasy is staged in terms of a rape in which his "fellow-senses" are taken away and replaced by unnamed new identities:

On all sides prurient prokers stiffening my limbs,
Straining the udder of my heart for its witheld drip,
Behaving licentious toward me, taking no denial,
Depriving me of my best as for a purpose,
Unbuttoning my clothes, holding me by the bare waist.
    (57)

11. Whitman's most thorough explanation of the variable voice is "Song of the Answerer" where the poet describes himself as a translator rather than an inspired author, one who responds rather than inaugurates. The human condition that he witnesses speaks in a variety of idiolects:

Every existence has its idiom, every thing has an idiom and tongue,
He resolves all tongues into his own and bestows it upon men, and
    any man translates, and any man translates himself also,
One part does not counteract another part, he is the joiner, he sees how they join.
    (168)

12. According to Brad Gooch's biography, O'Hara did love to cruise bars, parks, and public spaces for casual (and promiscuous) sex (194). The potential for violence, whether from plainclothes police in the bars or rough trade encounters, informs

much of the disjunctiveness of this poem and qualifies the traditional view of O'Hara as happy peripatetic stroller.

13. Robert von Hallberg has described the salient tonal feature of these poets as "cosmopolitan," which he links to Wordsworth's preface to *Lyrical Ballads*. Quoting Wordsworth, von Hallberg notes that a poet "makes a formal engagement that he will gratify certain known habits of association, that he not only thus apprizes the Reader that certain classes of ideas and expressions will be found in his book, but that others will be carefully excluded" (18).

14. I am grateful to Robert von Hallberg for suggesting the two poems discussed in this section.

15. See "Paris, Capital of the Nineteenth Century."

16. For a useful, extensive reading of this passage, see Byrne Fone, *Masculine Landscapes* (27).

CHAPTER FIVE

1. Andrew Ross connects O'Hara's epiphany at the 5 Spot with Norman Mailer's essay, "The White Negro" in which moments of authenticity for the white hipster are purchased by connection with black culture. Ross notes that although O'Hara appears to be moved by Holiday's performance, his typical milieu is seldom the jazz club, suggesting that the poet is engaging in a bit of cultural slumming. Ross goes on to point out that although the poem is obviously parodic, it is difficult to figure out "who and what is being parodied or *imitated*"—whether it is O'Hara's own high culture proclivities or his use of black vernacular traditions to underwrite those proclivities (67).

2. O'Hara does name at least one black person in his poem, Mal Waldron, to whom Billie Holiday "whispered" her song. Her intimate, private contact with a fellow black performer creates a degree of intimacy in direct contrast to O'Hara's frenzied lunch hour and alienated social life. In fact, the verb, "whispered," signals the quiet vitality that O'Hara seeks in his otherwise "breathless" day.

3. Of course Pan-Africanism has a much older tradition in African American culture and was a primary focus of political life during the Harlem Renaissance. The dialogue that I am describing here is one between U.S. black intellectuals within the specific framework of decolonization and nationalist struggles in the wake of World War II.

4. At this time, Jones was living in the Lower East Side, publishing *Yugen* magazine with his wife, Hettie, and editing *Floating Bear* with Diane DiPrima. And within this Greenwich Village milieu, he was soon to publish in magazines such as *Umbra*, which was one of the first publications in what was to become the Black Arts movements.

5. It is significant that Jones himself does not name Billie Holiday in *Blues People*, a significant absence given his attention to other female blues singers such as Bessie Smith. I am grateful to Don Wayne for pointing this fact out to me.

6. On the unnaming of black women in Black Arts fiction, see Joyce Hope Scott's "From Foreground to Margin" (305–7).

7. On Malcolm X and masculinity, see Saldana-Portillo. It would be wrong to assert that only men expressed misogyny or homophobia. Manning Marable quotes the work of Nikki Giovanni, Lucille Clifton, and others who manifest the same nationalist patriarchalism as that of male poets. Similarly, the attack on homosexuals as a threat to the nationalist project is sustained in Jayne Cortez's "Race" with its invocation of gay men "unable to grasp the fact / and responsibility / of manhood black" and whose "ability to create what? / A Race called Faggot" (*Pisstained Stairs* n.p.). In a recent interview, however, Cortez says that the poem does not indict homosexuals: "I think it talks about the contradictions of a particular person. The poem is about contradictions and inconsistencies" ("Interview" 207).

8. Komozi Woodward makes a convincing case for black women's leadership in the formation of CFUN (Committee for Unified Newark) and other nationalist organizations. And while Woodward acknowledges gender discrimination in these organizations, he focuses primarily on male authority, generally, and Baraka's leadership role, specifically. His otherwise excellent history of black nationalism is limited by its strict institutional and historical focus. By not attending to cultural representations, he is unable to account for the more virulent strands of gender discrimination within the movement.

9. See, for example, Lipsitz, *The Possessive Investment in Whiteness* (84–85).

10. A summary selection of those responses appears at the back of Rainwater and Yancey, *The Moynihan Report and the Politics of Controversy* (395–478).

11. When I speak of misogyny and homophobia as "constitutive" within black nationalism, I am referring only to the version that surfaced in the wake of the civil rights movement. Previous nationalist movements allowed a much greater opportunity for women's participation and much greater latitude for alliances to be formed across racial lines. Abolitionism, antilynching protests, and slave revolts often were inspired and articulated by women such as Harriet Jacobs, Sojourner Truth, Maria Stewart, Ida B. Wells, and others. As Joyce Hope Scott notes, black women were at the center of nationalist movements as early as the eighteenth century. And writings of Frederick Douglass, Martin Delany, Robert Purvis, James Forten, Charles Lenox Remond, and William Nell "advocated through their oratories and their writings the centrality of women in the struggle for freedom and justice in America" (Scott, *Nationalism and Sexualities* 298). While this simplifies a considerably more complicated sexual politics within earlier black male rhetoric, the black nationalist movement of the 1960s made patriarchy a cornerstone of its program.

12. Baraka has modified his stance on homosexuals somewhat. In an interview published in 1990, he declares, "I don't think I believe in any gratuitous attacks on homosexuals as such. I've tried to stop saying that, calling people 'faggots,' even though, still I would say when the majority of black people say 'faggot,' they're not talking about homosexuals . . . you're talking about him being a weak, jive person." Despite

his belief that the civil rights of gays should not be violated, he goes on to say that he wouldn't want his child to be educated by one: "But obviously I don't want the child to be taught homosexuality, and I don't want the child to *be* a homosexual. I don't want that to be raised up as a positive thing, because I do believe that homosexuality is a social aberration" ("Interview" 240).

13. This attack on homosexuality and lesbianism coincides with a cultural critique of the Harlem Renaissance, which had included a number of gay men and women, including several of its most distinguished authors, among them Langston Hughes, Countee Cullen, and Alain Locke.

14. The example of the Nation of Islam suggests that its appeal was less in its origins in a specific national site in the Middle East or Africa than in its invocation of an international movement.

15. One could make similar claims about the ways that critics of the same period gendered "heroic" abstract expressionism. In both Black Art and Action Painting, the gestural quality of language, its spontaneity and freeform movement, was counterposed to more constrained, figural language. On the gendering of abstract expressionism, see Wagner.

16. Baraka makes a similar distinction about the femininity (and inadequacy) of the blues in *The Dutchman:* "If Bessie Smith had killed a few white people she wouldn't have had to sing the blues" (Baraka and Neal 163).

17. On the formation of the Black Arts Repertory Theater, see Woodard (62–68).

18. Benston reads this inversion of modernism as Baraka's most revolutionary contribution: his poetry "appropriates a classic Euro-American form, inverts its imagery and themes, and molds it into a new structure by wedding furious critique to traditional Afro-American expressions and the language of Pan-African mythologies" (*Baraka* 119).

19. On Crow Jane as negative muse, see the interview in *Conversations with Amiri Baraka* (174–75).

20. Ntozake Shange speaks of infibulation and genital mutilation of girls in her response to critics of *For Colored Girls . . .* in *Black Scholar* (28).

21. Baraka, in his later interviews, has acknowledged the importance of Olson's influence. See *Conversations with Amiri Baraka* (173).

22. Larry Neal summarizes Baraka's positions by speaking of poems as "physical entities: fists, daggers, airplane poems, and poems that shoot guns. Poems are transformed from physical objects into personal forces" (187).

23. bell hooks notes that "Baraka did not celebrate this male violence against women in isolation. His plays were performed before audiences of women and men who were not shocked, disgusted and outraged by what they saw" (107). hooks goes on to point out that the dramatization of black male woman-hating led, in one case, to a black actress being bludgeoned to death on stage.

24. A good example of this use of self-criticism to further demonize others can

be seen in his new preface to his *Autobiography*. Acknowledging his "previous" male chauvinism, he attacks his former wife, Hettie (Cohen) Jones for presenting him in an unkind light in her own memoir, *How I Became Hettie Jones*. The invective that he delivers against Jones is extreme, even by Baraka's standards, but it seems directed as much at criticisms he has received from black feminists. By bludgeoning his former wife for undermining his political commitment through her depiction of his sexism, he may claim to have been "wronged" by a bad white woman (a "cryptoracist" he calls her) who is "an animated agent of straight-out lies and harassment" (xxii).

25. Marcellus Blount notes that this desire extends to the nineteenth century. Describing Anna Julia Cooper, he notes that she "bemoaned the desire of black male leaders to speak for the entire black race, and she posited instead the centrality of her black female consciousness" (*Engendering Men* 225).

26. Aldon Nielsen has reminded me that although Baraka's title implies "self-mutilation," the fact that it refers to a "preface" to a "20 Volume Suicide Note" qualifies the seriousness of his suicidal intent (personal correspondence, 12 Feb. 1998).

CHAPTER SIX

1. Or so it seemed at the time. In going back to that anthology in preparation for writing this chapter, I discovered that Kennedy does acknowledge that his reading of the poem "may be overly biographical." He mentions essays by Wendy Martin and Erica Jong who propose alternate, feminist readings (227).

2. See, for example, Wendy Martin, "From Patriarchy to the Female Principle," and Erica Jong, "Visionary Anger."

3. On "lesbian continuum," see Rich, "Compulsory Heterosexuality and Lesbian Existence" (203–23).

4. Halberstam notes that masculinity in action films such as the James Bond series "has little, if anything to do with biological maleness and signifies more often as a technical special effect" (*Female* 3). Masculinity in such films is often performed not by Bond but by female characters such as M in *Goldeneye* who expose "the sham of Bond's own performance" (4). This prosthetic aspect of Bond's masculinity has been parodied recently in the Mike Meyers's Austin Powers films, which are built entirely around Bondian gadgets—cars, techno-devices, futuristic weapons—and gestures that explode Bond's supposed sexual prowess—and allure. Halberstam has discussed the Austin Powers phenomenon in her *GLQ* essay.

5. The controversy surrounding Billie Tipton poses a set of interesting challenges to the usual taxonomies of sex and gender. As Diane Middlebrook shows in her recent biography, Tipton was a woman who cross-dressed as a man throughout his career as a jazz pianist and entertainer. Tipton successfully managed to pass as a male, despite the complexities of maintaining an active sexual life with two of his three wives and touring with an all-male combo throughout the 1940s and 1950s. Female-to-male

(f2m) transsexuals have faulted Middlebrook's biography for seeing Tipton as engaged in an elaborate charade or con job. "[When] I look at the pictures in the book I see female-to-male written all over them," says Jamison Green, president of FTM International (Japenga E4). And Holly Devor agrees, saying that "Billy Tipton needed to be a man" (Japenga E4). For transsexuals, Tipton is not a female in male attire but a masculine female who participated sexually with consenting female partners.

6. Joan Nestle, speaking of 1950s butch-femme self-expression, defines it as a "lesbian-specific way of deconstructing gender that radically reclaims women's *erotic* energy. . . . The pinky ring flashing in a subway car, the DA haircut combed more severely in front of a mirror always made me catch my breath, symbolizing as they did a butch woman announcing her erotic competence. A language of courtship and seduction was carefully crafted to allow for expression of both lust and love in the face of severe social repression" (Penn 375).

7. The example of Billy Tipton offers a good example of female masculinity as a gender position outside of both heterosexual and lesbian circles. According to Diane Middlebrook, Tipton lived within a largely male, heterosexual environment of musicians and showed little interest in gay or lesbian lifestyles. One feature of Tipton's onstage monologues was a series of misogynist, homophobic comedy routines. Interviews with former wives of Tipton, all of whom claim to have been unaware of "her" actual gender, suggest that although they were attracted to "his" sensitivity and kindness, "he" played the role of patriarchal head of household in every respect.

8. On the demonization of lesbians under Production Code rules, see Donna Penn, "The Sexualized Woman."

9. On the formation of the Mattachine Society, see D'Emilio, "Gay Politics and Community in San Francisco" (460).

10. This response from the DOB was to a recent attack on homosexuals in San Francisco during its current election. Using a platform statement by the Mattachine Society at its annual convention, a candidate for mayor, Russell Wolden, accused the incumbent mayor, George Christopher, of allowing "sex deviates" to make San Francisco its headquarters. The most damning evidence of this fact, Wolden claimed, was the presence of "organized homosexuals" in the city, by which he meant the Mattachine Society and the Daughters of Bilitis. A summary of the article and responses to it were printed in the November 1959 number of *The Ladder*.

11. What I have been describing as an assimilationist posture within the DOB is class-inflected and does not necessarily reflect the views of many working-class lesbians who were making their own culture outside of institutional venues like *The Ladder*. As Elizabeth Lapovsky Kennedy and Madeline Davis demonstrate in their study of Buffalo during the postwar era, butch-femme styles were prominent in the largely working-class lesbian community of that city. For black and white lesbians, the "salience and tenacity of butch-fem roles . . . derives from their functioning as both a powerful personal code of behavior and as an organizing principle for community life" (152).

12. The film is different from Cain's novel in many respects, not the least of

which is the fact that in the latter Mildred has an affair with both Wally and Monte. In the novel, Veda becomes a famous opera star, whereas in the film she attempts a brief career as a sexy singer in a cheap nightclub. The film's final shootout at Monte's beach house is a total fabrication, but it serves to provide a standard Hollywood conclusion to the gender trouble introduced within the melodrama/domestic frame.

13. Jeanne Heuvig notes that Moore's "poetry of understatement is structured by her paradoxical attempt to give expression to a universality and also to herself as a woman" (167).

14. See Rich's essay, "When We Dead Awaken" (171).

15. On Bishop's relation to the cold war, see Camille Roman, *Elizabeth Bishop's World War II–Cold War View.*

16. On Bishop's relation to Lacerda, see Millier (352–53). Maria Carlota Costallat de Macedo Soares was a remarkable woman in her own right. A painter, sculptor, architect, city planner, and politician, she was very much at the center of Brazilian cultural and political life during the 1950s and 1960s. She was the architect of a major project of urban renewal in Rio de Janeiro—a park that was part of the Aterro redevelopment project. She was also the architect of a distinctive modern house in Samambaia where she lived for some years with Bishop. On Bishop's relationship to Soares, see Oliveira.

17. See Betsy Erkkila's commentary on this correspondence in *Wicked Sisters* (124–26).

18. In an early poem, "The Gentleman of Shalott," the main presence in the poem is in fact part mirror and part male:

Which eye's his eye?
Which limb lies
next the mirror?
For neither is clearer
nor a different color
than the other

. . . . . .

To his mind
it's the indication
of a mirrored reflection
somewhere along the line
of what we call the spine.
        (9)

The question of which is mirror and which reality ("his person was / half looking glass") produces a perceptual confusion that Bishop thematizes in many of her poems.

19. As Betsy Erkkila summarizes Moore's response, "Not only was Bishop in some sense behaving like a hussy; she was also failing to observe Moore's ladylike code of aesthetic reticence" (138).

20. Millier points out that Bishop reread *Robinson Crusoe* before writing the poem and said, in an interview, that "her intention had been to retell the story without Defoe's message of Christian consolation. But the poem is as close as Elizabeth came to a verse autobiography" (447).

21. In her interview with George Starbuck, Bishop explains that when she was in college, "there were women's anthologies, and all-women issues of magazines, but I always refused to be in them. I didn't think about it very seriously, but I felt it was a lot of nonsense, separating the sexes. I suppose this feeling came from feminist principles, perhaps stronger than I was aware of" (Schwartz and Estes 322).

22. The biographies of Plath all indicate that she was aggressively involved in getting Hughes published and spent long hours correcting proofs and typing final drafts. Her journals indicate that she also shared in his fame once poems were accepted or else worried that certain poems had not been accepted.

23. Marjorie Perloff has discussed the disparity between Plath's letters to her mother and her poetry contemporaneous with those letters in "Sylvia Plath's 'Sivvy' Poems: A Portrait of the Poet as Daughter" (155–78).

24. Susan Van Dyne, in a fascinating essay on the manuscripts of Plath's bee poems, reports that many of Plath's most violent late poems were written on drafts of *The Bell Jar*, the recto of prose bleeding through to the verso of poetry.

25. The character of Joan may or may not have been based on a real character, but at least one historical woman, Jane V. Anderson, a Harvard psychiatrist, thought that the portrayal resembled her enough to sue the Plath estate in 1987. Anderson *did* meet Plath during the period that Plath was in a mental hospital, but her suit complains that she never made sexual advances as the novel claims and that this portrayal cost her (Anderson) severe mental stress and trauma. What Anderson claims was the actual threat offered to Plath was the threat of being a successful "career woman in the 1950s. . . . She wanted to get rid of me and what I represented" (MacPherson 90).

26. Introductory remarks to a reading for the BBC radio imply that the applicant is also a consumer: "In this poem . . . the speaker is an executive, a sort of exacting super-salesman. He wants to be sure the applicant for his marvelous product really needs it and will treat it right" (*Collected Poems* 293).

27. In "Face Lift," Plath speaks of the "Jovian voices of surgeons" (156).

28. Furthermore, he wrote a lengthy series of poems, *Birthday Letters*, that reinforce the heterosexual and "feminine" side of Plath while exposing her irrational behavior.

CHAPTER SEVEN

1. John Canaday in *The Nuclear Muse* notes that Oppenheimer's utterance of these words from the *Bhagavad-Gita* lends a certain prophetic quality to the event, "the weight of direct revelation, muting and disguising the anachronism involved in his

use of them" (184). Canaday goes on to point out that many of the Los Alamos scientists used literary allusions and rhetoric "to construct narratives capable of expressing and containing the moral ambiguities of their involvement with nuclear weapons" (184).

2. As Richard Ohmann points out, when "the lines of the Cold War firmed up, English was a pastoral retreat within the university. Its practitioners celebrated verbal art and Anglo-American high culture. Little disturbed their tranquility beyond a dispute as to whether textual analysis or historical and philological scholarship was to ground their claims to disciplinarity" (Ohmann 73).

3. In a letter to Robert Payne, who published "The Kingfishers" in *Montevallo Review,* Olson complains, "I have never forgiven Eliot for stealing Dry Salvages from me: if his 'poetic' use of same, and of the Lady of Good Voyage, and of the longshore fisherman in TW [*The Waste Land*] is a measure of his use of other experience, then he lacks economic root" (*Selected Letters* 94).

4. On Olson's life at Harvard, see Henry Abelove, Tom Clark, and Ralph Maud.

5. Within a year of completing "The Kingfishers," Olson traveled to the Yucatan Peninsula where he conducted fieldwork on Mayan glyphs and meso-American culture.

6. George Butterick identifies Fernand as John Gernand "who worked as a kind of associate curator at the Phillips Gallery in Washington" who was "perhaps slightly effeminate" (qtd. in Maud 25).

7. There are numerous other connections between the kingfisher among the Maya and the East. George Butterick discovered that the lines that conclude section 1 ("'The pool the kingfishers' feathers were wealth why / did the export stop?'") refer to Osbert Sitwell's book, *Escape with Me!* which describes the export of kingfisher feathers to China and their decorative use in Chinese wedding fashions (35). Although this detail is not explicit in the poem, it serves as one of several links between the "East" that was the New World and its trade with the Asian East.

8. Ralph Maud disagrees with Guy Davenport in seeing any reference to Pound's canto in these lines. Rather, Maud feels that they more properly derive from a biblical story about Samson's killing of a lion. When Samson returns to the scene, he finds "a swarm of bees in the body of the lion, and honey" (99). Yet, Olson's address to "you" ("I pose you your question") seems rather obviously to refer to Pound's lines in Canto 74, "That maggots shd / eat the dead bullock." We must also hear, in these remarks, a contrast to Olson's final lines in which he hunts "among stones" instead of among the carcasses of dead history.

9. In "The Songs of Maximus," Olson compares the "whiteness" of bird droppings and decaying fish to the forces of commercialization in his native Gloucester: "And I am asked—ask myself (I, too, covered / with the gurry of it) where / shall we go from here, what can we do / when even the public conveyances / sing?" (*Maximus* 17).

10. On orientalism and the cold war, see William Pietz, "The Post-Colonialism of Cold War Discourse."

11. Perry Anderson is one of the few historians to note Olson's early use of the term. He notes the importance of "The Kingfishers" in defining a postmodern world, one that "lay beyond the imperial age of the Discoveries and the Industrial Revolution" (7). Anderson also situates Olson's development of the term within the poet's concept of space as the "mark of new history, and the measure of work now afoot" (8).

12. The question of whether Korea is a postcolonial country has been the subject of some debate. When it received independence from Japan in 1945, Korea rapidly became colonized by other forces—a nationalist movement within the country, supported by the United States. Hence it might be better to think of Cha's poem as marking not Korea's postcoloniality but the endurance of its colonial status within various rhetorics of decolonization posed by the West.

13. A recent exhibition of her films and video installations at the University of California, Berkeley, Art Museum was the first retrospective survey of Cha's work. The catalogue produced for that exhibit, *The Dream of the Audience: Theresa Hak Kyung Cha (1951–1982)*, is particularly helpful in situating her within the world of visual and performance art.

14. Although by comparing Olson's "The Kingfishers" with Cha, I am implying that *Dictee* is a poem, I have tried to use the term *work* or *text* throughout this essay in order to keep the issue of genre open. At the same time, by stressing Cha's work as a filmmaker and theoretician, I want to emphasize the ways that *Dictee* challenges the generic boundaries of film by adapting its features to a textual medium.

15. Elizabeth Frost notes that the acupuncture chart is printed "in negative: white-on-black. That formal choice is fitting for the first image in the 'Astronomy' section; its white points on a black background bring to mind the night sky and stars" (186). Frost goes on to point out that in an earlier period of Chinese history, cosmology and medicine were linked.

16. Like so much else in *Dictee,* the letter to her mother utilizes the outward form of a genre (in this case, epistolary form) to discuss historical materials that could never be contained in an actual letter. The address to her mother gradually merges into a meditation on the collapsing of temporal elements around repeated historical oppression: "I am in the same crowd, the same coup, the same revolt, nothing has changed. I am inside the demonstration I am locked inside the crowd and carried in its movement" (81). Such stylistic code-switching is indicative of a speaker who inhabits several historical moments and who, in addressing her mother, is also addressing many other displaced women in her life.

17. MacArthur, quoted in Connery (41).

18. See for example Paul Bové's *Destructive Poetics: Heidegger and Modern American Poetry,* William V. Spanos's "Breaking the Circle: Hermeneutics as Dis-closure," and Charles Altieri's *Enlarging the Temple.*

1. See Dana D. Nelson, *National Manhood: Capitalist Citizenship and the Imagined Fraternity of White Men*; Gail Bederman, *Manliness and Civilization: A Cultural History of Gender and Race in the United States, 1880–1917*; Joseph A. Boone and Michael Cadden, *Engendering Men: The Question of Male Feminist Criticism*; and Maurice Berger, Brian Wallis, and Simon Watson, *Constructing Masculinity*.

Works Cited

Abelove, Henry. "American Studies, Queer Studies." *Deep Gossip*. Minneapolis: University of Minneapolis Press, forthcoming.

Adorno, Theodor W. "Lyric Poetry and Society." *Telos* 20 (summer 1974): 56–71.

Agamben, Giorgio. *The End of the Poem: Studies in Poetics*. Trans. Daniel Heller-Roazen. Stanford, Calif.: Stanford University Press, 1999.

Allen, Donald M., ed. *The New American Poetry*. New York: Grove Press, 1960.

Almaguer, Tomás. *Racial Fault Lines: The Historical Origins of White Supremacy in California*. Berkeley: University of California Press, 1994.

Altieri, Charles. *Enlarging the Temple: New Directions in American Poetry during the 1960s*. Lewisburg, Pa.: Bucknell University Press, 1979.

Anderson, Perry. *The Origins of Postmodernity*. London: Verso, 1998.

Arac, Jonathan. "F. O. Matthiessen: Authorizing an American Renaissance." In *The American Renaissance Reconsidered*. Ed. Walter Benn Michaels and Donald E. Pease. Baltimore: Johns Hopkins University Press, 1985. 90–112.

Armstrong, Nancy. *Desire and Domestic Fiction: A Political History of the Novel*. New York: Oxford University Press, 1987.

Austin, J. L. *How to Do Things with Words*. Cambridge, Mass.: Harvard University Press, 1975.

Baldwin, James. "The Black Boy Looks at the White Boy." *The Price of the Ticket: Collected Nonfiction 1948–1985*. New York: St. Martin's Press, 1985.

Baraka, Amiri. *The Autobiography of LeRoi Jones*. Chicago: Lawrence Hill Books, 1997.

———. *Blues People: Negro Music in White America*. New York: William Morrow, 1963.

———. *Conversations with Amiri Baraka*. Ed. Charlie Reilly. Jackson: University Press of Mississippi, 1994.

———. *Dutchman: The LeRoi Jones/Amiri Baraka Reader*. Ed. William J. Harris. New York: Thunder's Mouth Press, 1991.

——— [LeRoi Jones]. *Home: Social Essays*. New York: William Morrow, 1966.

———. "Interview with Amiri Baraka (LeRoi Jones)." In *Heroism in the New Black Poetry: Introductions and Interviews*. Ed. D. H. Melhem. Lexington: University Press of Kentucky, 1990. 223–63.

———. *Madheart: Four Black Revolutionary Plays*. New York: Bobbs-Merrill, 1969.

———. *Selected Poetry of Amiri Baraka/LeRoi Jones*. New York: William Morrow, 1979.

——— [Jones, LeRoi]. "Slice of Life." *Yugen* 1 (1958): 16.

———. *Transbluesency: Selected Poems*. New York: Marsilio, 1995.

Baraka, Amiri [LeRoi Jones], and Larry Neal, eds. *Black Fire: An Anthology of Afro-American Writing*. New York: William Morrow, 1968.

Barthes, Roland. "The Reality Effect." *The Rustle of Language*. Trans. Richard Howard. New York: Hill and Wang, 1986. 141–48.

Baudrillard, Jean. "Consumer Society." *Selected Writings*. Ed. Mark Poster. Stanford, Calif.: Stanford University Press, 1988. 29–56.

Beach, Christopher. *Poetic Culture: Contemporary American Poetry between Community and Institution*. Evanston, Ill.: Northwestern University Press, 1999.

Bederman, Gail. *Manliness and Civilization: A Cultural History of Gender and Race in the United States, 1880–1917*. Chicago: University of Chicago Press, 1995.

Belgrad, Daniel. *The Culture of Spontaneity: Improvisation and the Arts in Postwar America*. Chicago: University of Chicago Press, 1998.

Bell, Daniel. *The End of Ideology: On the Exhaustion of Political Ideas in the Fifties*. Glencoe, Ill.: Free Press, 1960.

Benjamin, Walter. "Paris, Capital of the Nineteenth Century." *Reflections: Essays, Aphorisms, Autobiographical Writings*. Trans. Edmund Jephcott. Ed. Peter Demetz. New York: Harcourt Brace Jovanovich, 1978. 146–62.

Benston, Kimberly W. *Baraka: The Renegade and the Mask*. New Haven, Conn.: Yale University Press, 1976.

———. "I Yam What I Am: The Topos of (Un)naming in Afro-American Literature."

In *Black Literature and Literary Theory.* Ed. Henry Louis Gates, Jr. New York: Methuen, 1984. 151–72.

Berger, Maurice, Brian Wallis, and Simon Watson, eds. *Constructing Masculinity.* New York: Routledge, 1995.

Bierce, Ambrose. "The Haunted Valley." *The Complete Short Stories of Ambrose Bierce.* Ed. Ernest Jerome Hopkins. New York: Doubleday, 1970. 117–26.

Bishop, Elizabeth. *The Complete Poems 1927–1979.* New York: Farrar, Straus, and Giroux, 1983.

———. *One Art: Letters, Selected and Edited.* Ed. Robert Giroux. New York: Noonday Press, 1994.

Black Scholar 10 (Mar.–Apr. 1979). "Black Male/Female Relationships."

Bloom, Harold. *Poetry and Repression: Revision from Blake to Stevens.* New Haven, Conn.: Yale University Press, 1976.

Blount, Marcellus. "Caged Birds: Race and Gender in the Sonnet." In *Engendering Men: The Question of Male Feminist Criticism.* Ed. Joseph A. Boone and Michael Cadden. New York: Routledge, 1990. 225–38.

Bly, Robert. "I Came out of the Mother Naked." *Sleepers Joining Hands.* New York: Harper, 1973. 29–50.

Boone, Bruce. "Gay Language as Political Praxis: The Poetry of Frank O'Hara." *Social Text* 1 (winter 1979): 59–92.

Boone, Joseph A., and Michael Cadden, eds. *Engendering Men: The Question of Male Feminist Criticism.* New York: Routledge, 1990.

Bové, Paul. *Destructive Poetics: Heidegger and Modern American Poetry.* New York: Columbia University Press, 1980.

Bredbeck, Gregory. "B/O—Barthes's Text/O'Hara's Trick." *PMLA* 108 (Mar. 1993): 268–82.

Breines, Wini. "Postwar White Girls' Dark Others." In *The Other Fifties: Interrogating Midcentury American Icons.* Ed. Joel Foreman. Urbana: University of Illinois Press, 1997. 53–77.

Breslin, James. *From Modern to Contemporary: American Poetry, 1945–1965.* Chicago: University of Chicago Press, 1984.

Brooks, Gwendolyn. *Blacks.* Chicago: Third World Press, 1992.

Brunner, Edward. *Cold War Poetry.* Urbana: University of Illinois Press, 2001.

Butler, Judith. *Bodies That Matter: On the Discursive Limits of "Sex."* New York: Routledge, 1993.

———. *Gender Trouble: Feminism and the Subversion of Identity.* New York: Routledge, 1990.

Butterick, George. "Charles Olson's 'The Kingfishers' and the Poetics of Change." *American Poetry* 6 (winter 1989): 28–69.

Cadden, Michael. "Engendering F.O.M.: The Private Life of *American Renaissance.*" In *Engendering Men: The Question of Male Feminist Criticism.* Ed. Joseph A. Boone and Michael Cadden. New York: Routledge, 1990. 25–35.

Campbell, David. *Writing Security: United States Foreign Policy and the Politics of Identity.* Minneapolis: University of Minnesota Press, 1992.

Canaday, John. *The Nuclear Muse: Literature, Physics, and the First Atomic Bomb.* Madison: University of Wisconsin Press, 2000.

Case, Sue-Ellen. "Toward a Butch-Femme Aesthetic." In *The Lesbian and Gay Studies Reader.* Ed. Henry Abelove, Michèle Aina Barale, and David Halperin. New York: Routledge, 1993. 294–306.

Castle, Terry. *The Apparitional Lesbian: Female Homosexuality and Modern Culture.* New York: Columbia University Press, 1993.

Cha, Theresa Hak Kyung. *Dictee.* New York: Tanam Press, 1982.

———. *The Dream of the Audience: Theresa Hak Kyung Cha (1951–1982).* Ed. Constance M. Lewalen. Berkeley: University of California Press, 2001.

Chan Is Missing. Dir. Wayne Wang. Perf. Wood Moy, Marc Hayashi, Laureen Chew, Judy Nihei, Peter Wang. Wayne Wang, 1981.

Cheung, King-Kok. "The Woman Warrior versus the Chinaman Pacific." In *Conflicts in Feminism.* Ed. Marianne Hirsch and Evelyn Fox Keller. New York: Routledge, 1990. 234–51.

Chinatown. Dir. Roman Polanski. Perf. Faye Dunaway, Jack Nicholson, John Huston. Paramount, 1974.

Chomsky, Noam, et al. *The Cold War and the University: Toward an Intellectual History of the Postwar Years.* New York: New Press, 1997.

Chow, Rey. *Woman and Chinese Modernity: The Politics of Reading between West and East.* Minneapolis: University of Minnesota Press, 1991.

Ciardi, John. *Mid-Century American Poets.* New York: Twayne, 1950.

Clark, Tom. *Charles Olson: The Allegory of a Poet's Life.* New York: Norton, 1991.

Cleaver, Eldridge. *Soul on Ice.* New York: Delta, 1968.

Connery, Christopher. "Pacific Rim Discourse: The U.S. Global Imaginary in the Late Cold War Years." *boundary 2* 21 (spring 1994): 30–56.

Cook, Pam. "Duplicity in *Mildred Pierce.*" In *Women in Film Noir.* Ed. E. Ann Kaplan. London: British Film Institute, 1980. 68–82.

Coontz, Stephanie. *The Way We Never Were: American Families and the Nostalgia Trap.* New York: Harper/Collins, 1992.

Corber, Robert J. *Homosexuality in Cold War America: Resistance and the Crisis of Masculinity.* Durham, N.C.: Duke University Press, 1997.

Cortez, Jayne. "Interview with Jayne Cortez." In *Heroism in the New Black Poetry: Introductions and Interviews.* Ed. D. H. Melhem. Lexington: University Press of Kentucky, 1990. 195–212.

———. *Pisstained Stairs and the Monkey Man's Wares.* New York: Phrase Text, 1969.

Costello, Bonnie. *Elizabeth Bishop: Questions of Mastery.* Cambridge, Mass.: Harvard University Press, 1991.

Creeley, Robert. *The Collected Poems of Robert Creeley.* Berkeley: University of California Press, 1982.

Cumings, Bruce. *Parallax Visions: Making Sense of American–East Asian Relations at the End of the Century.* Durham, N.C.: Duke University Press, 1999.

Damon, Maria. *The Dark End of the Street: Margins in American Vanguard Poetry.* Minneapolis: University of Minnesota Press, 1993.

Davenport, Guy. "Scholia and Conjectures for Olson's 'The Kingfishers.'" *boundary 2* 2 (fall 1973, winter 1974): 250–62.

Davidson, Cathy. *The Experimental Fictions of Ambrose Bierce: Structuring the Ineffable.* Lincoln: University of Nebraska Press, 1984.

Davidson, Michael. *Ghostlier Demarcations: Modern Poetry and the Material Word.* Berkeley: University of California Press, 1997.

———. *The San Francisco Renaissance: Poetics and Community at Mid-Century.* Cambridge: Cambridge University Press, 1989.

Davidson, Michael, Lyn Hejinian, Ron Silliman, and Barrett Watten. *Leningrad.* San Francisco: Mercury House, 1991.

Dawson, Fielding. *The Black Mountain Book.* New York: Croton, 1970.

Deleuze, Gilles, and Félix Guattari. *A Thousand Plateaus: Capitalism and Schizophrenia.* Trans. Brian Massumi. Minneapolis: University of Minnesota Press, 1987.

D'Emilio, John. "Gay Politics and Community in San Francisco since World War II." In *Hidden from History: Reclaiming the Gay and Lesbian Past.* Ed. Martin Duberman, Martha Vicinus, and George Chauncy Jr. New York: Meridian, 1990.

———. *Sexual Politics, Sexual Communities: The Making of a Homosexual Minority in the United States, 1940–1970.* Chicago: University of Chicago Press, 1983.

D'Emilio, John, and Estelle B. Freedman. *Intimate Matters: A History of Sexuality in America.* Chicago: University of Chicago Press, 1997.

Diamond, Sigmund. *Compromised Campus: The Collaboration of Universities with the Intelligence Community, 1945–1955.* New York: Oxford University Press, 1992.

Diehl, Joanne Feit. "Bishop's Sexual Poetics." In *Elizabeth Bishop: The Geography of Gender.* Ed. Marilyn May Lombardi. Charlottesville: University Press of Virginia, 1993. 17–45.

Dirlik, Arif. "The Asia-Pacific Idea: Reality and Representation in the Invention of a Regional Structure." In *What Is in a Rim? Critical Perspectives on the Pacific Region Idea.* Ed. Arif Dirlik. Lanham, Md.: Rowman and Littlefield, 1998. 15–36.

———. "Introduction: Pacific Contradictions." In *What Is in a Rim? Critical Perspectives on the Pacific Region Idea.* Ed. Arif Dirlik. Lanham, Md.: Rowman and Littlefield, 1993. 3–13.

Dorn, Edward. *The North Atlantic Turbine.* London: Fulcrum Press, 1967.

Duberman, Martin. *Black Mountain: An Exploration in Community.* New York: Dutton, 1972.

Duncan, Robert. "Poem Beginning with a Line by Pindar." *Opening of the Field.* New York: Grove Press, 1960. 62–69.

———. "The Underside." Unpublished manuscript.

Eat a Bowl of Tea. Dir. Wayne Wang. Perf. Cora Miao, Russell Wong, Victor Wong, Lau Siu Ming. PBS *American Playhouse* production, 1989.

Edelman, Lee. "The Geography of Gender: Elizabeth Bishop's 'In the Waiting Room.'" In *Elizabeth Bishop: The Geography of Gender.* Ed. Marilyn May Lombardi. Charlottesville: University Press of Virginia, 1993. 91–107.

Ehrenreich, Barbara. *Fear of Falling: The Inner Life of the Middle Class.* New York: Harper, 1989.

———. *The Hearts of Men: American Dreams and the Flight from Commitment.* New York: Anchor, 1983.

Eliot, T. S. *The Complete Poems and Plays: 1909–1950.* New York: Harcourt, Brace, and World, 1962.

Ellingham, Lewis, and Kevin Killian. *Poet Be Like God: Jack Spicer and the San Francisco Renaissance.* Hanover, N.H.: Wesleyan University Press, 1998.

Enloe, Cynthia. *The Morning After: Sexual Politics at the End of the Cold War.* Berkeley: University of California Press, 1993.

Erkkila, Betsy. *The Wicked Sisters: Women Poets, Literary History, and Discord.* New York: Oxford University Press, 1992.

Etzold, Thomas H., and John Lewis Gaddis. *Containment: Documents on American Policy and Strategy, 1945–1950.* New York: Columbia University Press, 1978.

Faderman, Lillian. *Odd Girls and Twilight Lovers: A History of Lesbian Life in Twentieth-Century America.* New York: Penguin, 1991.

Faludi, Susan. *Stiffed: The Betrayal of the American Man.* New York: William Morrow, 1999.

Feldstein, Ruth. "'I Wanted the Whole World to See': Race, Gender, and Constructions of Motherhood in the Death of Emmett Till." In *Not June Cleaver: Women and Gender in Postwar America, 1945–1960.* Ed. Joanne Meyerowitz. Philadelphia: Temple University Press, 1994. 263–303.

Fenn, William Purviance. *Ah Sin and His Brethren in American Literature.* Peking: College of Chinese Studies, 1933.

Field, Edward. *Stand Up, Friend, with Me.* New York: Grove Press, 1963.

Flinn, Carol. "Sound, Woman, and the Bomb." *Wide Angle* 8, nos. 3–4 (1986): 115–27.

Folsom, Ed. "Talking Back to Walt Whitman: An Introduction." In *Walt Whitman: The Measure of His Song.* Ed. Jim Perlman, Ed Folsom, and Dan Campion. Minneapolis: Holy Cow! Press, 1981. xxi–liii.

Fone, Byrne. *Masculine Landscapes: Walt Whitman and the Homoerotic Text.* Carbondale: Southern Illinois University Press, 1992.

Frazier, E. Franklin. *Black Bourgeoisie.* New York: Free Press, 1957.

Friedan, Betty. *The Feminine Mystique.* New York: Dell Publishing, 1983.

Frost, Elizabeth. "'In Another Tongue': Body, Image, Text in Theresa Hak Kyung Cha's *Dictée.*" In *We Who Love to Be Astonished: Experimental Women's Writing and Performance Poetics.* Ed. Laura Hinton and Cynthia Hogue. Tuscaloosa: University of Alabama Press, 2002. 181–92.

Fuss, Diana. *Essentially Speaking: Feminism, Nature, and Difference.* New York: Routledge, 1989.

Gaddis, John Lewis. *Strategies of Containment: A Critical Appraisal of Postwar American National Security Policy.* New York: Oxford University Press, 1982.

———. *The United States and the Origins of the Cold War: 1941–1947.* New York: Columbia University Press, 1972.

Garber, Marjorie. *Vested Interests: Cross-Dressing and Cultural Anxiety.* New York: Harper Collins, 1992.

Garcia, Ramón. "Historicizing Horror: Ambrose Bierce's 'The Haunted Valley' and the American Ghost Story." University of California, San Diego. Unpublished manuscript.

García Lorca, Federico. *Poet in New York.* Trans. Ben Belitt. New York: Grove, 1955.

———. "Theory and Function of the Duende." Trans. J. L. Gili. In *Poetics of the New American Poetry.* Ed. Donald Allen and Warren Tallman. New York: Grove, 1973. 91–103.

Gibson, Morgan. *Revolutionary Rexroth: Poet of East-West Wisdom.* Hamden, Conn.: Archon, 1986.

Gilbert, Sandra M., and Susan Gubar. *The Madwoman in the Attic: The Woman Writer and the Nineteenth-Century Imagination.* New Haven, Conn.: Yale University Press, 1979.

Gilroy, Paul. *The Black Atlantic: Modernity and Double Consciousness.* Cambridge, Mass.: Harvard University Press, 1993.

Ginsberg, Allen. *Collected Poems, 1947–1980.* New York: Harper & Row, 1988.

Gioia, Dana. *Can Poetry Matter? Essays on Poetry and American Culture.* St. Paul, Minn.: Graywolf, 1992.

Gladman, Renee. "Arlem." In *An Anthology of New (American) Poets.* Ed. Lisa Jarnot, Leonard Schwartz, and Cris Stroffolino. Jersey City, N.J.: Talisman House, 1998. 68–76.

Golding, Alan. *From Outlaw to Classic: Canons in American Poetry.* Madison: University of Wisconsin Press, 1995.

———. "The *New American Poetry* Revisited, Again." *Contemporary Literature* 39, no. 2 (1998): 180–211.

Gooch, Brad. *City Poet: The Life and Times of Frank O'Hara.* New York: Alfred Knopf, 1993.

Gordon, Avery. *Ghostly Matters: Haunting and the Sociological Imagination.* Minneapolis: University of Minnesota Press, 1997.

Gray, Francine du Plessix. "Charles Olson and an American Place." *Yale Review* 76 (June 1987): 341–52.

Gray, Timothy. "Gary Snyder: Poet-Geographer of the Pacific Rim." *Studies in Humanities* 26 (June–Dec. 1999): 18–40.

Greenberg, Clement. "Avant-Garde and Kitsch." *Art and Culture: Critical Essays.* Boston: Beacon Press, 1961. 3–21.

Guys and Dolls. Music and lyrics by Frank Loesser. New York: Frank Music Corp., 1953.

Halberstam, David. *The Fifties*. New York: Fawcett Columbine, 1993.

Halberstam, Judith. *Female Masculinity*. Durham, N.C.: Duke University Press, 1998.

———. "'Oh Behave': Austin Powers and the Drag Kings." *GLQ* 7, no. 3 (2001): 425–52.

Hall, Donald, Robert Pack, and Louis Simpson, eds. *New Poets of England and America*. New York: New American Library, 1957.

Harper, Phillip Brian. *Are We Not Men? Masculine Anxiety and the Problem of African-American Identity*. New York: Oxford University Press, 1996.

Harte, Bret. "Plain Language from Truthful James." *The Poetical Works of Bret Harte*. Boston: Houghton Mifflin, 1912. 129–31.

Harvey, David. *Spaces of Hope*. Berkeley: University of California Press, 2000.

Hecht, Anthony. *The Venetian Vespers*. New York: Atheneum, 1979.

Hernton, Calvin. "The Sexual Mountain and Black Women Writers." In *Wild Women in the Whirlwind: Afra-American Culture and the Contemporary Literary Renaissance*. Ed. Joanne M. Braxton and Andree Nicola McLaughlin. New Brunswick, N.J.: Rutgers University Press, 1990. 195–212.

Heuving, Jeanne. *Omissions Are Not Accidents: Gender in the Art of Marianne Moore*. Detroit: Wayne State University Press, 1992.

Hofstadter, Richard. "The Paranoid Style in American Politics." *"The Paranoid Style in American Politics" and Other Essays*. New York: Knopf, 1965. 3–40.

Hook, Sidney. "Our Country and Our Culture." *Partisan Review* 19 (Sept.–Oct. 1952): 569–74.

hooks, bell. *Ain't I a Woman: Black Women and Feminism*. Boston: South End Press, 1981.

Horowitz, Steven P. "An Investigation of Paul Goodman and Black Mountain." *American Poetry* 7 (fall 1989): 2–30.

Howe, Irving. "Mass Society and Post-Modern Fiction." *Partisan Review* 26 (summer 1959): 420–36.

Hudson, Theodore R. *From LeRoi Jones to Amiri Baraka: The Literary Works*. Durham, N.C.: Duke University Press, 1973.

Hughes, Ted. "Ted Hughes and the Plath Estate." *Times Literary Supplement* (24 Apr. 1992): 15.

Hull, Gloria T. "Afro-American Women Poets: A Bio-Critical Survey." In *Shakespeare's Sisters: Feminist Essays on Women Poets*. Ed. Sandra M. Gilbert and Susan Gubar. Bloomington: Indiana University Press, 1979. 165–82.

Huyssen, Andreas. *After the Great Divide: Modernism, Mass Culture, Postmodernism*. Bloomington: Indiana University Press, 1986.

Japenga, Ann. "The Great Pretender" (review of Diane Wood Middlebrook, *Suits Me: The Double Life of Billy Tipton*). *Los Angeles Times* (Fri., 17 Jul. 1998): E1–4.

Jarraway, David R. "'O Canada!': The Spectral Lesbian Poetics of Elizabeth Bishop." *PMLA* 113, no. 2 (Mar. 1998): 243–57.

Jarrell, Randall. *Selected Poems*. Ed. William H. Pritchard. New York: Farrar, Straus, and Giroux, 1990.

Johnson, Joyce. *Minor Characters: A Beat Memoir*. New York: Penguin, 1999.

Jones, Hettie. *How I Became Hettie Jones*. New York: Grove Press, 1990.

Jones, LeRoi. *See* Baraka, Amiri.

Jong, Erica. "Visionary Anger." In *Adrienne Rich's Poetry*. Ed. Barbara Charlesworth Gelpi and Albert Gelpi. New York: W. W. Norton, 1975. 171–74.

Joyce, Joyce A. *Ijala: Sonia Sanchez and the African Poetic Tradition*. Chicago: Third World Press, 1996.

Kalaidjian, Walter. *Languages of Liberation: The Social Text in Contemporary American Poetry*. New York: Columbia University Press, 1989.

Kennan, George. "The Long Telegram" (Moscow Embassy Telegram #511, 22 Feb. 1946). In *Containment: Documents on American Policy and Strategy, 1945–1950*. Ed. Thomas H. Etzold and John Lewis Gaddis. New York: Columbia University Press, 1978. 50–63.

———. "The Sources of Soviet Conduct." *American Diplomacy*. Chicago: University of Chicago Press, 1984.

Kennedy, Elizabeth Lapovsky, and Madeline D. Davis. *Boots of Leather, Slippers of Gold: The History of a Lesbian Community*. New York: Penguin, 1993.

Kennedy, X. J. *Literature: An Introduction to Fiction, Poetry, and Drama*. 2d ed. Boston: Little, Brown, 1979.

Kerouac, Jack. *The Dharma Bums*. New York: New American Library, 1958.

———. "The Philosophy of the Beat Generation." *Esquire* 49 (Mar. 1958): 24–25.

Kim, Elaine. "Poised on the In-Between: A Korean American's Reflections on Theresa Hak Kyung Cha's *Dictée*." In *Writing Self Writing Nation*. Ed. Elaine Kim and Norma Alarcon. Berkeley, Calif.: Third Woman Press, 1994. 3–30.

Kim, Elaine, and Norma Alarcon. *Writing Self Writing Nation*. Berkeley, Calif.: Third Woman Press, 1994.

Kinsey, Alfred, et al. *Sexual Behavior in the Human Female*. Philadelphia: W. B. Saunders, 1953.

———. *Sexual Behavior in the Human Male*. Philadelphia: W. B. Saunders, 1948.

Kirk, Don. "2 Koreas Celebrate Decision to Reconnect a Railway." *New York Times* (Thurs., 19 Sept. 2002): A8.

Kiss Me Deadly. Dir. Robert Aldrich. Perf. Ralph Meeker, Cloris Leachman, Gaby Rogers. United Artists, 1955.

Knight, Etheridge. *The Essential Etheridge Knight*. Pittsburgh: University of Pittsburgh Press, 1986.

The Ladder. Reprint, *Homosexuality: Lesbians and Gay Men in Society, History, and Literature*. New York: Arno Press, 1953.

The Lady from Shanghai. Dir. Orson Welles. Perf. Rita Hayworth, Orson Welles, Glenn Anders, Everett Sloan. Columbia, 1948.

Lasch, Christopher. "The Cultural Cold War: A Short History of the Congress for Cultural Freedom." In *Towards a New Past: Dissenting Essays in American History.* Ed. Barton J. Bernstein. New York: Pantheon, 1968. 322–59.

Lee, Don L. *See* Madhubuti, Haki.

Lewontin, R. C. "The Cold War and the Transformation of the Academy." In *The Cold War and the University: Toward an Intellectual History of the Postwar Years.* By Noam Chomsky et al. New York: New Press, 1997. 1–34.

Lipsitz, George. "Land of a Thousand Dances: Youth, Minorities, and the Rise of Rock and Roll." In *Recasting America: Culture and Politics in the Age of Cold War.* Ed. Lary May. Chicago: University of Chicago Press, 1989. 267–84.

———. *The Possessive Investment in Whiteness: How White People Profit from Identity Politics.* Philadelphia: Temple University Press, 1998.

———. *Rainbow at Midnight: Labor and Culture in the 1940s.* Urbana: University of Illinois Press, 1994.

Lockwood, William. "Toward a Reappraisal of Kenneth Rexroth: The Poems of His Middle and Late Periods." *Sagetrieb* 2 (winter 1983): 113–32.

Lombardi, Marilyn May, ed. *Elizabeth Bishop: The Geography of Gender.* Charlottesville: University Press of Virginia, 1993.

Lorde, Audre. *Undersong: Chosen Poems Old and New.* New York: Norton, 1968.

———. *Zami: A New Spelling of My Name.* Freedom, Calif.: Crossing Press, 1982.

Lott, Eric. "All the King's Men: Elvis Impersonators and White Working-Class Masculinity." *Race and the Subject of Masculinities.* Ed. Harry Stecopoulos and Michael Uebel. Durham, N.C.: Duke University Press, 1997. 192–227.

Lowe, Lisa. *Critical Terrains: French and British Orientalisms.* Ithaca, N.Y.: Cornell University Press, 1991.

———. "Unfaithful to the Original: The Subject of *Dictee.*" In *Writing Self Writing Nation.* Ed. Elaine Kim and Norma Alarcon. Berkeley, Calif.: Third Woman Press, 1994. 35–69.

Lowell, Robert. *Selected Poems.* Rev. ed. New York: Farrar, Straus, and Giroux, 1986.

Loy, Mina. *The Last Lunar Baedeker.* Ed. Roger L. Conover. Highlands, N.C.: The Jargon Society, 1982.

Macdonald, Dwight. "Masscult and Midcult." *Against the American Grain.* New York: Random House, 1962. 3–75.

Mackey, Nathaniel. *Discrepant Engagement: Dissonance, Cross-Culturality, and Experimental Writing.* Cambridge: Cambridge University Press, 1993.

MacPherson, Pat. *Reflecting on The Bell Jar.* London: Routledge, 1991.

Madhubuti, Haki [Don L. Lee]. *Directionscore: Selected and New Poems.* Detroit: Broadside Press, 1971.

———. *Dynamite Voices: Black Poets of the 1960s.* Detroit: Broadside Press, 1971.

Mailer, Norman. "The White Negro." In *The Portable Beat Reader.* Ed. Ann Charters. New York: Penguin, 1992. 582–605.

Malcolm, Janet. "The Silent Woman." *New Yorker* (23 and 30 Aug. 1993): 84–159.

Mann, Paul. *The Theory-Death of the Avant-Garde*. Bloomington: Indiana University Press, 1991.

Marable, Manning. *How Capitalism Underdeveloped Black America*. Boston: South End Press, 1983.

Marchetti, Gina. *Romance and the "Yellow Peril": Race, Sex, and Discursive Strategies in Hollywood Fiction*. Berkeley: University of California Press, 1993.

Martin, Robert K. *The Homosexual Tradition in American Poetry*. Austin: University of Texas Press, 1979.

Martin, Wendy. "From Patriarchy to the Female Principle: A Chronological Reading of Adrienne Rich's Poems." In *Adrienne Rich's Poetry*. Ed. Barbara Charlesworth Gelpi and Albert Gelpi. New York: W. W. Norton, 1975. 175–88.

Matthiessen, F. O. *American Renaissance: Art and Expression in the Age of Emerson and Whitman*. New York: Oxford University Press, 1968.

Maud, Ralph. *What Does Not Change: The Significance of Charles Olson's "The Kingfishers."* Madison, Wis.: Fairleigh Dickinson University Press, 1998.

May, Elaine Tyler. *Homeward Bound: American Families in the Cold War Era*. New York: Basic Books, 1988.

May, Lary, ed. *Recasting America: Culture and Politics in the Age of Cold War*. Chicago: University of Chicago Press, 1989.

McCormick, Thomas J. *America's Half-Century: United States Foreign Policy in the Cold War and After*. Baltimore: Johns Hopkins University Press, 1995.

Melley, Timothy. *Empire of Conspiracy: The Culture of Paranoia in Postwar America*. Ithaca, N.Y.: Cornell University Press, 2000.

Meltzer, David, ed. *The San Francisco Poets*. New York: Ballantine, 1971.

Merrill, James. *Collected Poems*. Ed. J. D. McClatchy and Stephen Yenser. New York: Alfred A. Knopf, 2001.

Meyerowitz, Joanne, ed. *Not June Cleaver: Women and Gender in Postwar America, 1945–1960*. Philadelphia: Temple University Press, 1994.

Michaels, Walter Benn, and Donald E. Pease, eds. *The American Renaissance Reconsidered*. Baltimore: Johns Hopkins University Press, 1985.

Middlebrook, Diane. *Suits Me: The Double Life of Billy Tipton*. Boston: Houghton Mifflin, 1998.

Mildred Pierce. Dir. Michael Curtiz. Perf. Joan Crawford, Jack Carson, Zachary Scott, Eve Arden, Ann Blyth, Bruce Bennett. Warner Bros., 1945.

Miller, J. Hillis. *Poets of Reality: Six Twentieth-Century Writers*. New York: Atheneum, 1969.

Miller, Nancy K., ed. *The Poetics of Gender*. New York: Columbia University Press, 1985.

Millier, Brett C. *Elizabeth Bishop: Life and the Memory of It*. Berkeley: University of California Press, 1993.

Molesworth, Charles. *The Fierce Embrace: A Study of Contemporary American Poetry*. Columbia: University of Missouri Press, 1979.

Moon, Michael. *Disseminating Whitman: Revision and Corporality in Leaves of Grass.* Cambridge, Mass.: Harvard University Press, 1991.

Mooney, Richard. "Visitor, Cameramen up Early: Khrushchev Twits Allen Dulles." *New York Times* (Thurs., 17 Sept. 1959): 20.

Moore, Marianne. *The Complete Poems of Marianne Moore.* New York: Macmillan, 1967.

———. "A Modest Expert: *North & South.*" In *Elizabeth Bishop and Her Art.* Ed. Lloyd Schwartz and Sybil P. Estes. Ann Arbor: University of Michigan Press, 1983. 177–79.

Morrison, Toni. *Playing in the Dark.* New York: Random House, 1993.

Mulvey, Laura. "Visual Pleasure and Narrative Cinema." *Screen* 16, no. 3 (1975): 6–18.

Nadel, Alan. *Containment Culture: American Narratives, Postmodernism, and the Atomic Age.* Durham, N.C.: Duke University Press, 1995.

Neal, Larry. "The Black Arts Movement." In *Within the Circle: An Anthology of African American Literary Criticism from the Harlem Renaissance to the Present.* Ed. Angelyn Mitchell. Durham, N.C.: Duke University Press, 1994.

Nelson, Cary. *Repression and Recovery: Modern American Poetry and the Politics of Cultural Memory, 1910–1945.* Madison: University of Wisconsin Press, 1989.

Nelson, Dana. *National Manhood: Capitalist Citizenship and the Imagined Fraternity of White Men.* Durham, N.C.: Duke University Press, 1998.

Nestle, Joan. *A Restricted Country.* Ithaca, N.Y.: Firebrand Books, 1987.

Newton, Esther. "Just One of the Boys: Lesbians in Cherry Grove, 1960–1988." In *The Lesbian and Gay Studies Reader.* Ed. Henry Abelove, Michèle Aina Barale, and David M. Halperin. New York: Routledge, 1993. 528–41.

———. *Mother Camp: Female Impersonators in America.* Chicago: University of Chicago Press, 1979.

Nielsen, Aldon. *Writing between the Lines: Race and Intertextuality.* Athens: University of Georgia Press, 1994.

Nitze, Paul. National Security Communication 68 ("United States Objectives and Programs for National Security"). In *Containment: Documents on American Policy and Strategy, 1945–1950.* Ed. Thomas H. Etzold and John Lewis Gaddis. New York: Columbia University Press, 1978. 385–442.

Oates, Joyce Carol. "The Death Throes of Romanticism." In *Sylvia Plath: The Woman and the Work.* Ed. Edward Butscher. New York: Dodd, Mead, 1977. 206–24.

O'Hara, Frank. *The Collected Poems of Frank O'Hara.* Ed. Donald Allen. New York: Alfred A. Knopf, 1971.

———. *Standing Still and Walking in New York.* Bolinas, Calif.: Grey Fox Press, 1975.

Ohmann, Richard. "English and the Cold War." In *The Cold War and the University: Toward an Intellectual History of the Postwar Years.* By Noam Chomsky et al. New York: New Press, 1997. 73–105.

Oliveira, Carmen L. *Rare and Commonplace Flowers: The Story of Elizabeth Bishop and Lota de Macedo Soares*. Trans. Neil K. Besner. New Brunswick, N.J.: Rutgers University Press, 2002.

Olson, Charles. *Call Me Ishmael*. In *Collected Prose*. Ed. Donald Allen and Benjamin Friedlander. Berkeley: University of California Press, 1997. 1–106.

———. *Charles Olson and Frances Boldereff: A Modern Correspondence*. Ed. Ralph Maud and Sharon Thesen. Hanover, N.H.: Wesleyan University Press, 1999.

———. *The Collected Poems of Charles Olson*. Ed. George F. Butterick. Berkeley: University of California Press, 1987.

———. *Collected Prose*. Ed. Donald Allen and Benjamin Friedlander. Berkeley: University of California Press, 1997.

———. *The Maximus Poems*. Ed. George Butterick. Berkeley: University of California Press, 1983.

———. "The Mayan Letters." *Charles Olson: Selected Writings*. Ed. Robert Creeley. New York: New Directions, 1966. 69–130.

———. "On Black Mountain." *Muthologos: The Collected Lectures and Interviews*. Vol. 2. Ed. Donald Allen. Bolinas, Calif.: Four Seasons Foundation, 1979. 55–79.

———. "Reading at Berkeley." *Muthologos: The Collected Lectures and Interviews*. Vol. 1. Ed. Donald Allen. Bolinas, Calif.: Four Seasons Foundation, 1979. 97–156.

———. *Selected Letters*. Ed. Ralph Maud. Berkeley: University of California Press, 2000.

Oppen, George. *The New Collected Poems of George Oppen*. Ed. Michael Davidson. New York: New Directions, 2002.

———. *The Selected Letters of George Oppen*. Ed. Rachel Blau DuPlessis. Durham, N.C.: Duke University Press, 1990.

"Our Country and Our Culture." *Partisan Review* 19 (May–June 1952): 282–326.

Parkes, Francis Ernest Kobina. "African Heaven." *New World Writing*. New York: New American Library, 1959. 230–32.

Pease, Donald. *Visionary Compacts: American Renaissance Writings in Cultural Context*. Madison: University of Wisconsin Press, 1987.

Penn, Donna. "The Sexualized Woman: The Lesbian, the Prostitute, and the Containment of Female Sexuality in Postwar America." In *Not June Cleaver: Women and Gender in Postwar America, 1945–1960*. Ed. Joanne Meyerowitz. Philadelphia: Temple University Press, 1994. 358–81.

Perlman, Jim, Ed Folsom, and Dan Campion, eds. *Walt Whitman: The Measure of His Song*. Minneapolis: Holy Cow! Press, 1981.

Perloff, Marjorie. "Charles Olson and the 'Inferior Predecessors': 'Projective Verse' Revisited." *ELH* 40 (summer 1973): 285–306.

———. *The Dance of the Intellect: Studies in the Poetry of the Pound Tradition*. Cambridge: Cambridge University Press, 1985.

———. *Frank O'Hara: Poet among Painters*. Austin: University of Texas Press, 1976.

———. "Sylvia Plath's 'Sivvy' Poems: A Portrait of the Poet as Daughter." In *Sylvia*

Plath: New Views on the Poetry. Ed. Gary Lane. Baltimore: Johns Hopkins University Press, 1979. 155–78.

Pietz, William. "The Post-Colonialism of Cold War Discourse." *Social Text* 19–20 (fall 1988): 55–75.

Plath, Sylvia. *The Bell Jar*. New York: Bantam, 1972.

———. *The Collected Poems*. Ed. Ted Hughes. New York: Harper & Row, 1981.

———. *Letters Home: Correspondence 1950–1963*. Ed. Aurelia Schober Plath. New York: Harper & Row, 1975.

———. *The Unabridged Journals of Sylvia Plath, 1950–1962*. Ed. Karen V. Kukil. New York: Anchor, 2000.

Plummer, Brenda Gayle. *Rising Wind: Black Americans and U.S. Foreign Affairs, 1935–1960*. Chapel Hill: University of North Carolina Press, 1996.

Pound, Ezra. *The Cantos of Ezra Pound*. New York: New Directions, 1972.

———. *Personae*. New York: New Directions, 1926.

———. *Selected Prose 1909–1965*. Ed. William Cookson. New York: New Directions, 1973.

Rahv, Philip. "Commentary." In "Our Country and Our Culture," *Partisan Review* 19 (May–June 1952): 304–10.

Rainwater, Lee, and William L. Yancey, eds. *The Moynihan Report and the Politics of Controversy*. Cambridge, Mass.: MIT Press, 1967.

Ransom, John Crowe. "Poetry: A Note in Ontology." In *Critical Theory since Plato*. Ed. Hazard Adams. New York: Harcourt Brace Jovanovich, 1971. 871–81.

Rasula, Jed. *The American Poetry Wax Museum: Reality Effects, 1940–1990*. Urbana, Ill.: National Council of Teachers of English, 1996.

———. "Gendering the Muse." *Sulfur* 35 (fall 1994): 159–75.

Rexroth, Kenneth. *An Autobiographical Novel*. Ed. Linda Hamalian. New York: New Directions, 1991.

———. *The Burning Heart: Women Poets of Japan*. New York: Seabury, 1977.

———. *Li Ch'ing Chao: Complete Poems*. New York: New Directions, 1979.

———. *The Love Poems of Marichiko*. In *Flower Wreath Hill: Later Poems*. New York: New Directions, 1979. 105–38.

———. *The Orchid Boat: Women Poets of China*. New York: Herder and Herder, McGraw Hill, 1972.

———. "San Francisco Letter." *Evergreen Review* 1, no. 2 (1957): 5–14.

———. "San Francisco's Mature Bohemians." *The Nation* 184 (Sat., 23 Feb. 1957): 159–62.

Rich, Adrienne. *Adrienne Rich's Poetry and Prose*. Ed. Barbara Charlesworth Gelpi and Albert Gelpi. New York: Norton, 1993.

Riesman, David, with Nathan Glazer and Reuel Denney. *The Lonely Crowd*. New Haven, Conn.: Yale University Press, 1961.

Rifkin, Libbie. *Career Moves: Olson, Creeley, Zukofsky, Berrigan, and the American Avant-Garde*. Madison: University of Wisconsin Press, 2000.

Roediger, David R. *The Wages of Whiteness: Race and the Making of the American Work-ing Class*. London: Verso, 1991.

Rogin, Michael. *Blackface, White Noise: Jewish Immigrants in the Hollywood Melting Pot*. Berkeley: University of California Press, 1998.

———. *Ronald Reagan, the Movie, and Other Episodes in Political Demonology*. Berke-ley: University of California Press, 1987.

Roman, Camille. *Elizabeth Bishop's World War II–Cold War View*. New York: Palgrave, 2001.

Rose, Jacqueline. *The Haunting of Sylvia Plath*. Cambridge, Mass.: Harvard Univer-sity Press, 1991.

Ross, Andrew. *No Respect: Intellectuals and Popular Culture*. New York: Routledge, 1989.

Said, Edward. *Orientalism*. New York: Vintage, 1979

Saldana-Portillo, Maria Josefina. "Consuming Malcolm X: Prophecy and Performa-tive Masculinity." *Novel* 30 (spring 1997): 289–308.

Sanchez, Sonia. "Interview with Toni Cade Bambara and Sonia Sanchez." *Wild Women in the Whirlwind: Afra-American Culture and the Contemporary Literary Renaissance*. New Brunswick, N.J.: Rutgers University Press, 1990.

———. *I've Been a Woman: New and Selected Poems*. Sausalito, Calif.: Black Scholar Press, 1978.

Saunders, Frances Stonor. *The Cultural Cold War: The CIA and the World of Arts and Letters*. New York: New Press, 1999.

Savran, David. *Communists, Cowboys, and Queers: The Politics of Masculinity in the Work of Arthur Miller and Tennessee Williams*. Minneapolis: University of Min-nesota Press, 1992.

———. *Taking It Like a Man: White Masculinity, Masochism, and Contemporary Ameri-can Culture*. Princeton, N.J.: Princeton University Press, 1998.

Saxton, Alexander. *The Indispensable Enemy: Labor and the Anti-Chinese Movement in California*. Berkeley: University of California Press, 1971.

Schlesinger, Arthur. *The Vital Center: The Politics of Freedom*. New York: Houghton Mifflin, 1949.

Schwartz, Delmore. "The Present State of Poetry." In *American Poetry at Mid-Century*. By John Crowe Ransom, Delmore Schwartz, and John Wheelock. Washington, D.C.: U.S. Library of Congress, 1958. 15–26.

Schwartz, Lloyd, and Sybil P. Estes, eds. *Elizabeth Bishop and Her Art*. Ann Arbor: University of Michigan Press, 1983.

Scott, Joyce Hope. "From Foreground to Margin: Female Configurations and Mascu-line Self-Representation in Black Nationalist Fiction." *Nationalisms and Sexu-alities*. Ed. Andrew Parker, Mary Russo, Doris Sommer, and Patricia Yaeger. New York: Routledge, 1992. 296–312.

Sedgwick, Eve Kosofsky. *Between Men: English Literature and Male Homosocial Desire*. New York: Columbia University Press, 1985.

———. *Epistemology of the Closet*. Berkeley: University of California Press, 1990.

————. "Nationalisms and Sexualities in the Age of Wilde." In *Nationalisms and Sexualities*. Ed. Andrew Parker et al. New York: Routledge, 1992. 235–45.

Shange, Ntozake. *for colored girls who have considered suicide / when the rainbow is enuf*. New York: Macmillan, 1977.

Silliman, Ron. "The Political Economy of Poetry." *The New Sentence*. New York: Roof, 1987.

Silverman, Kaja. *The Acoustic Mirror: The Female Voice in Psychoanalysis and Cinema*. Bloomington: University of Indiana Press, 1988.

Sloan, Mary Margaret, ed. *Moving Borders: Three Decades of Innovative Writing by Women*. Jersey City, N.J.: Talisman House, 1998.

Snyder, Gary. *The Back Country*. New York: New Directions, 1968.

————. *Mountains and Rivers without End*. Washington, D.C.: Counterpoint, 1996.

————. *Myths and Texts*. New York: New Directions, 1978.

————. *The Real Work: Interviews and Talks, 1964–1979*. New York: New Directions, 1980.

Spahr, Juliana. *Everybody's Autonomy: Connective Reading and Collective Identity*. Tuscaloosa: University of Alabama Press, 2001.

Spanos, William V. "Breaking the Circle: Hermeneutics as Dis-closure." *boundary 2* 4 (winter 1977): 421–57.

Spicer, Jack. *The Collected Books of Jack Spicer*. Ed. Robin Blaser. Los Angeles: Black Sparrow, 1975.

————. "Homosexuality and Marxism." *Capitalist Bloodsucker*. N.p., 1962.

————. *The House That Jack Built: The Collected Lectures of Jack Spicer*. Ed. Peter Gizzi. Hanover, N.H.: Wesleyan University Press, 1998.

Spigel, Lynn. *Make Room for TV: Television and the Family Ideal in Postwar America*. Chicago: University of Chicago Press, 1992.

Staples, Robert. "The Myth of Black Macho: A Response to Angry Black Feminists." *Black Scholar* 10 (Mar.–Apr. 1979): 24–67.

Starr, Kevin. *Americans and the California Dream: 1850–1915*. New York: Oxford University Press, 1973.

Stevenson, Anne. *Bitter Fame: A Life of Sylvia Plath*. New York: Viking, 1989.

Takaki, Ronald. *Strangers from a Different Shore: A History of Asian Americans*. New York: Penguin, 1989.

Telotte, J. P. "The Fantastic Realism of Film Noir." *Wide Angle* 14 (Jan. 1992): 4–18.

Tompkins, Jane P. "The Other American Renaissance." In *The American Renaissance Reconsidered*. Ed. Walter Benn Michaels and Donald E. Pease. Baltimore: Johns Hopkins University Press, 1985. 34–57.

Towne, Robert. *"Chinatown," "The Last Detail": Screenplays*. New York: Grove, 1997.

Trachtenberg, Alan. *Reading American Photographs: Images as History, Mathew Brady to Walker Evans*. New York: Hill and Wang, 1989.

Trilling, Diana. "The Other Night at Columbia: A Report from the Academy." *Partisan Review* 26 (spring 1959): 214–30.

Trilling, Lionel. *Beyond Culture: Essays on Literature and Learning*. New York: Harcourt Brace Jovanovich, 1965.

Van Dyne, Susan R. "'More Terrible Than She Ever Was': The Manuscripts of Sylvia Plath's Bee Poems." In *Critical Essays on Sylvia Plath*. Ed. Linda W. Wagner. Boston: G. K. Hall, 1984. 154–70.

von Hallberg, Robert. *American Poetry and Culture, 1945–1980*. Cambridge, Mass.: Harvard University Press, 1985.

Wagner, Anne Middleton. *Three Artists (Three Women)*. Berkeley: University of California Press, 1996.

Wallerstein, Emmanuel. "The Unintended Consequences of Cold War Area Studies." In *The Cold War and the University: Toward an Intellectual History of the Postwar Years*. By Noam Chomsky et al. New York: New Press, 1997. 195–231.

Walley, David G. *Nothing in Moderation: A Biography of Ernie Kovacs*. New York: Drake Publishers, 1975.

Weinberger, Eliot. "At the Death of Kenneth Rexroth." *Sagetrieb* 2 (winter 1983): 45–52.

White, Patricia. *unInvited: Classical Hollywood Cinema and Lesbian Representability*. Bloomington: Indiana University Press, 1999.

Whitfield, Stephen J. *The Culture of the Cold War*. Baltimore: Johns Hopkins University Press, 1991.

Whitman, Walt. *Leaves of Grass*. Ed. Sculley Bradley and Harold W. Blodgett. New York: Norton, 1965, 1985.

Wiener, Norbert. *Cybernetics: Or Control and Communication in the Animal and the Machine*. Cambridge, Mass.: MIT Press, 1961.

Wieners, John. *The Hotel Wentley Poems*. San Francisco: Dave Haselwood, 1965.

Wilbur, Richard. *The Poems of Richard Wilbur*. San Diego, Calif.: Harcourt Brace Jovanovich, 1963.

Williams, William Carlos. *The Collected Poems of William Carlos Williams*. Vol. 2. Ed. Christopher MacGowan. New York: New Directions, 1988.

———. *The Selected Letters of William Carlos Williams*. Ed. John C. Thirlwall. New York: McDowell, Obolensky, 1957.

Williamson, Alan. "*A Cold Spring*: The Poet of Feeling." In *Elizabeth Bishop and Her Art*. Ed. Lloyd Schwartz and Sybil P. Estes. Ann Arbor: University of Michigan Press, 1983. 96–108.

Winks, Robin W. *Cloak and Gown: Scholars in the Secret War, 1939–1961*. New Haven, Conn.: Yale University Press, 1987.

Wong, Shelley Sunn. "Unnaming the Same: Theresa Hak Kyung Cha's *Dictée*." In *Writing Self Writing Nation*. Ed. Elaine Kim and Norma Alarcon. Berkeley, Calif.: Third Woman Press, 1994. 103–40.

Woodard, Komozi. *A Nation within a Nation: Amiri Baraka (LeRoi Jones) and Black Power Politics*. Chapel Hill: University of North Carolina Press, 1999.

Wylie, Philip. *Generation of Vipers*. New York: Rinehart, 1955.

Yeats, William Butler. *The Poems of W. B. Yeats*. Ed. Richard J. Finneran. New York: Macmillan, 1983.

Yingling, Thomas. *Hart Crane and the Homosexual Text: New Thresholds, New Anatomies*. Chicago: University of Chicago Press, 1990.

Index

blues music, 134, 242 n. 16

Bly, Robert, 30

body: female, and poem, 229 n. 2; as
    metaphor, 215–16

Bogan, Louise, 21, 118

Boldereff, Frances, 34–35, 203, 208

Boone, Bruce, 110

Bové, Paul, 20

Boyle, Kay, 106

Bradley, Mamie Till, 63

Bradstreet, Anne, 3

Brando, Marlon, 2, 51

Bredbeck, Gregory W., 114

Breines, Wini, 7

Breslin, James, 20

Brooks, Gwendolyn, 11, 22, 54, 135; "A
    Bronzeville Mother Loiters in Missis-
    sippi," 63–65; on stereotypes, 61;
    "Strong Men, Riding Horses," 61–62

Brown v. Board of Education (1954), 64, 127

Bruchac, Joseph, 107

Brunner, Edward, 231

Bryant, Carolyn, 63–64

Bryant, Roy, 63

Buchanan, Patrick, 99–100, 110

Buchanan, Robert, 106

Buddhism, 87–88

bureaucracy, 13, 32, 56

Burroughs, William S., 7

butch-femme: definitions of, 158–59,
    162; in film, 164–65; and social
    class, 244 n. 11

Butler, Judith, 3, 26–27, 47

Butterick, George, 247 n. 6

Cadden, Michael, 108

Cain, James M., 165

California: and Asian culture, 78, 93;
    and cultural myth of the West, 80;
    immigrants in, 76–77

Campbell, David, 55

Campion, Dan, 107

Canaday, John, 246–47 n. 1

canon, 107–8

Carmichael, Stokely, 128–29

Case, Sue-Ellen, 159

Cassady, Carolyn, 16

Cassady, Neal, 2, 16

Castle, Terry, 161, 165

censorship, 5

Central Intelligence Agency, 5, 56, 202

Césaire, Aimé, 113

Cha, Theresa Hak Kyung: *Dictee*, 3, 23–
    24, 198, 210–17; education of, 210,
    212; films of, 210–11; and genre, 248
    n. 14; and Korea, 198–99, 211–12,
    216, 219; and naming, 220; and
    women's speech, 213–14, 219

Chandler, Zala, 150

Chan Is Missing (1981, Wayne Wang), 21,
    95–96

Cheney, Richard, 108

Chiang Kai-shek, 197

Chin, Frank, 98, 237 n. 19

Chinatown: as political unconscious, 81;
    as urban area, 77, 236 n. 7

Chinatown (1974, Roman Polanski), 80–
    81

Chinese Exclusion Law (1882), 77

Chinese immigrants, 77–79

Chomsky, Noam, 4

Chow, Rey, 236 n. 4

Christopher, George, 244 n. 10

Chu, Louis, 96

Ciardi, John, 21, 49, 51

citationality, 3–4

Citizen Kane (1941, Orson Welles), 236
    n. 6

City Lights Books, 52

Civil Rights Act (1964), 127

civil rights movement, 72, 125

Clark, Tom, 231 n. 5

Cleaver, Eldridge, 128

Clinton, Bill, 26

cold war: and area studies, 198, 201; and containment, 55–56; and cultural anxiety, 2, 16, 54; defined, 4–5; end of, 221–22; and gender, 222–23; historiography of, 6, 21; and Pacific Rim, 78, 95, 218

colonialism: and gender, 208; in Korea, 198–99, 211–12, 216; and nationalism, 111–12; in New World, 207; and the other, 126

Coltrane, John, 133–35

communism: and domesticity, 66; and Mattachine Society, 163; research on, 201; as threat, 5–6, 8, 55

community: formation of, 18; of gay men, 21–22, 31, 59–61; poetic, 13–19, 47–48

confession, 4–5

conformity, 9, 95

Congress for Cultural Freedom, 5

Connery, Christopher, 197–98, 235 n. 3

Conrad, Alfred, 158

consensus, 6, 107

consumerism: and agency, 8, 230 n. 8; and family, 56–56; and masculinity, 57, 95; and Whitman, 107; and women, 53

containment, 5, 55–56, 95

Cook, Pam, 167

Coontz, Stephanie, 7

Corber, Robert, 6

Corn, Alfred, 118

Corso, Gregory, 5, 53

Cortez, Jayne, "Race," 241 n. 7

Costello, Bonnie, 180

Crane, Hart, 105

Crawford, Christina, 167

Crawford, Joan, 23, 165–67

creative writing programs, 19, 226

Creeley, Robert, 22, 34, 53, 55–56; "The Lover," 57–58; and Olson, 201, 206; "The Way," 58–59

cross-dressing: and female masculinity, 160; and formalism, 118–20; and gender, 101; as metaphor, 22–23, 100, 116, 121; and Whitman, 102–3

Cuban Revolution, 71

Cullen, Countee, 156

Cumings, Bruce, 197, 201

cybernetics, 209

dadaism, 52

Damon, Maria, 21, 73

Daughters of Bilitis, 162–64

Davenport, Guy, 203, 208

Davidson, Cathy, 85

Davis, Angela, 130

Davis, Madeleine D., 160, 244 n. 11

Dawson, Fielding, 34, 37–39

Dean, James, 2, 51

deconstruction, 50

Deep Image movement, 30, 233 n. 20

Defense Intelligence Agency (DIA), 56

Defoe, Daniel, *Robinson Crusoe*, 177

Deleuze, Gilles, 78

DeLillo, Don, 7

D'Emilio, John, 11, 31, 56

democracy, 107–9

Devor, Holly, 244 n. 5

Diamond, Sigmund, 201

Dickinson, Emily, 3, 101, 168, 182

Diehl, Joanne Feit, 178

Dirlik, Arif, 197, 199

Dorn, Ed, 199

Dr. Strangelove (1964, Stanley Kubrick), 7

Du Bois, W. E. B., 125

Duchamp, Marcel, 18, 52

Dulles, Alan, 234 n. 9

Dunaway, Faye, 80

Duncan, Robert, 19, 54, 88; and Black Mountain poets, 17, 34, 41, 232–33 n. 17; and Whitman, 100

Dunn, Joe, 44

Eat a Bowl of Tea (1989, Wayne Wang), 96–97

écriture féminine, 170

Edelman, Lee, 172

Edwards, Harry, 153

Ehrenreich, Barbara, 56–57

Eisenhower, Dwight D., 66

Eliot, T. S., 20, 70, 105; "The Four Quartets," 205; *The Waste Land,* 192, 202

Ellington, Duke, 133

Ellison, Ralph, 20, 125

Emerson, Ralph Waldo, "Experience," 105

Enloe, Cynthia, 222–23

environmentalism, 87–88

Erkkila, Betsy, 245 n. 19

Evans, Mari, 135

Evers, Medgar, 156

Everson, Landis, 42

excess, 5, 106–7

existentialism, 55

Faderman, Lillian, 31, 160

Faludi, Susan, *Stiffed,* 25–26

Falwell, Jerry, 237–38 n. 1

family, 6–7, 56–57

Fanon, Franz, 125

feedback, 209

Feldstein, Ruth, 234 n. 8

femininity: and agency, 8; and black men, 9, 131, 142–43; critiques of, 23; as normative, 10–11; and poetics, 42. *See also* gender; masculinity; women

feminism: and Black Power movement, 130; and gender, 223; as term, 158; and women poets, 181, 195

Ferlinghetti, Lawrence, 107

Field, Edward, 22; "Ode for Fidel Castro," 71–73

film noir, 21, 167

Film Production Code, 2, 165

film theory, 26–27

Fiore, Mary, 37

Flaubert, Gustav, *Madame Bovary,* 53

Folsom, Ed, 107

formalism, 21, 53, 168, 194; and cross-dressing, 106, 117–20; in narrative, 224

Foucault, Michel, 127

fraternal organizations, 17

Frazier, E. Franklin, 129, 137

Freud, Sigmund, 26

Friedan, Betty, *The Feminine Mystique,* 10–11, 25, 168, 183

Frost, Elizabeth, 248 n. 15

Fuss, Diana, 26

futurism, 18

Galbraith, John Kenneth, 8

Garber, Marjorie, 101–2

Garbo, Greta, 165

Garcia, Ramón, 85

García Lorca, Federico, 20, 45–47, 233 n. 20

Gardner, Erle Stanley, 51

Garvey, Marcus, 131

gay men: communities of, 21–22, 31, 41, 59–61; and femininity, 43; stereotypes of, 2, 115–16; and Whitman, 100–101. *See also* homosexuality; Mattachine Society

gender: as binary, 128; and colonialism, 208; and hermeneutics, 195; and mass culture, 183–85; and normalcy, 8, 57–58, 85; as performative, 3, 26, 63, 101, 159–60, 180; and poetics, 29, 42, 131, 194; and politics, 222–23; and race, 65, 126; as socially constructed, 223. *See also* femininity; masculinity

George, Stefan, 41

Gibson, Morgan, 90

Gilbert, Sandra, 4

Gilroy, Paul, 65

Ginsberg, Allen, 5, 24, 32, 50, 71; "America," 74–75; and Asian culture, 89; and homosociality, 13–14, 19; *Howl,* 7–8; misogyny of, 30–31; and Whitman, 52, 107

Gioia, Dana, 226

Giovanni, Nikki, 132, 135

Gladman, Renee, 225

globalism, 218

Golding, Alan, 21, 200–201, 233 n. 1

Gold Rush, 82

Gooch, Brad, 114, 239 n. 12

Goodman, Paul, 38–40, 42

Gordon, Avery, 14

Grahn, Judy, 153

Gray, Francine du Plessix, 19, 36–37

Gray, Timothy, 88

Green, Jamison, 244 n. 5

Greenberg, Clement, 6, 51, 52

Griffin, Joanna, 153

Guattari, Félix, 78

Gubar, Susan, 4

Gundolf, Friederich, 41

Hagedorn, Jessica, 98, 153

Halberstam, David, 234 n. 5

Halberstam, Judith, 23, 26, 159–60, 195, 243 n. 4

Hall, Donald, 49

Hamalian, Linda, 90

Hammett, Dashiell, 77

Hansberry, Lorraine, 164

happenings, 19

Harlem Renaissance, 131, 155, 240 n. 3, 242 n. 13

Harper, Phillip Bryan, 132

Harte, Bret, 22, 79; "Plain Language from Truthful James," 82–83

Harvey, David, 221

Hay, Henry, 163

Hayworth, Rita, 79–80, 236 n. 5

Hecht, Anthony, "The Deodand," 118–19

Hejinian, Lyn, 223–24

Hemingway, Ernest, 20

Hepburn, Katharine, 165

Hernton, Calvin, 130

heterosexuality: as compulsory, 28–29, 59, 61; and homosociality, 16, 29, 79; as normative, 158, 185; as subversive, 31

Heuvig, Jeanne, 169, 245 n. 13

Heyen, William, 107

Higginson, Thomas Wentworth, 3

Hiss, Alger, 56

Hofstadter, Richard, 230 n. 7

Holiday, Billie, 125, 133–34, 240 n. 2

Hollander, John, 51, 118

Holmes, John Clellon, 13, 16

homophile movement. *See* Daughters of Bilitis; Mattachine Society

homophobia: and black nationalism, 128–30, 241 n. 7, n. 11; during 1950s, 59, 108, 163–64; and politics, 100, 238 n. 2

homosexuality: and Asian immigrants, 83–85; in black culture, 130, 144–45; defined, 238 n. 5; and Harlem Renaissance, 242 n. 13; and identity, 59, 61; in Kinsey report, 9; and misogyny, 44; and national security, 59, 232 n. 7; and politics, 99; as subversive, 161–62; and Whitman, 122–23. *See also* gay men; lesbians; sexuality

homosociality: of Asian Americans, 95–97; of Beat poets, 30, 93–95; defined, 16–17; and heterosexuality, 16, 29, 79; and masculinity, 9; and misogyny, 16; and poetic community, 13–19, 35, 47–48; and power, 17; as threat, 11; and the West, 83; of women, 32, 158; and World War II, 31, 59

Hook, Sidney, 230 n. 5

hooks, bell, 129–30, 242 n. 23
Hoover, J. Edgar, 8
Hoover Commission Task Force on Intelligence, 56
House Un-American Activities Committee, 12, 31, 56
Howe, Irving, 51
Hua, Hyung Soon, 213
Hudson, Theodore, 142
Hughes, Langston, 156
Hughes, Ted, 170, 182; and Plath, 187, 190–91, 193
Hunt, Erica, 225
Hurston, Zora Neale, 150
Huston, John, 80
Huyssen, Andreas, 53

identity: as discursive, 55, 66, 214–15; female, 183–85; as performative, 101; and postmodernity, 224–25; and sexuality, 59, 110. *See also* subjectivity
ideology, 52, 70
immigrants, 76–77; laws concerning, 78; in the West, 80. *See also* Asian immigrants
Immigration Act (1924), 77
individualism, 6–7
Intelligence Advisory Committee (IAC), 56
internment camps, 77

Jackson, Michael, 26
James, Henry, 20
James, William, 71
Jarrell, Randall, "Next Day," 70–71
Joan of Arc, 213–14
Johns, Jasper, 52, 53
Johnson, Joyce, 15; *Minor Characters*, 13–14, 16
Jones, Hettie, 145
Jones, LeRoi. *See* Baraka, Amiri

Jones, Terry, 152
Jordan, June, 132
Joyce, James, 20
Joyce, Joyce Ann, 148–49

Kalaidjian, Walter, 21
Kantorowicz, Ernst, 41
Karenga, Ron, 129, 153
Kauffman, Bob, 24, 52
Keats, John, 47
Kennan, George, 55–56, 71
Kennedy, Elizabeth Lapovsky, 160, 244 n. 11
Kennedy, X. J., 158
Kenyon Review, 50
Kerouac, Jack, 2, 9, 22, 61; and advertising, 14, 15, 32; and Asian culture, 93–95; and the Cassadys, 16; *Dharma Bums*, 14, 86, 93–95; and homosociality, 30, 93–95; and mass culture, 51–52; *On the Road*, 86; and the West, 79
Khrushchev, Nikita, 66–67, 234 n. 9
Kim, Elaine, 210
Kim Jong Il, 221
King, Martin Luther, 125, 156
Kingston, Maxine Hong, 22, 237 n. 19
Kinnell, Galway, 54
Kinsey, Alfred, 8–9, 161
Kiss Me Deadly (1955, Robert Aldrich), 11–13, 159
Kitasono, Kitsue, 203
Kline, Franz, 37, 39
Knight, Ethridge, 126–27
Koizumi Junichiro, 221
Koontz, Stephanie, 56
Korea: colonization of, 198–99, 211–12, 216, 248 n. 12; unification of, 220–21
Kovacs, Ernie, 1–2, 21, 226
Kunitz, Stanley, 118
Kyger, Joanne, 30